The Revels Plays COMPANION LIBRARY

SUSAN BROCK, SUSAN CERASANO, PAUL EDMONDSON and GRACE IOPPOLO
general editors

For over forty years *The Revels Plays* have offered the most authoritative editions of Elizabethan and Jacobean plays by authors other than Shakespeare. The *Companion Library* provides a fuller background to the main series by publishing important dramatic and non-dramatic material that will be essential for the serious student of the period.

Three seventeenth-century plays on women and performance
eds CHALMERS, SANDERS & TOMLINSON
Doing Kyd: A collection of essays on The Spanish Tragedy ed. CINPOEȘ
'Art made tongue-tied by authority' CLARE
Drama of the English Republic, 1649–60 CLARE
Three Jacobean witchcraft plays eds. CORBIN, SEDGE
The Stukeley Plays ed. EDELMAN
Three Renaissance usury plays ed. KERMODE
Beyond The Spanish Tragedy: *A study of the works of Thomas Kyd* ERNE
John Ford's political theatre HOPKINS
The works of Richard Edwards KING
Marlowe and the popular tradition: Innovation in the English drama before 1595 LUNNEY
Banquets set forth: Banqueting in English Renaissance drama MEADS
Thomas Heywood: Three marriage plays ed. MERCHANT
Three Renaissance travel plays ed. PARR
John Lyly PINCOMBE
A textual companion to Doctor Faustus RASMUSSEN
Documents of the Rose Playhouse RUTTER
John Lyly: Euphues: The Anatomy of Wit *and* Euphues and His England ed. SCRAGG
Pap with an Hatchet, *John Lyly: An annotated, modern-spelling edition* SCRAGG
Richard Brome: Place and politics on the Caroline stage STEGGLE

Three sixteenth-century dietaries

Manchester University Press

THE REVELS PLAYS COMPANION LIBRARY

Three sixteenth-century dietaries

edited by Joan Fitzpatrick

Manchester University Press

Copyright © Joan Fitzpatrick 2017

The right of Joan Fitzpatrick to be identified as the author of this work has been asserted by her in accordance with the Copyright, Designs and Patents Act 1988.

Published by Manchester University Press
Oxford Road, Manchester M13 9PL

www.manchesteruniversitypress.co.uk

British Library Cataloguing-in-Publication Data
A catalogue record for this book is available from the British Library

ISBN 978 0719 08113 2 hardback
ISBN 978 1 5261 6695 1 paperback

First published 2017
Published in paperback 2022

The publisher has no responsibility for the persistence or accuracy of URLs for any external or third-party internet websites referred to in this book, and does not guarantee that any content on such websites is, or will remain, accurate or appropriate.

Typeset
by Toppan Best-set Premedia Limited

CONTENTS

LIST OF FIGURES	vi
GENERAL EDITORS' PREFACE	vii
ACKNOWLEDGEMENTS	viii
INTRODUCTION	1
History and contexts	1
The dietaries	8
Note on the editorial history of the dietaries	35
Textual issues	35
Finding aids (indexing)	37
THE DIETARIES	39
The Castle of Health, Thomas Elyot	40
A Compendious Regiment, or a Dietary of Health, Andrew Boorde	158
The Government of Health, William Bullein	206
APPENDICES	
Appendix 1: Proems to the first and second editions of Thomas Elyot's *Castle of Health*	303
Appendix 2: The preface to the first edition of Andrew Boorde's *Compendious Regiment*	307
Appendix 3: The second address to the reader from the first edition of William Bullein's *Government of Health*	309
Appendix 4: Glossary of words commonly used in the dietaries	310
Appendix 5: Authorities and works cited or alluded to in the dietaries	315
WORKS CITED	327

LIST OF FIGURES

1 Portrait of Sir Thomas Elyot by Hans Holbein the Younger, c. 1532–34, Royal Collection Trust (RCIN 912203). © Her Majesty Queen Elizabeth II 2016 *page 8*
2 Andrew Boorde, woodcut, Wellcome Library, London (ICV No. 850). Reproduced under CC BY 4.0 19
3 William Bullein after unknown artist, possibly late sixteenth to early seventeenth century, woodcut, National Portrait Gallery, London (NPG D25457). © National Portrait Gallery, London 29

GENERAL EDITORS' PREFACE

Since the late 1950s the series known as The Revels Plays has provided for students of the English Renaissance drama carefully edited texts of the major Elizabethan and Jacobean plays. The series includes some of the best-known drama of the period and has continued to expand, both within its original field and, to a lesser extent, beyond it, to include some important plays from the earlier Tudor and from the Restoration periods. The Revels Plays Companion Library is intended to further this expansion and to allow for new developments.

The aim of the Companion Library is to provide students of the Elizabethan and Jacobean drama with a fuller sense of its background and context. The series includes volumes of a variety of kinds. Small collections of plays, by a single author or concerned with a single theme and edited in accordance with the principles of textual modernisation of The Revels Plays, offer a wider range of drama than the main series can include. Together with editions of masques, pageants and the non-dramatic work of Elizabethan and Jacobean playwrights, these volumes make it possible, within the overall Revels enterprise, to examine the achievements of the major dramatists from a broader perspective. Other volumes provide a fuller context for the plays of the period by offering new collections of documentary evidence on Elizabethan theatrical conditions and on the performance of plays during that period and later. A third aim of the series is to offer modern critical interpretation, in the form of collections of essays or of monographs, of the dramatic achievement of the English Renaissance.

So wide a range of material necessarily precludes the standard format and uniform general editorial control which is possible in the original series of Revels Plays. To a considerable extent, therefore, treatment and approach are determined by the needs and intentions of individual volume editors. Within this rather ampler area, however, we hope that the Companion Library maintains the standards of scholarship that have for so long characterised The Revels Plays, and that it offers a useful enlargement of the work of the series in preserving, illuminating and celebrating the drama of Elizabethan and Jacobean England.

ACKNOWLEDGEMENTS

Thanks are due to the staff at the British Library, Bodleian Library, Cambridge University Library, Royal College of Surgeons Library, and Wellcome Library for allowing me to consult exemplars of the dietaries in this edition. Thanks also to the staff at the Shakespeare Institute, University of Birmingham.

I am grateful to the British Academy for funding a trip to the US East Coast to spend six weeks researching in the Countway Library of Medicine rare books collection of Harvard University (Boston) and the History of Medicine Division of the US National Library of Medicine (Bethesda). This allowed me to examine three US exemplars of Boorde's dietary not available elsewhere. Special thanks goes to Jack Eckert and Jessica B. Murphy at Countway and to Susan Stravinski at Wisconsin Madison for lending a copy of Boorde's text for consultation at Countway. I am also grateful to Ian Gadd at Bath Spa University for his useful advice on making the application to the British Academy.

My employer, Loughborough University, granted me two periods of study leave to work on this project: the first allowed me to begin work on the volume and the second to complete it. Its support is much appreciated. I am also grateful to my editor Susan Cerasano and Matthew Frost at Manchester University Press for agreeing that these three dietaries deserved to be more readily available to a wider audience.

Thanks are also due to Ken Albala at University of the Pacific who read parts of the volume and helped me identify some obscure words and phrases in the dietaries and to Gabriel Egan at De Montfort University who also read parts of the volume and offered invaluable editorial and critical advice. Lastly, my copy editor at MUP, John Banks, proved to be a most careful, intelligent, and patient reader who saved me from numerous errors and whose thoughtful input greatly enhanced this volume. Any remaining errors are, of course, my own.

JOAN FITZPATRICK

INTRODUCTION

HISTORY AND CONTEXTS

The dietary genre

Dietaries, or regimens, are texts (usually prose) advising readers on how to best achieve and maintain good health, and they were immensely popular in the early modern period. Dozens of titles were published in the sixteenth century, with many reprinted several times, and some corrected, revised, and enlarged in subsequent editions. The market for these texts was clearly huge, and, following the success of the first titles, writers and publishers responded by producing further works aimed at a readership eager to learn more about their physical and mental well-being. Dietaries are an eclectic genre, with some titles aimed specifically at particular groups, such as old men or the melancholic, and some containing recipes or lengthy advice devoted to specific ailments, such as the plague. However most were aimed at a wide range of readers who could each consult the particular piece of advice that especially pertained to them. They all contain detailed advice on how to live a healthy life according to one's complexion (determined by the predominance or imbalance of a particular humour) but also taken into account are a person's age, gender, location, and even their occupation.

Advice is usually given on how to maintain bodily health by taking exercise and avoiding bad air, using purges, and bloodletting. Advice is also provided about which medicines are best suited to alleviate a particular ailment, with instructions given for how to make certain medicines at home. How to sleep (for how long and in what position) is also usually discussed as are other aspects of behaviour that impact upon bodily health such as when to wash and what to wear. The dietaries also usually attend to mental well-being, noting that a happy disposition is the best way to maintain physical and mental health.

What to eat and why forms an important part of any dietary. The following are all dealt with in detail: what foods are best suited to a particular complexion; whether foods are best consumed raw or cooked (usually the latter); how best to cook a particular food, usually according to one's complexion; how much to eat and when (in what season, at what time of the day); what combinations of foods are best avoided; how easily a particular food is digested. Specific food groups – for example animal flesh, fish, fruit and bread – are usually discussed in detail, with further detail provided according to which particular types of animal, fish, fruit or bread should be sought-out and which avoided. Herbs and spices are often given considerable attention, with their medical attributes stressed, and drinks are also considered. Typically the section on each food will consider the food's properties, to whom it is best suited, in what state it is best consumed (for example whether fresh if fruit, or young if animal flesh), and its effects upon the body. The reader is repeatedly urged to avoid excessive consumption of food and drink, with the merits of moderation often rehearsed.

A major influence on early modern dietary authors was the medieval text *Regimen sanitatis Salerni* (*The Salernitan Rule of Health*), attributed to Joannes De Mediolano, and translated into English by Thomas Paynell (De Mediolano 1528) and later in a verse translation by Sir John Harington (De Mediolano 1607). Harington's translation is closer in spirit to the original because the rhyming verses make the advice offered easy to remember, something that helped established the popularity of the medieval text. In this celebrated work we find what would become the common concerns of those dietaries published in English during the early modern period and outlined above. The debt to the *Regimen sanitatis Salerni* is evident in the three dietaries included in this edition, for example in their promotion of mirth as an aid to good health. Translating the *Regimen sanitatis Salerni* into English was an important step in the development of the dietary genre. In his dedication to Lord John, Earl of Oxford, and High Chamberlain of England, Paynell explains why he has translated the work:

> Oh how wholesome is it then to use good diet, to live temperately, to eschew excess of meats and drinks? Yea how greatly are we Englishmen bound to the masters of the universities of Salerno (Salerno is in the realm of Naples), which vouchsafed in our behalf to compile thus necessary and thus wholesome a book? But what availeth it to have gold or abundance of riches if one cannot use it? What helpeth costly medicines if one receive them not? So what profiteth us a book, be it never so expedient and fruitful, if we understand it not? Wherefore I considering the fruit that might come of this book if it were translated into the English tongue (forwhy every man understandeth not the Latin), I thought it very expedient at some times for the wealth of unlearned persons to busy myself therein, for learned persons and such as have great experience need no instructions to diet themself nor to conserve their health. (Present author's modernization of De Mediolano 1528, A3r)

The focus on increasing the understanding of those not educated in Latin or medical and dietary matters, on translating these "wholesome" ideas into English, was part of an emerging sense of egalitarianism and national pride found in humanist circles. This is apparent also in the printer's address to the reader that prefaces the later translation by Harington:

> Reader, the care that I have of thy health appears in bestowing these physical rules upon thee; neither needest thou be ashamed to take lessons out of this school, for our best doctors scorn not to read the instructions. It is a little *academa* where every man may be a graduate and proceed Doctor in the ordering of his own body. It is a garden where all things grow that are necessary for thy health. This medicinable tree first grew in Salerno, from thence it was removed and hath born fruit and blossoms a long time in England. (Present author's modernization of De Mediolano 1607, A3r)

The printer claims that "the author", perhaps Harington rather than De Mediolano, "is to me unknowne, and I put this child of his into the open world without his consent", urging the reader to hope, as the printer does, "that he will not be angry, finding this a traueler abroad, when by his trauel, so many of his owne country, are so manifoldly benefited" (De Mediolano 1607, A3v).

The humanists reached back even further than the medieval period and privileged classical learning, believing that the study of ideas and values found in writings by the ancients would unlock the intellectual and spiritual potential of humankind. By studying Latin and Greek, rhetoric, grammar, poetry, history, and moral philsophy, and considering ancient values in the context of Christianity, they believed that what it meant to be human could be brought into sharper focus. Humanist scholars sought to return to original writings as far as was possible so as to uncover the errors of earlier translations and commentaries. The printing press facilitated the dissemination of knowledge and further enabled humanists to impart the values learnt from the ancients, the benevolence towards one's fellow Christian through learning being a key aspect of humanist thought.

Medical humanism saw a renewed interest in bodily and mental health propagated by ancient authorities, as is evident in the well-known humanist phrase *mens sana in corpore sano* (a healthy mind in a healthy body), taken from the tenth satire of the Roman poet Juvenal. The spirit of medical humanism is perhaps most clearly evident in the career of Thomas Linacre, the physician and humanist scholar responsible for teaching Greek to Sir Thomas More. Linacre went back to the original Greek manuscripts of some of Galen's most important writings to provide fine Latin translations of volumes hitherto unavailable in print.

The development of dietary literature parallels the spread of humanist ideas in early modern England. Humanists formed an intellectual network and many were friends with one another. As noted in this volume's introduction to Elyot, Thomas Linacre is probably the physican praised by Elyot in the proem (= preface) to his *Castle of Health*, and Elyot's dietary was influenced by the ideas of More and Erasmus, men he might also have known personally. It is also perhaps not too fanciful to suggest that Andrew Boorde might have met More since both men spent time with the Carthusian monks in London, Boorde as a member of the order and More as a visitor. What is clear is that the dietary authors took even further than the humanists the concept of communicating learning to the people by making ancient views on maintaining a healthy body and mind available not only in Latin, the language of scholars, but in the vernacular.

The notion that all readers, and specifically English readers, ought to have access to medical knowledge, hitherto the preserve of specialists, led to a surge in new titles, written in English and aimed at the general public. A popular work was Thomas Moulton's *Mirror or Glass of Health* (Moulton 1531), which begins with a treatise on the pestilence, offering some advice on how to avoid it via diet and other measures such as bloodletting, but is mainly a list of medical ailments and how to treat them, with a particular focus on astrology. With *The Castle of Health* Thomas Elyot is the first author to present a dietary written in the vernacular – not one simply translated into English – that takes into account the English climate, English foods, and the particular habits of English people. For the first time this kind of advice was widely available to the layperson, albeit one who was well-educated enough to be able to read.

The three dietaries contained in this volume, Thomas Elyot's *Castle of Health*, Andrew Boorde's *Compendious Regiment*, and William Bullein *Government of Health*, were each republished several times and are typical of the genre. Elyot's dietary, the first of the three to be published, clearly influenced the other two, although each is distinct in its approach, with Boorde the least conservative in his attitude to traditional views on health. Boorde's *Compendious Regiment* is arguably the next most important dietary written in English to emerge after Elyot's *Castle of Health* and, although, unlike Elyot, Boorde was trained in medicine, his tone is light, indeed lighter than Elyot's, and the work aimed at the general reader. Like Elyot,

Boorde is keen to make his work particularly relevant to his English readers. Bullein's *Government of Health* is unlike the other two in that it takes the form of a dialogue between the the riotious John and the moderate Humphrey, but it shares their efforts to make matters relating to health understandable to all who can read in the vernacular and, again, there is a focus on matters specifically pertinent to England and the English people.

These popular and influential works deserve a modern readership because they offer an insight into early modern attitudes to food and diet, ideas about the body, psychological well-being, and identity. We know that they were widely read and popular because they were frequently reprinted in the decades after they first appeared. Today's scholars' investigations of this genre have hitherto been hampered by the lack of modern critical editions of them. It is hoped this volume will be of use to any reader interested in the history of food, medicine, and how these early printed books evolved through successive editions. Dietaries also illuminate early modern literary and dramatic texts where references and allusions to food and health were influenced by this fascinating but neglected genre.

Humoral theory

The ancient model of humoral theory dominated medieval and early modern thinking about how the body worked and was the key to understanding how to maintain bodily health. According to humoral theory, human personalities could be divided into four essential types: sanguine, choleric, melancholic, and phlegmatic. These were derived from the four cardinal humours: blood, choler (yellow bile), melancholy (black bile) and phlegm that they believed flowed through the body. The humours were described in terms of heat and moisture: blood was hot and moist; choler, hot and dry; melancholy, cold and dry; and phlegm cold and moist. Ideally a person had to have a properly proportioned mixture of the four humours since a predominance of one produced a person who was sanguine, phlegmatic, choleric, or melancholic. However, the balance of the humours was not equal, for example blood was present in more abundance than other humours, and it was considered normal for most people to suffer from a slight humoral imbalance. This imbalance was usually corrected by modifying one's diet as well as controlling external factors – termed "non-naturals", for example air and exercise – that could influence the internal humoural balance (Albala 2002, 49, 50).

Sir John Harington's verse translation of the *Regimen sanitatis Salerni* describes the four humours:

> Four humours reign within our bodies wholly,
> And these compared to four elements,
> The sanguine, choler, phlegm, and melancholy . . .
> Like aire, both warm and moist, is sanguine clear,
> Like fire doth choler hot and dry appear,
> Like water, cold and moist, is phlegmatic,
> The melancholy cold, dry earth is like.
> (Present author's modernization of De Mediolano 1607, C3r)

Various physical and personality traits are associated with each humour: the sanguine person tends to be fat, loving "wine, and women, and all recreation"; the choleric man tends to be thin and is described as "proud, bountifull enough, yet oft malicious"; the phlegmatic man is "fat and square" and "Giuen much vnto their ease, to rest and sloth"; the melancholic is "Suspitious in his nature, and mistrustfull" with a "heauy look" (De Mediolano 1607, C3r–C4r). The physical characteristics typical of a particular complexion are further elaborated upon and are worth quoting in full:

> If Sanguine humour do too much abound,
> These signs will be thereof appearing chief,
> The face will swell, the cheeks grow red and round,
> With staring eyes, the pulse bear soft and brief,
> The veins exceed, the belly will be bound,
> The temples and the fore-head full of grief,
> Unquiet sleeps, that so strange dreams will make
> To cause one blush to tell when he doth wake,
> Besides the moisture of the mouth and spittle,
> Will taste too sweet, and seem the throat to tickle.
>
> If Choler do exceed, as may sometime,
> Your ears will ring and make you to be wakeful,
> Your tongue will seem all rough, and oftentimes
> Cause vomits, unaccustomed and hateful,
> Great thirst, your excrements are full of slime,
> The stomach squeamish, sustenance ungrateful,
> Your appetite will seem in nought delighting,
> Your heart still grieved with continual biting,
> The pulse beat hard and swift, all hot, extreme,
> Your spittle sour, of fire-work oft your dream.
>
> If phlegm abundance have due limits past,
> These signs are here set down will plainly show,
> The mouth will seem to you quite out of taste,
> And apt with moisture still to overflow;
> Your sides will seem all sore down to the waist,
> Your meat wax loathsome, your digestion slow,
> Your head and stomach both in so ill-taking,
> One seeming ever griping tother aching:
> With empty veins, the pulse beat slow and soft,
> In sleep, of seas and rivers dreaming oft.
>
> But if that dangerous humour over-reign,
> Of melancholy, sometime making mad,
> These tokens then will be appearing plain,
> The pulse beat hard, the colour dark and bad,
> The water thin, a weak fantastic brain,
> False-grounded joy, or else perpetual sad,
> Afrighted oftentimes with dreams like visions,
> Presenting to the thought ill apparitions,
> Of bitter belches from the stomach coming,
> His ear (the left especial) ever humming.
> (Present author's modernization of De Mediolano 1607, C4v–C5r)

Humoral theory considered disease a consequence of humoral imbalance and so it needed to be avoided at all costs. Various kinds of behaviours and environmental factors discussed in dietary literature, the so called 'non-naturals', could help the reader bring about the perfect balance of the four humours, as noted in the *Regimen sanitatis Salerni*:

> Against these several humours overflowing,
> As several kinds of physic may be good,
> As diet-drink, hot baths, whence sweat is growing
> With purging, vomiting, and letting blood:
> Which taken in due time, nor overflowing,
> Each Malady's infection is withstood,
> The last of these is best, if skill and reason
> Respect age, strength, quantity, and season,
> Of seventy from seventeen, if blood abound,
> The opening of a vein is healthful found.
> (present author's modernization of De Mediolano 1607, C5v)

The early modern dietary authors also advocated bloodletting but this would have been suitable only for those bodies containing an excess of blood (the sanguine) and usually when the humoral imbalance was extreme and disease had already taken hold.

Diet was the more usual way of correcting an imbalance in the humours in order to keep disease at bay. The reason diet was so important in regulating the humours was that each food and drink had its own complexion: for example whilst the consumption of hot and dry herbs would help correct the excessively phlegmatic (a humour that was cold and moist), they ought to be avoided by those suffering from an excess of a humour with the same qualities, that is choler (hot and dry), since they would augment the imbalance already causing a problem and make the person sick. The humours produced by foods, and the process of digestion, must also be of the correct quality and magnitude according to the type of person consuming them. For example, a delicate constitution would have difficulty processing a heavy meat such as pork, that was better suited to a strong body, whereas a delicate food such as chicken would be unsuitable for a strong body better suited to processing pork. In the strong body a delicate meat could result in burnt or adust humours and in a delicate consitution a heavy meat could produce raw humours (Albala 2002, 49). The *Regimen sanitatis Salerni* recommends moderation in diet before providing detailed advice on specific foods. The following assertion is typical of the emphasis put upon food in establishing and maintaining a good humoral balance and thus good health:

> They that in physic will prescribe you food,
> Six things must note, we here in order touch,
> First what it is, and then for what 'tis good,
> And when, and where, how often, and how much . . .
> (present author's modernization of De Mediolano 1607, B5v)

These "six things" are typically the focus of attention for early modern dietary authors, including Elyot, Boorde, and Bullein.

Authorities
Although Elyot, Boorde, and Bullein were clearly influenced by the *Regimen sanitatis Salerni* they mention it rarely. It is cited by Bullein in the section "What is sage?" (pp. 257–8) and referred to by Elyot in the revised proem to the fourth edition of his

dietary (upon which this edition is based) but not in the dietary itself. It is not mentioned at all by Boorde. This is typical of the relaxed early modern attitude toward citing a debt to earlier authors. Harington's translation of the *Regimen sanitatis Salerni* advises that the reader "Vse three Physitians still, first Doctor *Quiet*, / Next Doctor *Merry-man*, and *Doctor Dyet*" (De Mediolano 1607, A6r) and Bullein also recommends these three doctors without specifically mentioning Harington's translation (p. 252). Elyot and Bullein are more likely than Boorde to credit their sources even if they are not consistent in naming them. Of course much of the advice given in the *Regimen sanitatis Salerni* can itself be found in earlier classical texts and these are often specifically cited or alluded to by Elyot, Bullein, and Boorde.

A major influence on the dietary authors was Galen of Pergamon, the Greek physician of the second century CE. Andrew Boorde is less likely than Elyot and Bullein to cite Galen, yet even he is heavily indebted to the ancient authority and all three authors do not demur from questioning Galen's opinions, invoking their own experience when relevant. Arab and Jewish authorities are also cited by the three dietary authors, although the influence of Galen and Galenic medicine in general tends to dominate. In the proem to the fourth edition Elyot lists the authorities with whom he is familiar:

> when I wrote first this book I was not all ignorant in physic, for before that I was twenty years old a worshipful physician, and one of the the most renowned at that time in England, perceiving me by nature inclined to knowledge, read unto me the works of Galen, of temperaments, natural faculties, the introduction of Johannitius, with some of the aphorisms of Hippocrates. And afterward, by mine own study, I read over in order the most part of the works of Hippocrates, Galen, Oribasius, Paulus Celius, Alexander of Tralles, Celsus, Pliny, the one and the other, with Dioscorides. Nor I did omit to read the long canons of Avicenna, the commentaries of Averroes, the practice of Isaac, Haly Abbas, Rasis, Mesue, and also of the more part of them which were their aggregators and followers.

As John Villads Skov pointed out, this list "includes the most important authorities of his time" (Elyot 1970, 12) and Elyot clearly wants to impress the medical men reading his dietary with his knowledge of medical experts. Indeed, as Skov noted, the authors cited by Elyot "appear on reading lists assigned to medical students, and it is quite likely that Elyot deliberately intended to suggest that he had the equivalent of a university education in medicine" (Elyot 1970, 12–13). Most of these authorities are cited by Boorde and Bullein also.

The majority of the authorities cited by the three dietary authors in this volume are experts on the body, diet, and related issues such as bloodletting but other topics also emerge, for example, theology, politics, history, and mathematics. While most of the authorities are classical and some medieval, early modern authorities also feature, for example Elyot mentions Augustine de Augustinus, the sixteenth-century Venetian doctor who was personal physician to Cardinal Wolsey and royal physician from 1540 to 1546. Bullein is the dietary author most likely to cite his contemporaries, some of whom were English, for example the physician, cartographer, and astronomer William Cunningham and the mathematician and surveyor Leonard Digges. Bullein also cites Elyot's *Castle of Health* as an authority when discussing radish roots (pp. 269–70). A full list of who and what is cited and by which dietary author is provided in Appendix 5.

THE DIETARIES

The Castle of Health

The author and the dietary

The following account of Elyot's life is derived from the standard sources (Hogrefe 1967; Elyot 1970, 1–124; Lehmberg 2004a; Lehmberg 2004b). Thomas Elyot was born around 1490 into a wealthy and influential family. His father, Richard, was a judge with powerful connections: acting as attorney-general to Queen Elizabeth. Richard also worked with Cardinal Wolsey and took part in the preliminary investigations into charges of treason against Edward Stafford, Duke of Buckingham (whose aunt was the wife of King Edward IV). Thomas Elyot spent his childhood in Oxfordshire and in the preface to the first edition of his Latin–English dictionary, published in 1538, claims he was educated by a private tutor until the age of twelve. It seems that he was subsequently largely self-taught; it is not clear whether he attended university or took any degrees. There is no evidence that he was trained in or practised

1 Portrait of Sir Thomas Elyot by Hans Holbein the Younger, c. 1532–34, Royal Collection

law but from 1510 to 1526 he served as clerk to the justices of assize for the western circuit, assisting his father and continuing for four years after his father's death.

Around 1510 he married Margaret à Barrow and it seems that the couple were friends of Sir Thomas More. After More's death, Elyot asked Thomas Cromwell to "lay apart the remembraunce of the amity betweene me and Sir Thomas More . . . I was never so moche adict [so much addicted] unto him as I was unto truthe and fidelity towards my sovereign lord" (Elyot Undated, fol. 260). In his biography of More, William Roper (More's son-in-) claims that Elyot reported to him a conversation he had with the Spanish Emperor Charles V about More's death, emphasizing More's worth as a counsellor to Elyot himself, his wife, and friends (Roper 1935, 104). If Elyot did know More then he would also have known the influential members of More's circle such as Erasmus and he certainly knew Hans Holbein because the artist produced drawings of Elyot and his wife, which are currently in the Royal Collection at Windsor Castle. It may have been through More that Elyot also met Thomas Linacre, the humanist scholar and physician who taught More Greek, and Linacre is probably the physician Elyot praises in the proem to *The Castle of Health*:

> before that I was twenty years old a worshipful physician, and one of the most renowned at that time in England, perceiving me by nature inclined to knowledge, read unto me the works of Galen, of temperaments, natural faculties, the introduction of Johannitius, with some of the aphorisms of Hippocrates.

Between 1515 and 1529 Elyot served as a Justice of the Peace for Oxfordshire and Wiltshire and in 1527 and 1529 he was named sheriff of the two counties. In 1523 he was appointed senior clerk of the King's council and served Cardinal Wolsey until his fall from power in 1529. Elyot's apparent friendship with More and advancement at the hands of Wolsey did not appear to cause him any lasting harm: he was knighted in 1530, and in 1531 appointed by King Henry as ambassador to the Spanish Emperor. Henry may have wanted Elyot to influence the Emperor's views on his divorce from Katherine of Aragon, Charles's aunt, but things clearly did not go well, presumably due to the fact that although Elyot was a loyal subject he was also sympathetic to Katherine's religious principles. He was recalled from Spain in January 1532 and replaced by Thomas Cranmer, the future archbishop of Canterbury. Elyot spent some time travelling through Germany with Cranmer and also spent some time in the Netherlands. He represented Cambridgeshire in the parliament of 1539 and also served as a Justice of the Peace for the region but did not get the preferment that he sought. Elyot continued undertaking various duties for the government in the final years of his life but lost any real influence when his patron, Thomas Cromwell, was charged with treason and executed in 1540. Elyot died on 26 March 1546 leaving his property to his wife (they had no children) and ordering that his books be sold and the money distributed to poor scholars.

With the death of his father in 1522 Elyot had inherited lands and a large library, containing French and Latin books as well as manuscript primers. The library was clearly put to good use: Elyot's reputation as a humanist scholar was established with *The Book of the Governor*, a treatise on government and the ideal ruler, first published in 1531 and dedicated to Henry VIII. Elyot's view of monarchy as the only proper form of government was indebted to a wide range of classical and medieval sources and in the book he recommends that future rulers be well-read in Greek and

Latin literature. His Latin–English dictionary, first published in 1538, was also dedicated to King Henry who was apparently interested in the project and had lent Elyot some books. It was the first Latin dictionary based on classical sources and applying humanist principles. Other works that deal with English matters with a view to influencing King Henry are *Pasquil the Plain*, first published in 1533, a Socratic dialogue that promotes the virtues of the free-speaking counsellor, and *Of the Knowledge Which Maketh a Wise Man*, also published in 1533, a prose dialogue featuring Plato and Aristippus that discusses, among other issues, the distinction between a king and a tyrant and what kind of knowledge the wise man possesses.

Elyot's *Castle of Health* was first published around 1537, with two further editions appearing in 1539, three in 1541, and subsequent editions appearing from 1547 onwards (making a total of eighteen). The textual situation is discussed in detail below. Elyot's title is an allusion to the traditional notion of the body as a fortress under siege from threatening forces, against which a strong regimen might launch a defence. The dietary begins with a proem in which Elyot explains his reasons for writing it and the various scholarly sources to which he is indebted. It is then divided into four books that incoporate the six topics of the regimen genre: air, food, evacuation, passions, exercise, and sleep. Throughout the dietary Elyot makes frequent use of lists and headings. As John Villads Skov pointed out, this way of dividing his material "owes a good deal to the Renaissance concept of 'method,' the reduction of an 'art,' or subject-matter field, to brief, clearly organized, summary form for quick reference and speed of comprehension" (Elyot 1970, x). Elyot also tends to use over-long sentences, some of which cannot be easily repunctuated due to his over-use also of subordinate clauses (for example in the penultimate paragraph of chapter seven, "Letting of blood", from the third book). Although this kind of writing can be frustrating for the modern reader (and the modern editor) it does lend the writing a modern 'stream of consciousness' effect, conveying a sense of excitement and urgency.

The first book is fairly short, containing what Elyot terms a "table" listing all the items and topics discussed in the dietary. It then lists what were known as the seven things natural (elements, complexion, humours, members, powers, operations and spirits); the six things not natural (air, meat and drink, sleep and watch, moving and rest, emptiness and repletion, affections of the mind) and the three things against nature (sickness, cause of sickness, and accident which follows sickness). Also listed, and annexed to the things natural, are age, colour, figure and diversity of kinds. He then discusses the things natural, not natural, and against nature in more detail, mainly in list form detailing also the effect meat and drink have upon the various parts of the body and specific humours.

Food and drink are the main focus of the second book: how much to consume; the nature of certain foodstuffs; the problems that emerge with excessive consumption, and the positive effects of moderation. Subsequent chapters are dedicated to specific foodstuffs, beginning with a short chapter on bread, then a longer one on the different kinds of animal flesh before proceeding to fowl, offal, fish, dairy products, fruits, nuts, vegetables, and herbs. The section on drinks begins with a discussion of water, then wine, milk, ale, cider, and whey. Honey and then sugar are dealt with before considering issues pertinent to health such as when to eat, which diet is best for which age group, and the merits of moderate sleep and exercise.

The third book begins with a discussion of the state of the body and bodily functions, for example repletion and purgations, before listing the foods (mainly herbs) that will help digest or purge a particular humour. Also discussed are bloodletting, scarifying the body, haemorrhoids, and the mental states of ire and dolour. It is suggested that certain foods will help the afflicted (again these are provided in a list) and, after briefly discussing the merits and dangers of joy, Elyot considers the combination of humours that might exist in one body, what time of the year certain humours are more prevalent, and which diets best suit particular complexions.

The fourth and final book discusses bodily ailments further – crudities (the imperfect concoction of humours or undigested matter in the stomach); distillations (catarrh); lassitude (weariness) – and proposes some remedies. It also details which illnesses are likely to strike at specific times of the year and to people of certain ages, and includes a list of the signs for telling which particular body part is afflicted. There is a detailed discussion of the diagnostic significance of urine before the "'Precepts of the Ancient Physician Diocles Unto King Antigonus'" are outlined: a brief description of medical symptoms and remedies. The book ends with a diet to be used in the time of pestilence.

Elyot's proem to his dietary was revised twice: the first time for the second edition of the work published in 1539 and again for the fourth edition, published in 1541, and upon which this new edition is based. The proem to the first edition, published some time between 1536 and 1539, addresses Thomas Cromwell, Elyot's patron, directly. In it Elyot claims that the main motivation for writing *The Castle of Health* is to help Cromwell to regain health, having recently discovered that the great man is suffering from a dyscrasy, a bodily disorder resulting from an imbalance among humours or qualities. Elyot tells how he was upset to hear of the illness of a friend but also that a wise and honourable counsellor to the King was ill because the King needs such men around him to help govern the kingdom. *The Castle of Health*, claims Elyot, will be of use to Cromwell but also to anyone who would "perfectly know the state of his body, being in the lattitude of health or declination to sickness, engendered by distemperance of the four natural humours". The reader may find in the work the means to effect a cure himself or "instruct his physician", and here Elyot pre-empts criticism for stepping on the physicians' toes by stating that "by wise physicians considered, they will not disdain that I write in this matter, their estimation (where few men do perish) being thereby increased". He also defends himself against accusations that writing a work on physic is not suitable for a knight by listing a number of great men, amongst them emperors, kings, and knights, who did the same. Isn't it better for a Christian knight to cure men than kill them? he asks, concluding his proem with the plea "let not men be offended with my labour, which I have taken for their universal commodity", returning to the point that it was Cromwell's illness that first moved him to compose the work.

In the revised proem to the second edition Elyot begins by explaining that he was so upset by Cromwell's illness and the desire to quickly build his *Castle of Health* that he rushed it and the work consequently contained errors, which were also due to Elyot's responsibilities as a Member of Parliament. He then praises moderation, announcing that "he that liveth moderately doth love always faithfully, for over him affections and passions have left authority and he that standeth just in the middle standeth most surely". The moderate person chooses sincere friends, indeed friendship is a treasure, and Elyot urges Cromwell not to forget that he is a friend, concluding by proclaiming that he will pray to God for Cromwell's continued good fortune and health.

In the final revision made by Elyot to his proem for the fourth edition no mention is made of Cromwell, no doubt because he had been executed for treason in 1540. Where Elyot briefly defended his decision to write about physic in the proem to the first edition he here defends himself at length against those who have criticized his *Castle of Health* and he aligns himself with Galen who also faced criticism for putting his interest in learning above financial reward. Elyot denounces those who hold books on physic in distain, repeating the point from the first edition that kings and emperors have studied physic, this time listing different powerful people and specifying their medical discoveries, mainly herbal cures, and later adding to the list of authorities by including traditional Arabic and classical medical authorities. He proclaims the esteem with which physic has been long held in England, hoping the king will take an interest in establishing it in the country, just as he is establishing "true and uncorrupted doctrines". If this were the case then his fellow Englishmen would "have less need of things brought out of far countries, by the corruption whereof innumerable people have perished". Although Elyot claims the physicians are not to blame for these deaths, he does note that some have been less than diligent in ensuring the safety of their drugs and ingredients. As David W. Swain pointed out, this is a dig at the Italian College of Physicians, "whose founder and early members had medical degrees from Padua and other continental schools" and implies also that "like native medicine, a native medical literature might also lessen English reliance on continental learning" (Swain 2008, 61).

The subtle criticism of physicians is evident throughout *The Castle of Health*, for example when Elyot concludes his advice on purgations, in chapter six of the third book, by commenting "These things I remembered because I have known right good physicians to have forgotten to instruct thereof their patients". His criticism is more overt in chapter two of the fourth book when he advises on the treatment of rheums, saying that men can follow his advice if they wish "although some physicians more considering their market than their duty to God and their country will be never so much offended with mine honest enterprise". Throughout the dietary Elyot advises the reader to consult "honest physicians", "good and well-learned physicians", "honest and perfect physicians", clearly a rhetorical strategy to suggest that not all physicans are to be trusted.

Elyot continues on the defensive in this proem, proclaiming that in writing his book he follows the example of King Henry VIII who wrote a book on grammar. Elyot specifically mentions the criticism he has received from the College of Physicians: "some of them hearing me spoken of have said in derision that although I were prettily seen in histories yet being not learned in physic I have put in my book diverse errors in presuming to write of herbs and medicines". He challenges this criticism by claiming that history is less trivial than the physicians believe and "may more surely cure men's affections than diverse physicians do cure maladies". Crucially, he also asserts that he is not ignorant when it comes to physic, listing the medical authorities he has read in his youth under the tutelage of "a worshipful physician, and one of the the most renowned at that time in England", presumably an allusion to Thomas Linacre. He knows not why the physicians would be angry with him since he wrote with a view to helping them better diagnose illness and better prescribe medicine and that men reading his work might, by following a suitable diet, prevent serious sickness and be sooner cured. Of course such claims were not likely to placate his critics and were perhaps even made to deliberately antagonize them: certainly the tone of Elyot's defence veers between apology and mockery of his critics.

Elyot defends writing his *Castle of Health* in the vernacular: "But if physicians be angry that I have written physic in English, let them remember that the Greeks wrote in Greek, the Romans in Latin, Avicenna and others in Arabic, which were their own proper and maternal tongues". If the physicians wanted to keep their skills a secret, he says, they ought to have written it in a secret language, and he compares them unfavourably with earlier authorities who were not guilty of trying to withhold learning and knowledge from the untrained. He concludes by claiming he is not interested in "glory, reward, nor promotion" and that his book will prove advantageous to the careful reader and "honest physicians", this being part of the rhetorical strategy mentioned above that works by suggesting that not all physicians are honest and that those who find fault with *The Castle of Health* are amongst the dishonest ones.

The focus on popularizing medical knowledge, writing in English, and the influence of the English physician Thomas Linacre mark Elyot out as distinctly humanist in his approach. As Skov indicated, Linacre was an important, medical humanist, producing numerous influential translations of the writings of Galen (Elyot 1970, 71–2). As noted above, Elyot recalls being read the works of Galen by "a worshipful physician" (probably Linacre) and he names Linacre explicitly in book two, chapter thirty-three of his dietary when he advises further reading on fricaces or rubbings before exercise "He that will know more abundantly thereof, let him read the book of Galen of the preservation of health, called in Latin *De sanitate tuenda*, translated more truly and eloquently out of Greek into Latin by Doctor Linacre, late physician of most worthy memory to our sovereign lord, King Henry the Eighth". Medical humanism became well known in intellectual circles in England, not least due to Linacre's translations of Galen, yet for the humanists most influential in England, Erasmus and More, human well-being moved beyond the physical and their approach to health was more "broadly humanistic in that they sought not only to preserve the body but also to reform the mind and spirit", their interest spurred not only by medicine but also "a fundamentally psychological, ethical, and religious orientation toward all things coming down from Plato and medieval Christiantity" (Elyot 1970, 73). Mental and spiritual well-being is especially evident in those chapters in the third book of *The Castle of Health* that deal with "the affects of the mind": however Elyot's main focus is the body and it is telling that, unlike Erasmus and More, Elyot expresses no dislike of athletics (Elyot 1970, 88).

By writing in English and making medical learning available to the non-expert Elyot was also apparently influenced by Erasmus's view that medical information should be more widely available: for example in his *Praise of Physic* Erasmus asserts that no man should be ignorant of "that parte of phisike whiche apperteyneth to the gouernance and preseruation of helth" although this is made difficult mainly due to the "blynde ignorance ... [and] the vayne glorie & ambition of leude phisitia[n]s" (Erasmus 1537, Civ). Similarly Elyot was likely influenced by More's view that medical knowledge, specifically that of Galen, could be put to practical use, as expressed in his *Dialogue of Comfort*. That good health could be maintained by following a healthy regiment is stressed also by Raphael in More's *Utopia*, for example in his description of Utopian habits in dining (Elyot 1970, 75–8; Erasmus 1537, C1v; More 1553, H5v–H6r; More 1551, K2r–K3v). David W. Swain has compared the humanist endeavours regarding medicine and the tensions this raised between lay authors and physicians as "congruent to religious conflicts over the English bible", although the arguments over ownership of Galen "entailed matters of academic politics, professional identity, and the rights of patients to know themselves medically and determine their care" (Swain 2008, 55). As noted above, in the proem to the fourth edition of *The Castle of Health*, Elyot's plea to use more English ingredients in medicine suggests that the English ought also to rely less on continental medical authorities. As Swain observed, Elyot's defence of writing his dietary in English, that the early physicians wrote in their own language, which "echoes Reformist arguments for universal access to the Bible" compared those physicans who mock him to "a cabalistic priesthood intent on guarding private knowledge from the Christian community of believers" (Swain 2008, 63). Elyot thus appeals to an emerging sense of national confidence, a desire to democratize medical learning, and a sense that medical theory ought to be balanced with empirical evidence via experience.

A growing national confidence is apparent not just in the use of the vernacular to communicate learning about physic but also in the use of English examples to illustrate points about physic that occur throughout *The Castle of Health*. In the second book Elyot repeatedly locates his discussion of foodstuffs and physical symptoms in an English context. For example in his discussion of the quantity of meat and whether the body can better digest gross or fine meats, from chapter one, he notes "men which use much labour or exercise, also of them which have very choleric stomachs (here in England), gross meats may be eaten in a great quantity, and in a choleric stomach beef is better digested than a chicken's leg". A similar point is made in chapter eight: "Beef of England, to Englishmen which are in health, bringeth strong nourishment but it maketh gross blood and engendereth melancholy". Also in chapter eight, the discussion of fallow deer is given a local context: "I suppose because there be not in all the world so many as be in England, where they consume a good part of the best pasture in the realm". In chapter twenty-one, discussing drinks, he says of ale "I can neither hear nor read that ale is made and used for a common drink in any other country than England, Scotland, Ireland, and Poland". In chapter twenty-seven, discussing times in the day that meals ought to be eaten, he emphasizes the importance of "the temperature of the country and person" in deciding when to eat, remarking "I suppose that in England young men until they come to the age of forty years may well eat the meals in one day", stipulating the time that ought to elapse between meals. In discussing breakfast he again returns to the local context:

> I think breakfasts necessary in this realm, as well for the causes before rehearsed as also forasmuch as choler being fervent in the stomach sendeth up fumosities unto the brain and causeth headache, and sometime becometh adust and smouldereth in the stomach, whereby happeneth perilous sickness and sometime sudden death, if the heat enclosed in the stomach have no other convenient matter to work on; this dayly experience proveth and natural reason confirmeth.

Here Elyot clearly privileges experience over traditional authorities who were writing for a Greek, Latin, or Arabic audience, not an English one. He further underlines the point about experience when he states "And here I will not recite the sentences of authors which had never experience of English men's natures or of the just temperature of this realm of England, only this counsel of Hippocrates shall be sufficient: we ought to grant somewhat to time, to age, and to custom". The classical authority serves merely to underline Elyot's point, that Englishmen should learn from foreign authorities, of course, but these theories should be modified in the light of what Englishmen know to be good for their health. Elyot repeatedly cites Galen as a respected authority in medical matters but he also occasionally disagrees with him, for example in his discussion of the feet of swine as a foodstuff. In chapter nine from book two, he observes:

> Galen commendeth the feet of swine, but I have proved that the feet of a young bullock – tenderly sodden and laid in a souse two days or three, and eaten cold in the evening – have brought a choleric stomach into a good digestion and sleep, and therewith hath also expulsed salt phlegm and choler. And this have I found in myself by often experience, alway forseen that it be eaten before any other meat, without drinking immediately after it.

Similarly in his discussion of radish amongst herbs, in the second book, chapter fifteen, he notes that "being eaten last they make good digestion and looseth the belly (though Galen write contrary) for I, among diverse other, by experience have proved it". It is specifically Galen's lack of knowledge about the English context that is emphasized when Elyot disagrees with him on mutton, in the second book, chapter eight: "Galen doth not commend it, notwithstanding experience proveth here in this realm that if it be young it is a right temperate meat and maketh good juice, and therefore it is used more than any other meat in all diseases".

Elyot also indicates when particular conditions are especially likely to occur in England, such as rheums, of which he says, in the fourth book, chapter two: "at this present time in this realm of England there is not any one more annoyance to the health of man's body than distillations from the head, called rheums". In the fourth book, chapter seven, he describes the sicknesses happening to children, noting that older children can suffer from "swellings under the chin, and in England commonly purples, measles, and smallpox". He also makes frequent references to the English word for particular medical conditions and foodstuffs. For example in chapter one of the third book, in a discussion of repletion, he describes a condition "where the body is enfarced, either with choler yellow or black, or with phlegm, or with watery humours, and is properly called in Greek *cacochymia*, in Latin *viciosus succus*; in English it may be called corrupt juice". Similarly in the third book, chapter six, listing the foods "which of their property do digest or purge superfluous humours", Elyot notes that his examples are taken from classical authors such as Galen, but he has not listed all examples "forasmuch as there be diverse things whereunto we have not yet found any names in English". Describing crudity and lassitude in chapter one of the fourth book he remarks that "although they be words made of Latin, having none apt English work, therefore yet, by the definitions and more ample declaration of them, they shall be understood sufficiently and from henceforth used for English". Elyot does not assume that his reader will understand Latin, unlike some elitist authors who, even today, do not bother to translate Latin or French.

There are moments in *The Castle of Health* when Elyot's personality emerges, sometimes because of what he tells the reader about himself and sometimes because of what is implied. In describing the diet of choleric persons, in chapter sixteen of book one, Elyot remarks:

> beside the opinion of best learned men, mine own painful experience also moveth me to exhort them which be of this complexion to eschew much abstinence, and although they be studious and use little exercise yet in the morning to eat somewhat in little quantity, and not to study immediately but first to sit a while and after to stand or walk softly, which using these two years I and also other that have long known me have perceived in my body great alteration, that is to say, from ill estate to better.

We also learn that he is prone to mental suffering in his discussion of dolour in chapter thirteen of the third book. He tells us that grief and sorrow can be caused by ingratitude:

> This vice therefore of ingratitude, being so common a chance, maketh no worldly friendship so precious that life or health therefore should be spent or consumed. I have been the longer in this place because I have had in this grief sufficient experience.

In a discussion of the sorrow caused by the death of a child he offers advice that sounds odd, even callous, to modern ears:

> If death of children be cause of thy heaviness, call to thy remembrance some children (of whom there is no little number) whose lives, either for incorrigible vices or unfortunate chances, have been more grievous unto their parents than the death of thy children ought to be unto thee, considering that death is the discharger of all griefs and miseries and to them that die well the first entry into life everlasting.

His advice on why the reader might not have got that longed-for promotion is more perceptive:

> Oftentimes the repulse from promotion is cause of discomfort, but then consider whether in the opinion of good men thou art deemed worthy to have such advancement or in thine own expectation and fantasy. If good men so judge thee, thank God of that felicity and laugh at the blindness of them that so have refused thee; if it proceed of thine own folly abhor all arrogance and enforce thyself to be advanced in men's estimation before thou canst find thyself worthy in thy proper opinion.

Skov comments upon Elyot's "sermonizing" and a general tone of "stern repression" (Elyot 1970, 34) in *The Castle of Health* but there are lighter moments when joy shines through, for example in the chapter on honey, from chapter twenty-two in the second book:

> this excellent matter most wonderfully wrought and gathered by the little bee, as well of the pure dew of heaven as the most subtle humour of sweet and virtuous herbs and flowers, be made liquors commodious to mankind, as mead, metheglin, and oxymel.

The joy is not simply Christian awe but also wonder at nature's inspired creation and industry, evident in both the bees who gather the honey and humanity who create the liquors from which they benefit.

The early editions and the present edition
Much of the material in this section is indebted to Skov's valuable bibliographical work (Elyot 1970, 155–64). Six editions of Thomas Elyot's *Castle of Health* were

published by Thomas Berthelet during Elyot's lifetime. The first is an octavo (STC 7642.5) probably published in 1537, with two more editions published in 1539: a quarto (STC 7642.7) and an octavo (STC 7643). Three subsequent editions were published in 1541: a quarto (STC 7644) and two more octavos (STC 7645 and STC 7646). A further eleven editions were published between the years 1546 (the year of Elyot's death) and 1610, with one edition, the 1541 quarto, reissued.

O1 (1537?), the first known edition, was clearly printed from manuscript or from an unknown predecessor edition. Q2 (1539) may have been produced from a manuscript or a marked-up copy of O1 and contains what appear to be authorial revisions, including a new proem. O3 (1539), which has the same new additions as Q2, seems to be set from an exemplar of O1 and is worse printed than Q2. Q4 (1541) has what appear to be authorial revisions not in earlier editions (matter not in Q2 or O3) and seems to be set from an exemplar of Q2. O5 and O6 (1541) have some of the same new further additions as Q4; until one-third of the way into the second book both seem to be set from an exemplar of O3 and the rest set from an exemplar of Q4 but with a new heading (in chapter two of the fourth book) not in O1-Q2-O3-Q4 that reads "By what tokens...". The order of O5 and O6 is uncertain and their numbering here relies only on the assumption that the fact that subsequent editions follow the details of STC 7646 instead of those of STC 7645 shows that STC 7646 is the later of the two (on the grounds that printers tend to reprint from the latest edition).

Skov reproduced the only known exemplar of O1, the first edition of Elyot's dietary (dated some time between 1536-1539), which is located in Yale University library but not reproduced in Early English Books Online (EEBO). Skov collated the six editions that appeared during Elyot's lifetime, arguing that since Elyot died in 1546 these later editions cannot have greater or independent authority. In fact, a posthumous edition may easily have additional authority derived from authorial labour – the words of fresh writing or the correction of existing writing – that lay unused by a publisher until after the author's death. In the present case there are no obvious signs of such authorial labour in the posthumous editions and they are henceforth ignored.

Skov thought that the 1539 quarto (STC 7642.7) represents Elyot's second and corrected edition, and that the 1539 octavo (STC 7643) is a somewhat less carefully made third edition. Amongst the three editions of 1541 (STC 7644, 7645, and 7646) Skov thought that the quarto (STC 7644) most faithfully embodies Elyot's last modifications of his text. Skov's conclusion is accepted here and STC 7644 (Q4), in the form of the exemplar in the Huntington Library, California (call number 53932), and reproduced in Early English Books Online (EEBO), is the copy text for the present edition. All six editions appearing in Elyot's lifetime text have been freshly collated and because all either certainly or possibly contain material from authorial manuscripts and/or authorial corrections, the variants (the differences from Q4) found in the other five are given in the collation notes.

The major difference between Q4 and earlier editions is a revised proem that omits all references to Thomas Cromwell, Elyot's former patron. The new proem is defensive against the criticism aimed at earlier editions, and critical of professional physicians, the source of these attacks (discussed in detail above). Also new to Q4 is chapter two of the fourth book: "Of distillations called commonly rheums and of some remedies against them right necessary". This revision is apparently authorial since here Elyot continues in the same acerbic tone of the revised proem, criticizing those physicians "more considering their market than their duty to God and their country", and wondering that they are not more skilled in providing remedies for rheums. Elyot also provides additional personal information, remarking that reading Galen persuaded him to disregard the advice of physicians and to self-medicate, with favourable results. There are other minor changes that are likely authorial, for example in chapter eighteen "Of drinks, and first of water" the addition of the clause "specially taken with superfluous eating of banqueting meats" and in chapter twenty-three on sugar from book two the addition of the clause "with sugar and vinegar is made syrup acetose".

Each collation note begins with a roman numeral and the reading (called the lemma) that appears in this edition, followed by a closing square bracket. Next comes either the source for the adopted reading – indicated by its siglum O1, Q2, O3, O5, O6 or *this ed.* (meaning this edition, the editor's own invention) – or else, where Q4 is the source of the adopted reading, an alternative reading that has not been adopted and its sigla (O1, Q2, O3, O5 or O6), followed if necessary by an italic semicolon and another alternative reading not adopted and its sigla, and so on (italic semicolon, reading, sigla) for other variants from Q4. Where the collation note is recording a lemma that departs from Q4, the note next has an italic semicolon followed by Q4's reading and its identifying siglum Q4 and the sigla of other sources that agree with Q4, followed if necessary by other alternative readings and their sigla, separated by italic semicolons. The collational notes for marginal notes follow this pattern but are included in the marginal notes themselves within square brackets – rather than appearing at the bottom of the page – and where the lemma is the entire marginal note it is omitted; explanatory notes to marginal notes also appear in the marginal notes themselves, again in square brackets and after the collational note if there is one.

A Compendious Regiment or a Dietary of Health

The author and the dietary

The following account of Boorde's life is derived from the standard sources (Boorde 1870; Boorde 1936; Furdell 2004). Andrew Boorde was born around 1490 at Borde Hill, near Cuckfield, Sussex, and grew up in Oxford. He was under age when he became a monk in 1515 by joining the Carthusian order at the London Charterhouse. He clearly flourished within the order because he was nominated as Suffragan (that is, assistant) Bishop of Chichester but in 1517, as reported in one of his letters, he was accused of being "*conversant with women*" (Boorde 1870, 44) and dismissed from the post by papal bull in 1521. In a letter to John Batmanson, the prior of Hinton Charterhouse in Somerset, dated 1528, Boorde announced himself unable to conform to the Carthusian's rigorous rules, which included vegetarianism and fasting, and asked to be released from his vows. Boorde then travelled abroad to study medicine at numerous universities. In 1530 he returned to England, during which time he provided medical assistance to Thomas Howard, Duke of Norfolk, to whom he would dedicate his *Compendious Regiment or Dietary of Health*. Boorde claims to have also waited on King Henry VIII, at Norfolk's request, which was presumably an informal arrangement since there is no record of payment for his services. By 1532 Boorde was again abroad and conferring with medical authorities in Orléans, Poitiers,

2 Andrew Boorde, woodcut, Wellcome Library, London

Toulouse, Wittenberg, and Rome, as well as travelling to Santiago de Compostela in Galicia and meeting with surgeons from the university there.

Having returned to England, Boorde took the oath of conformity, acknowledging King Henry VIII's supremacy, on 29 May 1534. His powerful friends included Thomas Cromwell, Principal Secretary and Chief Minister of the King. In a letter to Cromwell he complained of being kept imprisoned in the Charterhouse and upon his release seems to have spent some time at Cromwell's house in Hampshire. In 1535 Boorde was again abroad, apparently having been sent by Cromwell to report on continental views of the English King. Boorde travelled throughout France, Spain, and Portugal, writing to Cromwell complaining about a lack of sympathy for England in most countries, France excepted, and sending him rhubarb seeds from Barbary with instructions for growing the plant.

Boorde had returned from his travels by April 1536 and, in a letter to Cromwell, claimed to be practising medicine in Glasgow. He spent a year in Scotland before moving back to England where he sought help from Cromwell in the recovery of two horses stolen from him in London and the repayment of some money that was owed to him. In late 1537 or early 1538 Boorde again travelled abroad, to Jerusalem amongst other places, and in 1542 he was living in Montpellier. Whilst there he completed *The Compendious Regiment, or, Dietary of Health* and wrote a number of other works, including *The First book of the Introduction of Knowledge* (Boorde 1555), which describes the customs and manners of various nations, commenting on a range of issues including the weather, fashions, and food. He also appears to have written a treatise denouncing beards (now lost) since this work was responded to in the *Treatise Answering the Book of Beards*; its title page claims it was compiled "by Collyn clowte" and its last page suggests the author is one "Barnes" (1541), who Furdell claims is the satirist Milton Barnes (Furdell 2004). It is during his time at Montpellier that Boorde is reputed to have collected the humorous stories attributed to him in two publications: *Merry Tales of the Mad Men of Gotham* (Boorde 1565) and *Scoggins Jests* (Boorde 1625); this reputation for humour has led to the notion that Boorde was the original 'merry-Andrew'.

In 1547 Boorde was back in England and living in Winchester; 1547 also saw the publication of his *Breviary of Health* (described below), a work he repeatedly promotes in his *Compendious Regiment*. That same year Boorde was incarcerated in Fleet prison after being charged by John Ponet, later the Bishop of Winchester, with keeping three prostitutes in his chamber. Boorde's powerful friend Thomas Cromwell had died in 1540 so there was no possibility of appealing to him for help and Boorde died in prison in 1549. It is not known where he was buried.

Boorde's *Compendious Regiment or Dietary of Health* was first published in 1542. It contains two distinct sections: the first eight chapters provide details on where and how a man should build his house, exercise himself, and dress for the good of his health. These chapters were published separately in an anonymous work entitled *Book for to Learn a Man to be Wise in Building of his House* (Boorde 1550). It is unclear whether this work was written before the thirty-two chapters that form the rest of the *Compendious Regiment* or when it was published as a distinct volume (the STC date of 1550 is conjecture), but F.J. Furnivall suggests that it was printed before the first edition of the *Compendious Regiment* and then incorporated into the dietary rather than being a section later extracted from the dietary for separate publication (Boorde 1870, 396).

According to Don E. Wayne the *Book for to Learn a Man to be Wise in Building of his House*, also the first eight chapters of Boorde's *Compendious Regiment*, constitute "the earliest published work in English on the subject of building" (Wayne 1984, 114). Boorde advises the reader on the practicalities of house-building: one ought to build a house where there is easy access to water and wood, where a man has plenty of room and fresh air, avoiding marshy ground and other places where the air is not good; one should also choose a plot that is pleasing to the eye and thus the heart. Boorde advises against overspending, warning that "a man must consider the expense before he do begin to build" (the fourth chapter), not borrow from his neighbours, and have enough put aside for sundry expenses that may occur along the way. When the house has been built it is essential for the householder to properly exercise his body and soul by suitable physical activity and prayer. He must also set a good example to those who serve him and Boorde is especially critical of those who swear, claiming a particular propensity towards it amongst his own countrymen "for in all the world there is not such odible swearing as is used in England, specially among youth and children, which is a detestable thing to hear it and no man doth go about to punish it" (the seventh chapter).

The importance of sleep is emphasized by Boorde, who advises on the proper amount of sleep according to complexion, age, and health; in the eighth chapter he warns against sleeping on a full stomach, although if this must be done "then let him stand and lean and sleep against a cupboard, or else let him sit upright in a chair and sleep". Boorde also warns against having sex "before the first sleep", presumably a reference to segmented sleep, which seems to have been common in the early modern period, and probably consisted of a first sleep some time after dusk followed by a period of wakefulness and activity of various degrees, possibly including sex, before a second sleep (Ekirch 2001; Ekirch 2005). Boorde's reputation as the original 'merry Andrew' is apparent also in this chapter when he advises "To bedward be you merry, or have merry company about you, so that to bedward no anger nor heaviness, sorrow, nor pensivefulness do trouble or disquiet you". Sleeping on the stomach or the back is not recommended, nor is it wise to leave any part of the body uncovered, and on the head one should wear a scarlet nightcap. After a good stretch first thing in the morning, one should cough, spit and evacuate the bowels. Repeated hair-combing and washing, but only in cold water, is also recommended; washing in hot water is also specifically warned against in Bullein's dietary since it "engendereth rheums, worms, and corruption in the stomach because it pulleth away natural heat unto the warmed place which is washed" (p. 240). Later in his dietary, when recommending a diet for those suffering from a fever or ague, Boorde notes "Good it is for the space of three courses to wear continually gloves and not to wash the hands . . ." (the twenty-eighth chapter). According to Boorde, going for a walk, hearing mass or saying prayers, and then playing a game of tennis or bowls is the best way to round off morning activities before eating (the eighth chapter). This chapter also contains advice about what to wear in winter and summer: in winter a scarlet petticoat and a jacket lined with lambskin, and in summer a lighter scarlet petticoat and goatskin perfumed gloves.

The chapters on specific foodstuffs, what to eat and why, begin with a warning against surfeit and praise for moderation and abstinence; a labourer can eat three meals a day but a man who is less active ought to eat only two. Boorde often remarks upon the behaviour and diet of English people, noting that the English spend too long sitting at dinner and supper and feed on gross (heavy, inferior) meats before lighter ones, which is not good for their digestion (the ninth chapter). The tenth chapter, on drinks, warns Englishmen against drinking water because it is "cold, slow, and slack of digestion", preferring ale over beer since "ale for an Englishman is a natural drink" whereas beer "is a natural drink for a Dutchman". Other drinks are discussed, with Boorde explaining that he will not say too much about cordial drinks at this juncture: "To speak of a tisane, or of oxymel, or of aqua-vitae, or of hippocras, I do pass over at this time, for I do make mention of it in *The Breviary of Health*". Boorde was clearly alert to future book sales because promotion of this other volume occurs throughout *The Compenious Regiment*.

Boorde devotes subsequent chapters to specific foods with discussion of bread, broths, white meats (dairy products), fish, fowl, animal flesh, roots, herbs, fruits, and spices. He then proceeds to outline diets that ought to be followed by men who are sanguine, phelgmatic, choleric, or melancholy before moving on to diets that best suit specific ailments, for example a diet to follow during an outbreak of pestilence and a diet for those who are suffering from pain in the head. Boorde repeatedly comments on which foods are regularly consumed in England, for example: "Pottage is not so much used in all Christendom as it is used in England" (the twelfth chapter) and "in England there is no eggs used to be eaten but hen eggs" (the thirteenth chapter). In the sixteenth chapter, on the flesh of wild and tame beasts, he observes that "brawn is a usual meat in winter amongst Englishmen" and also offers the English reader advice, noting that "Beef is good meat for an Englishman so it be the beast be young and that it be not cow-flesh" and that venison "is a lord's dish and I am sure it is good for an Englishman, for it doth animate him to be as he is, which is strong and hardy".

Throughout *A Compendious Regiment* Boorde repeatedly invokes his experiences travelling the world, for example in his observations about hunting for venison: "I have gone round about Christendom and overthwart Christendom and a thousand or two and more miles out of Christendom yet there is not so much pleasure for hart and hind, buck and doe, and for roebuck and doe as is in England" (the sixteenth chapter). As H. Edmund Poole pointed out, "Boorde accepted the propositions of the ancients, but he had his own general opinions" and the reader can trace how "he refuses or accepts the ancient beliefs as they coincide or not with his experience" (Boorde 1936, 14). This is evident in Boorde's comments upon the deleterious effects of honeysops (a piece of bread soaked in honey) and what he terms "other broths", observing "they be not good nor wholesome for the colic, nor the iliac, nor other inflative impediments or sicknesses . . . the sayings of Pliny, Galen, Avicenna, with other authors, notwithstanding" (the twelfth chapter). Experience of how foreigners see things comes up repeatedly in Boorde's discussion of specific foodstuffs: for example he notes that garlic "is used and most praised in Lombardy and other countries annexed to it" (the nineteenth chapter) and he refers to High Almain (Germany) in his discussion of cheese, noting that although cheese ought not to be full of maggots "Yet in High Almain the cheese the which is full of maggots is called there the best cheese and they will eat the great maggot as fast as we do eat comfits" (the thirteenth chapter). In his section on pork Boorde compares how people of various nationalities keep their swine, observing that "Spaniards, with the other regions annexed to them, keep the swine more filthier than English persons doth" (the sixteenth chapter). In his description of the development of dietary literature Ken Albala categorized dietaries from the 1570s to 1650 (what he called "period 3") as distinct from earlier works:

> they were . . . willing to criticize the ancients and strike out with their own opinions. It is in this period that local custom began to outweigh nutritional dogma. Social prejudices also came to the fore. Personal experience became a valid criterion in making dietetic judgments, and although there was nothing like a revolution with the experimental method and quantification that characterized scientific investigation of later centuries, there were major departures from orthodoxy. (Albala 2002, 8)

Boorde is clearly ahead of his time since *A Compendious Regiment*, first published in 1542, prefigures the focus on experience Albala identified in dietary literature produced decades later.

Boorde's sense of fun is apparent throughout *A Compendious Regiment* and that this is intentional is made clear from the outset in the proem (which he also calls his preface) addressed to the Duke of Norfolk:

> diverse times in my writings I do write words of mirth, truly it is for no other intention but to make your grace merry, for mirth is one of the chiefest things of physic, the which doth advertise every man to be merry and to beware of pensivefulness.

Like William Bullein in *The Government of Health* who advised his readers to acquaint themselves with 'Dr Merry' (p. 252), Boorde repeatedly advises the reader to attend to their mood as well as their food: for instance the householder ought to show good example to those around him "then may he rejoice in God and be merry, the which mirth and rejoicing doth lengthen a man's life and doth expel sickness" (the seventh chapter). Also important is going to bed "with mirth" and getting up happy: "When you do rise in the morning, rise with mirth and remember God" (the eighth chapter). Generally, the message is that good diet and medicine alone are not sufficient and one must maintain a positive frame of mind: "let every man beware of care, sorrow, thought, pensivefulness, and of inward anger" (the thirty-ninth chapter).

The manner in which Boorde gives dietary advice also emphasises mirth, for example in the discussion of Martinmas beef in the sixteenth chapter, which Boorde warns against eating because "it is evil for the stone and evil of digestion and maketh no good juice", elaborating as follows:

> If a man have a piece hanging by his side and another in his belly, that the which doth hang by the side shall do him more good if a shower of rain do chance that that the which is in his belly, the appetite of man's sensuality nothwithstanding.

The notion that a man would be better off using the piece of beef as an impromptu umbrella than eating it adds colour to what might otherwise be a routine piece of dietary advice. Boorde adds such touches throughout the work, for example when he denounces bakers who adulterate their bread with inferior grains: "I would they might play bo-peep through a pillory" (the eleventh chapter). Yet Boorde also deals with darker subject matter, and his discussion of what appears to be the real case of a madman called Michael – who killed his wife and her sister before committing suicide – is disturbing, if perhaps unintentionally amusing, when Boorde warns "see that the mad-man have no knife nor shears . . . for hurting or killing himself" (the thirty-seventh chapter).

Boorde's *Breviary of Health*, a work he promotes throughout *A Compendious Regiment*, was first published five years after his dietary (Boorde 1547). *The Breviary of Health* is generally medical in its trajectory with 384 short chapters, arranged alphabetically, each devoted to a medical condition, which is described, its causes rehearsed, and a remedy proposed. The remedy typically includes pills or some other medicine but also advice about diet, specifically which food and drink to include or exclude in order to regain health. Douglas Guthrie characterized it as "the first medical book, by a medical man, originally written in the English language"; as Guthrie pointed out, Thomas Elyot's *Castle of Health* had been published in 1534 but Elyot was not a doctor and had "incurred the wrath of physicians" for his impertinence (Guthrie 1943, 508).

In the Prologue addressed to Physicans that prefaces *The Breviary of Health* Boorde contends that those offering medical advice ought to be properly qualified for otherwise he "shal kyll many more than he shall saue" (Boorde 1547, A3r). In the Proem to Surgeons he adds that surgeons should be "wyse, gentyll, sober, and nat dronken" and "to promyse no more than they be able to performe with goddes helpe" (Boorde 1547, A4r). The importance of diet is here emphasized: surgeons "muste knowe the operation of all maner of breades, of drynkes, and of meates" as well as having their instruments, salves, and ointments at the ready (Boorde 1547, A4v). In a "Preamble to sycke men and to those that be wounded" Boorde warns that the sick person should have patience and put his faith in Christ; only after he has called upon his "spyrytuall phisicion [spiritual physician]" should he "prouyde for his body, and take counsell of some expert phisicion" (Boorde 1547, A4v–B1r). Boorde aims his book at the general reader, explaining in the "Preface to reders of this boke" that he has translated foreign and obscure words into English so that everyone may understand them (Boorde 1547, B2r), although he adds that he is brief in his explication, so that "the archane science of phisicke shulde nat be to[o] manifest and open, for than [then] the eximious [excellent] science shulde fall in to great detriment and doctors the which hath studied the facultie shulde nat be regarded so well". Boorde claims that if he told all he knew then "every bongler [bungler] wolde practyce phisicke vpon my boke, wherfore I do omyt and leue [leave] out many thynges" (Boorde 1547, B2r). *The Second Book of the Breviary named the Extravagants*, attached to the *Breviary of Health*, adds certain ailments and their remedies not discussed in the first book, concluding with a discussion of various types of urine, the specific colour, containing blood and so on, and what this signifies.

The early editions and the present edition
There are six early editions of Andrew Boorde's *Compendious Regiment of Health*. The first is STC 3378.5, published by Robert Wyer in 1542, and the second is STC 3380, published by William Powell in 1547, and these quartos are here called Q1 and Q2 respectively. A roman numeral error makes the title page of Q2 claim to be published in 1567, but this is unlikely because as Furnivall noted "Boorde died in 1549, and the dedication is altered [compared to Q1] in a way that no one but an author could have altered it" (Boorde 1870, 13). It is possible that Boorde made the alterations before he died in 1549 and that they lay unactioned for two decades during which several other editions (described below) were printed. However, the alterations were apparently made by annotating an exemplar of Q1 so this possibility is remote. The survival, rediscovery and reprinting of such a marked-up exemplar is even more unlikely than the discovery of a fresh authoritative manuscript.

That Q2 is a reprint of Q1 is established by their agreement-in-error on the unwanted sentence break in "comfort the brayne. And the powers natural" (Q1 B4r, Q2 A2v). However, the exemplar of Q1 used to print Q2 was first extensively annotated by the author, for the latter advertises itself as "newly corrected" on the title page and includes a different preface from Q1 that, like the dedication, could have been written only by the author and has dozens of improved readings. For example, Q2 omits the spurious words "other of" in Q1's "fulfyllynge other of the .vii. werkes of mercy" (Q1 C4v, Q2 B2r) and recommends that beer reduces the heat of the liver if it is "wel brude and fyned" (well-brewed and refined) rather than "well serued and be fyned" (Q1 F2v, Q2 D2v). Such alterations are not beyond the capacities of an intelligent printshop editor or compositor, but Q2 also expands upon certain descriptions with additional knowledge only the author could provide, such as extending the description of the drink coyte to mention that "hit dothe but quench the thyrste" (Q2 D3v) without providing nutrition. Because of this layer of authorial improvement, Q2 is the copy text for this edition.

Part of Boorde's *Compendious Regiment* appeared in the quarto STC 3382.5 (published by Wyer and dated around 1550 by the ESTC), together with a short guide at the end indicating what quantity of medicines one ought to use, and this is here called Q3. This edition's title page markets itself as compiled by Thomas Linacre (c. 1460-1524) and several "Doctours in Physicke" with no mention of Boorde. John L. Thornton conjectured that, with Boorde in disgrace after his death in prison, the publisher Wyer chose to republish part of *Compendious Regiment* under the safer name of Linacre (Thornton 1948, 209). The alternative proposition that Boorde earlier took over Linacre's or another writer's work and expanded it to make *Compendious Regiment* is unlikely, since Boorde's book reads as a stylistically coherent whole. What Wyer used to set STC 3382.5 is uncertain, but it was not Q2 as the authorial improvements are absent. Assuming that the assigned dates are correct, the choice for copy text for STC 3382.5 is limited to Q1 or a fresh manuscript or a combination of the two. Q3 frequently agrees with later editions against Q1-Q2 yet it cannot have been printer's copy for those later editions since it lacks much of *Compendious Regiment*'s text, including parts where those later editions depart from Q1-Q2. Moreover, Q3 has a number of unique readings that are neither garblings nor innovations likely to arise in the printshop, which suggests an independent manuscript source. These are "breketh wynde", "immedyatly eaten", "reform the nature", "asshe wode or cole", "Antony a Physycion", "his curate", and "byd the sycke man remembre how christe suffred death & passyon for hym" (Q3 A4v, B1r, B1r, D4r, F3r, G2r, G3r). Because Q3 apparently preserves readings from an independent manuscript, wherever it differs from this modernized edition's copy text, Q2, its readings have been given special consideration.

The dietary was published again as a quarto by Wyer (STC 3380.5) in an edition conjecturally assigned to the year 1554 by the ESTC, and reprinted again as an octavo by Thomas Colwell in 1562 (STC 3381) and again as an octavo by Hugh Jackson in 1576 (STC 3382). The three editions are here identified as Q4, O5, and O6 on the assumption that the first's assigned date of 1554 is correct. P.B. Tracy's study of Wyer's type enabled her to produce a tentative chronology of his undated books and she assigned STC 3380.5 (under its former STC number of 3379) to the year "1550?" (Tracy 1980, item 111). Q4-O5-O6 form a distinct group agreeing on dozens of readings against Q1-Q2. Despite the difference in format, O5 was a slavish page-for-page reprint of Q4, copying even a catchword error "of" for "a" (Q4 F3r; O5 L3r). All of O5's differences from Q4 could have arisen in the printshop without authority. Presumably the manuscript used to set Q1 was destroyed in the process (this was usual), and hence Q4's agreement-in-error with Q1 on the readings "lyeth of digestion" (Q1 E4r; Q4 F3r) and "fulfyllynge other of the seuen workes of mercy" (Q1 C4v; Q4 C4v) shows that an exemplar of Q1 was the printer's copy for Q4. For the first of these two variants, O5 prints the correct "lyght of dygestion" (C7r), as does Q2 (C4v), but this could simply be a printshop correction.

However, Q4 also departs from Q1 in a number of small rephrasings that seem unlikely to have been made in the printshop:

thynges that shortneth mans lyfe (Q1 C1r)
thynges the whiche shulde shorten the lyfe of man (Q4 B4v)

consyderynge it doth compasse vs rounde aboute (Q1 B4r)
consyderynge it doth close and doth compasse vs rounde aboute (Q4 B2v)

as the influence (Q1 B4r)
The fyrst is the influence (Q4 B3r)

hath prepared (Q1 D1v)
hath prouyded (Q4 D2r)

nede not to be rehersed (Q1 D3r)
nede not greatly to be rehersed (Q4 D5r)

or ye water of buglos or the water of endyue (Q1 F1r)
or the water of Buglosse, or the water of Borage, or the water of Endyue (Q4 F4r)

vnto she be maried (Q1 F1v)
vnto the tyme she be maryed (Q4 G1r)

and deade ale the which doth stande (Q1 F2r)
and deed ale, and ale the whiche doth stande (Q4 G2r)

feble stomackes (Q1 G2v)
fell stomackes (Q4 H3v)

shall do hym more good (Q1 H3v)
shal do a man more good (Q4 K2r)

doth fede in Englande (Q1 H4r)
doth fede, specyallye in Englande (Q4 K3r)

of roste meate, of fryed meate, and of bake meate (Q1 I3r)
of roste meate, of fryed meate, of soden or boyled meate, of bruled meate, and of bake meate (Q4 L2v)

in ye broth of beef (Q1 K1r)
in the broth of Beefe or with beefe (Q4 M1v)

preseruatyues (Q1 L3r)
preseruacions (Q4 O1v)

take any open ayer (Q1 L4v)
take ye open ayre (Q4 O3r)

sowre brede (Q1 M3v)
sowre beere (Q4 P3r)

he that doth not the commandment (Q1 N3v)
he y^t doth not obserue the co[m]maundements (Q4 Q3v)

theyr brethes (Q1 N4r)
theyr hote breathes (Q4 Q4r)

man in suche agony (Q1 N4r)
man that is in suche agony (Q4 Q4r)

These mainly indifferent variations suggest that the exemplar of Q1 used to set Q4 was first annotated by reference to an authoritative manuscript, collateral to the one used to set Q1. This additional authority is not sufficient for us to prefer Q4 to Q2 as copy text for a modern edition, since Q2's additional authority (attested on the title page and in the prefatory material) is witnessed in dozens of improved readings. But if Boorde annotated an exemplar of Q1 to make copy for Q2, as seems likely, they will agree wherever he failed to correct Q1 and thus Q1-Q2 agreement against Q4 is not strong evidence that Q4 is wrong. For this reason, wherever Q4 departs from Q1 its readings have been given special consideration in this edition.

O6 is a page-for-page reprint of either Q4 or O5, and more likely the latter since it agrees in error with O5 against Q4 on "west wynde mutable", "performation on it", and "Aptisone" (O6 B1v, B3v, D3v), and without error on "and also other necessary thinges", "lyght of dygestion", "yet they be not commendable", "and so be chickens in sommer", "and redde wyne", "tyme of Pestylence", "beware the legges", "and hee muste exchewe", and "of lying" (O6 B4v, C7r, C7v, E5r, G4v, G5r, G8r, G8v, H4v). Where O6 agrees with another edition against O5 the correction is sometimes obvious enough to be a printshop alteration, as with "treateth of Potage" (O6 A2v) and "of Cullesses" (O6 D6r), but on a couple of occasions O6 departs from its O5 copy to agree with a good reading from Q1-Q2: "good for all ages" (O6 D4r) and "be not co[m]mendable" (O6 E5v). These two corrections seem beyond the capacity of anyone in the printshop, so we must conclude that either the exemplar of O5 used as copy for O6 was first corrected at just these points by reference to Q1-Q2 or an authoritative manuscript, or else those resources were consulted in the printshop; either procedure is hard to explain. We can be sure that such correction of O6's copy was not thoroughgoing because O5 and O6 show a series of agreements-in-error deriving from Q4: "docknet", "Wynes of operacion", "strayne coylyon", "oryfe", "Ieueue" and "skyn take of" (O6 C8r, D1r, D2v, E1r, E1v, E8r). O6 also has a few unique readings of its own that go beyond accidental variation by a compositor: "thy kynred, or nation", "for it doth doeth hynder and let much the memorye", "of yll digestion", and "do vse to go to the Church" (O6 A4v, B7v, C2r, C3r). These appear to be small rewordings made in the printshop, perhaps to save or waste space in order to preserve the pagination of this page-for-page reprint.

This edition uses as its copy text for *A Compendious Regiment of Health* the British Library exemplar of Q2 (classmark 1606/18). The readings of Q2 are followed except where they are manifestly wrong. Wherever Q1 or Q3 differ from Q2 their readings are recorded, and special consideration is given to Q3's differences from Q2 since these are evidence of independent manuscript authority. Where Q4 differs from Q1 the readings of both are recorded and special consideration is given to Q4's readings since these are evidence of independent manuscript authority. Throughout the text all roman numerals have been converted to arabic numerals and Boorde's Latin has been retained and explained in notes. In collation notes quotations from texts other than Q2 are not modernized.

Each collation note begins with a roman numeral and the reading (called the lemma) that appears in this edition, followed by a closing square bracket. Next comes either the source for the adopted reading – indicated by its siglum *Q1*, *Q3*, *Q4*, or *this ed.* (meaning this edition, the editor's invention) – or else, where Q2 is the source of the adopted reading, an alternative reading that has not been adopted and its sigla

(Q_1, Q_3, or Q_4), followed if necessary by an italic semicolon and another alternative reading not adopted and its sigla, and so on (italic semicolon, reading, sigla) for other variants. Where the collation note is recording a lemma that departs from Q_2, the note next has an italic semicolon followed by Q_2's reading and its identifying siglum Q_2 and the sigla of other sources that agree with Q_2, followed if necessary by other alternative readings and their sources, separated by italic semicolons. Where Q_1's reading is recorded solely to mark its difference from Q_4's reading, it appears at the end of the note. Where Q_1's reading is recorded solely to mark its difference from Q_2, it appears in the collation in its chronological position, which is at the beginning.

The Government of Health

The author and the dietary

The following account of Bullein's life is derived from the standard sources (Mitchell 1959; McCutcheon 1996; Wallis 2004; Maslen 2008). It is not clear exactly when William Bullein was born but it was probably around the year 1515 in the Isle of Ely, which was a county in what is now Cambridgeshire. He was the eldest son of William Bullen and Alice Tryvet and had two brothers one of whom, his younger brother Richard, apparently shared his interest in medicine. The family may have been related to Anne Boleyn and Bullein may have studied at both Cambridge and Oxford. There is no evidence that he went to either university, although he mentions (in the voice of Surgery) serving under "R.R." in his *Bulwark of Defence* (Bullein 1579, Gg1r), which may indicate Robert Record, the mathematician, astronomer, and physician, who taught at both Universities.

On 9 June 1550 Bullein became rector of Blaxhall in Suffolk and in *The Government of Health* claims to be related to the most important family in the town, although he does not indicate which family (p. 276). By 5 November 1554 he had resigned his post, presumably because, as a committed Protestant, he was unhappy under the reign of the Catholic monarch Mary I who had come to the throne in the summer of 1553. He remained in contact with the powerful Protestant noblemen he had met in Suffolk, among them Sir Robert Wingfelde, to whom he dedicated *A Comfortable Regiment . . . Against the Most Perilous Pleurisy* (Bullein 1562a), and Lord Henry Carey, Baron of Hunsdon, to whom he dedicated his *Bulwark of Defence*.

It is not clear where Bullein studied medicine (possibly Germany) but he does not appear to have taken a medical degree. He began to practise medicine in Northumberland and Durham where one of his patients, and patron, was Sir Thomas Hilton, Baron of Hilton and captain of Tynemouth Castle. Bullein lived in Hilton's home whilst writing his first book *The Government of Health* and dedicated it to him. Hilton died soon after the book was first published in 1558 and Bullein married Hilton's widow Agnes (or Anne). In the summer of 1560 the couple moved to London and rented a house in Grub Street in the parish of St Giles Cripplegate; Bullein had sent his goods ahead by ship from the Tyne but lost these when the ship was wrecked. Bullein's brother, Richard, was rector of the parish and evidence that he too was interested in medicine can be found in Bullein's description of him in the *Bulwark of Defence* as "a zealous Louer of Physicke" who "hath good Experience of many Infirmities and Sicknesses . . . and hath done many goodly Cures", including a treatise

3 William Bullein after unknown artist, possibly late sixteenth to early seventeenth century, woodcut, National Portrait Gallery, London

on the stone (Bullein 1579, Hh4r–Hh4v). Richard was probably the author of the commendatory verses signed "R.B." that were printed at the beginning of *The Government of Health*.

Whilst in London Bullein was accused by Hilton's brother, William, of murdering his patron, Sir Thomas Hilton, and was arraigned before the Duke of Norfolk. Bullein denied the charge and the case was dismissed, perhaps through the influence of his powerful Suffolk connections. William Hilton continued to pursue Bullein and in 1559 or 1560 prosecuted him and his wife for a debt which he claimed he had been owed by his brother, Sir Thomas. Hilton won the case and Bullein and his wife were imprisoned. It was whilst in prison that Bullein rewrote his *Bulwark of Defence* (the original manuscript had perished in the shipwreck along with his other goods), which contains his account of Hilton's accusations against him.

After his release from prison Bullein published his third book, *A Comfortable Regiment . . . Against the Most Perilous Pleurisy* in December of that year (Bullein 1562a). His last and most popular work was *A Dialogue Against the Fever Pestilence*, which he appears to have written in the home of Edward Barrette of Belhouse in Essex, to whom the work is dedicated (Bullein 1564).

Bullein continued to practise medicine in London, although he never became a fellow of the College of Physicians. His first wife died in the early 1560s, and in the autumn of 1566 he married Anne Doffield, with whom he had a daughter, Margaret. He appears to have written little after his *Dialogue Against the Fever Pestilence*, his last known publication being some commendatory verses prefacing John Sadler's translation of *De re militari* (*On Military Matters*), a Latin work from the fifth century (Flavius 1572).

Bullein was up in court again when at Christmas 1570 a Yule log set fire to his house and he answered accusations of carelessness by claiming that he and his family were unaware that the chimney had been built upon a floor of timber. He died on 7 January 1576 and was buried two days later in the church of St Giles Cripplegate. In the same grave was his brother, Richard, who had died in 1563, and a few years later the martyrologist John Foxe was also interred there; it was not unusual for unrelated persons to share graves in churchyards situated in overcrowded parts of London. An inscription over the tomb commemorates the three men and says of Bullein "*medicamina semper habebat, aeque pauperibus danda, ac locupletibus aeque*" ("he always had medicines, which he gave to rich and poor alike").

Bullein's *Government of Health* was first published in 1558. It consists of a dialogue between John, a self-confessed rioter, and Humphrey, a man of moderate habits. At the beginning of the dialogue John is confident in his gluttony, announcing that "Abstinence and fasting is a mighty enemy and nothing pleasant to me" (p. 221). When Humphrey suggests he is amongst the "lusty revellers and continual banquet makers" (p. 221) who will come to no good, John expresses irritation, telling Humphrey that he is an old man who ought to mind his own business. But, having heard Humphrey's report of the consequences of a life of excess, John soon comes round, apologizing for his opinions expressed earlier:

> I would be glad to learn some of thy knowledge, for thou hast a good order in talking, and seem to be grounded of authority. Therefore I am sorry that I have contended with thee. I pray thee be not angry with my former talk. (p. 224)

The dialogue begins with a discussion about physic before moving on to the humours, which Humphrey describes by way of singing a song upon his lute, a song that John concludes is "not very pleasant" but "profitable" (p. 227). After a discussion of the four elements (earth, water, air, and fire) and the seasons, Humphrey plays another song describing the complexions of "meats and medicines" (p. 229). There follows a detailed discussion of the complexions of men, women, and other animals, according to man's various ages and the different types of creatures. Humphrey then describes the human body, pointing out to John the various veins that ought to be cut so as to bleed the patient and thus alleviate certain conditions. Having also commented briefly upon what medicines might clean the blood and the number of bones in the body, Humphrey advises John on different kinds of purging and the value of remaining clean, specifically combing one's hair and washing one's hands, though not in hot water, which "engendereth rheums, worms, and corruption in the stomach because it pulleth away natural heat unto the warmed place which is washed" (p. 240). He also advises on what diet best suits a phlegmatic man like John, those with other complexions, and sick men, as well discussing the value of good air, exercise, and a good night's sleep. After explaining how to avoid "the stone" (kidney stones), which John tells

Humphrey "my father was sore vexed therewith" (p. 249), Humphrey provides two rhymes, one detailing how to read urine for signs of illness and the other how to read excrement for the same. Humphrey agrees with John that three doctors ought to be known if a man is to remain healthy and happy: Dr Diet, Dr Quiet, and Dr Merryman. It is at this point in the dialogue that the question and answer session on specific foodstuffs begins, with John enquiring "what is wormwood?" (p. 255).

The section discussing various foods considers their dietary and medicinal value as well as what John, and thus the reader, ought to avoid in order to maintain good health. Humphrey discusses how certain foods might alleviate both relatively minor conditions such as coughs and headaches, as well as more serious ones such as fevers and the death of a foetus in-utero. Foodstuffs are broadly divided into categories, beginning with herbs and vegetables before moving on to fruit, animal flesh, fowl, fish, and white meats (dairy products), drinks, bread, rice, nuts, condiments, and spices. Familiar foodstuffs appear, although Humphrey makes certain observations that would strike a modern reader as odd, for example that garlic "is hurtful to the eyes and head" but "is good for the haemorrhoids, applied to the sore place" (p. 260). Also included are a number of foods that we would regard as strange, for example the sparrow and robin redbreast that Humphrey recommends "either roasted or boiled" (p. 284) and the preference for women's breast milk over the milk of other mammals for adults as well as children (p. 289).

The section on foodstuffs is generally less discursive than the material on medicine, complexions, veins and so on, discussed above, with John tending to rephrase his questioning only slightly, for example "I would fain know what is chickenweed" and "What is sorrel" (p. 256). However, at one point in the dialogue the formerly spirited nature of John resurfaces when, in the discussion of pork, John questions what good may be reported of the meat, asserting "I think very little or nothing" (p. 277); when Humphrey praises pork John questions his advice, calling pigs filthy animals and invoking the biblical admonition against them. John later similarly gives his opinion of the damage done by conies to corn grown by English farmers. Like Elyot and Boorde, Bullein repeatedly comments on the English context when discussing certain foods and physical health, for example in chapters discussing the production of saffron, grapes, and salt. Where Boorde considered ale a proper drink for an Englishman, Bullein is similarly nationalistic in his warning against rotten hops imported from abroad (in the section headed "What is beer or ale", p. 292). He recommends English almanacs for knowing when to administer a purge (p. 238) and warns that the temperate English climate means that Englishmen, unlike those living further south, should avoid eating raw herbs, roots, and fruits (in the section "what be cucumbers?", pp. 259–60).

At one point in the dialogue John describes himself as one of the "plain men in the country" who "dwell far from great cities" and must rely on home-remedies when ill. R.W. Maslen suggests John is typical of the questioners in Bullein's dialogues, poor men who have much to teach their wealthy superiors (Maslen 2008, 121), yet although John is a country-dweller who knows less about medicine than Humphrey and cannot easily get access to it, he is clearly not poor since he can afford to indulge his love of food and drink and he refers to his "servants and labouring family" (p. 246). Having received advice from Humphrey on " the precious treacle called mithridatum" he is presented with "a pretty regiment for the pestilence" (p. 299).

The prefatory material in *The Government of Health* is also of interest since it provides information about Bullein himself. In the epistle Bullein is defensive about the accusation that he had poisoned his patron, Sir Thomas Hilton. There is some prefatory verse signed R.B., that is probably by his brother, Robert Bullein (see above), as well as verse that is apparently by Bullein. There is also an address to the reader in prose where Bullein indicates his debt to the classical authorities he will cite at length in the main dialogue.

Bullein's second work, *The Bulwark of Defence* (Bullein 1562b) is mentioned in his *Government of Health* in the section on clysters when he states his intention to elaborate upon their use "in my next book of healthful medicines" (p. 240) and in a concluding address to the reader when he mentions his next work in recommending *The Government of Health*:

> And thus, I beseech thee to bear with my rudeness, committing this book once again into thy hands, trusting that I have meant good will unto thee in the setting forth thereof so thou wilt thankfully embrace it and order thyself unto the rules thereof, which is all that I desire. And in the mean season, as I have begun, so, through God's help, I intend to make an end of another book of healthful medicines, which, like-wise, I trust thou wilt take in good worth and in that part that I make it for. (p. 302)

In the dedication to Lord Henry Carey, Baron of Hunsdon, in *The Bulwark of Defence*, Bullein describes the work as "this little fort . . . [a] worke of defence agaynst Sicknesse, or euill dyet" that has been influenced by Thomas Elyot's regimen, *The Castle of Health*, first published around 1537 (Bullein 1579, C2v). As Maslen pointed out, Bullein's debt to Elyot is also clear in his *Government of Health* since the title fused the name of Elyot's regimen with his political treatises *The Book Named the Governor*, first published in 1531, and *The Image of Governance*, first published in 1541 (Maslen 2008, 120). *The Bulwark of Defence* consists of four distinct works: "The Booke of Simples", which is a dialogue between Marcellus and Hilarius; "A Little Dialogve Betweene Soarenes, and Chirurgi [Soreness and Surgery]"; "The Booke of Compoundes", which is a dialogue between Sickness and Health; and "The Booke of the Vse of Sicke Men, and Medicines", also a dialogue between Sickness and Health. In the dialogue between Marcellus and Hilarius, Bullein expands upon the information given about various foodstuffs in *The Government of Health*; in the dialogue between Soreness and Surgery, Soreness asks questions about various physical conditions, such as wounds and ulcers, and how best to treat them; in "The Booke of Compoundes" Sickness enquires how to make specific medicines consisting of more than one ingredient (a "compound"); and in "The Booke of the Vse of Sicke Men, and Medicines" Health offers advice on when and how to use specific medicines and procedures as well as general advice regarding health. Bullein clearly thought the dialogue format from *The Government of Health* worked well and again sought to use it, fully exploiting its rhetorical advantages. He was also clearly still smarting from the accusations levelled against him by William Hilton, for in the section from "The Book of Simples" describing milk, butter, and cheese he discusses his persecution at the hands of Hilton "who accused me of no lesse cryme [crime] then [than] of most cruel murder of his own brother, who dyed of a feuer (sent onely of God) among his owne frends, fynishing his lyfe in the christen fayth" (Bullein 1579, O1v).

Bullein's next work was *A Regiment Against Pleurisy*, a short treatise, this time not in dialogue form, providing a history of the disease as well as a description of its symptoms and its causes, which Bullein claims is partly due to the drinking of cold water when good ale, beer, or wine is not available (Bullein 1562a). He provides instructions for various clysters, ointments, and plasters that will aid the patient. His final major work was *A Dialogue Against the Fever Pestilence*, which is not so much a dialogue as a narrative containing several dialogues between a number of different characters (Bullein 1564). These include a citizen and his wife who flee London in order to avoid the plague, the sick Antonius who is infected with the plague, Antonius's doctor and apothecary, and two lawyers who are after the dying man's money. Towards the end of the work the character Death comes for the citizen and Bullein provides this sinister figure with a chilling speech on death as the great leveller. It is the dialogue between Antonius and his physician Medicus about the nature of the plague, its symptoms and how to treat it, that is most typical of Bullein's other works.

The early editions and the present edition
Bullein's *Government of Health* was entered in the Stationers' Register amid undated entries that can from context be dated between 19 July 1557 and 9 July 1558 (Arber 1875, 1:77). The first edition – an octavo here designated O1 (STC 4039) – was printed early in 1558 but Bullein was unhappy about certain errors that appeared, something made clear in his address to the reader at the end of the work where he blames haste in preparing the volume:

> because I have had no conference with others, nor long time of premeditation in study, but with speed have conciliated this small entitled Government of Health, it cannot be but many things have missed in the print. (Bullein 1558, S4r–S4v)

Bullein gives some examples of words he knows to be incorrect. The printer must have let Bullein see the printed sheets before they were gathered since he was able to comment on the book in an address contained within the book. (Had Bullein seen the sheets during the print run his corrections could have been applied to the type by stop-press correction.). Bullein anticipates *The Government of Health* being printed again:

> And thus to conclude, I will, by God's grace, join another book called *The Healthful Medicines* into this Government, and at the next impression such amends shall be made that both syllable and sentence shall be diligently kept in true order to thy contentation, God willing, who ever kept thee in health. The first of March, the year of our salvation, 1558. (Bullein 1558, S4v)

Assuming that registration preceded publication, this first edition's address to the reader being dated 1 March 1558 makes that date the *terminus ad quem* for composition.

The other book Bullein refers to above as "The Healthful Medicines" is his *Bulwark of Defence*, first published in 1562. A second edition – O2 (STC 4040) – of *The Government of Health* containing corrections was published shortly after the first, and Bullein dates his address to the reader at its conclusion "the 20 of April 1558". We might suspect that the date 1 March 1558 written by Bullein in O1 was in fact 1 March 1559 by our reckoning if Bullein was the kind of devout person who did not increment the year number until after Lady Day (25 March) whereas we increment it on 1 January. If this were true the edition here identified as O2 might in fact (despite the title pages' dates) be the first and O1 the second. However the possibility of such misidentification is eliminated by O1's Stationers' Register entry appearing amid a group that can be dated no later than 9 July 1558 and also by the textual relationship between O1 and O2: the latter's improvements, and Bullein's comments in both editions about making corrections show that it is a reprint of the former.

In this address to the reader at the beginning of the second edition Bullein claims that he looked over the first edition and mended "certain faults that were escaped in the print", for example he rightly claims that "Wenzoar" is corrected to "Avenzoer". O2 seems to have been typeset from an exemplar of the first edition that had been marked up with corrections by the author and there are numerous examples of O2 improving upon O1 besides those specifically noted by Bullein. For example, in O2 Humphrey (responding to John's "I pray thee tell me something of exercise") refers to the idle who "love meats of light digestion" (O2, H5r), a reading which makes better sense than O1's reference to the idle who "abhore" such meats (since the idle would clearly like meats that are easy to digest); similarly Humphrey's rhyme on excrements corrects O1's "holler" to "choler" (O2, I1v). Although the spellings change, O2 is a line for line and page for page reprint of the main text of O1 up to the end of H3r and it seems that after this point in the text the changes Bullein presented in his marked-up exemplar of O1 were too many for the printer to retain the lineation and pagination of O1. Collation of O1 and O2 bears this out: there are many more authorial changes after H3r than before it.

A third edition (O3, STC 4041) of *The Government of Health* was published in 1559, which collation shows to be a reprint of the second edition with no additional authority, and a fourth edition (O4, STC 4042) was published in 1595 (Bullein died in 1576), which collation shows to be a reprint of the first edition with no additional authority. Because O2 contains Bullein's own improvements upon the first edition it is the copy text for this modern edition.

This edition uses as its copy text for *The Government of Health* the British Library exemplar of O2 (classmark Huth 76, wrongly dated 1559 by the British Library), which was collated against O1, O3, and O4. O3 and O4 are derivative editions in which there are no signs of additional authority, although they might of course occasionally reproduce press variants from their copy texts (exemplars of O2 and O1 respectively) that are not present in the exemplars of O2 and O1 used for this edition. (No collation within editions to detect press variants has been undertaken.) From their knowledge of the work and of the beliefs of the period the compositors of O3 and O4 might also have departed from their copy texts to correct error and so produce good readings not available in O1 or O2. For these reasons, readings from O3 and O4 appear in the collation notes wherever they contain a rejected variant reading that might none the less be correct. The readings of O2 are followed except where they are manifestly wrong. All O1-O2 differences are recorded in the collation notes, and O2-O3 and O2-O4 differences are recorded wherever O3's and O4's readings might be right but are not adopted

Each collation note begins with a roman numeral and the reading (called the lemma) that appears in this edition, followed by a closing square bracket. Next comes

INTRODUCTION 35

either the source for the adopted reading – indicated by its siglum *O1*, *O3*, *O4*, or *this ed.* (meaning this edition, the editor's own invention) – or else, where *O2* is the source of the adopted reading, an alternative reading that has not been adopted and its sigla (*O1*, *O3*, or *O4*), followed if necessary by an italic semicolon and another alternative reading not adopted and its sigla, and so on (italic semicolon, reading, sigla) for other variants from *O2*. Where the collation note is recording a lemma that departs from *O2*, the note next has an italic semicolon followed by *O2*'s reading and its identifying siglum *O2* and the sigla of other sources that agree with *O2*, followed if necessary by other alternative readings and their sigla, separated by italic semicolons. The collational notes for marginal notes follow this pattern but are included in the marginal notes themselves within square brackets – rather than appearing at the bottom of the page – and where the lemma is the entire marginal note it is omitted; explanatory notes to marginal notes also appear in the marginal notes themselves, again in square brackets and after the collational note if there is one.

NOTE ON THE EDITORIAL HISTORY OF THE DIETARIES

In 1970 John Villads Skov produced a critical edition of the first edition of Sir Thomas Elyot's *Castel of Health* from the only available copy, in Yale University Library (not available in EEBO). Skov's edition merely printed a photographic facsimile of the original text and so it is not a modern spelling edition, and, being an unpublished PhD thesis, it is not readily available. However Skov did provide a collation of the first six editions of Elyot's dietary (those published during his lifetime), useful introductory material, and explanatory notes.

Andrew Boorde's *Compendious Regiment* was printed in an abridged version, edited by H. Edmund Poole in a run of 550 copies in 1936 by the Garswood Press. It contains no explanatory notes but does include, without explanation, a random extract from one of Boorde's other works, *The Breviary of Health*. F.J. Furnivall's 1870 edition of Boorde's *Compendious Regiment* for the Early English Text Society is an original-spelling edition presented in the same volume as other works by Boorde, including extracts from his *Breviary of Health*. Furnivall reprints the first edition of Boorde's dietary, published in 1542, and collates it with another (undated) edition, probably published in 1554, the 1547 edition, and the 1562 edition. He provides only brief explanatory notes on Boorde's text.

William Bullein's *Government of Health* has not been published since the sixteenth century. This volume contains the first modern-spelling edition of this important work with a complete collation and full explanatory notes.

TEXTUAL ISSUES

In accordance with Revels Companion Library series practice, I have silently modernized spelling, expanded abbreviations and elisions (for example turning *lōg* into *long*), regularized *i/j* and *u/v* to modern usage, and corrected non-substantive misprints (such as doubled or turned letters, extra spaces, inked quads and so on). The only exception is that when a marginal note in the early modern edition is indecipherable it is presented literatim and its possible meaning suggested by an explanatory note. Where possible the punctuation of the copy text has been retained but, as with many early modern texts, the dietaries' punctuation is often erratic and does not follow modern grammatic rules, so the texts have been extensively repunctuated. On the rare occasion when it is unclear what letter or letters are intended by the copy text this is indicated by [.] and, where possible, the inferred meaning is given in an explanatory note.

The letter *y* is used in manuscripts and printed books to represent the lost Old and Middle English letter *þ* (called thorn), giving rise to the forms *ye* for modern *the* and *yt* for modern *that*; these are not collated as variants here. All the early editions use ¶ (the pilcrow) to highlight headings and the beginnings of paragraphs and (occasionally) significant points within paragraphs; Boorde's edition also uses manicules (☞) or a leaf symbol to direct the reader's eye. These have all been normalized to modern typographical forms, usually a new paragraph with its first line indented. Guidance on how to read collation notes is specific to each of the dietaries and is described above in the textual introduction for each text.

All Roman numerals (except when citing the Bible) have been converted to Arabic and Latin has been retained and explained in notes, except for persons' names which have been normalized to the canonical versions (such as Galen for Bullein's "Galenus"). In the marginal notes that appear in Bullein and Elyot all abbreviations (mostly of medical works cited) are silently expanded and a note indicates when expansion has not been possible because the meaning is unclear. Where marginal notes are clearly misaligned they have been moved to where they ought to be (never more than a few lines up or down); marginal notes are treated as headings and so there is no punctuation at the end of each one. In collation notes for the main text and its marginal notes, quotations from texts other than the copy text are not modernized.

When the author uses a word that requires explanation, this is given in the explanatory notes except for those words frequently used by an author, which are listed in Appendix 4. Works and authors cited in the main text and the marginal notes appear in Appendix 5.

When quoting from early modern English texts other than the three dietaries in this edition, specifically in the explanatory notes, the earliest edition is used unless a later edition is available as electronic text from the Text Creation Partnership (TCP) at the University of Michigan since these are easier to read, navigate and search than the early printed text, may contain text not present in an earlier edition, and are available to readers who cannot examine the rare books directly. Where possible out of copyright texts are cited rather than modern editions because they are freely available to any reader who can access the Internet. All longer (indented) quotations from early printed texts, in the introduction and throughout the volume, have been rendered into modern English by the present editor.

When the dietaries mention ancient authorities such as Galen I have not given precise references to these sources, although Elyot usually gives the name of the work, and the book in which it appears and often the chapter number. Even when it is clear which work is being cited it is not always clear which particular edition was consulted so I have not added to the references given except when works are directly quoted from (which is hardly ever) and are available in a reliable modern translation, which is not the case for much of Galen and other ancient authorities. Most obscure, rare, or obsolete words explained in the endnotes are indebted for their definitions to the *Oxford English Dictionary* (*OED*), consulted online in the period 2013–15, and these definitions are often directly quoted; in such cases the *OED* is cited only when the word concerned does not appear there as a headword. Authorities not glossed in the explanatory notes can be found in Appendix 5.

FINDING AIDS (INDEXING)

Ordinarily a volume like this would have an index, but the dietaries here presented provide such thorough finding aids (what the authors call "tables", which are equivalent to a modern index) that an additional index by the present author is unnecessary and instead readers are encouraged to use the tables provided by the original authors to find material. The alphabetization in the original tables by Elyot and Bullein was incomplete and is here corrected with page numbers corresponding to this modern edition and not the original texts. Additionally Appendix 5 indicates where in the dietaries specific authorities and their works are mentioned.

THE DIETARIES

THE CASTLE OF HEALTH

Corrected and in some places augmented by the first author thereof, Sir Thomas Elyot, Knight, the year of Our Lord 1541.

THE PROEM OF SIR THOMAS ELYOT, KNIGHT, INTO HIS BOOK CALLED THE CASTLE OF HEALTH[1]

De methodo medendi, liber 1, folio. 1

Galen, the most excellent physician, feared that in writing a compendious doctrine for the curing of sickness he should lose all his labour, forasmuch as no man almost did endeavour himself to the finding of truth but that all men did so much esteem riches, possessions, authority, and pleasures that they supposed them which were studious in any part of sapience[2] to be mad or distract of their wits, forasmuch as they deemed the chief sapience (which is in knowledge of things belonging as well to God as to man) to have no being. Since this noble writer found that lack in his time – when there flourished in sundry countries a great multitude of men excellent in all kinds of learning, as it yet doth appear by some of their works – why should I be grieved with reproaches wherewith some of my country do recompence me for my labours taken without hope of temporal reward, only for the fervent affection which I have ever born toward the public weal[3] of my country? "A worthy matter", sayeth one, "Sir Thomas Elyot is become a physician and writeth in physic, which beseemeth not a knight, he might have been much better occupied". Truly, if they will call him a physician which is studious about the weal of his country, I vouchsafe they so name me, for during my life I will in that affection alway continue. And why, I pray you, should men have in disdain or small reputation the science of physic, which being well understood, truly experienced, and discreetly ordered doth conserve health, without the which all pleasures be painful, riches unprofitable, company annoyance, strength turned to feebleness, beauty to loathsomeness, senses are dispersed, eloquence interrupted, rememberance confounded? Which hath been considered of wise men, not only of the private estate but also of emperors, kings, and other great princes, who for the universal necessity and incomporable utility which they preceived to be in that science of physic they did not only advance and honour it with special privileges but also diverse and many of them were therein right studious. In so much as Juba, the King of Mauritania and Libya, found out the vertuous qualities of the herb called *euphorbium*;[4] Gentius, King of Ilyria, found the virtues of gentian;[5] the herb *lysimachia* took

---

1 *The proem*] The proems, or prefaces, to O1 and Q2 differ significantly from other editions and are included in this edition as Appendix 1.

2 *sapience*] wisdom, understanding.

3 *weal*] welfare, well-being.

4 *euphorbium*] Here Elyot refers to the plant euphorbia but the name was also used for the drug derived from the succulent species euphorbia, which was valued for its purgative and emetic properties. Pliny the Elder claimed that the drug was named in honour of Euphorbus, the physician of Juba II, King of Mauritania (Anon 1910).

5 *gentian*] In the *Natural History* (book 25, chapter 35) Pliny claimed Gentius, King of Illyria, discovered gentian (Pliny 1956, 7:189).

his name of King Lysimachus;[1] Mithridates, the great king of Ponthus, found first the virtues of *scordion*[2] and also invented the famous medicine against poison called mithridate; Artemisia, Queen of Caria, found the virtues of motherwort, which in Latin beareth her name,[3] whereby her noble renown hath longer continued than by the making of the famous monument over her dead husband, called *mausoleum*,[4] although it were reckoned among the wonderful works of the world. And yet her name, with the said herb, still abideth whiles the said monument a thousand years passed was utterly destroyed. It seemeth that physic in this realm hath been well esteemed since the whole study of Salerno at the request of a king of England[5] wrote and set forth a compendious and profitable treatise called *The Government of Health*, in Latin *Regimen sanitatis*. And I trust in almighty God that our sovereign lord, the king's majesty, who daily prepareth to stablish among us true and uncorrupted doctrines, will shortly examine also this part of study in such wise as things apt for medicine growing in this realm – by conference with most noble authors – may be so known that we shall have less need of things brought out of far countries, by the corruption whereof innumerable people have perished, without blame to be given to the physicians saving only that some of them not diligent enough in beholding their drugs or ingredients at all times dispensed and tried.

Besides the said kings whom I have rehearsed, other honourable personages have written in this excellent doctrine – and not only of the speculative part but also of the practise thereof – whose works do yet remain unto their glory immortal, as Avicenna, Avenzoar, Rasis, Cornelius Celsus, Serenus, and which I should have first named, Machaon and Podalirius, noble dukes in *Grecia*,[6] which came to the siege of Troy and brought with them thirty great ships with men of war. This well considered, I take it for no shame to study that science or to set forth any books of the same, being thereto provoked by the most noble and virtuous example of my noble master, King Henry the Eighth, whose health I heartily pray God as long to preserve as God hath constitute man's life to continue. For his highness hath not disdained to be the chief author and setter forth of an introduction into grammar[7] for the children of his loving subjects whereby, having good masters, they shall most easily and in short time apprehend the understanding and form of speaking of true and eloquent Latin.

---

1 *the herb* lysimachia] Similar to gentian, above, Pliny claimed in the *Natural History* (book 25, chapter 35) that Lysimachus discovered the herb lysimachia, which was named after him (Pliny 1956, 7:189).

2 scordion] Latin for scordium, a plant that smells like garlic; formerly used as a sudorific (causing the patient to sweat) and as an antidote for poisons (*OED* scordium, *n*.).

3 *which in Latin beareth her name*] *Artemisia vulgaris*; the plant was often used to ease the pain of childbirth.

4 mausoleum] The monument to Mausolus, governor of Caria in south-western Asia Minor 377/6–353 BCE. Artemisa was his sister as well as his wife and her grief at his death was renowned; she succeeded him as ruler of Caria and was responsible for commissioning the monument in her husband's memory.

5 *a king of England*] presumably Robert Curthose, Duke of Normandy (1087–1106), son of William the Conqueror and claimant to the throne; according to tradition the *Regimen sanitatis Salernitanum* was written for him.

6 Grecia] Greece.

7 *the chief author and setter forth*] In 1542 Henry VIII instructed that William Lily's Latin grammar, *Rudimenta Grammatices* (1534) be used in English schools.

Oh royal heart, full of very nobility! Oh noble breast, setting forth virtuous doctrine and laudable study! But yet one thing grieveth me, that notwithstanding I have ever honoured and specially favoured the reverend college of approved physicians, yet some of them hearing me spoken of have said in derision that although I were prettily seen in histories yet being not learned in physic I have put in my book diverse errors in presuming to write of herbs and medicines. First, as concerning histories, as I have planted them in my works, being well understood, they be not so light of importance as they do esteem them but may more surely cure men's affections than diverse physicians do cure maladies. Nor when I wrote first this book I was not all ignorant in physic, for before that I was twenty years old a worshipful physician,[1] and one of the the most renowned at that time in England, perceiving me by nature inclined to knowledge, read unto me: the works of Galen, of temperaments, natural faculties; the introduction of Johannitius; with some of the aphorisms of Hippocrates. And afterward, by mine own study, I read over in order the most part of the works of Hippocrates, Galen, Oribasius, Paulus Celius,[2] Alexander of Tralles, Celsus, Pliny, the one and the other,[3] with Dioscorides. Nor I did omit to read the long canons of Avicenna, the commentaries of Averroes, the practice of Isaac, Haly Abbas, Rasis, Mesue, and also of the more part of them which were their aggregators[4] and followers. And although I have never been at Montpellier, Padua, nor Salerno,[5] yet have I found something in physic whereby I have taken no little profit concerning mine own health. Moreover, I wot not[6] why physicians should be angry with me since I wrote and did set forth *The Castle of Health* for their commodity, that the uncertain token of urines and other excrements should not deceive them but that by the true information of the sick man, by me instructed, they might be the more sure to prepare medicines convenient for the diseases. Also, to the intent that men observing a good order in diet and preventing the great causes of sickness, they should of those maladies the sooner be cured. But if physicians be angry that I have written physic in English, let them remember that the Greeks wrote in Greek, the Romans in Latin, Avicenna and others in Arabic, which were their own proper and maternal tongues. And if they had been as much attached with envy and covetise[7] as some now seem to be they

---

1 *a worshipful physician*] Most likely Thomas Linacre, reputed for his knowledge of medicine and Greek (Elyot 1970, 11).

2 *Paulus Celius*] As Skov notes, "Elyot's text reads, mysteriously, 'Paulus Celius'. Since Paulus can be readily identified as Paulus Aegineta, whose work Elyot cites a number of times in the body of his treatise, it remains to explain 'Celius'. The reference is probably to Caelius Aurelianus, a fifth-century Roman writer known mainly for his translation of Soranus of Ephesus, a first-century Greek physician. This identification is suggested by the fact that Oribasius and Caelius Aurelianus were published together in 1529. It was natural, therefore, that Elyot should juxtapose the two writers in this passage" (Elyot 1970, 19).

3 *Celsus, Pliny, the one and the other*] First-century Roman medical writers. As Skov points out, Pliny the Elder wrote about herbs, which makes him of medical interest, but it is not clear why Eliot would refer to the other Pliny since he did not engage with medical discourse (Elyot 1970, 12).

4 *aggregators*] collectors or compilers of medical remedies.

5 *Montpellier, Padua, ... Salerno*] all renowned centres of excellence for the study of medicine. Andrew Boorde refers to studying at Montpellier in the preface to his dietary.

6 *wot not*] know not.

7 *covetise*] inordinate or excessive desire, specifically desire for the acquisition and possession of wealth. In this context Elyot suggests that the physicians who criticize him, unlike the earlier authorities, are guilty of an excessive desire to keep hold of the valuable learning and knowledged they have acquired.

would have devised some particular language, with a strange cipher or form of letters, wherein they would have written their science, which language or letters no man should have known that had not professed and practised physic. But those, although they were paynims[1] and Jews, in this part of charity they far surmounted us Christians, that they would not have so necessary a knowledge as physic is to be hid from them which would be studious about it.

Finally, God is my judge, I write neither for glory, reward, nor promotion, only I desire men to deem well[2] mine intent, since I dare assure them that all that I have written in this book I have gathered of the most principal writers in physic, which being throughly studied and well remembered shall be profitable (I doubt not) unto the reader and nothing noyous[3] to honest physicians that do measure their study with moderate living and Christian charity.

THE TABLE[4]

It must be remembered that the [i]number in the table [ii]doth signify the leaf, [iii]and the letter A doth signify the first page or side, the letter B the second page or side.[5]

A

Abstinence	p. 115
Affects of the mind	p. 125
Ages	p. 69
Air	pp. 53, 71
Ale	p. 95
Almonds	p. 85
Aniseed	p. 89
Annexed to things natural	p. 53
Apples	p. 84
[iv]Autumn	p. 99

B

Beans	p. 89
[v]Beef	p. 76
[vi]Beer	p. 95
Beets	p. 88

---

i number] first number O1.   ii doth] do O1.
iii and the letter A doth signify the first page or side, the letter B, the second page or side] the second number the page or side O1.
iv Autumn] O1, Q2, O3 omit.   v Beef] O1, Q2, O3 omit.
vi Beer] Beer | By what tokens oone may know wheder the stomak and head be hot or cold] O5, O6.

---

1 *paynims*] pagans.
2 *deem well*] judge well.
3 *noyous*] vexatious.
4 THE TABLE] Alphabetization within the copy text is incomplete and is here corrected.
5 *It must be remembered ... side*] Elyot's signatures have been replaced in this modern edition with page numbers.

Birds	p. 78
Bittern	p. 79
Blackbird	p. 78
Blood	p. 61
[i]Bloodsuckers	p. 124
Borage	p. 91
Brain cold and dry	p. 56
Brain cold and moist	p. 56
Brain dry	p. 56
Brain exceeding in cold	p. 55
Brain exceeding in heat	p. 55
Brain hot and dry	p. 56
Brain hot and moist	p. 56
Brain moist	p. 56
Brain of beasts	p. 80
[ii]Brain sick	p. 149
Bread	p. 76
[iii]Breakfast	p. 102
[iv]Breast sick	p. 149
Bustard	p. 79
Butter	p. 81

C

Capers	p. 86
Capons, hens, and chickens	p. 78
[v]Carrots	p. 89
[vi]Causes whereby the air is corrupted	p. 71
[vii]Chances of fortune	p. 129
Cheese	p. 81
Cherries	p. 84
Chervil	p. 88
Chestnuts	p. 85
Chicory	p. 87
[viii]Children	p. 100
Choler	p. 61
Choleric body	p. 54
Choler natural	p. 62
Choler unnatural	p. 62
Cider	p. 95
Cloves	p. 92
Coleworts and Cabbages	p. 87
Colour	p. 69

---

i Bloodsuckers] O*1* omits.   ii Brain sick] O*1*, Q*2*, O*3* omit.   iii Breakfast] O*1* omits.
iv Breast sick] O*1*, Q*2*, O*3* omit.   v Carrots] O*1*, Q*2*, O*3* omit.
vi Causes whereby the air is corrupted] O*1*, Q*2*, O*3* omit.
vii Chances of fortune] O*1*, Q*2*, O*3* omit.   viii Children] O*1*, Q*2*, O*3* omit.

Colour of hair	p. 70
ⁱColour of inward causes	p. 70
ⁱⁱColour of outward causes	p. 70
ⁱⁱⁱColour of urines	p. 150
Comfortatives of the heart	p. 130
ⁱᵛCommodity happening by moderate use of the qualities of meat	p. 76
Complexion of man	p. 53
ᵛConcoction	p. 137
ᵛⁱConsiderations in abstinence	p. 115
Considerations of things belonging to health	p. 52
Cony	p. 77
ᵛⁱⁱCounsels against ingratitude	p. 128
Crane	p. 79
Crudity	p. 137
Cucumbers	p. 83
Custom	p. 75

D

Dates	p. 83
ᵛⁱⁱⁱDeath of children	p. 129
ⁱˣDeer, red and fallow	p. 77
ˣDiet concerning sundry times of the year	p. 98
Diet of choleric persons	p. 134
Diet of them which be ready to fall into sickness	p. 146
Diet in time of pestilence	p. 155
Diet of melancholic persons	p. 135
Diet of phlegmatic persons	p. 135
Diet of sanguine persons	p. 133
ˣⁱDigested	p. 114
Digestives of choler	p. 119
Digestives of phlegm	p. 120
ˣⁱⁱDistemperature happening by excess of sundry qualities of meat	p. 75
Diversity of meats	p. 103
Dominion of sundry complexions	p. 131
ˣⁱⁱⁱDrink at meals	p. 105
ˣⁱᵛDrink between meals	p. 103
Duck	p. 79

---

i Colour of inward causes] *O1, Q2, O3 omit.*
ii Colour of outward causes] *O1, Q2, O3 omit.*   iii Colour of urines] *O1, Q2, O3 omit.*
iv Commodity ... meat] *O1, Q2, O3 omit.*   v Concoction] *O1, Q2, O3 omit.*
vi Considerations in abstinence] *O1, Q2, O3 omit.*
vii Counsels against ingratitude] *O1, Q2, O3 omit.*
viii Death of children] *O1, Q2, O3 omit.*   ix Deer, red and fallow] *O1, Q2, O3 omit.*
x Diet ... of the year] *O1, Q2, O3 omit.*   xi Digested] *O1 omits.*
xii Distemperature happening by excess of sundry qualities of meat] *O1, Q2, O3 omit.*
xiii Drink at meals] *O1 omits.*   xiv Drink between meals] *O1 omits.*

E

[i]Earth	p. 53
Eggs	p. 81
Elements	p. 53
Endive	p. 87
Evacuation	p. 114
[ii]Excrements	p. 114
Exercise	pp. 109, 111

F

Feet of beasts	p. 81
Fennel	p. 88
Figs	p. 83
Filberts	p. 85
[iii]Fire	p. 53
Fish	p. 81
Flesh	p. 76
Fricaces or rubbings	p. 108
Fruits	p. 82

G

Garlic	p. 90
Genitors cold	p. 60
Genitors cold and dry	p. 60
Genitors cold and moist	p. 60
Genitors dry	p. 60
Genitors hot	p. 59
Genitors hot and dry	p. 60
Genitors hot and moist	p. 60
Genitors moist	p. 60
Gestation	p. 111
Ginger	p. 92
Gizzard of birds	p. 79
[iv]Gluttony	p. 104
Goose	p. 79
Gourds	p. 82
Grapes	p. 84

H

Haemorrhoids or piles	p. 124
Hare	p. 77
[v]Hazelnuts	p. 85

---

i Earth] O1, Q2, O3 *omit*.   ii Excrements] O1, O3 *omit*.   iii Fire] O1, Q2, O3 *omit*.
iv Gluttony] O1, Q2, O3 *omit*.   v Hazelnuts] O1, Q2, O3 *omit*.

Head of beasts	p. 80
Heart cold and dry	p. 58
Heart cold and moist	p. 58
Heart cold distempered	p. 57
Heart dry distempered	p. 57
Heart hot and dry	p. 57
Heart hot and moist	p. 57
Heart hot distempered	p. 57
Heart moist distempered	p. 57
Heart of beasts	p. 80
[i]Heart sick	p. 149
Heaviness or sorrow	p. 127
Herbs used in pottage or to eat	p. 86
Heron	p. 79
Honey	p. 97
Humours	p. 60
[ii]Humours superfluous	p. 114
Hyssop	p. 90

I

[iii]Ire	p. 125

J

Joy	p. 131

K

Kid	p. 77

L

[iv]Lack of promotion	p. 129
Lamb	p. 77
Lark	p. 78
Lassitude	pp. 145, 146
Leeches or bloodsuckers	p. 124
Leeks	p. 90
Letting of blood	p. 122
Lettuce	p. 86
Liver cold distempered	p. 58
Liver dry distempered	p. 59
Liver in heat distempered	p. 58
Liver moist distempered	p. 58
Livers of birds and beasts	p. 80
[v]Liver sick	p. 149

---

i Heart sick] O1, Q2, O3 omit.   ii Humours superfluous] O1, Q2, O3 omit.
iii Ire] O1, Q2, O3 omit.   iv Lack of promotion] O1, Q2, O3 omit.
v Liver sick] O1, Q2, O3 omit.

^(i)Loss of goods   p. 129
Lungs of beasts   p. 80

M

Maces   p. 92
Mallows   p. 87
Marrow   p. 80
Meals   p. 102
Meat and drink   p. 71
Meats engendering melancholy   p. 63
Meats hurting the eyen   p. 64
Meats hurting the teeth   p. 64
Meats making choler   p. 62
Meats making good juice   p. 71
Meats making ill juice   p. 72
Meats making oppilations   p. 64
Meats making phlegm   p. 62
Meats making thick juice   p. 73
Meats windy   p. 65
Medlars   p. 85
Melancholic body   p. 55
Melancholy   p. 62
^(ii)Melancholy natural   p. 62
^(iii)Melancholy unnatural   p. 62
Melons   p. 82
Members instrumental[1]   p. 64
Members of birds   p. 79
Milk   p. 95
Milt or spleen   p. 80
Moderation in diet   p. 101
Mutton   p. 77

N

^(iv)Navews   p. 89
Nutmegs   p. 92

O

^(v)Obstruction or rupture   p. 109
Official members   p. 63
^(vi)Old men   p. 101
Olives   p. 86

---

i Loss of goods] *O1, Q2, O3 omit.*   ii Melancholy natural] *O1, Q2, O3 omit.*
iii Melancholy unnatural] *O1, Q2, O3 omit.*   iv Navews] *O1, Q2, O3 omit.*
v Obstruction or rupture] *O1, Q2, O3 omit.*   vi Old men] *O1 omits.*

---

1 *instrumental*] having a special, vital function.

Onions	p. 90
Operations	p. 69
ⁱOppilations, what they are	p. 101
Oranges	p. 86
Order in eating and drinking	p. 105
ⁱⁱOrdure	p. 114

P

Parsley	p. 88
Parsnips	p. 89
ⁱⁱⁱParticular commodities of every purgation	p. 118
Partridge	p. 78
Parts similar[1]	p. 63
Peaches	p. 84
Pears	p. 85
Peason	p. 89
ⁱᵛPeculiar remedies of every humour	p. 133
Pennyroyal	p. 91
ᵛPepons	p. 82
Pepper	p. 92
Pheasant	p. 78
Phlegm	p. 61
Phlegmatic body	p. 54
Phlegm natural	p. 61
Phlegm unnatural	p. 61
Pigeons	p. 79
Plover	p. 78
Pomegranates	p. 85
Powers animal	p. 69
Powers natural	p. 68
Powers spiritual	p. 68
Precepts of Diocles	p. 152
ᵛⁱPrecise Diet	p. 106
Principal members	p. 63
Prunes	p. 86
Purgations by seige	pp. 117, 118
Purgers of choler	p. 120
Purgers of melancholy	p. 121
Purgers of phlegm	p. 121
Purslane	p. 88

---

i Oppilations, what they are] *O1, O3 omit.*   ii Ordure] *O1 omits.*
iii Particular commodities of every purgation] *O1, Q2, O3 omit.*
iv Peculiar remedies of every humour] *O1, Q2, O3 omit.*   v Pepons] *O1, Q2, O3 omit.*
vi Precise diet] *O1, O3, O5, O6 omit.*

---

1 *similar*] organs of a single substance or structure throughout.

Q

Quail	p. 78
Quality of meat	pp. 74, 75
Quantity of meat	p. 73
Quinces	p. 84

R

Radish	p. 89
Raisins	p. 84
Rapes	p. 89
Repletion	p. 112
[i]Rheums and remedies therefore	p. 140
Rocket	p. 91
[ii]Rosemary	p. 91

S

Saffron	p. 92
Sage	p. 90
Sanguine body	p. 53
Savory	p. 91
Scarifying	p. 123
Shoveler	p. 79
Sickness [iii]appropred to sundry seasons and ages	p. 147
Significations of sicknesses	p. 148
Sleep and watch	p. 106
Sorrel	p. 88
Sparrows	p. 79
Spirit animal	p. 69
Spirit natural	p. 69
Spirit vital	p. 69
[iv]Springtime	p. 98
Stomach cold	p. 59
Stomach dry	p. 59
Stomach hot	p. 59
Stomach in the which meat is corrupted	p. 154
Stomach moist	p. 59
[v]Stomach sick	p. 149
[vi]Stones of beasts	p. 80
[vii]Substance of urines	p. 151
Sugar	p. 98
[viii]Summer	p. 99
[ix]Supper	p. 102

i Rheums ... therefore] *O1, Q2, O3 omit.*   ii Rosemary] *O1, Q2 omit.*
iii *appropred*] appropriate.   iv Springtime] *O1, Q2, O3 omit.*
v Stomach sick] *O1, Q2, O3 omit.*   vi Stones of beasts] *O1, Q2, O3 omit.*
vii Substance of urines] *O1, Q2, O3 omit.*   viii Summer] *O1, Q2, O3 omit.*
ix Supper] *O1 omits.*

Swine's flesh	p. 77
ⁱSyrup acetose	p. 98

T

Temperature of meats	p. 75
Things against nature	p. 52
Things good for the eyes	p. 67
Things good for the head	p. 65
Things good for the heart	p. 66
Things good for the liver	p. 66
Things good for the lungs	p. 67
Things good for the stomach	p. 67
Things natural	p. 52
Things not natural	p. 52
Thyme	p. 91
Time	pp. 98, 99
Times appropred to every humour	p. 132
ⁱⁱTimes in the day concerning meals	p. 102
Tongue of beasts	p. 81
Town cresses[1]	p. 91
Tripes	p. 80
Turnips	p. 89

U

Udder	p. 80
Urines	p. 150

V

Veal	p. 77
Venison	p. 77
Virtue of meats	p. 154
Vociferation	p. 112
Vomit	p. 116

W

Walnuts	p. 85
Water	p. 92
Whey	p. 95
Winds	p. 71
Wine	p. 93
ⁱⁱⁱWinter	p. 98
Woodcocks	p. 79

---

i Syrup acetose] *O1, Q2, O3 omit.*
ii Times in the day concerning meals] *O1, Q2, O3 omit.*
iii Winter] *O1, Q2, O3 omit.*

---

1 *Town cresses*] garden cress.

^(i)Young men p. 100

Y

^(ii)Thus endeth the table[1]

^(iii)THE FIRST BOOK

^(iv)Chapter one

^(v)To the conservation of the body of mankind within the limitation of health – which, as Galen sayeth, is the state of the body wherein we be neither grieved with pain nor let from doing our necessary business – doth belong the diligent consideration of three sorts of things, that is to say:

De sanitate tuenda, liber 1

Things natural
Things not natural and
Things against nature

Things natural be seven in number:

Elements
Complexions
Humours
Members
Powers
Operations and spirits

These be necessary to the being of health according to the order of their kind and be alway in the natural body.

Things not natural be six in number:

Air
Meat and drink
Sleep and watch
Moving and rest
Emptiness and repletion and
Affections of the mind

Things against nature be three:

Sickness
Cause of sickness
Accident which followeth sickness

---

i Young men] O1, Q2, O3 *omit.*
ii Thus endeth the table] O1 *inserts a list of faults in printing after this sentence.*
iii THE FIRST BOOK] O3, O5; O1, Q2, Q4 *omit.*   iv Chapter one] *this ed.*; Q4 *omits*
v To the conservation ... water, air, and fire] O5, O6 *omit.*

---

1 *table*] At this point in the copy text there is a picture of Thomas Elyot's Coat of Arms featuring the Latin motto "*Face Avt Tace*" ("Act or be silent").

Annexed to things natural:

Age
Colour
Figure and
Diversity of kinds

The elements be those original things, unmixed and uncompound, of whose temperance and mixture all other things, having corporeal substance, be compact.[1] Of them be four, that is to say:

Earth
Water

Air and
Fire

Earth is the most gross and ponderous element and of her proper nature is cold and dry.

Water is more subtle and light than earth, but in respect of air and fire it is gross and heavy and of her proper nature is cold and moist.

Air is more light and subtle than the other two, and being not altered with any exterior cause is properly hot and moist.

Fire is absolutely light and clear, and is the clarifier of other elements if they be vitiate[2] or out of their natural temperance, and is properly hot and dry.

[i]It is to be remembered that none of the said elements be commonly seen or felt of mortal men as they are in their original being, but they which by our senses be perceived be corrupted with mutual mixture and be rather earthy, watery, airy, and fiery than absolutely earth, water, air, and fire.

Chapter two: Of the complexion of man

Complexion is a combination of two diverse qualities of the four elements in one body: as hot and dry of the fire, hot and moist of the air, cold and moist of the water, cold and dry of the earth. But although all these complexions be assembled in every body of man and woman, yet the body taketh his denomination[3] of those qualities which abound in him more than in the other, as hereafter ensueth.

The body where heat and moisture have sovereignty is called sanguine, wherein the air hath pre-eminence, and it is perceived and known by these signs which do follow:

Sanguine
Carnosity or fleshiness
The veins and arteries large
Hair plenty and red

---

i It is] This O3; This is O6.

---

1 *compact*] made up.
2 *vitiate*] vitiated: spoiled, infected.
3 *denomination*] designation, class.

The visage white and ruddy
Sleep much
Dreams of bloody things or things pleasant
Pulse great and full
Digestion perfect
Angry shortly
Siege, urine, and sweat abundant
Falling shortly into bleeding
The urine red and ⁱthick

Where cold with moisture prevaileth, that body is called phlegmatic, wherein water hath pre-eminence, and is perceived by these signs:

Plegmatic
Fatness, quaving,[1] and soft
Veins narrow
Hair much and plain
Colour white
Sleep superfluous
Dreams of things watery or of fish
Slowness
Dullness in learning
ⁱⁱSmallness of courage
Pulse slow and little
Digestion weak
Spittle white, abundant, and thick
Urine ⁱⁱⁱthick, white, and pale

Choleric is hot and dry, in whom the fire hath pre-eminence, and is discerned by these signs following:

Choleric
Leanness of body
Costiveness
Hair black or dark auburn curled
Visage and skin red as fire or sallow
Hot things noyful to him
Little sleep
Dreams of fire, fighting or anger
Wit sharp and quick
Hardy and fighting
Pulse swift and strong

---

i thick] grosse O1, Q2, O3, O5, O6.
ii Smallness of courage] cowardyse O1, Q2, O3, O5, O6.
iii thick] grosse O1, Q2, O3, O5, O6.

---

1 *quaving*] shaking, trembling.

Urine high coloured and clear
Voice sharp

Melancholic is cold and dry, over whom the earth hath dominion, and is perceived by these signs:

Melancholic
Leanness with hardness of skin
Hair plain and thin
Colour duskish or white with leanness
Much watch
Dreams fearful
Stiff in opinions
Digestion slow and ill
Timorous and fearful
Anger long and fretting
Pulse little
Seldom laughing
Urine watery and thin

Besides the said complexions of all the whole body, there be in the particular members complexions wherein if there be any distemperance it bringeth sickness or grief to the member. Wherefore to know the distemperature these signs following would be considered, forseen that it be remembered that some distemperatures be simple and some be compound. They which be simple be in simple qualities, as in heat, cold, moist, or dry; they which be compound are in compound or mixed qualities, as heat and moisture, heat and dryth, cold and moist, cold and dry. But now, first we will speak of the simple complexions of every principal member, beginning at the brain.

The brain exceeding in heat hath
The head and visage very red and hot
The hair growing fast, black, and curled
The veins in the eyen apparent
Superfluous matter in the nostrils, eyen, and ears
The head annoyed with hot meats, drinks, and savours
Sleep short and not sound

The brain exceeding in cold hath
Much superfluidity running out of the nose, mouth, ears, and eyen
Hair straight and fine, growing slowly and flaxen
The head disposed by small occasions to poses and murrs[1]
It is soon annoyed with cold
It is cold in touching
Veins of the eyen not seen
Sleepy somewhat

---

1 *murrs*] severe attacks of catarrh.

Moist in excess hath
Hairs plain
Seldom or never bald
Wit dull
Much superfluidities
Sleep much and deep

The brain dry hath
No superfluidities running
Wits good and ready
Watchful
Hairs black, hard, and fast growing
Bald shortly

                    Complexions compounded

Brain hot and moist distempered hath
The head aching and heavy
Full of superfluidities in the nose
The southern wind grievous
The northern wind wholesome
Sleep deep but unquiet, with often wakings and strange dreams
The senses and wit unperfect

Brain hot and dry distempered hath
None abundance of superfluidities, which may be expelled
Senses perfect
Much watch
Sooner bald than other
Much hair in childhood, and black, or brown, and curled
The head hot and ruddy

Brain cold and moist distempered hath
The senses and wit dull
Much sleep
The head soon replenished with superfluous moisture
Distillations and poses or murrs
Not shortly bald
Soon hurt with cold

Brain cold and dry distempered hath
The head cold in feeling and without colour
The veins not appearing
Soon hurt with cold
Often dyscrased
Wit perfect in childhood but in age dull
Aged shortly and bald

Of the heart

The heart hot distempered hath
Much blowing and puffing
Pulse swift and busy
Hardiness and manhood much
Promptness, activity, and quickness in doing of things
Fury and boldness
The breast hairy toward the left side
The breast broad, with the head little
The body hot, except the liver do let it

The heart cold distempered hath
The pulse very little
The breath little and slow
The breast narrow
The body all cold, except the liver doth inflame it
Fearfulness
Scrupulosity[1] and much care
Curiosity[2]
Slowness in acts
The breast clean without hairs

The heart moist distempered hath
The pulse soft
Soon angry and soon pacified
The body all moist, except the liver disposeth contrary

The heart dry distempered hath
The pulse hard
Not lightly angry, but being angry not soon pacified
The body dry, except the liver doth dispose contrary

The heart hot and moist [i]hath
The breast and stomach hairy
Promptness in acts
Soon angry
Fierceness, but not so much as in hot and dry
Pulse soft, swift, and busy
Breath or wind according
Shortly falleth into diseases caused of putrefaction

The heart hot and dry [ii]hath
The heart pulse great and swift
The breath or wind according

---

i hath] *this ed.;* Q4 *omits.*   ii hath] O1, Q2, O3, o5, O6 *omit.*

1 *scrupulosity*] suspiciousness, fear.
2 *Curiosity*] excessive care, fastidiousness.

The breast and stomach all hairy
Quick in his doings
Boldness and hardiness
Swift and hasty in moving
Soon stirred to anger and tyrannous in manners
The breast broad and all the body hot and dry

The heart cold and moist ⁱhath
The pulse soft
Fearful and timorous
Slow
The breast clean without hair
Not hastily angry nor retaining anger
The breast narrow
All the body cold and moist

The heart cold and dry hath
The pulse hard and little
The wind moderate
Seldom angry but when it happeneth it dureth[1] long
The breast clean without hair and little
All the body cold and dry

Of the liver

The liver in heat distempered hath
The veins ⁱⁱlarge and hard
The blood ⁱⁱⁱthick by reason of vehement heat consuming the subtle parts of moisture
The belly hairy
All the body hot, exceeding temperance
^{iv}Much red choler, and bitter in youth
Much black choler toward age by adustion of red choler

The liver cold distempered hath
The veins small
Abundance of phlegm
The blood thin and phlegmatic
All the body cold in feeling and the belly without hair

The liver moist distempered hath
The veins soft
Much blood and thin
All the body moist in feeling except the heart disposeth it contrary

---

i hath] *O1, Q2, O3, o5, O6 omit.*   ii large and hard] greate *O1, Q2, O3, o5, O6.*
iii thick ... moisture] more hote than temperate *O1, Q2, O3, o5, O6.*
iv Much ... youth / Much ... red choler] *O1, Q2, O3, o5, O6 omit.*

---

1 *dureth*] lasts, continues.

The liver dry distempered hath
The veins hard
The blood little and thick
All the body dry

The complexions compound may be discerned by the said simple qualities. And here it is to be noted that the heat of the heart may vanquish the cold in the liver, for heat is in the heart as in the fountain or spring and in the liver as in the river.

Galen in *Arte parva liber*, 2 [O6 omits; Galenus in arte parua, li, x O1.]

Of the stomach

The stomach hot distempered
He digesteth well, specially hard meats and that will not be shortly altered
Light meats and soon altered be therein corrupted
The appetite little and slow
He delighteth in meats and drinks which be hot, for every natural complexion delighteth in his semblable[1]

The stomach cold distempered
He hath good appetite
He digesteth ill and slowly, specially gross meats and hard
Cold meats doth wax sour, being in him undigested
He delighteth in meats and drinks which be cold and yet of them he is undamaged

The stomach moist distempered
He thirsteth but seldom yet he desireth to drink
With superfluous drink he is hurt
He delighteth in moist meats

The stomach dry distempered
He is soon thirsty
Content with a little drink
Diseased with much drink
He delighteth in dry meats

It is to be noted that the dispositions of the stomach natural do desire that which is of like qualities; the dispositions unnatural do desire things of contrary qualities.

Galen in *Arte parva*

Also, not the stomach only causeth a man to thirst or not thirst, but also the liver, the lungs, and the heart.

Of the genitories or stones of generation
The genitories hot distempered
Great appetite to the act of generation
Engendering men children
Heat soon grown about the members

---

1 *his semblable*] that which is similar.

The genitories cold distempered
Small appetite to the act of generation
Engendering women children
Slow growth of hair about the members

The genitories moist distempered
Seed abundant but thin and watery

The genitories dry distempered
Seed little but meetly[1] thick in stubstance

The genitories hot and moist
Less appetite to lechery than in them which be hot and dry
More puissance to do it[2] and with less damage
Hurt by abstaining from it
Less hairiness than in hot and dry

The genitories hot and dry
The seed thick
Much fruitfulness of generation
Great appetite and readiness to the act
Hair about the members soon grown
Swiftness in speeding of the act
Soon therewith satisfied
Damage by using thereof

The genitories cold and moist
The seed watery and thin
Little desire to the act, but more puissance than in them the which be cold and dry
Little hairs or none about the members

The genitories cold and dry
Hairs none or few
Little appetite, or none, to lechery
Little puissance to do it
Engendering more females than men children
That little seed that is, is thicker than in cold and moist

Of humours

In the body of man be four principal humours which, continuing in the proportion that nature hath limited, the body is free from all sickness. Contrariwise, by the increase or diminution of any of them in quantity or quality, over or under their natural assignment, inequal temperature cometh into the body, which sickness fol-

---

1 *meetly*] properly, sufficiently.
2 *to do it*] i.e. engage in sexual intercourse and possibly masturbation.

loweth more or less according to the lapse or decay of the temperatures of the said humours, which be these following:

Blood
Phlegm
Choler
Melancholy

Blood hath pre-eminence over all other humours in sustaining of all living creatures, for it hath more conformity with the original cause of living by reason of temperateness in heat and moisture. Also, nourisheth[1] more the body and restoreth that which is decayed, being the very treasure of life, by loss whereof death immediately followeth. The distemperature of blood happeneneth by one of the other three humours, by the inordinate or superfluous mixture of them.

Of phlegm

Phlegm is of two sorts: natural and unnatural.

Natural phlegm is a humour cold and moist, white and sweet, or without taste, engendered by insufficient decoction in the second digestion of the watery or raw parts of the matter decoct, called chyle,[2] by the last digestion made apt to be converted into blood; in this humour water hath dominion most principal.

Phlegm unnatural is that which is mixed with other humours or is altered in his quality, and thereof is eight sundry kinds:

Phlegm
Watery, which is found in spittle of great drinkers or of them which digest ill[3]
Slimy or raw
Glassy, like to white glass, thick, viscous, like bird-lime, and heavy
Plastery, which is very gross, and as it were chalky, such is found in the joints of them which have the gout
Salt, which is mingled with choler
Sour, mixed with melancholy, which cometh of corrupt digestion
Harsh, thick, and gross, which is seldom founden, which tasteth like green crabs[4] or sloes
Styptic or binding, is not so gross nor cold as harsh and hath the taste like to green red wine,[5] or other like, straining the tongue

Ponticum [the name for the kind of phlegm that is less than usually sour because it is mixed with melancholy.]

Choler doth participate with natural heat as long as it is in good temperance and thereof is also of two kinds: natural and unnatural.

---

1 *nourisheth*] the subject 'blood' is implied.
2 *chyle*] white milky fluid formed by the action of the pancreatic juice and the bile on the chyme, and contained in the lymphatics of the intestines.
3 *which digest ill*] i.e. have bad digestion.
4 *crabs*] crab-apples.
5 *green red wine*] young red wine.

Choler natural

Natural choler is the form of blood, the colour whereof is red and clear or more like to an orange colour, and is hot and dry wherein the fire hath dominion, and is light and sharp, and is ungendered of the most subtle part of matter decoct or boiled in the stomach whose beginning is in the liver.

Unnatural choler is that which is mixed or corrupted with other humours, wherof be four kinds:

Choler unnatural

Citrine[1] or yellow choler, which is of the mixture of natural choler and watery phlegm and therefore hath less heat than pure choler

Yolky, like to yolks of eggs, which is of the mixture of phlegm congealed and choler natural and is yet less hot than the other

Green, like to leeks, whose beginning is rather of the stomach than of the liver

Green, like to green canker of metal, and burneth like venom, and is of exceeding adustion of choler or phlegm, ⁱand by these two kinds nature is mortified[2]

Melancholy or black choler is divided into two kinds:

Natural which is the dregs of pure blood and is known by the blackness when it issueth either downward or upward and is verily cold and dry

Unnatural which proceedeth of the adustion of choleric mixture and is hotter and lighter, having in it violence to kill, with a dangerous disposition

Meats engendering choler
Garlic
Onions
Rocket
Cresses
Leeks
Mustard
Pepper
Honey
Wine much drunken
Sweet meats

Meats engendering phlegm
All slimy and cleaving meats
Cheese new
All fish, specially in a phlegmatic stomach
Inwards of beasts
Lamb's flesh

---

i and by these two kinds nature is mortified] Q2, O3, Q4, O5, O6.

1 *citrine*] light yellow or greenish-yellow.
2 *mortified*] deadened or destroyed.

The sinewy parts of flesh
Skins
Brains
Lungs
Rapes
Cucumbers
Repletion
Lack of exercise

Meats engendering melancholy
Beef
Goat's flesh
Hare's flesh
Boar's flesh
Salt flesh
Salt fish
Coleworts
All pulse, except white peason
Brown bread, coarse
Thick wine
Black wine[1]
Old cheese
Old flesh
Great fishes of the sea

Of the members

There be diversities of members, that is to say:

Principal members
The brain
The heart
The liver
The stones of generation

Official members
Sinews, which do serve to the brain
Arteries or pulses, which do serve to the heart
Veins, which do serve to the liver
Vessels spermatic, wherein man's seed lieth which do serve to the stones

Parts called similars,[2] for being divided they remain in themself like as they were
Bones
Gristle
Calles[3] betwixt the uttermost[4] skin and the flesh

---

1 *Black wine*] a very dark red, almost black, wine from the region of Cahors in France.
2 *similars*] organs of a single substance or structure throughout.
3 *Calles*] calluses.
4 *uttermost*] outermost.

Mussels or fillets
Fat
Flesh

Members instrumental[1]
The stomach
The reins
The bowels
All the great sinews
These of their virtue do appetite meat and alter it.

Meats which do hurt the teeth
Very hot meats
Nuts
Sweet meats and drinks
Radish roots
Hard meats
Milk
Bitter meats
Much vomit
Leeks
Fish fat
Lemons
Coleworts

ⁱThings which do hurt the eyes
Drunkenness
Lechery
Must
All pulse
Sweet wines and thick wines
Hempseed
Very salt meats
Garlic
Onions
Coleworts
Radish
Reading after supper immediately

Making great oppilations
Thick milk
All sweet things
Rye bread
Sweet wines

---

i Things] Meates O1, Q2, O3, O5, O6.

1 *instrumental*] having a special vital function.

Meats inflating or windy
Beans
Lupines
Cicer[1]
Mill[2]
Cucumbers
All juice of herbs
Figs dry
Rapes
Navews raw
Milk
Honey not well clarified
Sweet wine
Must

Things good for [i]**a cold head**
Cubebs[3]
Galangal
Lignum aloes
Marjoram
Balm-mints
Gladen[4]
Nutmegs
Musk
Rosemary
Roses
Peony
Hyssop
Spike
[ii]Ireos
Pennyroyal
Sage
Elecampane
Calamint
Betony
Savory
Fennel
Labdanum[5]
The leaves of laurel
Amber

---

i a cold] the O1, Q2, O3, O5, O6.   ii Ireos ... Amber] O1, Q2, O3, o5, O6 omit.

1 *Cicer*] chickpea.
2 *Mill*] millet.
3 *Cubebs*] the berry of a climbing shrub, similar in appearance and taste to pepper.
4 *Gladen*] presumably *gladolo* or sword-grass.
5 *Labdanum*] A gum-resin that comes from plants of the genus cistus.

Camomile
Melilot
Rue
Frankincense

^i^Hot things conserving a cold heart
Cinammon
Saffron
Coral
Cloves
Lignum aloes
Pearls
Maces
Balm-mints
Myrobalans[1]
Musk
Nutmegs
Rosemary
The bone of the hart of a red deer
Marjoram
Bugloss
Borage
Setwall
^ii^Gold
Amber
Cardamom
Basil
Beans red and white
Betony

Things good for the liver
Wormwood
Withwind[2]
Agrimony
Saffron
Cloves
Endive
Liverwort
Chicory
Plantain
Dragons[3]

---

i Hot things conserving a cold heart] Thynges good for the harte *O1, Q2, O3, O5, O6*.
ii Gold ... Betony] *O1, Q2, O3, O5, O6 omit*.

---

1 *Myrobalans*] astringent plum-like fruits from tropical trees.
2 *Withwind*] bindweed.
3 *Dragons*] gum-dragon or tragacanth.

Raisins great
Sanders
Fennel
Violets
Rosewater
Lettuce

Things good for the lungs
Elecampane
Hyssop
Scabious[1]
Licorice
Raisins
Maidenhair
Penides[2]
Almonds
Dates
Pistachios

Things good for the eyes
Eyebright
Fennel
Vervain
Roses
Celandine[3]
Agrimony
Cloves
Cold water

Things ⁱmaking the stomach strong
Myrobalans
Nutmegs
Organum
Pistachios
Quinces
Olibanum
Wormwood
Saffron
Coral
Agrimony
Fumitory

---

i making the stomach strong] good for the stomake O1, Q2, O3, O5, O6.

1 *Scabious*] herbaceous plants of the genus Scabiosa; thought to help cure certain skin diseases.
2 *Penides*] pieces or sticks of boiled sugar, similar to barley-sugar.
3 *Celandine*] plants with yellow flowers whose juice was thought to be a remedy for weak eyesight.

Galangal
Cloves
Lignum aloes
Mastics[1]
Mint
Spodium[2]
The innermost skin of a hen's gizzard
[i]Coriander prepared
[ii]Olive berries
Raisins
Nuts with figs
The rind of an orage
Rough wines
Wormwood steeped in wine or ale
Tart grapes
Aloes

Of powers

Animal
Spiritual
Natural

Natural power
Which doth minister
To whom is ministered

Which doth minister
Appetiteth
Retaineth
Digesteth
Expelleth

To whom is minstered
Ingendereth
Nourisheth
Feedeth

Power spiritual
Working, which dilateth the heart and arteries and eftsoons straineth them.
Wrought, which is stirred by an exterior cause to work, whereof cometh anger, [iii]indignation, subtlety, and care.

---

i Coriander prepared] O1 *omits*.　　ii Olive berries ... Aloes] O1, Q2, O3, O5, O6 *omit*.
iii indignation] indignation, victory, rule O1.

---

1 *Mastics*] aromatic gums or resins from the bark of the lentisk or mastic tree.
2 *Spodium*] A fine powder obtained from various substances by calcination.

Power animal
That which ordaineth, discerneth, and composeth
That moveth by voluntary motion
That which is called sensible, whereof do proceed the five wits

Of that which ordaineth do proceed
Imagination in the forehead
Reason in the brain
Remembrance in the noddle[1]

Operations
Appetite by heat and dryth
Digestion by heat and moisture
Retaining by cold and dryth
Expulsion by cold and moist

Spirit is an airy substance, subtle, stirring the powers of the body to perform their operations, which is divided into:

Spirit
Natural, which taketh ⁱhis beginning of the liver and by the veins which have no pulse spreadeth into all the whole body
Vital, which proceedeth from the heart and by the arteries or pulses is sent into all the body
Animal, which is engendered in the brain and is sent by the sinews throughout the body and maketh sense or feeling

Annexed to things natural

Ages be four
Adolescency to twenty-five years, hot and moist, in the which time the body groweth
Juventute[2] unto forty years, hot and dry, wherein the body is in perfect growth
Senectute[3] unto sixty years, cold and dry, wherein the body beginneth to decrease
Age decrepit until the last time of life, accidentally moist but naturally cold and dry, wherein the powers and strength of the body be more and more minished[4]

Colour

Of inward causes
Of outward causes

---

i his] *O1*; is *Q4*.

---

1 *noddle*] the back of the head.
2 *Juventute*] youth, early manhood.
3 *Senectute*] old age.
4 *minished*] diminished.

Colour of inward causes
Of equality of humours, as he that is red and white
Of inequality of humours, whereof do proceed black, [i]sallow, or white only
Do betoken dominion of heat: Red, Black, Sallow
White: cold of phlegm
Pale: cold of melancholy
Red: abundance of blood
Sallow: choler citrine[1]
Black: melancholy or choler adust

Colour of outward causes
Of cold or heat, as English men be white, Morians[2] be black
Of things accidental, as of fear, of anger, of sorrow, or other like motions

Colour of hair
Black: either of abundance of choler inflamed or of much incensing or adustion of blood
Red hair: of much heat not adust
Grey hairs: of abundance of melancholy
White hairs: of the lack of natural heat and by occasion of phlegm putrified

All the residue concerning things natural contained in the Introduction of Johannitius[3] and in the little craft of Galen I purposely pass over for this time, forasmuch as it doth require a reader having some knowledge in philosophy natural or else it is too hard and tedious to be [ii]understood.

The second table

Things not natural be so called because they be no portion of a natural body as they be which be called natural things, but yet by the temperance of them the body being in health [iii]is therein preserved. By the distemperance of them sickness is induced and [iv]health is dissolved.[4]

The first of things not natural is air or breath, which is properly of itself or of some material cause or occasion, good or ill.

That which is of itself good hath pure vapours and is [v]of good savour.

Also, it is of itself swift in alteration from hot to cold, wherein the body is not much provoked to sweat for heat nor to chill for vehemency of cold.

---

i sallow] sallow, paale *O1, O3, O5, O6*.
ii understood] understood. Moreouer this, whiche I haue written in this fyrste tables, shall be sufficiens, to the conseruation of helthe, I meane, with that whiche nowe foloweth in the other Tables *O1, Q2, O3, O5, O6*.
iii is therein preserved] so consysteth *O1, Q2, O3, O5, O6*.
iv health is] the body *O1, Q2, O3, O5, O6*.
v of good savour] odiferous *O1, Q2, O3, O5, O6*.

---

1 *citrine*] light yellow or greenish-yellow.
2 *Morians*] Moors.
3 *Introduction of Johannitius*] a reference to his *Isagoge*.
4 *dissolved*] weakened.

Air, among all things not natural, is chiefly to be observed forasmuch as it doth both enclose us and also enter into our bodies, specially the most noble member, which is the heart, and we cannot be separate one hour from it for the necessity of breathing and fetching of wind.

The causes whereby the air is corrupted be specially four:

Influences of sundry stars
Great standing waters, never refreshed
Carrion lying long above ground
Much people in small room living uncleanly and sluttishly

Winds bringing wholesome air
North, which prolongeth life by expelling ill vapours
East is temperate and lusty.

Winds bringing ill air
South corrupteth and maketh ill vapours
West is very mutable, which nature doth hate.

Of meat and drink

In meat and drink we must consider six things:

Substance
Quantity
Quality
Custom
Time
Order

Substance: some is good, which maketh good juice and good blood; some is ill and engendereth ill juice and ill blood.

Meats and drinks making good juice
Bread of pure [i]flour, somewhat leavened, well baked, not too old nor too stale
Eggs of pheasants, hens, or partridges, new-laid, poached mean between rear and hard
Milk new-milked, drunk fasting, wherein is sugar or the leaves of mints
Pheasants
Partridges or chickens
Capons or hens
Birds of the fields
Fish of stony rivers
Veal sucking
Pork young
Beef not passing three years
Pigeons

---

i flour] floure, of good whete O1, O3, O5, O6.

Venison of red deer
Pease pottage with mints
Feet of swine or calves
Before meals: figs ripe, raisins
Borage
Langue de boeuf[1]
Parsley
Mints
Rice with almond milk
Lettuce
Chicory
Grapes ripe
Wines good, moderately taken, well fined
Ale and beer six days old, clean brewed and not strong
Mirth and gladness
The liver and brains of hens and chickens and young geese

Meats and drinks making ill juice
Old beef
Old mutton
Geese old
Swan old
Ducks of the Cannel[2]
Inwards of beasts
Black puddings
The heart, liver, and kidneys of all beasts
The brains and marrow of the backbone[3]
Wood culvers
Shell-fish, except crayfish *d'eau doulce*[4]
Cheese hard
Apples and pears much used
Figs and grapes not ripe
All raw herbs, except lettuce, borage, and chicory
[i]Continually eaten specially [ii]of them which be choleric: Garlic, onions, leeks
Wine in must or sour
Fear, sorrow, [iii]pensiveness

---

i continually eaten] immoderatelye vsed O1, Q2, O3, O5, O6.
ii of them which be choleric] in Cholericke stomackes O1, Q2, O3, O5, O6.
iii pensiveness] and pensysenesse O1, O3, O5, O6.

---

1 *Langue de boeuf*] It is likely that Elyot refers to the plant with tongue-shaped leaves here, rather than the dish made from boiled and roasted ox tongue, since this item is listed between borage and parsley.
2 *cannel*] The natural bed of a stream of water; a watercourse.
3 *marrow of the backbone*] spinal marrow, the substance in the spinal canal.
4 d'eau doulce] fresh water.

^i^**Meats making thick juice:**
Rye bread
Must
Bread without leaven
Cake-bread
Sea-fish great
Shell-fish
Beef
The kidneys
The liver of a swine
The stones of beasts
Milk much sodden
Rapes
All round roots
Cucumbers
Sweet wine
^ii^Deep-red wine
Fennel
Cheese
Eggs, fried or hard
Chestnuts
Navews
Figs green
Apples not ripe
Pepper
Rocket
Leeks
Onions, ^iii^much used

^iv^THE SECOND BOOK

Chapter one: Of quantity

The quantity of meat must be proportioned after the substance and quality thereof and according to the complexion of him that eateth. First, it ought to be remembered that meats hot and moist, which are qualities of the blood, are soon turneth into blood and therefore much nourisheth the body. Some meats do nourish but little, having little conformity with blood in their qualities. Of them which do nourish,

---

i Meats making thick juice] *preceded in O1, Q2, O3, O5, O6 by a version of the sections appearing earlier in this edition as* "Meats engendering choler" *through to* "Meats engendering melancholy".

ii Deep-red wine] Deepe redde wyne / Garlyke / Mustard / Origanum / Hysope / Basylle O1, Q2, O3, O5, O6.

iii much used] *aligned (probably erroneously) alongside earlier items (from 'Pepper' to 'Leeks') in* O1, Q2, O3, O5, O6.

iv THE SECOND BOOK] *preceded in O1, Q2, O3, O5, O6 by a version of the sections appearing earlier in this edition as* "Meats which do hurt the teeth" *through to* "Things making the stomach strong".

Concoct or boiled [O1, Q2, O3, O5, O6 omit.]

Adust or burned [O1, Q2, O3, O5, O6 omit.]

Gourmandize or gluttony [O1, Q2, O3, O5, O6 omit.]

some are more gross, some lighter in digestion. The gross meat engendereth gross blood but where it is well concoct in the stomach and well digested it maketh the flesh more firm and the official members more strong than fine meats. Wherefore of men which use much labour or exercise, also of them which have very choleric stomachs (here in England), gross meats may be eaten in a great quantity, and in a choleric stomach beef is better digested than a chicken's leg, forasmuch as in a hot stomach fine meats be shortly adust and corrupted. Contrariwise, in a cold or phlegmatic stomach gross meat abideth long undigested and maketh putrified matter; light meats therefore be to such a stomach more apt and convenient. The temperate body is best nourished with a little quantity of gross meats, but of temperate meats in substance and quality they may safely eat a good quantity, forseen alway that they eat without gormandize¹ or leave with some appetite. And here it would be remembered that the choleric stomach doth not desire so much as he may digest, the melancholy stomach may not digest so much as he desireth, for cold maketh appetite but natural heat concocteth or boileth. Notwithstanding, unnatural or supernatural² heat destroyeth appetite and corrupteth digestion, as it appeareth in fevers. Moreover, fruits and herbs, specially raw, would³ be eaten in small quantity, although the person be very choleric, forasmuch as they do engender thin, watery blood, apt to receive putrifaction, which although it be not shortly perceived of them that use it, at length they feel it by sundry diseases, which are long in coming and shortly slayeth or be hardly⁴ escaped. Finally, excess of meats is to be abhorred ⁱfor, as it is said in the book called Ecclesiasticus, in much meat shall be sickness, and inordinate appetite shall approach unto choler.⁵ Semblaby,⁶ the quantity of drink would⁷ be moderated that it exceed not nor be equal unto the quantity of meat, specially wine, which moderately taken aideth nature and comforteth her. And ⁱⁱas the said author of Ecclesiasticus sayeth, "wine is a rejoicing to the soul and body",⁸ and ⁱⁱⁱTheognes sayeth, in Galen's work, "a large draught of wine is ill, a moderate draught is not only not ill but also commodius or profitable".⁹

Chapter two: Of quality of meats

Quality is in the complexion, that is to say it is the state therof, as hot or cold, moist or dry. Also, some meats be in winter cold in act and in virtue hot, and it would be

---

i for ... choler] *marginal note*: Eclesiastico. 37 O1, Q2, O3; Ecclesti O5, O6.
ii as ... body] *marginal note*: Eccl. 31 O1, Q2, O3, O5, O6.
iii Theognes ... ill] *marginal note*: Galen de tuenda sa O1, Q2, O3, O5, O6.

---

1 *gormandize*] gluttony.
2 *supernatural*] more than ordinary.
3 *would*] should.
4 *hardly*] with difficulty.
5 Ecclesiasticus ... *choler*] from the apocryphal biblical Book of Ecclesiasticus 37.30.
6 *semblably*] similarly.
7 *would*] should.
8 *Ecclesiasticus ... soul and body*] from Ecclesiasticus 31.36.
9 *a large draught ... profitable*] As Skov indicates, this quotation is from Galen's *Quod animi mores corporis temperatura sequantur* and the marginal reference attributing the quotation to Galen's *De sanitate tuenda* in editions other than Q4 is apparently an error (Elyot 1970, 392n17.17–19).

considered that every complexion, temperate and untemperate, is conserved in his state by that which is like thereto in form and degree, but that which exceedeth much in distemperance – by that which is contrary to him in form or quality but like in degree – moderately used. By form is understood grossness, fineness, thickness, or thinness by degree, as the first, the second, the third, the fourth, ⁱin heat, cold, moisture, or dryth.

Chapter three: Of custom

Custom in feeding is not to be contemned or little regarded, for those meats to the which a man hath been of long time accustomed, though they be not of substance commendable yet do they sometime less harm than better meats whereto a man is not used. Also, the meats and drinks which do much delight him that eateth are to be preferred before that which is better but more unsavoury. But if the custom be too pernicious, that it needs must be left, then would it be withdrawn by little and little in time of health and not of sickness. For if it should be withdrawn in time of sickness, nature should sustain terrible detriment, first by the grief induced by sickness, second by receiving of medicines, thirdly by forbearing the thing wherein she delighteth.

Hippocrates Aphorismo, 2

Galen [It is not clear if it is this point or the one immediately preceding that the gloss 'Galen' refers to.]

Chapter four: Of the temperature of meats to be received

To keep the body in good temper, to them whose natural complexion is moist ought to be given meats that be moist in virtue or power. Contrariwise, to them whose natural complexion is dry ought to be given meats dry in virtue or power. The body's[1] untemperate, such meats or drinks are to be given which be in power contrary to the distemperance, but the degrees are alway to be considered, as well of the temperance of the body as of the meats. For where the meats do much exceed in degree the temperature of the body they annoy the body in causing distemperance, as hot wines, pepper, garlic, onions, and salt be noyful to them which be choleric because they be in the highest degree of heat and dryth, above the just temperance of man's body in that complexion, and yet be they oftentimes wholesome to them which be phlegmatic. Contrariwise, cold water, cold herbs, and cold fruits moderately used be wholesome to choleric bodies by putting away the heat exceeding the natural temperature, and to them which be phlegmatic they be unwholesome and do bring into them distemperance of cold and moist.

Chapter five: What distemperance happeneth by the excess of sundry qualities in meats and drinks

Meats
Cold: do congeal and mortify[2]
Moist: do putrefy and hasten age
Dry: sucketh up natural moisture

---

i in heat, cold, moisture, or dryth] of any of the sayde qualitites O1.

1 *body's*] understood as 'body that is'.
2 *mortify*] deaden or destroy.

Clammy: stoppeth the issue of vapours and urine and engendereth tough phlegm and gravel
Fat and oily: swimmeth long in the stomach and bringeth in loathsomeness[1]
Butter: doth not nourish
Salt: [i]do fret much the stomach
Harsh: like the taste of wild fruits, do constipate and restrain
Sweet: chafeth[2] the blood and causeth oppilations or stoppings of the pores and conduits of the body
Sour: cooleth nature and hasteneth age

Chapter six: What commodity happeneth by the moderate use of the said qualities of meats and drinks

Meats
Cold: assuageth the burning of choler
Moist: humecteth that which is dried
Dry: consumeth superfluous moisture
Clammy: thicketh that which is subtle and piercing
Butter: cleanseth and wipeth off, also mollifyeth and expelleth phlegm
Salt: relenteth[3] phlegm clammy and dryeth it
Fat and unctious: nourisheth and maketh soluble
Styptic or rough on the tongue: bindeth and comforteth appetite
Sweet: doth cleanse, dissolve, and nourish

Chapter seven: [ii]*Of bread*

Bread of fine flour of wheat, having no leaven, is slow of digestion and maketh slimy humours but it nourisheth much; if it be leavened it digesteth sooner. Bread having much bran filleth the belly with excrements and nourisheth little or nothing but shortly descendeth from the stomach. The mean between both, sufficiently leavened, well moulded, and moderately baken is the most wholesome to every age. The greatest loaves do nourish most fast forasmuch as the fire hath not exhausted the moisture of them. Hot bread much eaten maketh fullness, and thirst, and slowly passeth. Barley bread cleanseth the body, and doth not nourish so much as wheat, and maketh colder juice in the body.

Chapter eight: Of flesh

Beef of England, to Englishmen which are in health, bringeth strong nourishment but it maketh gross blood and engendereth melancholy. But being of young oxen, not exceeding the age of four years, to them which have choleric stomachs it is more convenient than chickens and other like[4] fine meats.

---

i do] *O1 omits.*
ii *Of bread*] *Chapter seven "Of bread" down to chapter thirteen "Of eggs" occurs later (after the section on "Nutmegs" at end of chapter seventeen) in all other editions.*

---

1 *loathsomeness*] nausea.
2 *chafeth*] warms.
3 *relenteth*] dissolves.
4 *like*] similar.

Swine's flesh

Above all kinds of flesh in nourishing the body Galen most commendeth pork, not being of a old swine and that it be well digested of him that eateth it, for it maketh best juice. It is most convenient for young persons, and them which have sustained much labour and therewith are fatigate[1] and become weak. Young pigs are not commended before that they be one month old, for they do breed superfluous humours.

Lamb

Is very moist and phlegmatic, wherefore it is not convenient for aged men, except it be very dry roasted, nor yet for them which have in their stomach much phlegm.

Mutton

Galen doth not commend it, notwithstanding experience proveth here in this realm that if it be young it is a right temperate meat and maketh good juice, and therefore it is used more than any other meat in all diseases. And yet it is not like good in all places, nor the sheep which beareth finest wool is not the sweetest in eating nor the most tender. But I have found in some countries mutton which, in whiteness, tenderness, and sweetness of the flesh, might be well nigh compared to kid and in digestion have proved as wholesome. *De alimentorum facultatibus, liber 3*

Kid and veal

Of Galen is commended next unto pork, but some men do suppose that in health and likeness they be much better than pork, the juice of them both being more pure. And here it is to be noted that of all beasts which be dry of their nature, the youngest be most wholesome of them that are moist, the eldest are least hurtful.

Hare, cony

Maketh gross blood, it dryeth and stoppeth but yet it provoketh a man to piss. Cony maketh better and more pure nourishment and is sooner digested than hare. It is well proved that there is no meat more wholesome or that more clean, firmly, and temperately nourisheth than rabbit's. Hippocrates *De ratione victus in morbis acutis, liber 2*, chapter 19; Plin 28 [Plin presumably Pliny.]

Deer, red and fallow[2]

Hippocrates affirmeth the flesh of harts and hinds to be of ill juice, hard of digestion, and dry, but yet it moveth urine. Of fallow deer he nor any other old writer doth speak of, as I remember, I suppose because there be not in all the world so many as be in England, where they consume a good part of the best pasture in the realm and are in nothing profitable saving that of the skins of them is made better leather than is of calves, the hunting of them being not so pleasant as the hunting of other venery[3] or vermin, the flesh much more unwholesome and unpleasant than of a red deer, engendering melancholy and making many fearful dreams, and disposeth the body

---

1 *fatigate*] fatigued.
2 *Fallow*] pale brownish or reddish yellow in colour.
3 *venery*] wild animals hunted as game.

to a fever if it be much eaten. Notwithstanding, the fat thereof, as some learned men have supposed, is better to be digested than the lean.

Of birds

The flesh of all birds is much lighter than the flesh of beasts in comparison, most specially of those fowls which trust most to their wings and do breed in high countries.

Capons, hens, and chickens

The capon is above all other fowls praised, forasmuch as it is easily digested and maketh little ordure and much good nourishment; it is commodious to the breast and stomach. Hens in winter are almost equal unto the capon but they do not make so strong nourishment; Avicenna sayeth if they be roasted in the belly of a kid or lamb they will be the better. Chickens in summer, specially if they be cockerels, are very convenient for a weak stomach and nourisheth a little. The flesh of a cock is hard of digestion but the broth wherein it is boiled looseth the belly and having sodden in it coleworts, polypodium or carthamus,[1] it purgeth ill humours and is medicinable against gouts, joint-aches, and fevers, which come by courses.[2]

Pheasant

Exceedeth all fowls in sweetness and wholesomeness, and is equal to a capon in nourishing but he is somewhat drier, and is of some men put in comparison mean between a hen and a partridge.

Partridge

Of all fowls is most soonest digested and hath in him much nutriment; comforteth the brain, and maketh seed of generation, and receiveth lust, which is abated.

Quails

Although they be of some men commended, yet experience proveth them to increase melancholy and are of a small nourishing.

Larks

Be as well the flesh as the broth very wholesome; eaten roasted they do much help against the colic, as Dioscorides sayeth.

A plover

Is slow of digestion, nourisheth little, and increaseth melancholy.

Blackbirds or ouzels[3]

Among wild fowl hath the chief praise for lightness[4] of digestion, and that they make good nourishment and little ordure.

---

1 *carthamus*] safflower or bastard saffron.
2 *courses*] several successive attacks.
3 *ouzels*] the European blackbird.
4 *lightness*] ease.

Sparrows

Be hard to digest, and are very hot and stirreth up Venus,[1] and specially the brains of them.

Woodcocks

Are of a good temperance and meetly[2] light in digestion.

Pigeons

Be easily digested, and are very wholesome to them which are phlegmatic or pure melancholy.

Goose

Is hard of digestion; but being young and fat, the wings be easy to digest in a whole stomach and nourisheth competently.

Duck

Is hotter than goose and hard to digest, and maketh worse juice (saving the brawns on the breast-bone), and the neck is better than the remnant.

Crane and Bustard

Crane is hard of digestion and maketh ill juice, but being hanged up long in the air he is the less unwholesome. Bustard, being fat, and kept without meat a day or two afore that he be killed to expulse his ordure, and then drawn and hanged as the crane is, being roasted or baken is a good meat and nourisheth well if he be well digested.

Heron, bittern, and shoveler

Being young and fat, be lightlier[3] digested than crane, and the bittern sooner than the heron, and the shoveler sooner than any of them. But all these fowls must be eaten with much ginger or pepper, and have good old wine drunk after them, and so shall they be more easily digested and the juice coming of them be the less noyful.

Chapter nine: The parts and members of birds and beasts

The wings, brawns, and neck of geese, capons, hens, pheasant, partridge, and small birds, being fat, are better than the legs in digestion and lighter in nourishing. Of wild fowl and pigeons, being fat, the legs are better than the wings, the brawns of duck, teal, and widgeon[4] except, which is better to digest than the residue.

The Gizzard or stomach

Of a goose or hen, being fat with bran and milk, being well sodden or made in powder, is good for the stomach in making it strong to digest, and nourisheth competently.

---

1 *stirreth up Venus*] In the Prologue to *The Canterbury Tales* Chaucer describes the Summoner as "lecherous as a sparwe" (Chaucer 1989, l. 626).
2 *meetly*] properly, sufficiently.
3 *lightlier*] easier.
4 *widgeon*] wild duck.

The liver

Of a capon, hen, pheasant, or goose, being made fat with milk mixed with their meat, is not only easy to digest but also maketh good juice and nourisheth excellently. But the livers of beasts be ill to digest, passeth slowly, and maketh gross blood, but it is strong in nourishing.

The inwards of beasts, as tripes and chitterlings[1]

The flesh of them is more hard to digest, and therefore although they be well digested yet make they not juice naturally sanguine, or clean, but raw juice, and cold, and requireth a long time to be converted into blood.

The lungs or lights

Are more easy to digest than the liver and less nourisheth, but the nourishment that it maketh is phlegmatic, albeit the lungs of a fox is medicinable for them which have sickness of the lungs.

The Spleen or milt

Is of ill juice, for it is the chamber of melancholy.

The heart

Is of hard flesh and therefore is not well digested nor passeth shortly, but where he is well digested the juice that it maketh is not to be dispraised.

The brain

Is phlegmatic, of gross juice, slow in digesting, noyous[2] to the stomach, but where it is well digested it nourisheth much.

Marrow

Is more delectable than the brain; it is ill for the stomach, but where it is well digested it nourisheth much.

The stones and udders

Being well digested do nourish much, but the stones are hotter with their moistness, the udders cold and phlegmatic. They both do increase seed of generation, but the blood made of the udder is better than that which cometh of the stones, except it be of calves and lambs. Also, the stones of cocks maketh commendable nourishment.

The head

The flesh nourisheth much and augmenteth seed but it is slow of digestion and noyeth[3] the stomach, but to them which use much exercise it is not discommendable.[4]

---

1 *chitterlings*] the smaller intestines.
2 *noyous*] vexatious.
3 *noyeth*] annoys.
4 *discommendable*] i.e. it is recommended for those who use much exercise.

The tongue
Is of a spongy and sanguine substance, but the kernels[1] and gristle which are in the roots, if they be well digested, they make good nourishment; if they be not well digested they make phlegm.

The feet
Being well boiled and tender, in a whole stomach digesteth well and maketh good juice and passeth forth easily. Galen commendeth the feet of swine, but I have proved that the feet of a young bullock – tenderly sodden and laid in a souse[2] two days or three, and eaten cold in the evening – have brought a choleric stomach into a good digestion and sleep, and therewith hath also expulsed salt phlegm and choler. And this have I found in myself by often experience, alway forseen that it be eaten before any other meat, without drinking immediately after it.

Chapter ten: Of fish generally
The best fish, after the opinion of Galen, is that which swimmeth in the pure sea and is tossed and lift up with winds and surges; the more calm that the water is, the worse is the fish. They which are in muddy waters do make much phlegm and ordure, taken in fens and ditches ⁱbe worst. Being in fresh rivers and swift be sometime commendable, albeit generally all kinds of fish maketh more thinner blood than flesh so that it doth not much nourish and it doth sooner pass out by vapours. To a hot, choleric stomach or in fevers sometime they be wholesome, being new, fresh, and not very hard in substance or slimy. Hard fish is hard of digestion but the nourishment thereof is more firm than that which is soft; those which have much gross humours in them are best powdered.

Chapter eleven: Of butter
Butter is also nourishing and profiteth to them which have humours superfluous in the breast or lungs and lacketh riping[3] and cleansing of them, specially if it be eaten with sugar or honey. If it be well-salted it heateth and cleanseth the more.

Chapter twelve: Of cheese
Cheese, by the whole sentence of all writers, letteth digestion and is enemy unto the stomach; also, it engendereth ill humours and breedeth the stone. The cheese which doth least harm is soft cheese, reasonably salted, which some men do suppose nourisheth much.

Chapter thirteen: Of eggs
Eggs of pheasants, hens, and partridges be of all other meats most agreeable unto nature, specially if they be new laid. If they be rear they do cleanse the throat and breast, if they be hard they be slow in digestion but being once digested they do

---

ⁱ be] O1; by Q4.

1 *kernels*] glands.
2 *souse*] pickle.
3 *riping*] clearing.

nourish much. Mean between rear and hard, they digest conveniently and nourish quickly. ⁱEggs well poached are better than roasted. If they be fried hard they be of ill nourishment, and do make stinking fumes in the stomach, and do corrupt other meats with whom they be mingled. They be most wholesome when they be poached and most unwholesome when they be fried, Dioscorides sayeth. If they be supped warm before any other meat they do heal the griefs of the bladder and reins made with gravel, also soreness of the cheeks, and throat, and spitting of blood, and they be good against catarrhs or stilling out of the head into the stomach.

Chapter fourteen: Of fruits

Forasmuch as before that tillage of corn was invented – and that devouring of flesh and fish was of mankind used – men undoubtedly lived by fruits, and nature was therewith contented and satisfied. But by change of the diet of our progenitors there is caused to be in our bodies such alteration from the nature which was in men at the beginning, that now all fruits generally are noyful to man, and do engender ill humours, and be oft times the cause of putrified fevers if they be much and continually eaten. Notwithstanding, unto them which have abundance of choler they be sometime convenient to repress the flame which proceedeth of choler. And some fruits which be styptic or binding in taste, eaten before meals, do bind the belly, but eaten after meals they be rather ⁱⁱlaxative.

Of gourds

ⁱⁱⁱGourds raw be unpleasant in eating, ill for the stomach, and almost never digested. Therefore, he that will needs eat them must boil them, roast them, or fry them; every way they be, without savour or taste, and of their proper nature they give to the body cold and moist nourishment, and that very little. But by reason of the slipperiness of their substance, and because all meats which be moist of their nature be not binding, they lightly pass forth by the belly. And being well-ordered they will be meetly¹ concoct, if corruption in the stomach do not prevent them; they be cold and moist in the second degree.

Of melons and pepons

Melons and pepons be almost of one kind but that the melon is round like an apple and the innermost part thereof, where the seeds are contained, is used to be eaten. The pepon is much greater, and somewhat long, and the inner part thereof is not to be eaten. They both are very cold and moist and do make ill juice in the body if they be not well digested, but the pepon much more than the melon. They do least hurt if they be eaten afore meals, albeit if they do find in the stomach phlegm they be

---

i Eggs well poached ... they be mingled.] *O1 omits.*
ii laxative] laxative. Nowe shall it not be unexpedient to write of some fruites partycularly declarynge theyr noyfull qualities in appayrynge of Nature and how they may be used with lesse detriment *O1, Q2, O3, O5, O6.*
iii Gourds ... digested] *marginal note:* Galen de aliment 2 *O1, O3, O5, O6.*

1 *meetly*] properly, sufficiently.

turned into phlegm, if they find choler they be turned into choler. Notwithstanding, there is in them the virtue to cleanse and to provoke urine; they be cold and moist in the second degree.

Cucumbers

Cucumbers do not exceed so much in moisture as melons and therefore they be not so soon corrupted in the stomach, but in some stomachs, being moderately used, they do digest well. But if they be abundantly eaten or much used they engender a cold and thick humour in the veins, which never or seldom is turned into good blood and sometime bringeth in fevers; also, they abate carnal lust. The seeds – as well thereof as melons and gourds – being dyed and made clean from the husks, are very medicinable against sickness proceeding of heat, also the difficulty or let in pissing;[1] they be cold and moist in the second degree.

Galen De alimentorum facultatibus, 2

Dates

Be hard to digest, therefore being much eaten and not well digested they annoy the head, and cause gnawing in the stomach, and make gross juice, and sometime cause obstructions or stoppings in the liver and spleen. And where there is inflammation or hardness in the body they are unwholesome, but being well digested and temperately used they nourish, and make the flesh firm, and also bindeth the belly. Old dates be hot and dry in the first degree, new gathered are hot and moist in the first degree.

Of figs

Figs eaten do shortly pass out of the stomach and are soon distributed into all parts of the body and have the power to cleanse, specially gravel being in the reins of the back. But they make no substantial nourishment but rather somewhat loose and windy,[2] but by their quick passage the wind is soon dissolved;[3] therefore, if they be ripe, they do least harm of any fruits or almost none. Dry figs and old are more hot and dry than new gathered, but being much eaten they make ill blood and juice and (as some do suppose) do engender lice and also annoyeth the liver and the spleen if they be inflamed, but having the power to attenuate[4] or make humours current[5] they make the body soluble and do cleanse the reins. Also, being eaten afore dinner, with ginger, or pepper, or powder of thyme, or pennyroyal they profit much to them which have oppilations, or hard congealed matter in the inner parts of the body, or have distilations or rheums falling into the breast and stomach. New figs are hot and moist, old figs are hot in the first degree and dry in the second.

Aetius, 1

---

1 *let in pissing*] difficulty in urinating.
2 *loose and windy*] i.e. make the bowels loose and encourage flatulence.
3 *dissolved*] reduced, dispersed.
4 *attenuate*] make thinner.
5 *current*] fluid.

Of grapes and raisins

Galen *De alimentorum facultatibus*, 1

Dioscorides

Grapes do not nourish so much as figs but being ripe they make not much ill juice in the body, albeit newly gathered they trouble the belly and filleth the stomach with wind; therefore if they be hanged up a while ere they be eaten they are the less noyful. Sweet grapes are hottest, and do loose somewhat, and make a man thirsty. Sour grapes are cold and do also loose, but they are hard of digestion and yet they do not nourish; they which are in taste bitter or harsh be like to them that are sour. Raisins do make the stomach firm and strong, and do provoke appetite, and do comfort weak bodies being eaten afore meals; they be hot in the first degree and moist in the second.

Of cherries

Cherries, if they be sweet, they do soon slip down into the stomach, but if they be sour or sharp they be more wholesome, and do loose if they be eaten fresh and newly gatherered; they be cold and moist in the first degree.

Of peaches

Peaches do less harm and do make better juice in the body, for they are not so soon corrupted being eaten. Of the juice of them may be made a syrup very wholesome against the distemperance of choler, whereof proceedeth a stinking breath; they be cold in the first degree and moist in the second.

Of apples

All apples eaten soon after that they be gathered are cold, hard to digest, and do make ill and corrupted blood, but being well kept until the next winter or the year following, eaten after meals, they are right wholesome and do confirm[1] the stomach and make good digestion, specially if they be roasted or baken, most properly in a choleric stomach. They are best preserved in honey, so that one touch not another. The rough-tasted apples are wholesome where the stomach is weak by distemperance of heat or much moisture, the bitter apples where that grief is increased, the sour apples where the matter is congealed or made thick with heat. In distemperature of heat and dryth, by drinking much wine they have been found commodious, being eaten at night going to bed; without drinking to them, they be cold and moist in the first degree.

Of quinces

Quinces be cold and dry; eaten afore meals they bind and restrain the stomach that it may not digest well the meat, except that they be roasted or sodden. The core taken out and mixed with honey clarified, or sugar, then they cause good appetite and preserveth the head from drunkenness. Taken after meat it closeth and draweth the stomach together and helpeth it to digest, and mollifyeth the belly if it be abundantly taken; they be cold in the first degree and dry in the beginning of the second.

---

1 *confirm*] strengthen, invigorate.

Of pomegranates

Pomegranates be of good juice and profitable to the stomach, specially they which are sweet, but in a hot fever they that are sour be more expedient and wholesome, for then the sweet do incend[1] heat and puff up the stomach.

Of pears

Pears are much of the nature of apples but they are heavier. But taken after meat, roasted or baken, they are not unwholesome and do restrain and knit[2] the stomach, being ripe; they be cold and moist in the first degree.

Medlars

Medlars are cold and dry, and constrictive or straitening[3] the stomach, and therefore they may be eaten after meals as a medicine but not used as meat for they engender melancholy; they be cold and dry in the second degree.

Walnuts

Walnuts, if they be blanched, are supposed to be good for the stomach and somewhat loosing the belly; mixed with sugar they do nourish temperately. Of two dry nuts, as many figs, and twenty leaves of rue, with a grain of salt, is made a medicine whereof, if one do eat fasting, nothing which is venomous may that day hurt him, and it also preserveth against the pestilence, and this is the very right mithridate. They be hot and dry in the second degree, after some opinions: hot in the third degree, dry in the second.

Filberts and hazelnuts

They are more strong in substance than walnuts, wherefore they are not so easily or soon digested. Also, they do inflate the stomach and cause headache, but they engender fat and if they be roasted they are good to restrain rheums. Also, eaten with pepper they are good against torments of the belly and the stopping of urine; they be hot and dry in the first degree.

Of almonds

They do extenuate and cleanse without any binding, wherefore they purge the breast and lungs, specially bitter almonds. Also, they do mollify the belly, provoke sleep, and causeth to piss well. Five or six of them eaten afore meat keepeth a man from being drunk; they be hot and moist in the first degree.

Chesteines[4]

They being roasted under the embers or hot ashes do nourish the body strongly, and eaten with honey fasting do help a man of the cough.

---

1 *incend*] inflame.
2 *knit*] make hard.
3 *straitening*] make narrow, contract.
4 *Chesteines*] Chestnuts.

Prunes

Of the garden, and ripe, do dispose a man to the stool, but they do bring no manner of nourishment. To this fruit, like as to figs, this property remaineth: that being dried they do profit. The damask prune[1] rather bindeth than looseth and is more commodious unto the stomach; they be cold and moist in the second degree.

Olives

Condite in salt liquor, taken at the beginning of a meal, doth corroborate[2] the stomach, stirreth appetite, and looseth the belly, being eaten with vinegar. They which be ripe are temperately hot, they which be green are cold and dry.

Of capers

'They nourish nothing after that they be salted but yet they make the belly loose and purgeth phlegm which is therein contained. Also, stirreth appetite to meat and openeth the obstructions or stopping of the liver and spleen being eaten with oxymel before any other meat; they be hot and dry in the second degree.

Oranges

The rinds taken in a little quantity do comfort the stomach where it digesteth, specially condite with sugar and taken fasting in a small quantity. The juice of oranges, having a toast of bread put unto it, with a little powder of mints, sugar, and a little cinnamon, maketh a very good sauce to provoke appetite; the juice, eaten with sugar, in a hot fever, is not to be discommended.[3] The rind is hot in the first degree and dry in the second; the juice of them is cold in the second degree and dry in the first.

Chapter fifteen: Herbs used in pottage or to eat

Generally all herbs raw and not sodden do engender cold and watery juice if they be eaten customably[4] or in abundance, albeit some herbs are more comestible,[5] and do less harm unto nature, and moderately used maketh meetly[6] good blood.

Lettuce

Among all herbs none hath so good juice as lettuce, for some men do suppose that it maketh abundance of blood, albeit not very pure or perfect. It doth set a hot stomach in a very good temper[7] and maketh good appetite, and eaten in the evening it provoketh sleep, albeit it neither doth loose nor bind the belly of his own property. It increaseth milk in a woman's breasts but it abateth carnal appetite and much using thereof hurteth the eyesight; it is cold and moist temperately.

---

i They ... contained] *marginal note*: Galen. de aliment, 2 O1, O3, O5, O6.

1 *damask prune*] damson.
2 *corroborate*] strengthen.
3 *is not to be discommended*] i.e. it should be recommended.
4 *customably*] customarily, habitually.
5 *comestible*] edible.
6 *meetly*] properly, sufficiently.
7 *temper*] due proportion or mixture of qualities.

Coleworts and cabbages

Before that avarice caused merchants to fetch out of the east and south parts of the world the traffic of spice and sundry drugs to content the unsatiableness of wanton appetites, coleworts, for the virtues supposed to be in them, were of such estimation that they were judged to be a sufficient medicine against all diseases, as it may appear in the book of wise Cato wherein he writeth of husbandry. But now I will no more remember than shall be required in that which shall be used as meat and not pure medicine. The juice thereof hath virtue to purge, the whole leaves being half sodden, and the water poured out, and they being put eftsoons into hot water and sodden until they be tender, so eaten they do bind the belly. Some do suppose if they be eaten raw with vinegar before meat it shall preserve the stomach from surfeiting and the head from drunkenness, albeit much using of them dulleth the sight except the eyes be very moist. Finally, the juice that it maketh in the body is not so commmendable as that which is engendered of lettuce; it is hot in the first degree and dry in the second.

Of chicory or Succory

It is like in operation to lettuce and tempereth choler wonderfully, and therefore in all choleric fevers the decoction of this herb, or the water thereof, stilled, is right expedient. Semblably,[1] the herb and root boiled with flesh that is fresh, being eaten, keepeth the stomach and head in very good temper. I suppose that sow-thistle and dandelion be of like qualities, but not so convenient to be used of them which are whole because they are wild of nature and more bitter and therefore causeth fastidiousness[2] or loathsomeness[3] of the stomach. It is cold and dry in the second degree.

Endive and scariole[4]

Be much like in their operation to chicory but they are more convenient to medicine than to meat, albeit scariole, called white endive, having the tops of the leaves turned in and laid in the earth at the latter end of summer and covered becometh white and crisp, like to the great stalks of cabbage lettuce, which taken up and eaten with vinegar cooleth the heat of the stomach. And to them that have hot stomachs and dry they be right wholesome, but being too much used or in very great quantity they engender the humour which maketh the colic. ⁱThey be cold and moist in the first degree.

Mallows

Are not cold in operation but, rather, somewhat warm and have in them a slipperiness, wherefore being boiled and moderately eaten with oil and vinegar they make meetly[5] good concoction in the stomach and causeth the superfluous matter therein easily to pass and cleanseth the belly. It is hot and moist in the first degree.

Galen, 2 *De alimentorum facultatibus*

---

i They be] It is O*1*.

1 *semblably*] similarly.
2 *fastidiousness*] repulsiveness.
3 *loathsomeness*] nausea.
4 *scariole*] broad-leaved endive.
5 *meetly*] properly, sufficiently.

White beets

Are also abstertive and looseth the belly but much eaten annoyeth the stomach, but they are right good against obstructions or stopping of the liver; if they be eaten with vinegar or mustard, likewise it helpeth the spleen. It is cold in the first degree and moist in the second.

Purslane

Doth mitigate the great heat in all the inward parts of the body, semblably[1] of the head and eyes. Also, it represseth the rage of Venus[2] but if it be preserved in salt or brine it heateth and purgeth the stomach. It is cold in the third degree and moist in the second.

Chervil

Is very profitable unto the stomach but it may not sustain very much boiling; eaten with vinegar it provoketh appetite and also urine. The decoction thereof, drunk with wine, cleanseth the bladder.

Sorrel

Being sodden, it looseth the belly. In a time of pestilence – if one being fasting do chew some of the leaves and suck down the juice – it marvellously perserveth from infections, as a new practiser called Guainerius[3] doth write, and I myself have proved it in my household. The seeds therof, brayed[4] and drunk with wine and water, is very wholesome against the colic and fretting of the guts. It stoppeth fluxes and helpeth the stomach annoyed with repletion; it is cold in the third degree and dry in the second.

Dioscorides liber 2, chapter 106

Parsley

Is very convenient to the stomach and comforteth appetite and maketh the breath sweet. The seeds and root causeth urine to pass well and breaketh the stone, dissolveth winds. The roots boileth in water, and thereof oxymel being made, it dissolveth phlegm and maketh good digestion. It is hot and dry in the third degree.

Fennel

Being eaten, the seed or root maketh abundance of milk, likewise drunk with tisane or ale. The seed somewhat restraineth flux, provoketh to piss, and mitigateth frettings of the stomach and guts, specially the decoction of the root if the matter causing fretting be cold; but if it be a hot cause the use thereof is dangerous, for inflammation or exulceration[5] of the reins or bladder. It is hot in the third degree and dry in the first.

Galen De simplicium medicamentorum facultatibus liber 3, chapter 74

---

1 *semblably*] similarly.
2 *the rage of Venus*] lust.
3 *Guainerius*] Antonius Guainerius.
4 *brayed*] crushed to powder, usually in a mortar.
5 *exulceration*] ulceration, the early stage of ulceration.

Aniseed

Maketh sweet breath, provoketh urine, and driveth down things cleaving to the reins or bladder, stirreth up courage, and causeth abundance of milk. It is hot and dry in the third degree.

Beans

They make wind, howsoever they be ordered. The substance which they do make is spongy and not firm, albeit they be abstertive or cleansing the body. They tarry long ere they be digested and make gross juice in the body, but if onions be sodden with them they be less noyful.

Peason

Are much of the nature of beans but they be less windy and passeth faster out of the body. They be also abstertive or cleansing, specially white peason, and they also cause meetly[1] good nourishing, the husks taken away; and the broth wherein they be sodden cleanseth right well the reins and bladder.

Chapter sixteen: Rape roots and navews

The juice made by them is very gross and therefore being much eaten, if they be not perfectly concoct in the stomach, they do make crude or raw juice in the veins. Also, if they be not well boiled they cause winds, and annoy the stomach, and make sometime frettings. If they be well boiled, first in clean water and that being cast away, the second time with fat flesh, they nourish much and do neither loose nor bind the belly. But navews do not nourish so much as rapes, but they be even as windy.

Turnips

Being well boiled in water, and after with fat flesh, nourisheth much, augmenteth the seed of man, provoketh carnal lust. Eaten raw they stir up appetite to eat, being temperately used, and be convenient unto them which have putrified matter in their breasts or lungs, causing them to spit easily; but being much and often eaten they make raw juice and windiness.

Parsnips and carrots

They do nourish with better juice than the other roots, specially carrots, which are hot and dry and expelleth wind. Notwithstanding, much used they engender ill juice, but carrots less than parsnips; the one and the other expelleth urine.

Galen *De simplicium medicamentorum facultatibus liber 7*

Radish roots

Have the virtue to extenuate or make thin and also to warm; also they cause to break wind and to piss. Being eaten afore meats they let the meat that it may not descend, but being eaten last they

Paul of Aegina; Dioscorides

---

1 *meetly*] proper, sufficient.

Liber 7 De alimentorum facultatibus

make good digestion and looseth the belly (though Galen write contrary) for I, among diverse other, by experience have proved it. Notwithstanding, they be unwholesome for them that have continually the gout or pains in the joints.

Garlic

It doth extenuate and cut gross humours and slimy, dissolveth gross winds, and heateth all the body; also openeth the places which are stopped. Generally, where it is well digested in the stomach, it is wholesome to diverse purposes, specially in the body wherein is gross matter or much cold enclosed. If it be sodden until it looseth his tartness it somewhat nourisheth and yet looseth not his property to extenuate gross humours. Being sodden in milk it profiteth much against distillations from the head into the stomach.

Onions

Do also extenuate, but the long onions[1] more than the round, the red more than the white, the dry more than they which be green, also raw more than sodden. They stir appetite to meat, and put away loathsomeness,[2] and loose the belly; they quicken sight, and being eaten in great abundance with meat they cause one to sleep soundly.

Leeks

Galen 7, chapter 138

Be of ill juice and do make troublous dreams, but they do extenuate and cleanse the body and also make it soluble and provoketh urine. Moreover, it causeth one to spit out easily the phlegm which is in the breast.

Sage

It heateth and somewhat bindeth and therewith provoketh urine, the decoction of the leaves and branches being drunk; also, it stoppeth bleeding of wounds, being laid unto them. Moreover, it hath been proved that women which have been long time without children, and have drunk ten ounces of the juice of sage, with a grain of salt, a quarter of an hour before that they have companied with their husbands, have conceived at that time. It is hot and dry in the third degree; the using thereof is good against palsies.

Hyssop

Doth heat and extenuate, whereby it digesteth slimy phlegm; being prepared with figs it purgeth phlegm downward, with honey and water upward. Boiled in vinegar it helpeth the toothache, if the teeth be washed therewith; it is hot and dry in the third degree.

---

1 *long onions*] spring onions.
2 *loathsomeness*] nausea.

Borage

Comforteth the heart and maketh one merry eaten raw before meals or layed in wine that is drunk; also mollifieth the belly and prepareth to the stool. It is hot and moist in the middle of the first degree.

Savory

Purgeth phlegm, helpeth digestion, maketh quick sight, provoketh urine and stirreth carnal appetite. It is hot and dry in the third degree.

Rocket

Heateth much and increaseth seed of man, provoketh courage, helpeth digestion, and somewhat looseth. It is hot and moist in the second degree.

Thyme

Dissolveth winds, breaketh the stone, expulseth urine and ceaseth frettings; it is hot and dry in the third degree.

Pennyroyal

Doth extenuate heat and decoct; it reformeth the stomach oppressed with phlegm, it doth recomfort[1] the faint spirit, it expelleth melancholy by siege and is medicinable against many diseases. It is hot and dry in the third degree.

Town cress[2]

[i]Paulus[3] discommendeth,[4] saying that it resisteth concoction, and hurteth the stomach, and maketh ill juice in the body; taken as medicine it helpeth many diseases. It is hot and dry in the third degree.

[ii]Rosemary

Hath the virtue to heat, and therefore it dissolveth humour congealed with cold. It helpeth against palsies, falling-sickness, old diseases of the breast, torments or fretting; it provoketh urine and sweat, it helpeth the cough, taken with pepper and honey. It putteth away toothache, the root being chewed or the juice thereof put into the tooth. Being burned, the fume thereof resisteth the pestilence; the rind thereof sodden or burned and the fume received at the mouth stoppeth the rheum which falleth out of the head into the cheeks or throat, which I myself have proved. The green leaves bruised do stop the haemorrhoids if they be laid unto them. This herb is hot and dry in the third degree.

---

i Paulus ... stomach] *marginal note*: Lib. I O1, O3, O5, O6.
ii Rosemary] *O1 omits section on Rosemary.*

---

1 *recomfort*] soothe, strengthen anew.
2 *Town cress*] garden cress.
3 *Paulus*] Paul of Aegina.
4 *discommendeth*] advised against, did not recommend.

Chapter seventeen: *Spices growing out of this realm used in meat or drink*
Pepper
Black pepper is hottest and most dry, white paper is next, long pepper is most temperate. The general property of all kinds of pepper is to heat the body but, as Galen sayeth, it pierceth downward and doth not spread into the veins if it be gross beaten. It dissolveth phlegm and wind, it helpeth digestion, expulseth urine, and it helpeth against the diseases of the breast proceeding of cold. It is hot in the first degree and dry in the second.

Ginger
Heateth the stomach and helpeth digestion, but it heateth not so soon as pepper but afterward the heat remaineth longer and causeth the mouth to be moister. Being green[1] or well confectioned in syrup it comforteth much the stomach and head, and quickeneth remembrance if it be taken in the morrow fasting. It is hot in the second degree and dry in the first.

Saffron
Somewhat bindeth, heateth, and comforteth the stomach and the heart specially, and maketh good digestion being eaten or drunken in a small quantity. It is hot in the second degree and dry in the first.

Cloves
Hath virtue to comfort the sinews, also to consume and dissolve superfluous humours. They be hot and dry in the third degree; sodden with milk it comforteth the debility of nature.

Maces
Dioscorides commendeth to be drunk against spitting of blood and bloody fluxes and excessive laxes;[2] Paul of Aegina addeth to it that it helpeth the colic. They be hot in the second degree and dry in the third degree. It is to the stomach very commodious taken in a little quantity.

Nutmegs
With their sweet odour, comfort and dissolve, and sometime comforteth the power of the sight, and also the brain in cold diseases, and is hot and dry in the second degree.

Chapter eighteen: [i]*Of drinks, and first of water*
Undoubtedly water hath pre-eminence above all other liquors, not only because it is an element – that is to say a pure matter whereof all other liquors have their original substance – but also forasmuch as it was the very natural and first drink to all manner

---

i *Of drinks*] *Chapter seven "Of bread" down to chapter thirteen "Of eggs" occurs after the section on "Nutmegs" (at the end of chapter seventeen) in all other editions.*

1 *green*] the fresh root, often preserved.
2 *laxes*] looseness of the bowels, diarrhoea.

of creatures, wherefore the saying of Pindar the poet was ever well allowed, which sayeth water is best. And one thing is well considered, that from the creation of the world until the universal deluge or flood – during which time men lived eight or nine hundred years – there was none other drink used nor known but water. Also, the true followers of Pythagoras' doctrine drank only water and yet lived long, as Apollonius[1] and ⁱothers, and in the searching out of secret and mystical things, their wit excelled. Moreover, we have seen men and women of great age and strong body, which never or very seldom drank other drink than pure water, as by example in Cornwall (although that the country be in a very cold quarter), which proveth that if men from their infancy were accustomed to none other drink but to water only, moderately used it should be sufficient to keep natural moisture and to cause the meat that is eaten to pierce and descend unto the places of digestion, which are the purposes that drink serveth for. But now to the qualities of water after the sentence of ancient philosophers and physicians. The rainwater, after the opinion of most men, if it be received pure and clean, is most subtle and penetrative of any other waters; the next is that which issueth out of a spring in the east and passeth swiftly among great stones or rocks; the third is of a clean river, which runneth on great hard stones or pebbles. There be diverse means to try out which is the best water, for that which is lightest in poise[2] or weight is best, also that whereof cometh least scum or froth when it doth boil, also, that which will soonest be hot. Moreoever, dip linen clothes into sundry waters and after lay them to dry, and that which is soonest dry, ⁱⁱthe water wherein it was dipped is most subtle. After a great surfeit, ⁱⁱⁱspecially taken with superfluous eating of banqueting meats, cold water drunken is a general remedy. Hippocrates affirmeth that in sharp and fervent diseases none other remedy is to be required than water, and Galen will not that children should be *De ratione victus in morbis acutis, liber 3* let from drinking of water but that when they feel themselves very hot after meals and do desire to drink water, specially of a clean fountain, they should be suffered. Also, Hippocrates sayeth in such sickness whereas thou fearest lest the head should be vehemently grieved or the mind perished, there must thou give either water or white wine allayed with much water. Notwithstanding, there be in water causes of diverse diseases, as of swelling of the spleen and the liver; it also flitteth and swimmeth and it is long ere it pierceth, inasmuch as it is cold and slow in decoction. It looseth not the belly nor provoketh urine; also, in this it is vicious, that of his proper nature it maketh none ordure. Finally, alway respect must be had to the person that drinketh it, for to young men and them that be hot of complexion it doth less harm and sometime it profiteth, ⁱᵛbut to them that are feeble, old, phlegmatic or melancholy it is not convenient.

Chapter nineteen: Of wine

Plato, the wisest of all philosophers, doth affirm that wine, moderately drunk, nourisheth and comforteth as well all the body as the spirits of man. And therefore God

---

i others] *this ed.*; other Q4.   ii the water wherein it was dipped] O1 *omits*.
iii specially taken ... meats] O1, Q2, O3 *omit*.   iv but to them ... convenient] O1 *omits*.

1 *Apollonius*] Presumably Apollonius of Tyana.
2 *poise*] weight.

did ordain it for mankind as a remedy against the incommodities of age, that thereby they should seem to return unto youth and forget heaviness. Undoubtedly, wine heateth and moisteth the body, which qualities chiefly conserveth nature. And Galen, of all wines, commendeth that which is yellow and clear, saying that it is the hottest, and white wine least hot, and the colour mean between both of semblable temperature. The yellow wine, which is the proper colour of very hot wines, to old men doth bring these commodities: first, it heateth all their members; also it purgeth by urine the watery substance of the blood; moreover, the wines which be pale or yellow and full of substance, they do increase blood and nourish the body. But for the most part old men have need of such wines which do provoke urine forasmuch as in them do abound watery excrements or superfluitites, and they which do tarry long in the belly be not apt for aged men. Black or deep-red wines and thick do bind and congeal that which they do find in the body, and although some of them do not long abide in the belly yet they move not urine but rather [i]withdraweth. But yet they do harm to old men forasmuch as they do stop the conduits of the spleen, the liver, and the reins. Also, gross wines be best for them which desire to be fat, but it maketh oppilations; old wine and clear is better for them that be phlegmatic. Galen also prohibiteth children to drink any wine, forasmuch as they be of a hot and moist temperature and so is wine, and therefore it heateth and moisteth too much their bodies and filleth their heads with vapours. Moreover, he would that young men should drink little wine for it shall make them prone to fury and to lechery, and that part of the soul which is called rational it shall make troublous and dull; notwithstanding, yet it is sometime profitable to mitigate or expel ordure made of choler or melancholy. Also, [ii]it profiteth against dryth, which happeneth in the substance of the body either by too much labour or by the proper temperature of age, for wine moisteth and nourisheth that which is too dry, also mitigateth and dissolveth the sharpness of choler and purgeth it also by urine and sweat. Finally, as Theognes sayeth, much drinking of wine is ill but moderate drinking of wine is not only not ill but also commodious and profitable, which sentence is confirmed by Jesus Sirach in the book named Ecclesiastes, saying wine moderately drunk rejoiceth both the body and soul. Wherefore, to conclude this chapter, there is neither meat nor drink in the use whereof ought to be a more discreet moderation than in wine, considering that being good, and drunk in due time and measure, it not only conserveth natural and radical moisture, whereby life endureth, but also it helpeth the principal members which belong to digestion to do their office. On the other part, being ill or corrupt, or taken out of order and measure, it doth contrary to all the premises, besides that it transformeth a man or woman, making them beastly. More of the qualities of wine shall be touched hereafter in the order of diet.

liber 1, De sanitate tuenda [De sanitate tuenda] O1 omits.]

Ecclesiastes 134

---

i withdraweth] withdraweth, therfore they shulde be taken before meate *O1*.
ii it profiteth] *O1 omits*.

Chapter twenty: Of milk

Milk is compact[1] of three stubstances: cream, whey, and curds. The most excellent milk is of a woman, the milk of a cow is thickest, the milk of a camel is most subtle, the milk of a goat is between cow-milk and camel-milk, ewes' milk is between cow-milk and asses' milk. Also, the milk of beasts feeding in large pastures and out of fens and marshes is better than of them which be fed in little closes or in watery grounds. In springtime milk is most subtle and milk of young beasts is wholesomer than of old. To children, old men, and to them which be oppressed with melancholy or have the flesh consumed with a fever ethic,[2] milk is convenient, and generally to all of them which do not feel the milk rise in their stomachs after that they have eaten it. And in those persons it doth easily purge that which is in the belly superfluous, and afterward it entereth into the veins and bringeth good nourishment. Whosoever hath an appetite to eat or drink milk to the intent that it shall not arise or abraid[3] in the stomach, let him put into a vessel out of the which he will receive it a few leaves of mints, sugar, or pure honey, and into that vessel cause the beast to be milked and so drink it warm from the udder. Or else let him do as Paul of Aegina teacheth, that is to say boil first the milk with an easy fire,[4] and seethe it after with a hotter fire, and skim it clean, and with a sponge dipped in cold water take that clean away which would be burned to the vessel, then put to the milk, salt, and sugar and stir it often. Moreover, milk taken to purge melancholy would be drunk in the morning abundantly, new milked as is before written. And he that drinketh should abstain from meat and exercise until the milk be digested and have somewhat purged the belly, for with labour it becometh sour and therefore it requireth rest and watch or to walk very softly. Finally, where men and women be used from their childhood for the most part to milk, and do eat none or little other meat but milk and butter, they appear to be of good complexion and fashion[5] of body and not so much vexed with sickness as they which drink wine or ale; notwithstanding, much use of milk in men sanguine or choleric doth engender the stone.

Aetius

Oribasius De confectione ciborum, liber 3

[i]Chapter twenty-one: Of ale, beer, cider, and whey

I can neither hear nor read that ale is made and used for a common drink in any other country than England, Scotland, Ireland, and Poland. The Latin word *cerevitia*[6] is indifferent as well to ale as to beer. If the corn be good, the water wholesome and

---

i Chapter twenty-one] this ed.; Q4 omits.

1 compact] made up.
2 fever ethic] common fever. In the poem *Willoughby His Avisa* (probably written by Henry Willoughby under the pseudonym Hadrian Dorrell) Willoughby relates how the first sight of Avisa has caused him to be "sodenly infected with the contagion of a fantasticall fit" and he complains "I haue the feauer Ethicke right, / I burne within, consume without" (Dorrell 1594, L1v; L2v, canto 44).
3 abraid] to rise in the stomach and make one feel nauseous.
4 easy fire] i.e. gently.
5 fashion] shape, bulid.
6 cerevitia] a drink brewed from corn.

clean, and the ale or beer well and perfectly brewed and cleansed – and by the space of six days or more settled and defecate[1] – it must needs be a necessary and convenient drink, as well in sickness as in health, considering that barley-corn whereof it is made is commended and used in medicine in all parts of the world and accompted[2] to be of a singular efficacy in reducing the body into a good temper, specially which is in a distemperature of heat. For what ancient physician is there that in his works commendeth not tisane, which is none other than pure barley brayed[3] in a mortar and sodden in water? The same thing is small and clean ale or beer, saving that perchance the drying of the malt is cause of more dryth to be in the ale than in tisane, and the hops in beer maketh it colder in operation. But to say as I think, I suppose that neither ale nor beer is to be compared to wine – considering that in them do lack the heat and moisture which is in wine – for that being moderately used is most like to the natural heat and moisture of man's body. And also the liquor of ale and beer being more gross do engender more gross vapours and corrupt humours than wine, both being drunk in like excess of [i]quantity.

As for cider, [ii]it may not be good in any condition considering, as I said, that all fruits do engender ill humours and do cool too much natural heat. But to them which have abundance of red choler, moderately used it somewhat profiteth in mitigation of excessive heat. But who that will, diligently mark in the countries where cider is used for a common drink the men and women have the colour of their visage pallid and the skin of their visage rivelled,[4] although that they be young. Whey, if it be left of the butter, being well-ordered and not drunk until it have a thick curd of milk over it, like to a hat, is a right temperate drink forasmuch as by the unctuosity of the butter, whereof the whey retaineth some portion, it is both moist and nourishing and cleanseth the breast, and by the subtleness of itself it descendeth soon from the stomach and is shortly digested. Also, by reason of the affinity which it hath with milk it is convertible into blood and flesh, specially in those persons which do inhabit the north parts in whom natural heat is conglutinate,[5] and therefore is of more pussiance and virtue in the office of concoction. Also, custom from childhood doth elevate the power of meats and drinks in their position, notwithstanding that the four

---

i quantity] quantity. And one thynge is to be noted, whiche was lately wel marked, of a man of excellent lerning, being vexed with the syknes of the stone, That in them which do alway vse to drink ale or bere, the stone & grauel ingendered in them, is white of colour: And in the[m], which use to drink wine for the more parte, the stones and grauell whiche be ingendred in theym be reede of colour. Moreouer, who so euer useth ingurgitation of ale of biere, his breathe shall be more lothesome, than the breathes of theym whiche do take the excesse of wyne: for the wyne, by the reason of his heate, is sooner digested, and dothe leaue behynde hym, fewer dregges O1, Q2, Q3. *Before "Moreouer, who so euer" Q2 and O3 insert the following*: Not withstandynge commonly the colour of the stone foloweth the humour, whiche dothe moste abound in the pacient. As coler maketh the grauell more redde, fleme maketh it more white, also some men do suppose that red grauell is engendred in the raynes, white grauell in the bladder.
ii it may] *this ed.; may Q4 omits.*

---

1 *defecate*] purified of dregs.
2 *accompted*] accounted, reckoned.
3 *brayed*] crushed to powder, usually in a mortar.
4 *rivelled*] shrivelled or wrinkled.
5 *conglutinate*] concentrated.

humours, sanguine, choler, phlegm, and melancholy, [i]must also be considered, as it shall appear in diverse places hereafter.

Chapter twenty-two: Of honey

Honey, as well in meat as in drink, is of incomparable efficacy for it not only cleanseth, altereth, and nourisheth but also it long time preserveth that uncorrupted which is put into it, insomuch as Pliny sayeth, such is the nature of honey that it suffereth not the bodies to putrefy; and he affirmeth that he did see an hippocentaur – which is a beast half-man, half-horse – brought in honey to Claudius the Emperor, out of Egypt to Rome. And he telleth also of one Pollio Romulus who was above a hundred years old, of whom Augustus the Emperor demanded by what means he lived so long and retained still the vigour or liveliness of body and mind. Pollio answered that he did it inward with mead (which is drink made with honey and water), outward with oil, which saying agreed with the sentence of Democritus, the great philosopher, who, being demanded how a man might live long in health, he answered "if he wet him within with honey, without with oil".[1] The same philosopher, when he was a hundred years old and nine, prolonged his life certain days with the evaporation of honey, as Aristoxenus writeth. Of this excellent matter most wonderfully wrought and gathered by the little bee, as well of the pure dew of heaven as the most subtle humour of sweet and virtuous herbs and flowers, be made liquors commodious to mankind, as mead, metheglin, and [ii]oxymel. Mead, which is made with one part of honey and four times so much of pure water and boiled until no scum do remain, is much commended of Galen, drunk in summer for perserving of health. The same author alway commendeth the using of honey either raw, eaten with fine bread, somewhat leavened, or sodden and received as drink. Also, mead perfectly made cleanseth the breast and lungs, causeth a man to spit easily and to piss abundantly, and purgeth the belly moderately. Metheglin, which is most used in Wales by reason of hot herbs boiled with honey, is hotter than mead and more comforteth a cold stomach if it be perfectly made and not new or very stale. [iii]Oxymel is where to one part of vinegar is put double so much of honey, four times as much of water, and that being boiled unto the third part, and clean skimmed with a feather, is used to be taken wherein the stomach is much phlegm or matter undigested so that it be not red choler; look the use thereof in Alexander of Tralles. Many other good qualities of honey I omit to write of until some other occasion shall happen to remember them, particularly where they shall seem to be profitable.

Pliny, *liber* 22

Galen *De sanitate tuenda, liber* 4

---

i must also be considered] do cause moche alteration *O1*.
ii oxymel] the one with water and honye oonely, the other puttynge to sondry herbers, and some spyces *O1*.
iii Oxymel ... Tralles] *O1 omits*.

---

1 *Democritus ... oil*] Democritus was reputed to have lived until very old; when asked how to keep healthy he answered, "moisten the inside with honey and the outside with oil", that is, eat honey and moisturize the body with oil. The advice is attributed to Democritus by Athenaeus, author of *The Deipnosophistai* (*Banquet of the Sophists*) (Taylor 1999, 66, 262).

Chapter twenty-three: Sugar

Of sugar I do find none ancient author of Greeks or Latins do write by name but only Paul of Aegina, who sayeth in this wise after that he hath treated of honey: moreover, sugar which they call honey, that is brought to us from Arabia, called *felix*,[1] is not so sweet as our honey but is equal in virtue and doth not annoy the stomach nor causeth thirst; these be the wonders of Paul.[2] It is now in daily experience that sugar is a thing very temperate and nourishing, and where there is choler in the stomach or that the stomach abhoreth honey, it may be used for honey in all things wherein honey is required to be; [i]with sugar and vinegar is made syrup acetose.

Syrup acetose

Chapter twenty-four: Of time

Winter [O1, Q2, O3, O5 omit.]

In the consideration of time for taking of meats and drinks it is to be remembered that in winter meats ought to be taken in great abundance and of a more gross substance than in summer, forasmuch as the exterior air which compasseth the body, being cold, causeth the heat to withdraw from the inner parts, where being enclosed and [ii]gathered nigh together in the stomach and entrails it is of more force to boil and digest that which is received into it. Also, meats roasted are better than sodden, and flesh and fish powdered is then better than in summer. Herbs be not then commendable, specially raw, neither fruits, except quinces roasted or baked. Drink should then be taken in a little quantity, moreover wines shall need no water or very little, and that to choleric persons; red wines and they which be thick and sweet may be then more surely taken of them which have none oppilations or the stone. Alway remember that in winter phlegm increaseth by reason of rain and the moistness of that season, also the length of nights and much rest. And therefore in that time choleric persons are best at ease, semblably are young men, but to old men winter is enemy. It beginneth the eighth day of November and endureth until the eighth day of February.

Drink [O1, Q2, O3, O5, O6 omit.]

Galen in comment in *Aphorisms* 2, liber 3

Springtime [O1, Q2, O3 omit.]

Hippocrates *De natura humana*

The springtime doth participate the first part with winter, the latter part with summer, wherefore if the first part be cold then shall the diet be according to winter, if the end be hot then shall the diet be of summer. If both parts be temperate then should there be also a temperancy in diet, alway considering that phlegm yet remaineth and blood then increaseth, and meat would be less in quantity than in winter and drink somewhat more. Springtime beginneth the eighth day of February and continueth until the eighth day of May.

---

i with sugar ... acetose] O1, Q2, O3 *omit*.
ii gathered nigh] contract O1, Q2, O3.

---

1 felix] Latin for happy, lucky, or blessed.
2 Paul] Paul of Aegina.

In summer the inward heat is but little and the stomach doth not digest so strongly nor quickly as in winter, wherefore in that season eating often and a little at once is more convenient. And Damascene sayeth that fasting in summer dryeth the body, maketh the colour sallow, engendereth melancholy, and hurteth the sight. Also, boiled meat, bread steeped in white broth with sodden lettuce or chicory are then good to be used. Also, variety in meats, but not at one meal, pottages made with cold herbs, drink in more abundance, wine allayed with water, to hot complexions much, to cold, less. In this season blood increaseth and toward the end thereof, choler, and therefore they which be cold of nature and moist are then best at ease, hot natures and dry, worst. Moreover, children and very young men in the beginning of summer are wholest, old folk in the latter end and in harvest. Summer beginneth the eighth day of May and continueth until the eighth day of August.

Summer [O1, Q2, O3 omit.]

Galen comment in *Aphorisms* 18 liber 1

Hippocrates *De humoribus*

Galen in comment in *Aphorisms*

Autumn beginneth the eighth day of August and endeth the eighth day of November. That season of the year is variable and the air changable, by occasion whereof happen sundry sicknesses, and blood decreaseth, and melancholy aboundeth, whereof all summer fruits would then be eschewed forasmuch as they make ill juice and winds in the body. ⁱIn this time meat would be more abundant than in summer, but somewhat drier; drink must be less in quantity, but less mixed with water. This time is dangerous to all ages, all natures, and in all countries, but the natures hot and moist be less endamaged.¹

Autumn [O1, Q2, O3, O5, O6 omit.]

ⁱⁱ*Chapter twenty-five: Diet concerning sundry times of the year, written by the old physician, Diocles, to King Antigonus*

From the twelfth day of December, at the which time the day is at the shortest, until the ninth day of March, which do contain ninety days, rheums and moistures do increase; then meats and drinks naturally very hot would be moderately used. Also, to drink wine abundantly – without allay or with little water – and to use liberally the company of a woman² is not unwholesome to the body.

From the ninth day of March, at which time is *aquinoctium vernum*,³ unto the twenty-fifth day of April, sweat, phelgm, and blood do increase; therefore use then things having much juice and sharp, exercise the body diligently, then may ye use safely the company of a woman.

From the twenty-fifth day of April to the fourteenth day of June, choler increaseth; then use all things that are sweet and do make the belly soluble, forbear carnal company with women.

From the fourteenth day of June – at which time the day is at the length – unto the twelfth day of September doth melancholy reign; forbear ⁱⁱⁱcarnal company or use it moderately.

---

i In this time] *O1 omits.*   ii Chapter twenty-five] *this ed.; Q4 omits.*
iii carnal company] lechery *O1, Q2, O3.*

---

1 *endamaged*] injured.
2 *to use liberally the company of a woman*] i.e. have sex.
3 *aquinoctium vernum*] spring equinox.

From the twelfth day of September unto the seventeenth day of October do abound phlegm and thin humours; then would all fluxes and distillations be prohibited, then all sharp meats and drinks and of good juice are to be used, and ⁱcarnal occupation should then be eschewed.

From the seventeenth day of October to the twelfth day of December increaseth gross phlegm; use therefore all bitter meats, sweet wines, fat meat, and much exercise.

Chapter ⁱⁱtwenty-six: Of ages

Children, Galen *De sanitate tuenda, liber primo*

Children would be nourished with meats and drinks which are moderately hot and moist, notwithstanding Galen doth prohibit them the use of wine because it moisteth and heateth too much the body and filleth the heads of them which are hot and moist with vapours. Also, he permitteth them in hot weather to drink clear ⁱⁱⁱwater.

Children, Oribasius *De virtute simplicium, liber 1* [Children] *O1, Q2, O3, O5, O6 omit.*]

A child growing fast in his members toward a man – so that he seemeth well fed in the body – is then to be feared of fullness of humours, and if it be perceived that he is replete, then must be withdrawn and minished¹ some part of that nutriment and, according unto his age, some evacuation would be desired otherwhile,² by exercise, walking up and down, fasting. And before that they eat any meat let them exercise themselves with their own labours, and do their accustomed business, and eat the meats whereunto they be most used, so that it be such that may not hurt them. And this need they not to know of physicians, but by experience and diligent search by their stool ⁱᵛtheir nurses shall perceive what digesteth well and what doth ᵛthe contrary.

But if it appear that by excessive feeding the belly of the child is fuller and greater than it was wont to be, and that which passeth by the belly is corrupted or his sweat stinketh, these things known: if they eat strong meats give them not one kind of meat but diverse, that the novelty of the meat may help that they may go more easily to the stool. For if any have an unreasonable appetite, he is sooner recovered if he be purged by a boil or impostume come forth and broken before that the meat be corrupted, and after that let him eat fine meats, and being once whole, returned by little and little to his old custom.

Young men

Young men exceeding the age of fourteen years shall eat meats more gross of substance, colder and moister, also salads of cold herbs, and to drink seldom wine except it be allayed with water. Albeit all these things must be tempered according to their complexions, and exercise, and quietness in living, whereof ye shall read in their proper places hereafter.

---

i carnal occupation should then be] lechery *O1, Q2, O3*.
iii water] water of the fountayne *O1, Q2, O3, O5, O6*.
v the contrary] nat *O1, Q2, O3, O5, O6*.
ii twenty-six] this ed.; 25 *Q4*.
iv their nurses] they *O1*.

1 *minished*] deminished.
2 *otherwhile*] occasionally.

Old men – in whom natural heat and strength seemeth to decay – should use alway meats which are of quality hot and moist and therewithal easy to be digested, and abstain utterly from all meats and drinks which will engender thick juice and slimy, semblaby from wine which is thick, sweet, and dark red wines, and rather use them which will make thin humours and will purge well the blood by urine. Therefore white or yellow wines and perchance French claret wines are for them very commendable, also wine prepared with pure honey clarified wherein roots of parsley or fennel be steeped, specially if they suspect anything of the stone or gout. And if they more desire to clean their reins and bladder, then is it good to use small white wine, as racked[1] Rhenish wine[2] or other like to it, and sometime to steep overnight therein a parsley root, slit and somewhat bruised, and a little liquorice.

Old men

Paul of Aegina, *liber* 1, chapter 13

Finally, let them beware of all meats that will stop the pores and make obstructions or oppilations, that is to say with clammy matter stop the places where the natural humours are wrought and digested, the which meats I have before set in a table. But if it chance them to eat any such meat in abundance, let them take shortly such things as do resist oppilations or resolve[3] them, as white pepper (bruised and mixed with their meats or drink), garlic also, or onions, if they abhor them not. Alway remember that aged men should eat often and but little at every time, for it fareth by them as it doth by a lamp the light whereof is almost extinct, which by pouring in of oil little and little is long kept burning and with much oil poured in at once it is clean put out. Also, they must forbear all things which do engender melancholy, whereof ye shall read in the table before, and bread clean without leaven is to them unwholesome.

Oppilations, what they are [O1 omits.]

Chapter twenty-seven: Moderation in diet, having respect to the strength or weakness of the person

Now here it must be considered that although I have written a general diet for every age yet, none the less, it must be remembered that some children and young men – either by debility of nature or by some accidental cause, as sickness or much study – happen to gather humours phlegmatic or melancholy in the places of digestion, so that concoction or digestion is as weak in them as in those which are aged. Semblably, some old men find nature so beneficial unto them that their stomachs and livers are more strong to digest than the said young men; some perchance have much choler remaining in them. In these cases, the said young men must use the diet of old men, or nigh unto it, until the dyscrasy be removed, having alway respect to their universal complexions, as they which are naturally choleric to use hot things in a more temperance than they which be phlegmatic or melancholy by nature. The same observation shall be to old men, saving that age, of his own property, is cold and dry. Therefore the old man that is choleric shall have more regard to moisture in meats than the young man being of the same complexion, forseen alway that

Hippocrates *Aphorisms*, Galen in commentary

---

i *twenty-seven*] this ed.; 26 Q4.

1 *racked*] drawn from the lees so as to leave the sediment behind.
2 *Rhenish wine*] wine from the Rhineland.
3 *resolve*] dissolve, disintegrate.

where nature is offended or grieved she is cured by that which is contrary to that which offendeth or grieveth, as cold by heat, heat by cold, dryth by moisture, moisture by dryth. In that whereby nature should be nourished in a whole and temperate body, things must be taken which are like to the man's nature in quality and degrees: as where one hath his body in a good temper[1] things of the same temperance doth nourish him but where he is out of temper, in heat, cold, moisture, or dryth, temperate meats or drinks nothing do profit him. For being out of the mean and perfect temperature, nature requireth to be thereto reduced by contraries, remembering not only that contraries are remedy unto their contraries but also in every contrary consideration be had of the proportion in quantity.

Chapter twenty-eight: Times in the day concerning meals

Besides the times of the year and ages there be also other times of eating and drinking to be remembered, as the sundry times in the day, which we call meals, which are in number and distance according to the temperature of the country and person, as where the country is cold and the person lusty and of a strong nature there may more meals be used or the less distance of time between them. Contrariwise, in contrary countries and personages, the cause is afore rehearsed where I have spoken of the diet of the times of the year. Nothwithstanding, here must be also consideration of exercise and rest, which do augment or appair the natural disposition of bodies, as shall be more declared hereafter in the chapter of exercise. But concerning the general usage of countries, and admitting the bodies to be in perfect state of health, I suppose that in England young men until they come to the age of forty years may well eat three meals in one day, as at breakfast, dinner, and supper, so that between breakfast and dinner be the space of four hours at the least, between dinner and supper six hours, and the breakfast less than the dinner, and the dinner moderate, that is to say less than satiety or fullness of belly. And the drink thereunto measurable according to the dryness or moistness of the meat, for much abundance of drink at meal drowneth the meat eaten and not only letteth convenient concoction in the stomach but also causeth it to pass faster than nature requireth and therefore engendereth much phlegm and consequently rheums, and crudeness in the vein, debility and slipperiness of the stomach, continual flux, and many other inconveniences to the body and members.

Breakfast
[O1 omits.]

But to return to meals, I think breakfasts necessary in this realm, as well for the causes before rehearsed as also forasmuch as choler being fervent in the stomach sendeth up fumosities unto the brain and causeth headache, and sometime becometh adust and smoldereth in the stomach, whereby happeneth perilous sickness and sometime sudden death, if the heat enclosed in the stomach have no other convenient matter to work on; this daily experience proveth and natural reason confirmeth. Therefore men and women not aged – having their stomachs clean, without putrified matter, sleeping moderately and soundly in the night, and feeling themself light in the morning and sweet-breathed

---

i *twenty-eight*] this ed.; 27 Q4.

1 *temper*] due proportion or mixture of humours or qualities.

– let them on God's name break their fast, choleric men with gross meat, men of other complexions with lighter meat, forseen that they labour somewhat before; semblably their dinner and supper, as I have before written, so that they sleep not incontinent after their meals. And here I will not recite the sentences of authors which had never experience of English men's natures or of the just temperature of this realm of England, only this counsel of Hippocrates shall be sufficient: we ought to grant somewhat to time, to age, and to custom. Notwithstanding, where great weariness or dryth grieveth the body, there ought the dinner to be the less and the longer the distance between dinner and supper; also, much rest, except a little soft walking, that by an upright moving the meat being stirred may descend. This is alway to be remembered, that where one feeleth himself full and grieved with his dinner, or the savour of his meat by eructation ascendeth, or that his stomach is weak by late sickness or much study, then is it most convenient to abstain from supper and rather provoke himself to sleep much than to eat or drink anything. Also, to drink between meals is not laudable, except very great thirst constraineth, for it interrupteth the office of the stomach in concoction and causeth the meat to pass faster than it should do, and the drink being cold, it rebuketh natural heat that is working, and the meat remaining raw, it corrupteth digestion and maketh crudness in the veins. Wherefore he that is thirsty, let him consider the occasion, if it be of salt phlegm let him walk fair and softly and only wash his mouth and his throat with barley water or with small ale, or lie down and sleep a little, and so the thirst will pass away or at the least be well asuaged. If it happen by extreme heat of the air, or by pure choler, or eating of hot spices, let him drink a little julep[1] made with clean water and sugar or a little small beer or ale so that he drink not a great glut[2] but in a little quantity, let it still[3] down softly into his stomach as he sitteth and then let him not move suddenly. If the thirst be in the evening, by eating too much and drinking of wine, then – after the opinion of the best learned physicians, and as I myself have often experienced – the best remedy is, if there be no fever, to drink a little draught of cold water immediately, or else if it be not painful for him to vomit, to provoke him thereto with a little warm water and after to wash his mouth with vinegar and water and so to sleep long and soundly if he can. And if in the morning he feel any fumosities rising, then to drink julep[4] of violets or, for lack thereof, a good draught of very small ale or beer, somewhat warmed, without eating anything after it.

<small>Hippocrates *Aphorisms* 18, *liber* 1; Galen *De sanitate tuenda*</small>

Chapter twenty-nine: Of diversity of meats whereby health is appaired
Now let this be a general rule: that sundry meats, being diverse in substance and quality, eaten at one meal is the greatest enemy to health that may be and that which

---

i *twenty-nine*] this ed.; 28 Q4.

1 *julep*] a sweet drink prepared in different ways; considered comforting or gently stimulating.
2 *glut*] gulp, full swallow.
3 *still*] trickle down or fall in minute drops.
4 *julep*] a sweet drink prepared in different ways; considered comforting or gently stimulating.

engendereth most sickness. For some meats being gross and hard to digest, some fine and easy to digest, do require diverse operations of nature and diverse temperatures of the stomach, that is to say much heat and temperate heat, which may not be together at one time. Therefore when the fine meat is sufficiently boiled in the stomach, the gross meat is raw, so both the juices – the one good and perfect the other gross and crude – at one time digested and sent into the veins and body, needs must health decay, and sickness be engendered. Likewise, in diverse meats being diverse qualities, as where some are hot and moist, some cold and moist, some hot and dry, some cold and dry, according thereunto shall the juice be diverse which they make in the body. And like as between the said qualities is contrariety, so thereby shall be in the body an unequal temperature, forasmuch as it is not possible for man to esteem so just a proportion of the qualities of that which he receiveth that the one shall not exceed the ⁱother, wherefore of the said unequal mixture needs must ensure corruption and consequently sickness. And therefore to a whole man it were better to feed at one meal competently on very gross meat only, so that it be sweet and his nature do not abhor it, than on diverse fine meats of sundry substance and qualities. I have known and seen old men and old women which, eating only beef, bacon, cheese or curds have continued in good health, whom I have proved that when they have eaten sundry fine meats at one meal have soon after felt themselves grieved with frettings and headache. And after that they have been whole again there hath been given to them one kind of light meat, they have done as well therewith as they were wont to do with gross meats when they eat it alone, which proveth to be true that which I have rehearsed. And it is good reason, for after the general opinion of philosophers and physicians the nature of mankind is best content with things most simple and unmixed, all things tending to unity wherein is the only perfection. Also, it is a general rule of physic that where a sickness may be cured with simples, that is to say with one only thing that is medicinable, there should the physician give no compound medicine mixed with many things. These things considered, it may seem to all men that have reason what abuse is here in this realm in the continual gormandize[1] and daily feeding on sundry meats at one

Gluttony meal, the spirit of gluttony triumphing among us in his glorious chariot called welfare,[2] driving us afore him as his prisoners into his dungeon of surfeit where we are tormented with catarrhs, fevers, gouts, pleurisies, fretting of the guts, and many other sicknesses and, finally, cruelly put to death by them, oftentimes in youth or in the most pleasant time of our life when we would most gladly live. For the remedy whereof, how many times have there been devised ordinances and acts of counsel, although perchance bodily health was not the chief occasion thereof but rather provision against vain and sumptuous expenses of the mean people? For the nobility was exempted and had liberty to abide still in the dungeon if they would and to live less while than other men. But when, where, and

i other] other in quantitie $O1$, $Q2$, $O3$, $O5$, $O6$.

1 *gormandize*] gluttony.
2 *welfare*] abundance.

how long were the said good devices put in due execution for all that thereof should succeed double profit, that is to say health of body and increase of substance by eschewing of superfluous expenses in sundry dishes? Alas, how long will men fantasy[1] laws and good ordinances and never determine[2] them? Fantasy proceedeth of wit, determination of wisdom; wit is in the devising and speaking but wisdom is in the performance, which resteth only in execution. Here I had almost forgotten that my purpose was to write of the order of diet and not of laws but the fervent love that I have to the public weal[3] of my country constrained me to digress somewhat from my matter, but now will I proceed forth to write of order, which in taking of meats and drinks is not the least part of diet.

Chapter ⁱthirty: Of order in receiving of meat and drink

Herbs, as well sodden as unsodden, also fruits which do mollify and loose the belly, ought to be eaten before any other meat, except that sometime for the repressing of fumosities rising in the head by much drinking of wine, raw lettuce, or a cold apple, or the juice of oranges or lemons may be taken after meals in a little quantity. Moreover, all broths, milk, rear eggs, and meats, which are purposely taken to make the belly soluble, would be first eaten. All fruits and other meats that are styptic or binding would be eaten last of all other. Fruits confectionate, specially with honey, are not to be eaten with other meats, but here it is to be diligently noted that where the stomach is choleric and strong, gross meats would be first eaten. Where the stomach is cold or weak, there would fine meats be first eaten, for in a hot stomach fine meats are burned while the gross meat is digesting; contrariwise in a cold stomach the little heat is suffocate[4] with gross meat and the fine meat left raw for lack of concoction where, if the fine meat be first taken moderately, it stirreth up and comforteth natural heat and maketh it more able to concoct gross meats if they be eaten afterward so that it be but in small quantity. Notwithstanding, as I late affirmed, one manner of meat is more sure to every complexion, forseen that it be alway most commonly in conformity of qualities with the person that eateth. Moreover, take heed that slipper[5] meats be not first eaten lest it draw with it too hastily other meats ere they be digested, nor that styptic or restraining meats be taken at the beginning, as quinces, pears, and medlars, lest they may let other meats that they descend not into the bottom of the stomach where they should be digested. Notwithstanding, the confection made with the juice of quinces called *diacytonites*, taken two hours afore dinner or supper is commended of Galen and others for restoring appetite and making good concoction. Also, concerning drink at meals, it would not be afore that somewhat[6] were eaten, and at the beginning the drink would be strongest and so toward the end   Drink at meals [O1, Q2, O3 omit.]

---

i *thirty*] this ed.; 29 Q4.

1 *fantasy*] create (with the sense of a lack of substance).
2 *determine*] set limit to.
3 *weal*] welfare, well-being.
4 *suffocate*] suffocated.
5 *slipper*] slippery; specifically, readily passing through the body.
6 *it would not be afore that somewhat*] it should not be before that something; i.e. don't drink before eating.

more small, if it be ale or beer, and if it be wine, more and more allayed with water. And after the better opinion of physicians, the drink would rather be mixed with the meat by sundry little draughts than with one great draught at the end of the meal, for the mixture tempereth well the meat without annoyance. A great draught with much drink drowneth the meat, rebuketh natural heat that then worketh in concoction, and with his weight driveth down the meat too hastily. Hot wines, and sweet or confectioned with spices, or very strong ale or beer are not convenient at meals, for the meat is by them rather corrupted than digested and they make hot and stinking vapours ascend up to the brains. Albeit if the stomach be very windy, or so cold and feeble that it cannot concoct such a quantity of meat as is required to the sufficient nourishment of the body of him that eateth, or hath eaten raw herbs or fruits whereby he feeleth some annoyance, then may he drink last, incontinent after his meal a little quantity of sack or good aqua-vitae[1] in small ale. But if he have much choler in his stomach or a head full of vapours, it were much better that he did neither drink the one nor the other but rather eat a little coliander[2] seed prepared or a piece of a quince roasted or in marmalade, and after rest to amend the lack of nature with sleep, moderate exercise, and plasters provided for comforting of the stomach. And here will I leave to write any more of the diet in eating and drinking, saving that I would that the readers should have in rememberance these two counsels: first, that to a whole man too precise a rule is not convenient in diet, and that the diseases which do happen by too much abstinence are worse to be cured than they which come by repletion. And as Cornelius Celsus sayeth, a man that is whole, and well at ease, and is at his liberty ought not to bind himself to rules or need a physician. But yet, where the stomach is feeble, as is of the more part of citizens, and well nigh all they that be studious in learning or weighty affairs, there ought to be more circumspection that the meat may be such as that either in quality or quantity, nature, being but feeble, be not rebuked or too much oppressed.

Cornelius Celsus liber 1, chapter 1

Idem, chapter 2 [Idem] the same.]

Chapter ⁱthirty-one: Of sleep and watch

The commodity of moderate sleep appeareth by this: that natural heat – which is occupied about the matter wereof proceedeth nourishment – is comforted in the places of digestion and so digestion is made better or more perfect by sleep, the body fatter, the mind more quiet and clear, the humours temperate, as by much watch all things happen contrary. The moderation of sleep must be measured by health and sickness, by age, by time, by emptiness or fullness of the body, and by natural complexions. First, to a whole man having no debility of nature and digesting perfectly the meat that he eateth, a little sleep is sufficient, but to them which have weak stomachs and do digest slowly, it requireth that sleep be much longer; semblable,

---

i *thirty-one*] this ed.; 30 Q4.

1 *aqua-vitae*] water of life (Latin); any form in which ardent spirits, such as whiskey or brandy, have been drunk.

2 *coliander*] coriander.

temperance is required in youth and age, winter and summer. The body being full of ill humours, very little sleep is sufficient, except the humours be crude or raw for then is sleep necessary, which digesteth them better than labour. Semblably, where the body is long empty by long sickness or abstinence, sleep comforteth nature as well in the principal members as in all the other. Also, regard must be had to the complexion, for they that are hot and do eat little and digest quickly, a little sleep serveth, specially to choleric persons for in them much sleep augmenteth heat, more than is necessary, whereby hot fumes and inflammations are often engendered and sometime the natural choler is adust or putrified, as experience teacheth. Plegmatic persons are naturally inclined to sleep, and because they engender much humours they require more sleep than sanguine or choleric. Persons having natural melancholy not proceeding of choler adust do require very much sleep, which in them comforteth the powers animal, vital, and natural, which ye may find written in the tables preceding. Sleep would be[1] taken not immediately after meals and before that the meat is descended from the mouth of the stomach,[2] for thereby is engendered pains and noise in the belly, and digestion corrupted, and the sleep by ill vapours ascending made unquiet and troublous. Moreover, immoderate sleep maketh the body apt unto palsies, apoplexis, falling-sickness, rheums, and impostumes; also, it maketh the wits dull and the body slow and unapt to honest exercise. Semblably, immoderate watch dryeth too much the body and doth debilitate[3] the powers animal, letteth digestion, and maketh the body apt to consumptions, wherefore in these two things, as well as all other, a diligent temperance is to be used. The moderation is best conjected,[4] for it is hard perfectly to know it, by the sensible lightness of all the body, specially of the brain, the brows, and the eyes, the passage down of the meat from the stomach, the will to make urine, and to go to the stool. Contrariwise, heaviness in the body and eyes and savour of the meat before eaten signifieth that the sleep was not sufficient. They that are whole must sleep first on the right side because the meat may approach to the liver, which is to the stomach as fire under the pot and by him is digested. To them which have feeble digestion it is good to sleep prostrate on their bellies[5] or to have their bare hand on their stomachs. Lying upright on the back is to be utterly abhorred.

Chapter [i]thirty-two: The commodity of exercise and the time when it should be used

Every moving is not an exercise, but only that which is vehement, the end whereof is alteration of the breath or wind of a man. Of exercise do proceed two commodities:

---

i *thirty-two*] this ed.; 31 Q4.

1 *would be*] should be.
2 *mouth of the stomach*] probably the gastroduodenal junction (the lower part of the stomach that connects to the small intestine) rather than the gastroesophageal junction (Scurlock and Andersen 2005, 135).
3 *debilitate*] weaken, enfeeble.
4 *conjected*] conjectured.
5 *good to sleep ... on their bellies*] Boorde advises against sleeping on the stomach in chapter eight of his dietary.

Evacuation excrements [O1, Q2, O3, O5, O6 omit.]

evacuation of excrements and also good habit of the body. For exercise, being a vehement motion, thereof needs must ensue hardness of the members, whereby labour shall the less grieve and the body be the more strong to labour. Also, thereof cometh augmentation of heat, whereby happeneth the more attraction of things to be digested, also, more quick alteration and better nourishing. Moreover, that all and singular parts of the body be therewith somewhat humected, whereby it happeneth that things hard be mollified, moist things are extenuate, and the pores of the body are more opened, and by the violence of the breath or wind the pores are cleansed and the filth in the body naturally expelled. This thing is so necessary to the preservation of health that without it no man may be long without sickness, which is affirmed

Cornelius Celsus, liber 1

by Cornelius Celsus saying that sluggishness dulleth the body, labour doth strength it; the first bringeth in commodities of age shortly, the last maketh a man long time lusty. Notwithstanding, in exercise ought to be four things diligently considered, that is to say: the time, the things preceding, the quality, and the quantity of exercise.

First, as concerning the time convenient for exercise, that it be not when there is in the stomach or bowels great quantity of meat not sufficiently digested, or of humours crude or raw, lest thereby peril might ensue by conveyance of them into

Galen *De sanitate tuenda*, liber 2

all the members before those meats or humours be concoct or boiled sufficiently. Galen sayeth that the time most convenient for exercise is when both the first and the second digestion is complete, as well in the stomach as in the veins, and that the time approach to eat eftsoons. For if ye do exercise sooner or later ye shall either fill the body with crude humours or else augment yellow choler. The knowledge of this time is perceived by the colour of the urine: for that which resembleth unto clear water betokeneth that the juice which cometh from the stomach is crude in the veins; that which is well coloured, not too high or base,[1] betokeneth that the second digestion is now perfect; where the colour is very high or red it signifyeth that the concoction is more than sufficient. Wherefore when the urine appeareth in a temperate colour, not red nor pale but, as it were, gilt, should exercise have his beginning.

Chapter [1]*thirty-three: Of the fricaces or rubbings preceding exercise*

Galen; Paul of Aegina; Oribasius; Aetius

As touching things preceding exercise, forasmuch as it is to be feared left by vehement exercise any of the excrements of the belly or bladder should hastily be received into the habit of the body by the violence of heat kindled by exercise. Also, lest something which is whole be by heaviness of excrements or violent motion broken or pulled out of his place, or that the excrements by violence of the breath should stop the pores or conduits of the body, it shall be necessary, llittle and little, by chafing the body, first to mollify the parts consolidate,[2] and to extenuate or make thin the

---

1 *thirty-three*] this ed.; 32 Q4.

1 *base*] deep.
2 *consolidate*] solidified.

humours, and to loose open the pores, and then shall ensue to him that exerciseth no peril or obstruction or rupture. And to bring that to pass it shall be expedient after that the body is cleansed to rub the body with a coarse linen cloth, first softly and easily and after to increase more and more to a hard and swift rubbing until the flesh do swell and be somewhat ruddy, and that not only downright but also overthwart[1] and round. Some do use fricaces in this form: in the morning after that they have been at the stool, with their shirt sleeve, or bare hand if their flesh be tender, they do first softly and afterward faster rub their breast and sides downward and overthwart, not touching their stomach or belly and after cause their servant semblably to rub overthwart their shoulders and back, beginning at the neckbone and not touching the reins of their back except they do feel there much cold and wind, and afterward their legs from the knees to the ankle, last their arms from the elbow to the handwrist. And in this form of fricace I myself have founden an excellent commodity. Old men, or they which be very dry in their bodies, if they put to some sweet oils as *yrinum, nardinum, chamemelinum*,[2] or other like, mixed with a little sweet oil of roses, I suppose they do well. I will not here speak of ointments used in old time among the Romans and Greeks in fricaces or rubbings, for I suppose that they were never here used and in the said places they be also left, unless it be in the palsies, or apoplexies, or against the rigour which happeneth in fevers. Only I will remember the saying of Hippocrates: fricace hath power to loose, to bind, to increase flesh, and to minish it. For hard fricaces do bind or consolidate,[3] soft rubbing doth loose or mollify, much doth minish flesh, mean rubbing doth augment or increase it. He that will know more abundantly thereof, let him read the book of Galen of the preservation of health, called in Latin *De sanitate tuenda*, translated more truly and eloquently out of Greek into Latin by Doctor Linacre, late physician of most worthy memory to our sovereign lord, King Henry the Eighth. The same matter is written more briefly of Paul of Aegina, Oribasius, Aetius, and some other late writers, but unto Galen not to be compared.

Obstruction or rupture [O1, Q2, O3, O5, O6 omit.]

Chapter ⁱthirty-four: The diversities of exercises

The quality of exercise is the diversity thereof, forasmuch as therein be many differences in moving, and also some exercise moveth more one part of the body, some another. In difference of moving, some is slow or soft, some is swift or fast, some is strong or violent, some be mixed with strength and swiftness. Strong or violent exercises be these: delving, specially in tough clay and heavy; bearing or sustaining of heavy burdens; climbing or walking against a steep, upright hill; holding a rope and climbing up thereby; hanging by the hands on anything above a man's reach, that his feet touch not the ground; standing and holding up or spreading the arms with the hands fast closed and abiding so a long time; also, to hold the arms steadfast, casting

---

i *thirty-four*] this ed.; 33 Q4.

1 *overthwart*] across, crosswise.
2 *yrinum, nardinum, chamemelinum*] all plants providing medicinal oils.
3 *consolidate*] combine, make solid.

another man to assay[1] to pull them out and, notwithstanding, he keepeth his arm steadfast in forcing thereunto the sinews and muscles. Wrestling also, with the arms and the legs if the persons be equal in strength, it doth exercise the one and the other; if the one be stronger then is it to the weaker a more violent exercise. All these kinds of exercises and other like them do augment strength, and therefore they serve only for young men which be inclined or be apt to the wars. Swift exercise without violence is running, playing with weapons, tennis or throwing of the ball, trotting a space of ground forward and backward, going on the toes and holding up the hands; also, stirring up and down his arms without plummets. Vehement exercise is compound of violent exercise and swift when they are joined together at one time, as dancing of galliards,[2] throwing of the ball and the running after it; football play may be in the number thereof, throwing of the long dart, and the continuing it many times, running in harness and other like. The moderate exercise is long walking or going a tourney.[3] The parts of the body have sundry exercises appropred[4] unto them: as rounding and going is the most proper for the legs; moving of the arms up and down, or stretching them out and playing with weapons, serveth most for the arms and shoulders; stouping and rising often time, or lifting great weights, taking up plummets or other like poises[5] on the ends of staves, and in likewise lifting up in every hand a spear or morris-pike[6] by the ends, specially crossing the hands and to lay them down again in their places, these do exercise the back and loins; of the bulk[7] and lungs the proper exercise is moving of the breath in singing or crying; the entrails, which be underneath the midriff, be exercised by blowing, either by constraint or playing on shawms,[8] or sackbuts,[9] or other like instruments which do require much wind; the muscles are best exercised with holding the breath in a long time, so that he which doth exercise hath well digested his meat and is not troubled with much wind in his body. Finally, loud reading, counterfeit battle, tennis or throwing the ball, running, walking, add to shooting[10] – which in my opinion exceed all the other – do exercise the body commodiously. Alway remember that the end of violent exercise is difficulty in fetching of the breath, of moderate exercise alteration of breath only or the beginning of sweat. Moreover, in winter running and wrestling is convenient, in summer wrestling a little but not running. In very cold weather much walking, in hot weather rest is more expedient. They which seem to have moist bodies and live in idleness, they have need of violent exercise. They which are lean and choleric must walk softly and exercise themselves very temperately. The plummets, called of Galen halteres, which are now

Celsus, 1

---

1 *assay*] try, in order to test fitness.
2 *galliards*] quick and lively dances.
3 *going a tourney*] taking part in tournaments, i.e. exercises in combat on horseback.
4 *appropred*] appropriate.
5 *poises*] weights.
6 *morris-pike*] a type of pike thought to be of Moorish origin.
7 *bulk*] chest, thorax.
8 *shawms*] a shawm was a medieval instrument, precursor of the modern oboe.
9 *sackbuts*] Renaissance instruments; bass trumpets with a slide like a trombone.
10 *shooting*] It is possible that Elyot here means shouting since Q4's reading "shotynge" was valid for either.

much used with great men, being of equal wright and according to the strength of him that exerciseth, are very good to be used fasting a little before breakfast or dinner, holding in every hand one plummet[1] and lifting them on high and bringing them down with much violence or moderate, after the poise[2] of the plummets, heavier or lighter, and with much or little labouring with them.

Chapter ithirty-five: Of gestation, that is to say where one[3] is carried and is of another thing moved and not of himself[4]

There is also another kind of exercise, which is called gestation and is mixed with moving and rest, forasmuch as the body sitting or lying seemeth to rest and, notwithstanding, it is moved by that which beareth it, as lying in a bed, hanging by cords or chains or in a cradle, sitting in a chair which is carried on men's shoulders with staves (as was the use of the ancient Romans) or sitting in a boot or barge which is rowed, riding on a horse which ambleth very easily or goeth a very soft pace. The bed, cradle, and chair carried serveth for them that are in long and continual sickness or be lately recovered of a fever, also them which have the frenzy or lethargy, or have a light tertian fever or a quotidian. This exercise sweetly assuageth troubles of the mind and provoketh sleep, as it appeareth in children which are rocked; also, it is convenient for them which have the palsy, the stone, or the gout. Gestation in a chariot or waggon hath in it a shaking of the body but some be vehement and some more soft. The soft serveth in diseases of the head and where any matter runneth down into the stomach and entrails but the vehement shaking is to be used in the griefs of the breast and stomach, also in swelling of the body and legs in dropsies, palsies, megrims, and scotomas,[5] which is an imagination of darkness being returned. At the end of his journey he must sit up and be easily moved; I have known, sayeth Aetius, many persons in such wise cured without any other help. Navigation or rowing nigh to the land in a calm water is expedient for them that have dropsies, lepries,[6] palsies, called of the vulgar people takings and frenzies. To be carried on a rough water, it is a violent exercise and induceth sundry affections of the mind: sometime fear, sometime hope, now coward heart, now hardiness, one while pleasure, another while displeasure. These exercises, if they be well tempered, they may put out of the body all long-during sickness, for that which is mixed with rest and moving, if anything else may, it most excellently causeth the body to be well nourished. Celsus doth prohibit gestation where the body feeleth pain and in the beginning of fevers, but when they cease[7] he alloweth it. Riding moderately and without grief it doth coroborate the spirit and body above other exercises, specially the stomach; it cleanseth the senses and maketh

Gestation; Paul of Aegina; Aetius [Gestation;] O1, Q2, O3, O5, O6 *omit.*]

Celsus, 2

---

i *thirty-five*] this ed.; 34 Q4.

1 *plummet*] leaden weight.
2 *poise*] weight.
3 *one*] i.e. something.
4 *of another ... not of himself*] i.e. doesn't move by itself.
5 *scotomas*] Scotoma caused dizziness and obscured vision.
6 *lepries*] leprosies, i.e. skin ailments in general.
7 *they cease*] i.e. if they cease.

them more quick, albeit to the breast it is very noyful. It ought to be remembered that as well this as other kinds of exercise would be used in a whole[1] country and where the air is pure and uncorrupted, forseen that he that will exercise do go first to the stool for the causes rehearsed in the last chapter.

Chapter thirty-six:[i] Of vociferation

The chief exercise of the breast and instruments of the voice is vociferation, which is singing, reading, or crying, whereof is the property that it purgeth natural heat, and maketh it also subtle and stable, and maketh the members of the body substantial and strong, resisting diseases. This exercise would be used of persons short-winded; and them which cannot fetch their breath but holding their neck straight upright; also of them whose flesh is consumed, specially about the breast and shoulders; also which have had apostumes[2] broken in their breasts. Moreover, of them that are hoarse by too much moisture and to them which have quartan fevers it is convenient; it looseth the humour that sticketh in the breast and dryeth up the moistness of the stomach, which properly the course of the quartan is wont to bring with him. It also profiteth them which have feeble stomachs, or do vomit continually, or do break up sourness out of the stomach; it is good also for griefs of the head. He that intendeth to attempt this exercise after that he hath been at the stool, and softly rubbed the lower parts, and washed his hands, let him speak with as bass a voice as he can and, walking, begin to sing louder and louder but still in a bass voice. And to take no heed of sweet tunes or harmony, for that nothing doth profit unto health of the body, but to enforce himself to sing great, for thereby much air drawn in by fetching of breath thrusteth forth the breast and stomach and openeth and enlargeth the pores. By high crying and loud reading are expelled superfluous humours, therefore men and women having their bodies feeble and their flesh loose and not firm must read oftentime loud and in a bass voice, extending out the wind pipe and other passages of the breath. But, notwithstanding, this exercise is not used alway and of all persons; for they in whom is abundance of humours corrupted or be much diseased with crudity in the stomach and veins, those do I counsel to abstain from the exercise of the voice lest much corrupted juice or vapours may thereby be into all the body distributed. And here I conclude to speak of exercise, which of them that desire to remain long in health is most diligently and, as I might say most scrupulously, to be observed.

THE THIRD BOOK

Chapter one: Of repletion

Repletion is a superfluous abundance of humours in the body and that is in two manner of wise, that is to say in quantity and in quality. In quantity, as where all the four humours are more in abundance than be equal in proportion to the body that

---

i *thirty-six*] this ed.; 35 Q4.

---

1 *a whole country*] i.e. one free from infections and disease.
2 *apostumes*] abscesses.

containeth them, or where one humour much exceedeth the remnant in quantity. In quality, as where the blood or other humour is hotter or colder, thicker or thinner than is convenient unto the body. First, where all the humours being superfluously increased filleth and extendeth the receptories of the body, as the stomach, the veins, and bowels, and is most properly called fullness, in Greek *plethora*, in Latin *plenitudo*. The other is where the body is enfarced,[1] either with choler yellow or black, or with phlegm, or with watery humours, and is properly called in Greek *cacochymia*, in Latin *viciosus succus*; in English it may be called corrupt juice. I will not here write the subtle and abundant definitions and descriptions of Galen in his books *De plenitudine* and in his commentaries upon the aphorisms of Hippocrates, for it shall here suffice to show the operations of repletion good or ill, remitting[2] them which be curious and desire a more ample declaration to the most excellent works of Galen, where he may be satisfied if he be not determined to repugn[3] against reason. Hippocrates sayeth where meat is received much above nature, that maketh sickness; Galen, declaring that place,[4] sayeth more meat than accordeth with nature's measure is named repletion, and afterward he expoundeth that word above nature to signify too much and superfluously, as who sayeth where the meat is superfluously taken it maketh sickness. For meat but a little exceeding temperance may not forthwith make sickness but may yet keep the body within the lattitude or bounds of health, for the meat that shall make sickness must not a little exceed the exquisite[5] measure. The incommodity[6] which happeneth thereby is that moistness is too much extended and natural heat is debilitate.[7] Also, natural heat resolveth[8] somewhat of the superfluous meat and drink, and of that which is resolved[9] of meat undigested proceedeth fumosity, gross and undigested which, asending up into the head and touching the rim[10] wherein the vein is wrapped, causeth headache, trembling of the members, duskishness of the sight and many other sicknesses. Also, by the sharpness thereof, it pricketh and annoyeth the sinews which make sensibility, the roots of whom are in the brain, and from thence passeth through all the body. Finally, the said fumosity engendered of repletion, piercing the innermost part of the said sinews called sensible, it grievously annoyed the power animal there consisting[11] by the occasion, whereof

Aphorisms, liber 2

Aphorisms 15, *vbi cibus praeter natura plus ingest est hic morbū facit.* [vbi cibus ... facit] when more food than is natural has been consumed it causes sickness. This is from section 2, aphorism 17.]

Galen in commentary *loco praedicto* [loco praedicto] place aforesaid.]

---

1 *enfarced*] stuffed, congested.
2 *remitting*] referring.
3 *repugn*] resist.
4 *declaring that place*] i.e. explaining this part of Hippocrates' text.
5 *exquisite*] carefully chosen.
6 *incommodity*] disadvantage.
7 *debilitate*] weakened, enfeebled.
8 *resolveth*] dissolves, disintegrates.
9 *resolved*] dissolved, disintegrated.
10 *rim*] outer covering, membrane.
11 *consisting*] remaining.

understanding and reason as to the use of them are let and troubled. And also the tongue, which is reason's expositor, is deprived of his office, as it appeareth in them which are drunk and them which have grievous pains in their head proceeding of repletion. Signs of repletion be these: loss of appetite, delight in nothing, slothfulness, dullness of the wit and senses, more sleep than was accustomed to be, cramps in the body, starting or saltion[1] of the members, fullness of the veins and thickness of the pulses, horror[2] or shrivelling of the body mixed with heat. The remedies are abstinence and all evacuations, whereof I will make mention in the next chapter.

Chapter two: Of evacuation

The meats and drinks received into the body, if the stomach and liver do their natural office, be altered by concoction and digestion in such wise that the best part thereof goeth in the nourishment of the body; the worst, being separate by the members official from the residue, are made excrements in sundry forms and substances, which are like in quality to the natural humour which then reigneth most in the body. These excrements be none other but matter superfluous and unsavoury, which by natural powers may not be converted into flesh but remaining in the body corrupt the members, and therefore nature, abhoring them, desireth to have them expelled. These excrements be three in number: ordure, urine, humour superfluous. Moreover, there be two sorts of ordure, that is to say, one digested, which passeth by siege, the other undigested, which is expelled by vomit; where I say digested I mean that it is passed to the stomach and turned into another figure, likewise I call that undigested which still retaineth the figure of meat. Urine is the watery substance of the blood, like as whey is of milk, which out of the meat that is altered and concoct or boiled in the stomach is strained in the veins called *mesaraic*, which proceedeth from the hollow part of the liver and, sent by the reins into the bladder, passeth by the instrument the which is ordained as well to that purpose as for generation. Humour superfluous is in three forms: either mixed with any of the four humours called natural; or else it is gathered into the brain; or it is between the skin and the flesh, or lieth among the sinews, muscles, or joints. Of humours, some are more gross and cold, some are subtle and hot and are called vapours. Now, for to expel the said excrements are nine sundry kinds of evacuations, that is to say: abstinence; vomit; purgation by siege; letting of blood; scarifying, called cupping; sweating; provocation of urine; spitting; bleeding at the nose, or by haemorrhoids, and in women their natural purgations. Of these evacuations I will briefly [i]declare, with the commodities which, by [ii]the discreet use of them, do happen unto the [iii]body.

Excrements
[O1 omits.]
Ordure
Digested [O1, O3 omit.]
Urine

Humour superfluous

---

i declare] declare the tyme to vse theym O1.   ii the discreet use of] O1 omits.
iii body] body, if they be discretelye and temperately ordered O1.

---

1 *starting or saltion*] jumping or leaping.
2 *horror*] shuddering or shivering.

Chapter three: Of abstinence

Abstinence is a forbearing to recieve any meat or drink, for if it be but in part it is then called rather temperance than abstinence. It ought to be used only after repletion as the proper remedy therefore and then, if it be moderate, it consumeth superfluities and in consuming them it clarifyeth the humours, maketh the body fair coloured, and not only keepeth out sickness but also, where sickness is entered, nothing more helpeth if it be used in season. To them which have very moist bodies hunger is right expedient, for it maketh them more dry; notwithstanding, there ought to be considerations in the meat before eaten, in the age of the person, in the time of the year and custom. First in the meat before eaten, if it be much in excess, or very gross, or not much exceeding, or light of digestion, and according thereto would abstinence more or less be proportioned. Concerning age, Hippocrates sayeth old men may sustain fasting easily, next unto them men of middle age, young men may worse bear it, children worst of all, specially they that be lusty, notwithstanding here Galen correcteth Hippocrates, saying that he should have excepted men very old who, as experience declareth, must eat often and little. As touching time, it must be remembered that in winter and springtime the stomachs be naturally very hot and sleep is long, and therefore in that time meats would be more abundant, and although much be eaten it will be sooner digested. Wherefore abstinence would not be then so much as in summer, albeit to abstain much in summer except it be after repletion, Damascene sayeth it dryeth the body, it maketh the colour sallow, it engendereth melancholy, and hurteth the sight. Moreover, custom may not be forgotten, for they which are used from childhood to eat sundry meals in the day would rather be reduced to fewer meals and little meat than be compelled to abstain utterly, to the intent that nature, which is made by custom, be not rebuked and the power digestive thereby debilitate.[1] And note well that by too much abstinence the moisture of the body is withdrawn and consequently the body dryeth and waxeth lean. Natural heat, by withdrawing of moisture, is too much incended,[2] and not finding humour to work in, turneth his violence to the radical or substantial moisture of the body, and exhausting that humour bringeth the body into a consumption. Wherefore Hippocrates sayeth that too scarce and exquisite[3] an order in meat and drink is for the more part more dangerous than that which is more abundant. Contrariwise, moderation in abstinence according to the said considerations is to ⁱhealth a sure bulwark.

Cels[us] liber 2, Hippocrates Aphorisms, liber 7

Considerations in abstinence [O1 omits.]

Aphorisms, liber 1

Damascene Aphorisims

Aphorisms, liber 2

---

i health] bodily health O1.

---

1 *debilitate*] weakened, enfeebled.
2 *incended*] inflamed.
3 *exquisite*] carefully chosen.

Chapter four: Of vomit

Aetius, *liber* 1

The meat or drink superfluous or corrupted in the stomach is best expelled by vomit if it be not very grievous to him which is diseased. Also, the moderate use of it purgeth phlegm, lighteth the head, causeth that the excess of meats or drinks shall not annoy or bring sickness; moreover, it amendeth the effects of the reins, the bladder, and the fundament. It also helpeth against lepries,[1] cankers, gouts, dropsies, and also diverse sicknesses proceeding of the stomach, for if any grief happeneth of the head, vomit is then uncommodious. It is better in winter than in summer, also good for them which are replete or very choleric if they have not well digested, but it is ill for them that be lean or have weak stomachs. And therefore where one feeleth bitter vapours rising out of his stomach, with grief and weightiness in the overparts[2] of his body, let him run forth with to this remedy. It is also good for him that is heart-burned, and hath much spittle or his stomach wambleth,[3] and for him that removeth[4] into sundry places. Yet I counsel, sayeth Celsus, him that will be in health and would not be too soon aged, that he use not this daily. And I myself have known men which daily using it have brought thereby their stomachs into such custom that whatsoever they did eat they could not long retain it, whereby they shorten their lives. Wherefore it would not be used but only where great surfeit or abundance of phlegm do require it. He that will vomit after meat, let him drink sundry drinks mixed together and, last of all, warm water, or if that be too easy[5] let him mix therewith salt or honey. If he will vomit fasting, let him drink water and honey sodden together, or hyssop with it, or eat of a raddish root and drink warm water upon it, also water wherein radish is boiled, and afterward provoke himself to it. Them that will have more violent purgations I remit[6] to physicians learned, but yet I do eftsoons warn them that therein they be circumspect and do not much use it. Moreover, in vomits the matter brought forth would be considered according to the rules of Hippocrates in his second book of prognostications, that is to say: if it be mixed with phlegm and choler it is most profitable if it be not in very great quantity, nor thick; the less mixture it hath the worse is it; if it be green, like to leek blades, thin or black, it is to be judged ill; if it have all colours it is extreme perilous; if it be leady coloured and savoureth horribly, it signifieth a short abolition or dissolution of nature. For as Galen affirmeth there in his comment, such manner of vomit declareth corruption, with extincting of nature; also, every putrified and stinking savour in vomit is ill. These things be right necessary to be looked for where one doth vomit without any difficulty, but to enforce one to vomit which cannot is very odious and to be abhorred.

Celsus, *liber* 1

Hippocrates *Prognostigs* 2, chapter 7

Galen *De locis affectis*, *liber* 1

---

1 *lepries*] leprosies, i.e. skin ailments in general.
2 *overparts*] upper or outer parts.
3 *wambleth*] rolls over, thus making one feel nauseaous.
4 *removeth*] moves (from place to place).
5 *easy*] mild.
6 *remit*] refer or direct for information.

Chapter five: Of purgations by siege

If the head be heavy or the eyen dim, or if there be pain felt of the colic, or in the lower part of the belly, or in the hips, or some choleric matter or phlegm in the stomach, also if the breath be hardly[1] fetched, if the belly of himself sendeth forth nothing, or if, being costive, one feeleth ill savour or bitterness in his mouth, or that which he maketh hath an horrible savour, or if abstinence do not at the first put away the fever, or if the strength of the body may not sustain letting of blood, or else the time therefore convenient is past, or if one have drunk much before his sickness, or if he which oftentimes unconstrained hath had great sieges be suddenly stopped, in all these cases, and where it is painful to vomit, and in gnawing or frettings of the stomach, finally in all repletions where a man cannot or will not be let blood or vomit it is expedient to provoke siege by purgations, which are received by two ways: upward at the fundament by suppositories or clysters; downward at the mouth by potions, electuaries, or pills. Suppositories are used where the patient is weak and may not receive any other purgations, sometime forasmuch as the straight gut[2] is stopped with excrements, which are dry and hard; sometime where there needeth none other purgation, specially in burning fevers whereof the matter asendeth into the head, then clysters may do harm and by the benefit of suppositories excrements are brought forth without any annoyance, and oftentimes it bringeth forth that which clysters may not. Suppositories are made sometime with honey only, sodden, rolled on a board and made round, smaller at the one end than at the other and of the length and greatness according to the quantity of the body that taketh it. Sometime there is mixed with the honey salt dried, or saltpetre, or the powder of such things as do either purge the humour which offendeth or dissolveth gross winds or other matter. They be sometime made with rosin,[3] pitch, wax, or gums, sometime of roots or the leaves of mercury green, very small bruised, also with figs or raisins, the stones taken out, or of white soap, made in the figure aforesaid ⁱand being made in the form aforesaid. They must be put up in at the fundament to the great end and the patient must keep it there the space of half an hour or more. Clysters are made of liquor, sometime simple, as water sodden, milk, oil or wine; sometime mixed, as water and oil together or decoctions, as where herbs, roots, fruits, seeds, or gums, having property to make soft, dissolve, draw forth, or expel matter that grieveth be boiled and the liquor thereof, sometime warm, sometime hot, is received at the fundament into the body by a little pipe of gold or silver, ivory or wood, therefore ordained and called a clyster-pipe. This is necessary where the stomach is weak and may not sustain the working of medicines received at the mouth, also in fevers, colics, and other diseases in the bowels, grief in the reins of the back or huckle-bone,[4] ventosity in the belly, inflammation or exulceration[5] in the guts or

Celsus, *liber* 2;
Aetius, *liber* 1

---

i and being made ... more] *O1 omits.*

1 *hardly*] with difficulty.
2 *straight gut*] rectum.
3 *rosin*] a kind of resin.
4 *huckle-bone*] hip-bone (*OED* huckle, *n.* 1)
5 *exulceration*] ulceration, the early stage of ulceration

bladder. It is a convenient and sure medicine and less hurt doth ensue of it. The making and ordering thereof I will omit to write in this place, partly that I would not that physicians should too much note in me presumption, partly that another place may be more apt to that purpose.

Chapter six: The particular commodities of every purgation

In potions, electuaries, and pills ought to be much more observation than in clysters or suppositories forasmuch as these do enter no further than into the gut where the ordure lieth and by that place only bringeth forth the matter which causeth disease. But the other, entering in that way that meats and drinks do cometh into the stomach, and there is boiled and sent into the places of digestion, and afterward is mixed with the juice whereof the substance of the body is made, and expelling the adversary humours, somewhat thereof doubtless remaineth in the body. Wherefore men have need to beware what medicines they receive, that in them be no venenosity,[1] malice, or corruption, lest for the expelling of a superfluous humour, which perchance good diet, or some broths made of good herbs, or the said evacuation with suppositories or clyster, might bring forth at leisure. By desiring of too hasty remedy, they receive in medicine that which shall engender a venomous humour and inevitable destruction unto all the body. And therefore happy is he which in sickness findeth a discreet and well-learned physician, and so true apothecary, and hath alway drugs uncorrupted, and whom the physician may surely trust to dispense his things truly. But now to return to the said form of purgation, I will now let forth some counsels concerning that matter which I have collected out of the chief authors of physic: bodies hot and moist may easily sustain purgation by the stool; they which be lean or thin, having the members tender, may take harm by purgations; to men that are choleric and them that eat little, purgations are grievous; in young children and old men it is dangerous to loose much the belly; to them that are not wont to it, purgation is noyful; he that liveth in a good order of diet needeth neither purgation nor vomit. After that the purgation hath wrought, thirstiness and sound sleep be signs that the body is sufficiently purged; by daily taking of medicines nature is corrupted. When ye will purge anything make first the matter flowing and soluble; medicine to purge ought not to be mingled with meat but to be taken four hours at the least before meals or three hours after meals, except certain easy[2] pills made to cleanse and comfort the stomach, which would be taken at the beginning of supper ⁱor after supper, a little before that one goeth to bed, making a light supper or none. After purgation taken, the patient should rest and not walk until the medicine hath wrought nor eat or drink in the mean space. ⁱⁱThis is a general rule concerning excrements: that the cause of retaining of them being perceived, the contraries unto that cause would be given, as if a little quantity

Hippocrates
Aphorisms

Galen *De sanitate tuenda*, liber 1 [O1, Q2, O3, O5, O6 omit.]

---

i or ... none] *O1* omits.   ii This ... convenient quantity] *O1, Q2, O3, O5, O6* omit.

1 *venenosity*] poisonous quality or property.
2 *easy*] mild.

and dryeth be the cause then to take more in quantity and that which is moist; if dryeth be the cause only, then not to increase the quantity but that which is moist; if the cause be of taking sour things or bitter, then to use competently things sweet or fat. Likewise, in order of meals: as if he which was wont to eat twice in one day eateth but once and thereby is diseased, he must feed not only twice in one day but also oftener, having respect to a convenient quantity. These things have I remembered because I have known right good physicians to have forgotten to instruct thereof their patients. Now will I set forth the table of such things which of their property do digest or purge superfluous humours, particularly which I have gathered out of the books of Dioscorides, Galen, Paul of Aegina, Oribasius, and Aetius, and other late writers, notwithstanding I have not written all, forasmuch as there be diverse things whereunto we have not yet found any names in English.

Digestives of choler
Endive
Lettuce
Chicory
Scabious[1]
Maidenhair
Mallows
Mercury
The juice of pomegranates
Purslane
Poppy
Barberries
Roses
Violets, the leaf and flower
Sorrel
Liverwort
Sorrel de bois[2]
Whey clarified
The great four cold seeds, that is to say: of gourds, cucumbers, melons, and citruls[3]
Psyllium
Vinegar
Sanders
Barley water
Prunes
Tamarinds

---

1 Scabious] herbaceous plants of the genus Scabiosa; thought to help cure certain skin diseases.
2 Sorrel de bois] wood-sorrel.
3 *citruls*] water-melons and pumpkins.

Purgers of choler
Wild hops
Wormwood
Centaury
Fumitory
Whey of butter
Violets
Mercury
Juice of roses
Prunes
Agrimony
Tamarinds, half an ounce in a decoction
Manna, six drams at the least and so too twenty-five in the broth of a hen or capon
Rhubarb, by itself from two drams unto four, infused or steeped in liquor from four drams unto eight

Digestives of phlegm
The roots: fennel, parsley
Smallage
Capers
Laurel
Syrup
Puly[1]
Marjoram
Pennyroyal
Wild parsnip seed
Mint
Pimpernel
Horemint[2]
Gladen[3]
Agrimony
Calamint
Nep[4]
Betony
Sage
Radish
Mugwort
Juniper
Hyssop
Peony

---

1 *Puly*] Poly, an aromatic germander of southern Europe.
2 *Horemint*] some hoary species of mint; or perhaps horehound.
3 *Gladen*] presumably gladolo or sword-grass.
4 *Nep*] catmint or catnip.

Balm
Honey
Ginger
Squilla[1]
Aristolochia[2]
Cinnamon
Pepper
Cumin

Purgers of phlegm
Centaury
Nettle
Agrimony
Alder
Polypody of the oak
Myrobalani chebule,[3] infused from half an ounce to an ounce and two drams; in substance from two drams to half an ounce.
Agaricus,[4] from a dram to two drams, infused from two drams to five
Ireos
Maidenhair
Stechados[5]

Purgers of melancholy
The broth of coleworts light boiled
Balm-mint
Stechados
Thyme
Sene,[6] boiled in white wine or in the broth of a hen
Laced savory[7]
Epithimus[8]
Unwrought silk
Organum
Calamint
Borage
Hart's tongue
Quickbeam
Maidenhair

---

1 *Squilla*] the squill or sea-onion.
2 *Aristolochia*] a kind of shrub; a species found in Britain is the common Birthwort.
3 *Myrobalani chebulei*] dried prune-like astringent fruits from tropical trees, imported commercially under the name of myrobalan (*OED* chebule, *n.* 1).
4 Agaricus] agaric.
5 *Stechados*] French lavender.
6 *Sene*] senna.
7 *Laced savory*] savory entwined with a climbing plant.
8 *Epithimus*] flower of thyme (Patai 1994, 563n62).

Withwind[1]
Pennyroyal mountain
Honey
Sugar

Melancholy, for the thinness and subtleness of the humour, needeth no digestive.

They which will take sharper purgations or compound with diverse things, let them take the counsel of an honest and perfect physician and not adventure to mix things together without knowing the temperance of them in degrees; and that he can proportion them to the body that shall receive them in simples as they be written,[i] and so he may use them without peril against the humours whereunto they serve.

Chapter [ii]seven: Letting of blood

The part of evacuation by letting of blood is incision or cutting of the vein, whereby the blood which is the cause of sickness or grief to the whole body, or any particular part thereof, doth most aptly pass. The commodities whereof, being in a moderate quantity and in a due time taken, be these that follow: it clarifieth the wit and maketh good memory, it cleanseth the bladder, it dryeth the brain, it warmeth the marrow being in the bones, it openeth the hearing, it stoppeth tears or droppings of the eye, it taketh away loathsomeness[2] and confirmeth[3] the stomach, it nourisheth that which is proper to nature and the contrary expelleth. It is thought that thereby life is prolonged and the matter making sickness shortly consumed. Wherefore letting of blood is not only expedient for them which are full of blood or have abundance of strength but also for them in whom without plenitude, called fullness, inflammations begin to be in their bodies, or by some outward stroke the blood being gathered within by collection thereof do feel grief or disease, also where there is much pain felt or disabilty of some member whereof is supposed to be engendered some grievous disease. Moreover, they which use excess of meats and drinks may be cured by letting of blood but those which be temperate, keeping good diet, be holpen without letting of blood, as by fricaces; using of baths; exercise; walking and riding moderately; also, unctions with oils and ointments called *diaphoretice*, which by evaporation do shortly evacuate the fullness, albeit if the fullness be of melancholy blood, then alway needs must be letting of blood. Abundance of melancholy blood is known by these signs: there is felt in the entrails or within the bulk[4] of a man or woman a weightiness, with tension or thrusting outward, and all that part which is above the navel is more heavy that it was wont to be; also, much urine and fatty, the residence or bottom thick, troublous, and fat, sometime black pushes[5] or boils, with inflammation and much pain. They must be shortly let blood, and the melancholy humour also purged by siege. They which have crude or

Marginal notes: Arnoldus de Villa Nova; Oribasius suę medicinę compendio [suę medicinę compendio] his medical compendium.]

---

i and so] *O1* omits.   ii seven] 6 *O1, Q2, O3, O5, O6*.

1 *Withwind*] bindweed.
2 *loathsomeness*] nausea.
3 *confirmeth*] strengthen, invigorate.
4 *bulk*] chest, thorax.
5 *pushes*] pustules, pimples, or boils.

raw humours must be warily let blood before that sickness engender, but having the fever, in no wise. Concerning letting of blood, these things following would be had in continual remembrance and be afore thought on: in abundance of the blood, the quality and quantity; the greatness of the sickness and, if it be present or looked for; also, the diet preceding; the age and strength of the person; the natural form of his body; the time of the year; the region or country; the present state of the air; the disuse of accustomed exercise; the ceasing of evacuations used before. In quality consider of what humour the fullness proceedeth; in quantity, the abundance of that which is to be purged; in sickness if it be dangerous or tolerable. If the sickness be present it requireth the more diligence, if it be looked for it may be the better proportioned. In diet the custom in eating and drinking must be specially noted. In young men and women letting of blood would be more liberal; in old men and young children it would be scarcer; strong men may sustain bleeding, they which are feeble may not endure it; large bodies have greater vessels than they which be little, lean men have more blood, corporate[1] men have more flesh. The time of the year must be specially marked, for in the beginning of springtime is the best letting of blood, as Oribasius sayeth, and so doth continue, after the opinion of Arnold,[2] unto the eight calends[3] of June. Aetius affirmeth that in winter, or in a cold country, or where the person is of a very cold nature the veins should not be opened. And Damascene[4] sayeth that which in youth have used to be much let blood, after they be three score years old their nature waxeth cold and natural heat is in them suffocate, specially if they were of a cold complexion. But that is to be understood where they that are in health are often let blood, for in the lapse from health and in diverse diseases wherein the blood is corrupted, or where it engendreth impostumes, or restoreth to any place where it ought not to be, or passeth by any other conduit than nature hath ordained, or where it is furious or inflamed, or by any other means breedeth grievous diseases, in all these cases it ought to be practised, yea sometime in aged persons, women with child, and young infants, for in extreme necessity it were better experience some remedy than to do nothing. All other things concerning this matter pertain to the part curative, which treateth of healing of sickness, whereof I will not now speak but remit[5] the readers to the counsel of discreet physicians.

Aetius, liber 3

Cornelius Celsus, liber 3

Oribasius; Arnoldus de Villa Nova De flebotomia; Io Damascenus in arte med [De flebotomia ... Damascenus in arte med] *Of bloodletting ... Damascene in The art of medicine.*]

Chapter ⟨eight: Of scarifying called boxing or cupping

Forasmuch as it is not convenient to be let blood oftentimes in the year because much of the vital spirit passeth forth with the blood, which being exhaust the body waxeth cold and natural operations

Galen

Aetius, liber 3

---

i *eight*] 7 O1, Q2, O3, O5, O6.

---

1 *corporate*] corpulent.
2 *Arnold*] Arnold of Villanova.
3 *calends*] the first day of the month on the Roman calender.
4 *Damascene*] John Damascene.
5 *remit*] refer or direct for information.

become the more feeble, I therefore do counsel, sayeth Galen, that the base parts of the body, as the legs, be scarified, which is the most sure remedy, as well in conserving health as in repairing thereof, being decayed, for it cureth the eyen being annoyed with long distillations; it profiteth also to the head and over part of the body against sundry diseases. In what member the blood is gathered, the body being first purged by scarification, the grief may be cured. Also, Oribasius affirmeth the same and also added thereto that it helpeth squinances or quinsies in the throat and dissolveth the constipations or stoppings made of all places if the places be scarified. Notwithstanding, application of boxes about the stomach in hot fevers where reason is troubled are to be eschewed for fear of suffocation; likewise, put to the head undiscreetly it hurteth both the head and the eyes. The late authors do affirm that scarifying is in the stead of letting blood where for age, debility, or time of the year, or other like consideration a man may not sustain bloodletting, and it bringeth forth the thin blood, which is next to the skin.

[marginal notes: Oribasius in *medicine compendio* [medicine compendio] his medical compendium called the *Collectiones Medicae*.]
Aetius

Chapter [i]nine: *Of bloodsuckers or leeches*

There is also another form of evacuation, by worms found in waters, called bloodsuckers or leeches, which being put unto the body or member do draw out blood; and their drawing is more convenient for fullness of blood than scarifying is, forasmuch as they fetch blood more deeper and is more of the substance of blood. Yet the opinion of some men is that they do draw no blood but that which is corrupted and not proportionable unto our body, and therefore in griefs which happen between the skin and the flesh of blood corrupted these are more convenient than scarifying. But before that they be put unto any part of the body they must be first kept all one day, before giving unto them a little blood in fresh flesh, and then put them in a clean water, somewhat warm, and with a sponge wipe away the slime which is about them. And then lay a little blood on the place grieved, and put them then to it, and lay on them a sponge that when they be full they may fall away, or if ye will sooner have them off, put a horse hair between their mouths and the place and draw them away, or put to their mouths salt, or ashes, or vinegar and forthwith they shall fall, and then wash the place with a sponge. And if there do issue much blood, lay on the place the powder of a sponge, and pitch burned, or linen cloth burned, or galls[1] burned, or the herb called *bursa pastoris*[2] bruised. And this sufficeth concerning bloodsuckers.

[marginal notes: Oribasius in *medicine compendio* [medicine compendio] his medical compendium called the *Collectiones Medicae*.]

Chapter [ii]ten: *Of haemorrhoids or piles*

Haemorrhoids be veins in the fundament of whom do happen sundry passions: sometime swelling without bleeding; sometime superfluous blood by the puissance of

---

i *nine*] 8 O1, Q2, O3, O5, O6.   ii *ten*] 9 O1, Q2, O3, O5, O6.

1 *galls*] probably a reference to oak-galls, an excrescence produced on trees by the action of insects and used in medicine, or a reference to the bog-myrtle.

2 bursa pastoris] also known as shepherd's-purse, a member of the mustard family.

nature is by them expelled and then be they very convenient, for by them a man shall escape many great sicknesses which be engendered of corrupt blood or of melancholy. Semblably, if they be hastily stopped from the course which they have been used to, thereby do increase the said sicknesses which by them were expelled, as dropsies, consumptions, madness, frenzies, and diverse diseases of the head, and other sicknesses, paleness of the visage, grief in the reins of the back and thighs. And if they flow too much, there ensueth feebleness, leanness of the body, alteration of colour, great pains in the lower parts of the body. And if the flux be unmoderate it engendereth mischievous diseases, wherefore it would be diligently taken heed that they run in measure or else to use some things moderately which may restrain them.

Concerning other evacuations, I do purposly omit to write of them in this place, forasmuch as in this realm it hath been accompted[1] not honest to declare them in the vulgar tongue but only secretly.

Chapter [i]eleven: Of affects of the mind

The last of things called not natural is not the least part to be considered, the which is of affects and passions of the mind. For if they be immoderate they do not only annoy the body and shorten the life but also they do appair and sometime lose utterly a man's estimation. And that much more is, they bring a man from the use of reason and sometime in the displeasure of almighty God, wherefore they do not only require the help of physic corporal but also the counsel of a man wise and well learned in moral philosophy. Wherefore after that I have recited what they be, I will briefly declare such counsels as I have gathered. And as concerning remedies of physic, saving a few simples which do comfort the heart and spirits, the residue I will remit[2] to the counsel of physicians, like as I have done in evacuation. Affects of the mind whereby the body is annoyed and do bring in sickness be these: ire or wrath, heaviness or sorrow, gladness or rejoicing.

Chapter [ii]twelve: Of ire

Ire is kindled in the heart, inordinately chafing the spirits there, and then is sent forth into the members and doth superfluously heat them and disturbeth reason where the bodies be hot afore. Where natural heat is feeble the heat may not be dispersed unto the extreme parts, and then doth the extreme members, that is to say which are far from the heart, remain cold and trembling. Of this affection cometh sometime fevers, sometime apoplexies, or privation of senses, trembling, palsies, madness, frenzies, deformity of usage and, that worse is, outrageous swearing, blasphemy, desire of vengeance, loss of charity, amity, credence; also forgetfulness of benefit preceding, and of obedience, duty, and reverence. There also do succeed contention, chargeable suit,[3] unquietness of mind, lack of appetite, lack of sleep, feeble digestion, scorn, distain and hatred of other, with peril of losing of all good reputation. These

---

i *eleven*] 10 O1, Q2, O3, O5, O6.   ii *twelve*] this ed.; 11 Q4.

1 *accompted*] accounted, reckoned.
2 *remit*] refer or direct for information.
3 *chargeable suit*] presumably a troublesome suit of court.

incommodities of ire, perfectly had in remembrance and at the first motion thereof one of them thought on, may happen to bring in his fellows, and thereby the flame may be quenched. Or let him that is angry, even at the first, consider one of these things: that like as he is a man so is also the other with whom he is angry, and therefore it is as lawful for the other to be angry as unto him, and if he so be then shall that anger be to him displeasant and stir him more to be angry, whereby it appeareth that ire is to him loathsome. If the other be patient then let him abhor that thing in himself, the lack whereof in the other contenteth him and assuage his malice. Moreover, let him before that occasion of ire doth happen accustom himself to behold and mark well them that be angry, with the success of that anger, and ruminate it in his mind a good space after, and in that time let him remember how Christ, the son of God, and God, who (as he himself said) might have had of God his father, if he would have asked them, legions of angels, to have defended him, yea with less than a wing might have slain all his adversaries. Yet he, notwithstanding rebuked, scorned, falsely accused, plucked hither and thither, stripped, bounden with halters, whipped, spit on, buffeted, crowned with sharp thorn, laded[1] with a heavy piece of timber, his own proper torment haled[2] and driven forth like a calf to the slaughterhouse, eftsoons beaten and overthrown, retched[3] forth with ropes, arms and legs laid on the cross, and thereunto with long iron nails through the hands and feet nailed, with many strokes of hammers, with many prickings or ever the nails might pierce by his tender and most blessed flesh and sinews quite through the hard timber up to the heads of the nails, and all this being done for the offence of mankind and not his. Yet with the men which did it, his most unkind countrymen, his most unnatural kinsmen, whom he first made of nothing, preserved by miracles, delivered from perils, and cured of diseases, in all his vexation and trouble he was never seen or perceived angry. If one will say that anger is natural let him also consider that in Christ's manhood were all natural powers; if he will, say that ire is token of courage, and in Christ it lacked not, whom both angels and devils trembled and feared. The premises often resolved[4] and born in the mind I will not say shall utterly extinct all motions of wrath, which is not possible, but it shall when it kindleth lightly repress it and let, that it shall not grow into flame. And in speaking here of wrath I do not mean that which good men have against vices, or wise and discreet governors and masters against the defaults or negligences of their subjects or servants, used in rebuking them or moderately punishing them, for that is not properly ire but rather to be called displeasure and is that whereof God speaketh by his prophet David, saying "be you angry and do not sin",[5] and that manner of anger hath been in diverse holy men, prophets, and other. And it appeared in Christ when he drove out them which made their market in the holy temple of God where there ought to be nothing but prayer, and likewise when he rebuked the hypocrites. But if none of these things may come so

Psalm 4; Genesis 31; Exodus 32; Leviticus 10; Mark 11

---

1 *laded*] loaded.
2 *haled*] harried.
3 *retched*] stretched.
4 *resolved*] freed from uncertainty, settled.
5 *be you angry ... sin*] "Be ye angry, and sin not", from Ephesians (4.26).

shortly to his remembrance that is moved with anger, at the least let him think on the lesson that Apollodorus, the philosopher, taught to the emperor Octavian, that before he speak or do anything in anger he do recite in order all the letters of the ABC, and remove[1] somewhat out of the place that he is in and seek ocassion to be otherwise occupied. This shall for this time suffice for the remedies of ire, and he that will know more of this matter let him read in my work called *The Governor*,[2] where I thereof do write more abundantly.

Chapter thirteen: Of dolour or heaviness of mind

There is nothing more enemy to life than sorrow, also called heaviness, for it exhausteth both natural heat and moisture of the body and doth extenuate or make the body lean, dulleth the wit, and darkeneth the spirits, letteth the use and judgement of reason and oppresseth memory. And Solomon sayeth that sorrow dryeth up the bones and also, like as the moth in the garment and the worm in the tree, so doth heaviness annoy the heart of a man. Also, in the book called Ecclesiastes sorrow hath killed many and in itself is found no commodity. Also, by heaviness death is hastened, it hideth vertue or strength, and heaviness of heart boweth down the neck. [Proverbs 17 [17] 17.25 O1, O3, O6.] [Ecclesiastes 25.28 [28] 38 O1, O3, O6.] This is so puissant an enemy to nature and bodily health that to resist the malice and violence thereof are required remedies as well of the wholesome counsels found in holy scripture and in the books of moral doctrine as also of certain herbs, fruits, and spices having the property to expel melancholy humours and to comfort and keep lively the spirits which have their proper habitation in the heart of man, and moderate nourishing of the natural heat and humour called radical, which is the base or foundation whereupon the life of man standeth, and that failing, life falleth in ruin and the body is dissolved.[3] Now, first I will declare some remedies against sorrowfulness of heart concerning necessary counsel.

Sometime this affect happeneth of ingratitude, either where for benefit or special love employed one receiveth damage, or is abandoned in his necessity, or is deceived of him whom he trusted, or findeth him of whom he hath great expectation forgetful or negligent in his commodity, or perceiveth the person whom of long time he hath loved to be estranged from him, or to have one of later aquaintance in more estimation. This affection nippeth the heart, yea of most wise men, for they love most heartily, not provoked by carnal affection but rather by good opinion, engendered by similitude of honest studies and vertuous manners of long time mutually experienced. And it is not only unto man grievous but also unto God most displeasant and odious, as it is abundantly declared in scripture. Wherefore the person which feeleth himself touched with this affect, before that it grow into a passion and waxeth a sickness, let him call to resemblance these articles following, or at the leastways some

---

i *thirteen*] this ed.; 12 Q4.

1 *remove*] go away.
2 The Governor] Elyot's *Book of the Governor*, first printed 1531 and dedicated to King Henry VIII, set forth the ideal education for a governor-to-be.
3 *dissolved*] weakened.

of them, for every each[1] of them may ease him, though perchance they cannot forthwith perfectly cure him.

Counsels against ingratitude

Appianus in Varia historia [Elyot perhaps means to cite another work by Appianus (See Appendix 5.]

Consider that the corruption of man's nature is not so much declared in anything as in ingratitude, whereby a man is made worse than diverse brute beasts. The little ant or emmet[2] helpeth up his fellow whom he seethe overthrown with burden or by other occasion; also when elephants do pass over any great water, the greatest and most puissant of them divide themselves and, setting the weakest in the middle, part go before trying the deepness and perils, part come after succouring the weakest or least with their long noses when they see them in danger. The same beasts have been seen not only bringing men out of deserts which have lost their ways but also revenge the displeasures done to them the which gave them meat, as one that slew him which had committed adultery with his master's wife. The terrible lions and panthers have been seen in their manner to render thanks to their benefactors, yea and to object[3] their own bodies and lives for their defence; the same we may daily behold in our own dogs. Then in whom thou findest the destestable vice of ingratitude, reputing him among the worst sort of creatures, think not that thou hast lost a friend but think that thou art delivered from a monster of nature that devoured thy love, and that thou art now at liberty and hast won experience to choose thee a better. But if this may not suffice,

Seneca De beneficiis 7

then eftsoons consider that if thou look well on thyself, perchance thou mayst find the fault whereof thou complainest within thy own bosom. Call to thy rememberance if thou hast alway rendered unto every man condign thanks[4] or benefit of whom thou hast kindness received, or if thou hast alway remembered every one of them that have done to thee any commodity or pleasure. Thou shalt well perceive that what thing thou receivest in childhood thou forgatest or didest little esteem when thou camest to the state of a man. And what thou didest remember in youth, in age thou didest little think on: thy nurse's pap, her rockings, her watchings, thou hast not alway remembered or equally recompensed. The school master's study, his labour, his diligence, in a like degree thou hast not requited. What greater friends hast thou had, of whom thou couldst receive any greater benefits than thy nourishing and preserving of thy life in thy most feebleness or thine erudition whereby thy nature was made more excellent? Remembering this, leave to be angry or sorrowful for so common a vice. Yet if it cease not to grieve thee, compare the ingratitude that doth vex thee with that ingratitude which was showed by the Israelites whom God chose for his own people: delivered from servage;[5] showed for them wonders; preserved them forty years in desert; destroyed for them kings; gave to them the country which flowed milk and honey; defended them against all outward hostility; sent unto them such abundance of riches that silver was in Jerusalem as stones in the street; had his

---

1 *every each*] each one.
2 *emmet*] ant.
3 *object*] subject.
4 *condign thanks*] i.e. thanks equal in worth or dignity.
5 *servage*] servitude.

tabernacle and afterward his most holy temple among them, which he did daily visit with his divine majesty; made their kings to reign gloriously, and spake with their prophets familiarly, and corrected their errors most gently. And yet for all this they embracing the paynim's[1] idolatry, they left so gracious and loving a lord and living God, and to his great despite gave divine honours to calves of brass and other monstrous images, and at the last put to most cruel death the only son of God that had done so much for them.

And if we Christian men do look well on ourselves, resolving the incomparable benefit which we have received by Christ's passion, and consider the circumstance of his most excellent, patience and most fervent love toward us, with our forgetfulness, and the daily breach of our promise which we made at our baptism concerning our mutual unkindness thereunto, there shall appear none ingratitude that should offend us. Finally, for a conclusion, behold well about thee and thou shalt all day find the children ingrate[2] to their parents and wives to their husbands. And wilt thou look that thy benefit, or vain expectation should make thee more free from ingratitude of thy friend whom chance hath sent thee than nature may the parents toward their children, or the conjunction of bodies by lawful marriage take unkindness from the wives toward their husbands? This vice therefore of ingratitude, being so common a chance, maketh no worldly friendship so precious that life or health therefore should be spent or consumed. I have been the longer in this place because I have had in ⁱthis grief sufficient experience.

If death of children be cause of thy heaviness, call to thy remembrance some children (of whom there is no little number) whose lives, either for incorrigible vices or unfortunate chances, have been more grievous unto their parents than the death of thy children ought to be unto thee, considering that death is the discharger of all griefs and miseries and to them that die well the first entry into life everlasting.   *Death of children*

The loss of goods or authority do grieve none but fools, which do not mark diligently that like as neither the one nor the other doth alway happen to them that are worthy, so we have in daily experience that they fall from him suddenly who in increasing or keeping them seemeth most busy.   *Loss of goods*

Oftentimes the repulse from promotion is cause of discomfort, but then consider whether in the opinion of good men thou art deemed worthy to have such advancement or in thine own expectation and fantasy. If good men so judge thee, thank God of that felicity and laugh at the blindness of them that so have refused thee; if it proceed of thine own folly abhor all arrogance and enforce thyself to be advanced in men's estimation before thou canst find thyself worthy in thy proper opinion.   *Lack of promotion*

All other chances of fortune esteem as nothing and that long before they do happen. The oft recording of misery prepareth the   *Chances of fortune*

---

i this grief] the crafte O1.

1 *paynim's*] pagan's.
2 *ingrate*] ungrateful.

mind to feel less adversity and the contempt of fortune is sure quietness and most perfect felicity.

This now shall suffice concerning remedies of moral philosophy. Now will I write somewhat touching the counsel of physic, as in relieving the body, which either by the said occasions or by the humour of melancholy is brought out of temper.

The first counsel is that during the time of that passion eschew to be angry, studious, or solitary, and rejoice thee with melody or else be alway in such company as best may content thee.

Avoid all things that be noyous[1] in sight, smelling, and hearing, and embrace all-thing[2] that is delectable.

Flee darkness, much watch, and business of mind, much companying with women, the use of things very hot and dry, often purgations, immoderate exercise, thirst, much abstinence, dry winds, and cold.

Abstain from daily eating of much old beef or old mutton; hard cheese; hare-flesh; boar's flesh; venison; saltfish; coleworts; beans, and peason; very coarse bread; great fishes of the sea, as thurlepole, porpoise, and sturgeon, and other of like natures; wine red and thick; meats being very salt or sour; old, burned or fried garlic; onions, and leeks.

Use meats which are temperately hot and therewith somewhat moist; boiled rather than roasted; light of digestion and engendering blood clear and fine, as milk hot from the udder or at the least new milked, ruen cheese;[3] sweet almonds; the yolks of rear eggs; little birds of the bushes; chickens and hens; wine white or claret, clear or fragrant; sweet savours, in winter hot, in summer cold, in the meantime, temperate.

Comfortatives of the heart hot
Borage, the flower or leaf
Bugloss
Balm-mint
Elecampane
Cloves
Cardamom
Rosemary
Lignum aloes
Musk
Ambergris
Saffron
The bone of the heart of a red deer
Mints
The rind of citron
Bean
Cubebs[4]
Basil

---

1 *noyous*] vexatious.
2 *all-thing*] everything.
3 *ruen cheese*] a kind of soft cheese.
4 *Cubebs*] berries of a climbing shrub, similar in appearance and taste to pepper.

Comfortatives of the heart cold
Violets
Pearls
Coral
The unicorn's horn
Old apples which be good
Roses
Sanders
The elephant's tooth
Waterlilies
Coriander prepared

Comfortives temperate
Jacinth[1]
Sapphire
Emeralds
Myrobalans called chebule[2]
Bugloss
Gold, silver

Chapter [i]fourteen: Of joy

Joy or gladness of heart doth prolong the life; it fatteth the body that is lean with troubles, [ii]bringing the humours to an equal temperance and drawing natural heat outward. But if it be sudden and fervent, it oftentimes fleeth, forasmuch as it draweth too suddenly and excessively natural heat outward. And therefore diverse men and women have been seen to fall in a sound[3] when they have suddenly beholden the persons whom they fervently loved.

As a woman in Rome, hearing first that her son was slain in battle, after, when he came to her, she seeing him alive, embracing each other, she died in his arms. This well considered, against such inordinate gladness the best preservative is to remember that the extreme parts of mundane joy is sorrow and heaviness and that nothing of this world may so much rejoice us but occasion may cause it to be displeasant unto us.

Titus Livius

Chapter [iii]fifteen: The dominion of sundry complexions

It seemeth to me not inconvenient that I do declare as well the counsels of ancient and approved authors as also mine own opinion – gathered by diligent marking in daily experience – concerning as well the necessary diet of every complexion, age, and declination of health, as also the mean to resist diseases of the body before sickness be therein confirmed, leaving the residue unto the substantial learning and

---

i *fourteen: Of*] this ed.; Of Q4.   ii *bringing*] bytynge O3, O5, O6.
iii *fifteen*] this ed.; 13 Q4.

---

1 *Jacinth*] a reddish-orange gem.
2 *Myrobalans called chebulei*] dried prune-like astringent fruits from tropical trees, imported commercially under the name of myrobalan (*OED* chebule, *n.* 1).
3 *fall in a sound*] have a swoon or fainting fit.

circumspect practice of good physicians, which shall the more easily cure the patients if their patients do not distain to bear away and follow my counsel.

And first it ought to be considered that none of the four complexions have solely such dominion in one man or woman's body that no part of any other complexion is therewith mixed. For when we call a man sanguine, choleric, phlegmatic, or melancholy we do not mean that he hath blood only without any of the other humours, or choler without blood, or phlegm without blood or melancholy, or melancholy without blood or choler. And therefore the man which is sanguine, the more that he draweth into age, whereby natural moisture decayeth, the more is he choleric by reason that heat surmounting moisture needs must remain heat and dryeth. Semblably, the choleric man, the more that he waxeth into age, the more natural heat in him is abated, and dryeth surmounting natural moisture, he becometh melancholic. But some sanguine man hath in the proportion of temperatures a greater mixture with choler than another hath; likewise, the choleric or phlegmatic man with the humour of sanguine or melancholy. And therefore late practisers of physic are wont to call men according to the mixture of their complexions which man receiveth in his generation, the humours whereof the same complexions do consist,[1] being augmented superfluously in the body or members by any of the said things called not natural. Every of them do semblably augment the complexion which is proper unto him and bringeth unequal temperature unto the body. And for these causes the sanguine or phlegmatic man or woman, feeling any dyscrasy by choler happened to them by the said things called not natural, they shall use the diet described hereafter to him which is naturally choleric. Semblably the choleric or melancholic man or woman having any dyscrasy by phlegm, to use the diet of him which is naturally phlegmatic, alway remembering that sanguine and phlegmatic men have more respect unto dryeth, choleric and melancholic unto moisture, and that alway as the accidental complexion decayeth, to resort by little and little to the diet pertaining to his natural complexion.

Chapter [i]sixteen: The times appropred[2] to every natural humour

But first it must be considered that where the four humours be alway in man, and in some man commonly one humour is more abundant than another naturally, that is to say, from his generation, the said humours have also peculiar times aligned to every one of them wherein each of them is in his most power and force, as after ensueth after the description of [ii]Soranus.

Soranus Ephesius [Soranus] Horanus O1.]

Phlegm hath more puissance in winter, from the eighth ides of November unto the eighth ides of February,[3] whereby are engendered catarrhs or rheums, the uvula,[4] the

---

i *sixteen*] this ed.; 14 Q4.   ii Soranus] Horanus O1.

1 *consist*] remain.
2 *appropred*] appropriate.
3 *eighth ides ... February*] 13 November and 13 February.
4 *the uvula*] inflammation of the uvula, which is the conical fleshy prolongation hanging from the middle of the pendent margin of the soft palate.

cough, and the stitch.¹ This humour is part in the head, part in the stomach; it hath dominion from ⁱthe third hour of night until the ninth hour of the same night.

Blood increaseth in springtime, from the eighth ides of February unto the eighth ides of May,² whereof are engendered fevers and sweet humours, which do shortly putrefy. The power of this humour is about the heart and hath dominion from ⁱⁱthe ninth hour of night until the third hour of the morning.

Red choler hath power in summer, from the eighth ides of May until the eighth ides of August,³ whereby are engendered hot and sharp fevers; this humour is specially in the liver and hath dominion from the third hour of day until the ninth hour of the same day.

Yellow choler, whereof is engendered the phlegm of the stomach, is nourished in autumn, which beginneth the eighth ides of August and dureth⁴ unto the eighth ides of November,⁵ and maketh shaking fevers and sharp. The black choler then increaseth and then followeth thickness of the blood in the veins; black choler or melancholy most reigneth in the spleen ⁱⁱⁱand it reigneth from the ninth hour of day until the third hour of night.

Chapter ⁱᵛseventeen: Peculiar remedies against the distemperance of every humour

If the distemperance be of blood, help it with things cold, sharp, and dry, for blood is moist, hot, and sweet. If it be of red choler, give things cold, moist, and sweet, for red choler is bitter and fiery. If it be of black choler, give things hot, moist, and sweet, for black choler is sharp and cold. If the disease be of salt phlegm, give things sweet, hot, and dry, thus sayeth Soranus. Notwithstanding, where there is abundance of cold phlegm not mixed with choler, there things very sharp and hot be most convenient, as tart vinegar with hot roots and seeds or wines strong and rough, honey being sodden in the one and the other; or where choler is mixed with phlegm, syrup acetose made with vinegar and sugar, boiled sometime with herbs, roots, or seeds, which may dissolve phlegm and digest it.

Soranus *In artem medendi isagoge* [O1 omits.]

Chapter ᵛeighteen: Diet of them which are of sanguine complexion

Forasmuch as in sanguine men blood most reigneth, which is soon corrupted, it shall be necessary for them which are of that complexion to be circumspect in eating meat

---

i the third hour of night until the ninth hour] thre at the clocke in the euening, vntyl. ix. at the clock O1.
ii the ninth hour of night until the third hour of the morning] ix of the clocke at nyght, vntyll thre at the clocke in the mornynge O1.
iii and ... night] O1 omits.   iv seventeen] this ed.; Q4 16. O1 omits this chapter.
v eighteen] this ed.; 15 Q4.

---

1 *stitch*] a sharp and sudden pain, usually in the side.
2 *eighth ides ... May*] 13 Februrary and 15 May.
3 *eighth ides ... August*] 15 May and 13 August.
4 *dureth*] lasts, continues.
5 *eighth ides ... November*] 13 August and 13 November.

that shortly will receive putrifaction: as the more part of fruits, specially not being perfectly ripe; also meats that be of ill juice, as flesh of beasts too old or too young, udders of beasts, brains, except of capons and chickens, marrow of the back bone;[1] much use of onions, leeks, garlic; much use of old figs; much use of raw herbs; and all-thing[2] wherein is excess of heat, cold, or moisture; meats that be stale; fishes of the fens or muddy waters; and too much sleep, as experience showeth.

Chapter [i]nineteen: Diet of choleric persons

To them which be choleric – being in their natural temperature and having not from their youth used the contrary – gross meats moderately taken be more convenient than the meats that be fine, and better shall they digest a piece of good beef than a chicken's leg, choler of his property rather burning than well digesting meats of light substance. Notwithstanding, some gentlemen which be nicely brought up in infancy may not so well sustain that diet as poor men, being the more part used to gross meats, wherefore their diet must be in a temperance, as young beef, old veal, mutton and venison powdered, young geese and such like, conserving their complexion with meats like thereunto in quality and degree according to the counsel of Hippocrates. And as he perceiveth choler to abound so to interlace meats which be cold in a moderate quantity, and to allay their wine more or less with water, eschewing hot spices, hot wines, and excessive labour, whereby the body may be much chafed.[3] Also, he may eat oftener in the day than any other, forseen that there be such distance between his meals as the meat before eaten be fully digested, which in some person is more, in some less, according to the heat and strength of his stomach, noting alway that the choleric person digesteth more meat than his appetite desireth, the melancholic person desireth by false appetite more than his stomach may digest. And to a choleric person it is right dangerous to use long abstinence, for choler, finding nothing in the stomach to concoct it, fareth then as were a little pottage or milk being in a vessel over a great fire: it is burned to the vessel and unsavoury fumes and vapours do issue out thereof. Likewise, in a choleric stomach by abstinence these inconveniences do happen: humours adust; consuming of natural moisture; fumosities and stinking vapours ascending up to the head, whereof is engendered dusking of the eyes, headaches hot and thin, rheums after every little surfeit, and many other inconveniences. Wherefore, beside the opinion of best learned men, mine own painful experience also moveth me to exhort them which be of this complexion to eschew much abstinence, and although they be studious and use little exercise yet in the morning to eat somewhat in little quantity, and not to study immediately but first to sit a while and after to stand or walk softly, which using these two years I and also other that have long known me have perceived in my body great alteration, that is to say, from ill estate to better. Alway remember that if any other humour do abound in the choleric person, as phlegm or melancholy, then until that humour be expelled the diet must be cor-

---

i *nineteen*] this ed.; 16 Q4.

1 *marrow of the backbone*] spinal marrow, the substance in the spinal canal.
2 *all-thing*] obsolete word meaning everything.
3 *chafed*] warmed.

rective of that humour and therefore more hot and fine than the natural diet before rehearsed, but yet there would be alway respect had to the natural complexion, sometime suffering the person to eat or drink that which nature working fervently desireth.

Chapter ^i twenty: Diet of phlegmatic persons

It is to be remembered that pure phlegm is properly cold and moist and lacketh taste. Salt phlegm is mixed with choler and therefore hath not in him so much cold nor humidity as pure phlegm hath, and therefore it requireth a temperance in things hot and dry, whereby phlegm is digested or expulsed. To phlegmatic persons all meats are noyful which are very cold, viscous or slimy, fat, or soon putrified, eating much and often, specially meats engendering phlegm, which be remembered in the table preceding. All things be good which are hot and dry, also meats and drinks which be sour; onions also and garlic, moderately used, be very commendable in pure phlegm, not mixed with choler. Much using of salt, specially dried; pepper, gross-beaten and eaten with meat, ought to be with all phlegmatic persons familiar; also ginger is right convenient but not to be so frequently used as pepper, forasmuch as the nature of pepper is that being eaten it passeth throught the body, heating and comforting the stomach, not entering into the veins or annoying the liver, which virtue is not in ginger. Ginger condite, the which we do call green ginger,[1] specially candied with sugar if it may be gotten, and also myrobalans called chebule, condite in India,[2] be most excellent remedies against phlegm. Also, the herbs which are remembered afore in the table of digestives of phlegm, and roots of parsley, fennel, ireos, elecampane, and carrots be very commendable. Exercise twice in the day, the stomach being almost empty, so that sweat begin to appear is very expedient, cleansing of the body from all filthiness, with rubbing and wiping, oftentimes with washing, specially the head and parts thereabout. Moderate sweating in hot baths or stufes[3] be to this complexion necessary, specially when they have eaten or drunken excessively. The head and feet to be kept from cold and to dwell high and far from moors and marshes is a rule right necessary, also to abstain from eating herbs and roots not boiled and generally from all meats which will not be easily digested.

Chapter ^ii twenty-one: The division of melancholy and the diet of persons melancholic

Melancholy is of two sorts: the one is called natural, which is only cold and dry; the other is called adust or burned. Natural melancholy is, as Galen sayeth, the residence or dregs of the blood and therefore is colder and thicker than the blood. Melancholy adust is in four kinds: either it is of natural melancholy adust, or of the more pure part of the blood adust, or of choler adust, or of salt phlegm adust; but of all other,

---

i *twenty*] this ed.; 17 Q4.   ii *twenty-one*] this ed.; 18 Q4.

1 *Ginger condite ... green ginger*] fresh ginger that has been perserved.
2 *Myrobalans called chebule, condite in India*] dried prune-like astringent fruits from tropical trees, imported commercially under the name of myrobalan (*OED* chebule, *n.* 1) with perhaps a reference to preserving them in Indian spices.
3 *stufes*] hot-air baths.

that melancholy is worst which is engendered of choler. Finally, all adust melancholy annoyeth the wit and judgement of man, for when that humour is hot it maketh men mad and when it is extinct it maketh men fools, forgetful and dull.

<small>Ex Marsilio Ficino, *De vita sana* [*De vita sana*] Of healthy life, a reference to Ficino's *De vita libri tres* or *De triplici vita* (*Three Books on Life*).]</small> The natural melancholy kept in his temperance profiteth much to true judgement of the wit but yet if it be too thick it darkeneth the spirits, maketh one timorous, and the wit dull. If it be mixed with phlegm it mortifieth[1] the blood with too much cold, wherefore it may not be so little that the blood and spirits in their ferventness be, as it were, unbridled (whereof do happen unstableness of wit and slipper remembrance)[2] nor yet so much that by the weight thereof (for it is heavy, approaching night to the earth) that we seem to be alway in sleep and need a spur to prick us forward.

Wherefore it is right expedient to keep that humour as thin as nature will suffer it and not to have too much of it. But now to the diet pertaining to them whom this humour annoyeth. The knowledge that melancholy reigneth is oftentimes heaviness of mind or fear without cause; sleepiness in the members; many cramps, without repletion or emptiness; sudden fury; sudden incontinency of the tongue; much solicitude of light things, with paleness of the visage and fearful dreams of terrible visions; dreaming of darkness, deep pits, or death of friends or acquaintance, and of all-thing[3] that is black. The meats convenient are they which be temperate in heat but specially they that be moist; meats soon digested, and they rather boiled than roasted, temperately mixed with spices; milk, hot from the udder or late milked, is very convenient for that complexion; sweet almonds blanched and almond milk; the yolks of rear eggs; and finally, all things which engender pure blood and all that is written in the chapter of age. All these be ill for them: wine thick or troublesome, specially red wine; meats hard, dry, very salt or sour; burned meat; fried meat; much beef; hare's flesh; beans; rocket; coleworts; mustard; radish; garlic, except there be much wind in the body, for then it is very wholesome; onions; leeks. Finally all things which heateth too much, cooleth too much, or dryeth too much; also wrath; fear; compassion; sorrow; much study or care; much idleness or rest; all-thing that is grievous to see, to smell, or to hear, but most specially darkness. Moreover, much drying of the body, either with long watch or with much care and tossing of the mind; or with much lechery; or much eating and drinking of things that be hot and dry; or with immoderate evacuation; labour; abstinence; thirst; going in the air untemperately hot, cold, or dry; all these things do annoy them that be grieved with any melancholy. It is to be diligently considered that where melancholy happeneth of choler adust, there meats which be hot in working would be wisely tempered and drinking of hot wines would be eschewed; semblable, cautel[4] would be in savours. Notwithstanding, moderate use of small wines, clear and well verdured[5] is herein very commendable, the humour thereby being clarified and the spirits cleansed, but the abuse or excess

---

1 *mortifieth*] deadens or destroys.
2 *slipper rememberance*] slippery memory, i.e. not retentive; forgetful.
3 *all-thing*] obsolete word meaning everything.
4 *cautel*] caution.
5 *verdured*] having a (specified) taste.

thereof doth as much damage. Also, it is right expedient to put into wine or ale a gad[1] of silver or gold, glowing hot out of the fire; to temper[2] hot meats with roses, violets, sanders, rose water, borage, bugloss, balm called in latin *Melyssa*, or the water of all three, drunken with good wine, white or claret, or made in a julep[3] with sugar is wonderful wholesome. Chewing of licorice, or raisins, or currants is right expedient, but most of all other things, mirth, good company, gladness, moderate exercise with moderate feeding. And thus I leave to speak of diets aptly belonging to the four complexions.

THE FOURTH BOOK

Chapter one: What crudity is and remedies therefore

[i]I will somewhat write of two dyscrasies of the body which do happen by the excess or lack of things called not natural, whereof I have spoken before. The one is called crudity, the other lassitude, which although they be words made of Latin, having none apt English word, therefore yet, by the definitions and more ample declaration of them, they shall be understood sufficiently and from henceforth used for English. But first it shall be necessary to consider that concoction is an alteration in the stomach of meats and drinks according to their qualities whereby they are made like to the substance of the body. Crudity is a viscous concoction of things received, they not being wholly or perfectly altered; the cause thereof is sometime the distemperature of the stomach, sometime inflammations, sometime matter congealed or impostumes in the stomach, otherwhile in gurgitation of meat and drink, or for the viscous quality of the same meats or drinks, or the receiving thereof out of order, or lack of exercise, or of convenient evacuation. [ii]Galen sayeth that in crudity or viscous concoction it must be considered as well if the juice be utterly corrupted, and may not be sufficiently concoct, as also if it be in the way of concoction, for if it be corrupted it must be expelled by sweat or urine. If it be half concoct then must such things be ministered as may help to profit concoction, having regard to the quality and temperance of the juice, that is to say, whether it be thick or thin, phlegmatic or choleric, which shall be perceived by the diet preceding and also by other things named not natural. For phlegmatic meats eaten in great quantity or often maketh phlegmatic juice, likewise doth lack of convenient exercise, too much rest or idleness, as choleric meats and vehement labours do make choleric juices in summer and melancholic juice in autumn, specially where labours be continual or long-during. Also, where labour is with much sweat, there is the urine more gross; where it is without sweat, there is it thinner.

Concoction, what it is [O1, Q2, O3 omit.]

Crudity, what it is [O1, Q2, O3 omit.]

The cause of crudity [O1, Q2, O3 omit.]

Galen *De sanitate tuenda*, liber 4 [O1, Q2, O3 omit.]

---

i I will] Concernynge syckeness and thinges accident therevnto, I wylle not treate of, in this warke, sauynge onely sauynge onely that I will O1, Q2, O3.
ii Galen sayeth ... afterward to vomit] O1, Q2, Q3 *omit*.

---

1 *gad*] a spike or stick.
2 *temper*] bring to a suitable quality by mixing with something else.
3 *julep*] a sweet drink prepared in different ways; considered comforting or gently stimulating.

Moreover, the colour and substance of the urine declareth the temperance of the juice, which shall be hereafter declared in the table of urines. Semblably, the colour of the body declareth the juice that is in it: for being whiter than it was wont to be it signifieth abundance of phlegm, being more pale or yellow it signifieth excess of choler, if it be blacker it signifieth melancholy. If the ill juice be much in quantity and the blood little, the ill juice would be digested and expelled with such things as do serve for that temperature; but if the blood be much and the ill juice little in quantity, there would the vein be opened and, after sufficient bleeding, a convenient purgation given, having regard as well of the quantity of the juice as of the kind thereof. In case that, either for age or for timorousness, a man will not be let blood then must he be purged by siege in more abundance. But if he in whom is little good blood and much ill juice, and feeleth a lassitude or weariness in all his body, he should neither be let blood nor receive purgation, nor yet labour or walk much but abide in much quiet, and assay to sleep much, and receive such meats, drinks, and medicines which doth attenuate or make thin, cut, and digest gross humours without vehement heat, whereof it is written in the table of digestives in the number of whom is oxymel, being well made, or *acetosus simplex*.[1] Where the juice is much choleric or melancholic, semblably capers with oil and vinegar be praised of Galen. When there appeareth in the urine a residence light and white then wine white or claret moderately taken helpeth to concoction, maketh good juice, and provoketh urine; then increase frications and exercise by little and little and then let him return to his natural diet. In whom is abundance of raw juice and outwardly feeleth a lassitude, to them Galen counselth the second or third day to give mead wherein hyssop is boiled and afterward to vomit. The means to escape crudity is to be diligent in observation of the counsels before written concerning the things called not natural: not much using meats that be very hard to concoct; also fat meat and meats long kept, also corrupted or stinking; sweet fruits and banqueting dishes; hasty feeding without good chewing; also much or very oft drinking at meals; very much heat, or very much cold after meat.

[Galen sū liber 6 [sū] Elyot is perhaps abbreviating the Latin word *super*, meaning 'above', and is thus referring to the work cited above by Galen, *De sanitate tuenda*.]

[i]Furthermore, it must be considered that all things which bringeth grief to the body is engendered either of too much abundance of juice or of the viscous quality thereof. He that is sick of abundance, the diet of him wholly consisteth in reducing the juice to a convenient quality; he that is grieved with the viscous quality of the juices, his order resteth in making the juices equal in temperature. Moreover, where that which passeth out of the body is less than that which is received into the body there happeneth sickness, which cometh of abundance, in the which case it ought to be diligently foreseen that there be observed a convenient mean of meats and drinks in respect of that which is expelled out of the body, which may be done if

---

i Furthermore ... tables preceding] This affecte of crudytie, perceyued by somme ylle sauoure, rysynge oute of the stomacke, the moste spedy remedy is vomyte, yf that it maye be doone withoute great dyfficultie: but yf it be greuouse vnto the pacyente, than lete hym rest and absteyne all that daye or moore, yf that nede be: Afterwarde, with supposytoryes or other lyghte remedyes prouoke hym selfe to the stoole, O*1*, Q*2*, O*3*.

---

1 acetosus simplex] vinegar.

the quantity of each of them be wisely considered, and where abundance is, there the quantity or quality or both be temperered. Alway remember that of crude juice be diverse kinds: some be cold and phlegmatic, some be hot and choleric, other be more thin and watery, some of black choler or melancholy. They which do abound in any of them must abstain from such meats and drinks which do engender such juice as doth annoy them; those meats and drinks be declared in tables preceding. Aetius [i]also would that he should drink a draught of cold water, affirming that thereby the stomach being coroborate driveth out of him down into the belly that which cleaveth fast to it. I myself using to drink fasting very small beer or ale when I have been in that case have found ease by it. Paul of Aegina willeth that at the beginning the legs and arms should be rubbed with a coarse linen cloth, the legs downward to the feet, the arms to the tops of the fingers, and when they be well chafed, then to rub them again with some oil that doth open the pores and discuss[1] the vapours, as oil of camomile, oil of anet,[2] and other like. He praised much mulse[3] or the water of honey, specially if some hyssop be boiled in it. Galen and all other do agree that, in this case, pepper bruised and eaten with meat is very expedient. And where there is much wind in the stomach then to eat all times of the day of the medicine made of the kinds of pepper, thyme, aniseed, and honey clarified which is called *diatrion pipereon*,[4] or that which is called *diaspoliticon* or *diapiganon*, which is made of cumin steeped one day and a night or longer in tart vinegar and after fried or layed on a burning hot stone and made in powder; also pepper and rue dried somewhat and made into powder, all in equal proportions and mixed with clarified honey. Galen added thereto saltpetre called in latin *nitrum*. The confection made with the juice of quinces, and is called *diacytoniten*,[5] is very excellent but it is to be diligently noted that where crudity is in a choleric person there would the said medicines be temperately used and the said *diacytoniten* to have little or no spices in it. And for my part, being [ii]of a choleric humour mixed with phlegm, many years continually in crudity, I never found anything better than fine rhubarb chewed with raisins of Corinth,[6] which I took by the counsel of the worshipful and well-learned physician Master Doctor Augustine,[7] who in his manners declareth the greatness of his ancient blood, which medicine I do not leave to use daily, fasting when I feel such

Aetius sermon 9

Paul of Aegina, liber 2

Galen *de menda sani*, liber 5 [de menda sani] it is not clear which of Galen's works is here being referred to.]

---

i also] *O1, Q2, O3 omit.*
ii of a choleric humour ... continually in] the space of foure yeres contynuallye in this *O1, Q2, O3*.

---

1 *discuss*] dispel or disperse.
2 *anet*] the herb dill.
3 *mulse*] honey mixed with water or wine.
4 diatrion pipereon] preparation consisting of three kinds of pepper, or of sanders (sandalwood) (*OED* dia-, *prefix* 2).
5 diacytoniten] from quinces.
6 *raisins of Corinth*] currants (*OED* currant, *n*.1.a.).
7 *Master Doctor Augustine*] Augustine de Angustinis.

crudity to begin. Also, syrup acetose, that is to say, sugar sodden in pure vinegar and little water until it be thick as a syrup, is sometime convenient, and that as well to choleric persons as unto phlegmatic; and if phlegm be abundant then with roots and seeds of fennel and parsley sodden with it. Also, in that case, oxymel, that is to say honey and water sodden together with the said roots and seeds, and a quantity of vinegar put thereto in the boiling, is very commendable. If the patient be very costive then the medicine of Galen, called *hiera picra*, from half an ounce to an ounce, taken in water of honey or ale or taken in pills the weight of a groat and a half, or two groats if the stuff be good, will purge the body sufficiently without making the body weaker. Also, that medicine by cleansing the stomach and body delivereth a man and woman from many perilous sicknesses. If the humours in the stomach be not putrified but that it is grieved with abundance of salt phlegm, I have found that milk new milked wherein is put a quantity of good honey or sugar, and three leaves of good spearmints, and a little boiled, so being drunk warm fasting, the quantity of a pint, and resting on it, wihtout eating or drinking any other thing the space of three hours after, have abundantly purged and comforted the stomach. But where there is no phlegm but only choler it is not so wholesome but rather hurteth, making fumosities in the head whereof cometh headache.

Chapter two: [1]*Of distillations called commonly rheums and of some remedies against them right necessary*

Forasmuch as at this present time in this realm of England there is not any one more annoyance to the health of man's body than distillations from the head, called rheums, I will not let to write[1] somewhat of them whereby men may take benefit if they will, although some physicians more considering their market than their duty to God and their country will be never so much offended with mine honest enterprise.

Distillation is a dropping down of a liquid matter out of the head and falling either into the mouth, or into the nostrils, or into the eyes, and sometime into the cheeks and ears. That which falleth into the mouth is received of the throat into that part which is the instrument of the voice, which at the first maketh hoarseness and in process of time maketh the voice little and uneath[2] to be heard. And if the rheum be sharp it raiseth the inner skin of the throat and sometime it doth exulcerate[3] the lungs. If it doth fall into the somach, the rheum being cold, it altereth the body into a cold distemperance. If it be hot, it maketh a hot distemperance and doth sometime exulcerate in process of time, and at the beginning abateth appetite and maketh feeble concoction. The cold rheum maketh concoction flow, and also crudity, and engendereth sour rheums in the mouth. If it be corrupted, it turneth also nourishment unto corruption, which maketh upbraidings fumish,[4] or sharp, or of some ill quality, which cannnot be expressed. If the matter do descend lower, it tormenteth the guts,

---

i *Of distillations ... discreet physicians*] *O1, Q2, O3 omit this chapter.*

1 *I will not let to write*] I will not refrain from writing.
2 *uneath*] with difficulty, not easily.
3 *exulcerate*] affect with an ulcer, blister.
4 *fumish*] emitting smoke or vapour.

called *leiunum* and colon, and toucheth other vessels from whence proceedeth digestion. In this dyscrasy two things are to be provided for: first to let that the rheum do not distil into the said places, or if it hath done that it be shortly expelled from thence; ⁱsecond, to let that it shall not distil, it shall be necessary to eat some meat, the sooner in the morning if there hath not preceded repletion.

Where the temperature of all the body is choleric and the stomach is weak, the stomach would be made strong with such things as of their property do comfort the stomach, forseen that they be moderately cold and moist. And that which is already fallen into the stomach must be expelled with vomit or siege, provoked with wormwood steeped all one day and a night in a little small white wine or small ale and stale, which hath virtue only to wipe away the filth from the stomach. But if it be soaked deep into the filth of the stomach, then it is better to take the medicine called *hiera picra*, either in powder with drink warmed or else in pills to the number of five or more in the morning, six hours before any other meat or drink taken, afterward to noint the mouth of the stomach with oil of mastic[1] or *nardinum*[2] temperately warm. Alway if a hot rheum do fall into a hot stomach then meats and drinks which be cold in virtue would only be used. Where the stomach is distempered with heat and the rheum distilled into a cold head, there is the dyscrasy hard to be cured and they which be so affect or diseased must take such things as may dissolve the phlegm and cleanse the stomach without heating thereof, of the which virtue we know oxymel to be of.

If the stomach and head be both distempered with cold then must be used meats, drinks, and ointments which only be hot and utterly to forbear all that is cold.

By these distillations or rheums happeneth many other grievous diseases, besides those whereof I have spoken: as in the head whirlings called in Latin *vertigines*; sudden soundings;[3] falling-sickness; poses; stinking of the nose called polypus;[4] sores in the mouth; toothache; pain and web in the eyes;[5] dullness of hearing; quinsies;[6] fretting of the bowels with fluxes; shortness of breath; grief in the heart; palsies; ache in the muscles and joints, wherefore it is not to be neglected. And I do much marvel that our physicians do not more studiously provide therefore remedies. I myself was by the space of four years continually in this dyscrasy and was counselled by diverse physicians to keep my head warm, and to use *diatrion pipereon*,[7] and such other hot things as I have rehearsed. At the last, feeling myself very feeble and lacking appetite and sleep, as I happened to read the book of Galen *De temperamentis*, which treateth *De inequali temperatura* and afterward the sixth book, *De sanitate tuenda*,

---

i second] *this ed.*; First Q4, O5, O6.

1 *noint ... mastic*] He probably means they should anoint the gastroduodenal junction (the lower part of the stomach that connects to the small intestine) with aromatic gums or resins from the bark of the lentisk or mastic tree. Presumably Elyot intends the patient to swallow the treatment.
2 *nardinum*] medicinal oil from the aromatic plant, nard.
3 *soundings*] swoonings or fainting fits.
4 *stinking of the nose called polypus*] nasal polyp; a fleshy growth within the nasal passage.
5 *web in the eyes*] thin white film or opacity growing over the eyes.
6 *quinsies*] swellings and inflamations producing sore throats.
7 diatrion pipereon] preparation consisting of three kinds of pepper, or of sanders or sandalwood (*OED* dia-, *prefix* 2).

I perceived that I had been long in an error, wherefore first I did throw away my quilted cap and my other cloth bonnets and only did lie in a thin coif,[1] which I have ever since used both winter and summer, and wore a light bonnet of velvet only. Then made I oxymel after the doctrine of Galen, saving that I boiled in the vinegar roots of parsley and fennel with endive, chicory, and betony, and after that I had taken it three days continually, everyday three spoonfuls in the morning warm, then took I of the same oximel wherein I had infused or steeped one dram of agaric[2] and half a dram of fine rhubarb the space of three days and three nights, which I received in the morning, eating no meat six hours after, and that but a little broth of a boiled hen, whereof ensued eight stools abundant of choler and phlegm. Soon after I slept soundly and had good appetite to eat, and after supper I would either eat a few coriander seeds prepared or swallow down a little fine mastic,[3] and forbear wine, and drank only ale, and that but little and stale and also warmed. And sometime in the morning would take a perfume of *storax calamita*[4] and now and then I would put into my nostrils either a leaf of green laurel, or betony, or water of marjoram bruised, which caused the humour to distil by my nostrils. And if I lacked *storax* I took for a perfume the rinds of old rosemary and burned them and held my mouth over the fume, closing mine eyes afterward to comfort my stomach and make it strong. Sometime I would eat with my meat a little white pepper, gross bruised; sometime Galen's electuary made of the juice of quinces, called *diacytonites*;[5] sometime marmalade of quinces or a quince roasted. And by this diet, I thank almighty God, unto whom only be given all glory, I was reduced to a better state in my stomach and head than I was sixteen years before, as it may appear unto them which have long known me. And this have I not written for vainglory or of presumption but to the intent that they which have their bodies in like temperature as mine was, that is to say, being choleric of complexion and having rheums falling out of a hot head, may, if they list, assay mine experience, or in the stead of my said infusion take *hiera picra* with ale or water to purge them, whereof shall not ensue so much peril as of corrupted syrups and other confections called magistrals,[6] made with old rotten drugs, though the physicians be never so well learned. In bodies of other temperature I would not that mine experience should be practised but with discretion, tempering the medicine as the qualitites of the stomach and head do require, remembering alway that hot rheums be thin and subtle, cold rheums be for the more part thick. Also, that they which be thin would be made thick that they pierce not too fast, and that they which be thick would be made thin that they may the sooner be purged, by what tokens one may know whether the stomach and head be hot or cold. Finally, this dare I affirm, that the rheums which of late time have been more frequent in this realm than they were wont to be forty years past have happened of none occasion more than of banquet-

---

1 *coif*] nightcap.

2 *agaric*] a type of fungus that grows on trees.

3 *mastic*] aromatic gums or resins from the bark of the lentisk or mastic tree.

4 storax calamita] *Storax* is a fragrant gum-resin; *storax calamita* (or *storax calamite*) is the name given to the substance when dried (*OED* storax, *n*. 1).

5 diacytonites] from quinces.

6 *confections called magistrals*] compounds created according to a physician's own formula; not included in the pharmacopoeia (*OED* magistral, *n*. 2. b.).

ings after supper and drinking much, specially wine a little afore sleep. Another thing is the keeping the head too hot or too long covered whereby the brain, which is naturally cold, is distempered with hot vapours ascending from the stomach, those same vapours being let[1] to evaporate or pass forth out of the head and therefore be concrete or gathered into humour superfluous, which stilleth down eftsoons out of the head into the places before rehearsed. Yet nowadays if a boy of seven years age or a young man of twenty years have not two caps on his head he and his friends will think that he may not continue in health. And yet if the inner cap be not of velvet or satin a serving man feareth to loose his credence. A parson, vicar or parish priest by using their velvet caps embroidered with laces do make some men think that they be ashamed of their crowns, that reverend token of the order of priesthood, the which notable abuse I much marvel that the bishops will suffer, specially they which have had leisure to read the works of Saint Cyprian, Saint Jerome, Chrisostomus,[2] Saint Ambrose, and sundry decrees made by the old fathers concerning the honest vesture of priests which, although it seem a light matter to some men, yet it augmenteth or minisheth not a little in priests the estimation of their conditions, Solomon confirming the same, saying the garment, the gait, and laughter of a man declareth what he is. But this matter will I leave to another place, where I intend to speak more abundantly of it if it be not the sooner amended. Now, to conclude, as long as the said occasions continue, so long men shall not be without rheums, although they were all perfect physicians.

[i]Now to return to the remedies against the said annoyance whereof happeneth so many great sicknesses. I will be bold to write a little out of the works of the most famous and expert physicians. First, the cause of the rheum must be digested; after expulsed; thirdly diverted, that is to say turned from the eyen or throat into the nose from whence it may be more easily purged; fourthly it may be stopped that it shall not distil. In hot distillations the head is very hot in feeling, the rheum being in the mouth is thin and warm, the tongue or cheeks within blistered, the face sometime redder than it is accustomed to be, sometime a burning within the nose. To them which have this hot rheum may be given the seed of white poppy, *diacodion*,[3] made of the heads of white poppy and rainwater; *amylum*,[4] with milk if there be no fever; penides;[5] mallows; orage;[6] gourds and spinach, boiled and eaten with oil of almonds; syrup of violets; nenuphar[7] or the wine of sweet pomegranates. The waters of a great cucumber, boiled with a little sugar, being drunk, doth mitigate choler, stoppeth the rheum, and easily looseth the belly; the seeds of melons, braised in a

---

i Now] *preceded by centered heading* "By what tokens one may knowe whether the stomache and heed be hotte or colde." in O5, O6.

---

1 *let*] stopped.
2 *Chrisostomus*] Presumably John Chrysostom.
3 diacodion] Latin for diacodium, which is a syrup prepared from poppy heads (*OED* diacodium, *n.*).
4 amylum] Latin for amyl, which is starch, finest flour (*OED* amyl, *n.* 1).
5 *penides*] pieces or sticks of boiled sugar, similar to barley-sugar.
6 *orage*] possibly borage or orange.
7 *nenuphar*] roots, leaves, flowers, or seeds of the waterlily used in medicinal preparations.

mortar with water and strained, with soft bread having sugar put to it, maketh an excellent good meat against the hot rheums; plasters made of barley bruised, violets, poppy, and camomile boiled in water, wherein sponges or linen clothes being dipped, should be laid on the head and the genitories or legs therewith washed. If the sick man cannot sleep then the said parts, with the belly and fundament, shall be nointed with the oils of violets and nenuphar; the savour of camphor in rosewater with violets is good in that case. Galen exhorteth, and I have proved, that in a very hot rheum which hath stilled fast, the pouring of cold water in upon one's head hath stinted the rheum. He that is therein diseased must eschew going in the sun, or to come nigh a great fire, or to stand, or be long covered, or to wear much on his head; he must rest much and provoke himself to sleep a-night, but not very long, and to lie on the one side on a hard bed, having his head high; also rubbing of his legs before meal[1] is very wholesome. Cold rheums be perceived by coldness of the humour and head, with paleness of the visage, all cold things increasing the rheum. These things are good against it: the decoction of cicer[2] with honey and raisins, filbert nuts toasted, eaten after meals; nothing is more wholesome than abstinence, specially in the evening. They which have it must beware of northern winds, the moonshine by night, washing in cold water, and to be long bareheaded. The seeds of nigella, a little toasted and put into a piece of thin sarsenet[3] and smelled unto, stoppeth the rheums.

Neezing in the beginning of the rheum is dispraised of Galen, but after that the matter is digested it is very wholesome that may be made with leaves of laurel or betony put into the nostrils. The juice of coleworts, the roots of red beets, water of marjoram, a pretty medicine for that purpose proved; the juice of young beets and marjoram (of every[4] one ounce), good white wine (four ounces), saffron (the weight of twopence), that being hot and taken in the mouth shall be drawn up with breath to the place whereby the distillation falleth out of the nose into the mouth. And if the rheum do distil into the cheeks and teeth, I have proved that the juice of ground-ivy and that herb which we call mouse-ear[5] taken within a quill into the nostrils oftentimes purgeth exceedingly the rheum and taketh away the ache of the teeth.

Gargling, if it be not discreetly used, may do more harm than good (bring down much abundance of matter undigested) but taken in order with water, honey, and pepper, or with hyssop and figs, boiled in white wine and taken very hot in a gargarise, is right convenient.

For compassion which I have of them that be vexed with toothache caused of rheums, I will (by the leave of physicians) conclude this chapter with an excellent medicine against the said passion,[6] which is written of an honourable physican of late years, which medicine also maketh teeth fast which be loose and also stoppeth the superfluous bleeding of gums, wherewith the breath is made unsavoury. Take the rinds of caper roots; the roots of brambles which do bear blackberries; the flowers of pomegranates called *balaustia*, of every of them the weight of two ducats; pellitory

---

1 *meal*] a singular understood as a plural.
2 *cicer*] chickpea.
3 *sarsenet*] a very fine and soft silk material.
4 *every*] each.
5 *mouse-ear*] *Pilosella officinarum*, a type of hawkweed.
6 *passion*] pain, suffering.

of Spain,[1] one ducat; seed of white henbane; the rinds of mandrake, of every of them one ducat and a half; spurge of the garden, one handful; alum of the rock, two ducats; boil all this in white wine, or claret which is very rough in taste, and strain it therewith. Let the patient oftentimes wash his mouth, albeit I will counsel them which will take this medicine, or any other, first to purge the cause of the rheum, as before is rehearsed or in any otherwise as they shall be counselled by well learned and discreet physicians.

Chapter three: Of lassitude

Lassitude is a disposition toward sickness wherein a man feeleth a soreness, a swelling, or an inflammation. Soreness happeneth of humours sharp and gnawing, as after great exercise and labours, which lassitude happeneth to them whose bodies are full of ill juice and excrements, also after crudity in them which are not exercised or do abide long in the heat of the sun. It may also be in the body wherein is good juice if he be fatigate[2] with immoderate exercise. In them which do feel this lassitude the skin appeareth thick and rough and there is felt a grief, sometime in the skin only, sometime also in the flesh, as it were of a sore. The cure thereof is by much and pleasant rubbing with sweet oils which have not the virtue to restrain or close, and that with many hands, and afterward to exercise moderately and to be bained[3] in water sweet and temperate in heat. Also, then must be given meats of good juice, pottage but seld;[4] wine is not to be forbidden, for unto wine uneth[5] anything may be compared that so well digesteth crude humours, it also provoketh sweat and urine and maketh one to sleep loudly. But if this lassitude do abide the night and day following, or waxeth more and more, then if the patient be of good strength, and young, and hath abundance of blood, let him be let blood, or provoke the haemorrhoids or piles to bleed if they do appear. But if it proceed of the malice of any humour, without abundance of blood, then resort to purgations apt for the humour that grieveth, the tokens whereof shall appear as well by the colour of the skin and diet preceding as by urine, ordure, sweat, thirst, and appetite, as it is rehearsed before in the complexions. If the ill blood be little in quantity and the crude humours abundant then shall he not be let blood nor vehmently purged, neither shall exercise or move himself, nor be bained,[6] for all exercise carryeth humours throughout all the body and stoppeth the pores. Wherefore these manner of persons should be kept in rest and such meats, drinks, and medicines should be given to them which should attentuate[7] or dissolve the grossness of the humours without notable heat, as oxymel, barley water, and mulse,[8] if the patient abhor not honey. And forasmuch as

Aetius, liber 3

Galen De sanitate tuenda, liber 5

---

1 *pellitory of Spain*] a daisy-like plant from North Africa, commonly formerly used as a remedy against toothache.
2 *fatigate*] fatigued.
3 *bained*] bathed.
4 *seld*] seldom.
5 *uneth*] with difficulty, not easily.
6 *bained*] bathed.
7 *attentuate*] make thinner.
8 *mulse*] honey mixed with water or wine.

in the said persons commonly there is abundance of wind about their stomachs, therefore pepper, specially long pepper or white, is very convenient to be used, and the medicine before written, called *diaspoliticum*. When the humours are dissolved,[1] then is it good to drink white wine or small claret wine moderately.

Chapter four: Lassitude extensive

When one thinketh that he doth feel a swelling or boiling of the body where indeed there doth not appear in sight or touching any swelling, that is called lassitude extensive, if it happeneth without exercise or vehement moving. This doth happen of excessive multitude of humours which do extend the muscles or fillets. In this no soreness is felt but only an heaviness, with extention or thrusting out of the body. And because that there is abundance of blood in the body, best remedy is to be letten blood about the elbow or ankle, after to be purged, then to use soft fricaces with oils afore rehearsed. Afterward much rest, and temperate baths, and meats lacking sharpness, and being abstertive.

Chapter five: Lassitude with the feeling of inflammation

If, without any moving, the muscles and flesh rise up in the body, as it swelled with great pains and exceeding heat, then soon after followeth most hottest fevers, except it be prevented by letting of blood, and that in abundance, and almost to sounding.[2] But it were more sure to be let blood twice in one day, the first time without swooning, at the next time sounding is not to be feared. If the grief be in the neck or head, the blood must be let of the vein called *cephalea*, or the shoulder vein. If it be in the bulk[3] or uppermost part of the body then must the vein be cut which is called *basilica*, or the innermost vein. If all the body be grieved then cut the vein which is named *mediana*, or the middle vein. If a fever remain after bloodletting then order him with the diet of them that have fevers, which ye shall find written hereafter. If no fever remain then use moderate fricaces, and little eating, and that of meats having good juice, increasing by little and little to the natural diet.

Aetius [O1, O5, O6 omits.]

Chapter six: Diet of them that are ready to fall into sickness

Now ⁱto return eftsoons to speak of diet, it is to be remembered that they which are ready to fall into diseases, they are prepared thereunto either by repletion of superfluous humours or else by crudity or malice of humours which are in them. As touching the first, the general diet must be such as thereby the humours may be attentuate[4] and by convenient evacuation brought to a moderate quantity. As for the second, must be corrected with meats and drinks of contrary qualities, having alway respect to the age of the person, time of the year, place of habitation and, most

---

i *to return*] this ed.; Q4 omits.

1 *dissolved*] dispersed.
2 *sounding*] swooning or fainting.
3 *bulk*] chest, thorax.
4 *attentuate*] made thinner.

specially, the universal complexion for choler. Offending in an old man in winter time, in a cold country, or the person being of his natural complexion phlegmatic or melancholy, would not be so abundantly expulsed or subdued as if it be in one young and lusty in the hot summer, in the countries where the sun fervently burneth, or the person of his proper nature is very choleric. And in likewise contrary, wherefore every man knowing his own natural complexion with the quality of the humour that offendeth, let him make temperance his chief cook and, remembering that which I have before declared, ordain to himself such diet as may reform the offence with none or little annoyance to his universal complexion. And if he can do, he shall happily escape not only diverse sicknesses but also the most pernicious danger proceeding of corrupted drugs or spices whereof some covetous apothecaries do make medicines, maugre the heeds[1] of good and well-learned physicians.

Chapter seven: Sickness most common to particular times of the year and ages

Although I do not intend to write of the cure of aegritudes[2] or sicknesses confirmed, as well because it might be reputed in me a great presumption as also forasmuch as it were very perilous to divulgate[3] that noble science to common people not learned in liberal sciences and philosophy, which be required to be sufficiently in a physician. And, moreover, many books of Hippocrates and Galen ought to be read before that one do take upon him the general cure of men's bodies. Yet, notwithstanding, I trust I may, without any note of arrogance, write what diseases do most commonly happen in sundry times of the year and ages of men and women, with some significations whereby the dyscrasy or distemperature of the body is perceived, to the intent that the physician, being far off, may be truly informed, considering that urines far carried do often deceive them, and likewise lack of the sight of the patient, and inquisition of things which do precede or follow the sickness. And with this I trust none honest and charitable physician will be offended but rather give to me thanks for my diligence in the advancing of their estimation, which by lack of perfect instruction hath been appaired.

Sicknesses of springtime

Diseases proceeding of melancholy: as madness, falling-sickness, bleedings, quinsies,[4] poses, hoarsness, coughs, lepries,[5] scabs, ache in the joints.

Sicknesses of summer

Many of the said diseases, also fevers continual, hot fevers, fevers tertian, quartans, vomits, fluxes, watering of eyes, pains of the ears, blisters and sores of the mouth and sweatings.

---

1 *maugre the heeds*] in spite of the careful attentions.
2 *aegritudes*] illnesses.
3 *divulgate*] make publicly known, publish abroad.
4 *quinsies*] swellings and inflammations producing sore throats.
5 *lepries*] leprosies, i.e. skin ailments in general.

Sicknessess of autumn

Diverse of summer sicknesses, also oppilations of the spleen, dropsies, consumptions, strangullions,[1] costiveness, ache in the huckle-bones,[2] shortness of wind, fretting of the bowels, falling-sickness and melancholic diseases.

Sicknesses of winter

Stitches and griefs in the sides; inflammation of the lungs; rheums; coughs; pains in the breast, sides, and loins; headache and palsies.

Sicknessess happening to children

When they be newborn there do happen to them sores of the mouth called aphtha,[3] vomiting, coughs, watching, fearfulness, inflammations of the navel, moisture of the ears.

When they breed teeth: itching of the gums, fevers, cramps and lasks.[4]

When they wax elder, then be they grieved with kernels;[5] openness of the mould of the head; shortness of wind; the stone of the bladder; worms of the belly; waters; swellings under the chin; and in England commonly purples,[6] measles, and smallpox.

Sickness happening to young men from fourteen years of age

Fevers quotidian, tertian, quartan; hot fevers; spitting or vomiting of blood; pleurisies; diseases of the sides; inflammation of the lungs; lethargies; frenzy; hot sicknessess; choleric passions; costiveness or vehement lasks.

Sicknesses of age

Difficulty of breath, rheums with coughs, strangullion[7] and difficulty in pissing, ache in the joints, diseases of the reins, swimmings in the head, palsies, itching of all the body, lack of sleep, moisture in the eyes and ears, dullness of sight, hardness of hearing, ⁱphthisicness or shortness of breath.

Although many of the said sicknesses do happen in every time and age, yet because they be most frequent in the said times and ages, I have written them to the intent that in the ages and times most inclined unto them such things might be then eschewed which are apt to engender the said diseases.

Chapter eight: The general significations and tokens of sickness

If the body be hotter, colder, moister, drier, leaner, fuller, the colour more pale or swart, the eyes more hollow than is accustomed to be, it signifieth that the body is disposed to sickness or already sick.

---

i phthisicness or shortness of breath] *O1 omits.*

---

1 *strangullions*] a quinsy: swelling and inflammation producing a sore throat.
2 *huckle-bones*] hip-bones (OED huckle, *n.* 1).
3 *aphtha*] an ulcer, especially in the mouth.
4 *lasks*] looseness of the bowels, diarrhoea.
5 *grieved with kernels*] suffer enlarged glands, probably specifically inflamed tonsils.
6 *purples*] dark red or purplish lesion of the skin.
7 *strangullion*] a quinsy: swelling and inflammation producing a sore throat.

The brain sick
Raving
Forgetfulness
Fantasy
Humours coming from the roof of the mouth, the eyes, the nose, or the ears
Watch
Sleep

The heart sick
Difficulty of breath
Trembling of the heart
Beating of the pulse
Fevers
Cold
Diversity of colours
Grief about the heart

The liver sick
Lack or abundance of humours
The form of the body altered
Paleness
Concoction
Digestion
Alteration of excrements accustomed
Pain in the place of the liver
Swelling
Difficulty of breath

The stomach sick
Concoction slow or quick
Appetite of moist or dry, dull or quick
Separation of excrements moist or hard with their colours
Yering,[1] belking[2]
Vomiting with pain and difficulty of breath
Urine much or little, with the colour and substance too red or too pale, too thick or too thin

The ⁱbreast sick
Difficulty of breath
Cough
Spitting
Pain in the breast

This have I written not to give judgement thereby but only for the patient to have in a readiness, to the intent that whatsoever he feeleth or perceiveth in every of the said things thereof to instruct his physican whereunto he may adapt his counsel and remedies.

---

i breast sick] O6; breast Q4, O1, O3, O5.

---

1 *Yering*] desire, longing.
2 *Belking*] belching.

Chapter nine: Of urines

Forasmuch as nowadays the most common judgement in sickness is by urines, which being far carried, or much moved, or standing long after that it is made, the form thereof is so altered that the physician shall not perfectly perceive the natural colour nor contents, although it be never so well chafed at the fire, as Actuarius and other great learned men do affirm. I will therefore somehat speak of urines, not so much as a physician knoweth but as much as is necessary to every man for to perceive the place and cause of his grief, whereby he may the better instruct the physician.

First, in urine four things are to be considered, that is to say: the substance, the colour, the regions or parts of the urine, and the contents or things therein contained.

Also, forasmuch as in the body of man be four qualities: heat, cold, moisture, and dryeth. Two of them, heat and cold, are causes of the colour; dryeth and moisture are causes of the substance.

Moreover, in urine, being in a vessel apt thereunto to be seen, are three regions: the lowest region in the bottom of the urinal, containing the space of two fingers or little more; the middle region from whence the lowest ended, unto the circle; the highest region is the circle.

The highness of the colour signifyeth heat; the pale, black, or green, signifieth cold.

Also, the grossness or thickness of the urine signifyeth moisture; the clearness or thinness signifyeth dryeth.

The colours of urines

Perfect digestion
Colour of bright gold
Colour of gilt

Excess of digestion
Red as a red apple or cherry
Base red,[1] like to bole armeniac or saffron dry
Red, glowing like fire

Adustion of humours
Colour of a beast's liver
Colour of dark red wine
Green, like to coleworts

[i]**Feebleness or mortification**[2] [ii]**of nature, except it be in purging of melancholy**
Leady colour
Black as ink
Black as horn

---

i Feebleness or] *O1 omits.*   ii of nature] or death *O1.*

1 *Base red*] deep red.
2 *mortification*] deadening or destruction.

Lack of digestion
White, clear as water
Grey as a horn
White as whey
Colour of a camel's hair

The beginning of digestion
Pale like to broth of flesh sodden

The middle of digestion
Citron colour or yellow
Sub-citron or paler
White and thin betokeneth melancholy to have dominion
White and thick signifyeth phlegm
Red and thick betokeneth sanguine
Red and thin betokeneth choler to have the sovereignty

Chapter ten: The substance of the urine
At the first pissing all urines well nigh do appear thin, as long as they abide warm, for natural heat during the time that it prevaileth suffereth not that the liquor, which is the substance of the urine, to congeal or be thick for any occasion; but after that heat is gone some urines shortly, some a longer time after, wax thick. Likewise, sometime some are pissed thicker and after wax clear, some remain still as they were made, some be meetly[1] thick, as they were troubled, some very thick and gross. They that wax clear soon do gather that which is thick into the bottom of the urinal; some remain troubled, the grossness nothwithstanding, gathered in the bottom. Semblably, the diversity of thin or subtle urines must be perceived, that is to say that some are very subtle as water, some less subtle, some in a mean between thick and thin.

Of things contained in the urine some do descend down to the bottom and be called in a Greek word *hypostasis*, in English some call it the grounds, some the residence, which if it be white, light, rising up from the bottom of the urinal like a pear, it signifyeth health; if it be of any other figure or colour it betokeneth some annoyance. If like things be seen in the middle of the urinal they be called sublations, if they approach unto the highest region of the urine they be named clouds, in Latin *nebule*. The grounds or residences not perfect, some is like little red vetches and is called in Latin *grobea*; some is like to bran of wheat ground and severed from the meal and is called branny residence, in Latin *furfurea*; some be like unto plates, having breadth and length without thickness and may be named platy residence, in Latin *laminea*; some is like to meal, wheat, or barley and may be named mealy residence, in Latin *similacea*.

There is also seen in the urine like to white hairs, some longer, some shorter, sometime like to rags, somewhat red. There is also seen in the uppermost part of the urine sometime a foam or froth, sometime bells[2] or bubbles; sometime there swimmeth in the urine a thing like a cobweb; otherwhile there is about the circle, as it

---

1 *meetly*] properly, sufficiently.
2 *bells*] bubbles formed in liquid.

were, the renting of cloth; sometime there is in the urine like motes[1] of the sun; sometime like the matter of a sore; otherwhile like the seed of a man; also, gravel or sand. And in these things may be diverse colours: some white, some red, some between both, some yellow, some grey, and some black. All this must be diligently marked, and thereof separately, to advertise the physician unto whom I refer the judgement of the sickness for the cause afore rehearsed [i]and forasmuch as the judgement of them is very subtle.

Semblably, of ordure: whether it be very thin or very thick; what other matter issueth out with it; what colour it is of; the savour very great, little, or none; if it were easily expulsed or painfully; how oft or how seldom.

Moreover, of sweat: what colour it is of; and of what savour; if in tasting it be salt, sour, bitter, or unsavoury.

Also, the vomit: if it be of one colour or many, if it do smell horribly, of what humour it had most abundance, if it were fasting or after meals, if it were painful or easy.

Likewise spittle: whether it be thick or thin; or mixed with blood or matter corrupt accordingly, of the humour issuing out at the nose; and if that be blood, then whether it be red, watery, or black.

Moreover, it may not be forgotten to advertise the physician of the diet used by the patient, as well afore the sickness as in the time of the sickness; his age; the strength of his body; his exercise; and place where he longest abode in his youth, whether it were high or low, watery or dry, hot or cold.

This, I trust, shall be sufficient to instruct a physician. He that desireth to know more, particularly hereof, let him read the books of Hippocrates, Galen, Cornelius Celsus, Actuarius, Paul,[2] and diverse other late writers, for this little treatise may not receive it.

Chapter eleven: The precepts of the ancient physician Diocles unto King Antigonus

We will now divide the body of man into four parts: the head; the bulk, called in Latin *thorax*, which containeth the breast; the sides; the stomach and entrails. The belly, called in Latin *venter*, containeth the paunch and the bowels, also the bladder, called in Latin *vesica*, in the which name is also contained the cundites,[3] by the which urine passeth. When any disease approacheth to the head these tokens do commonly precede: swimming in the head, headache, heaviness of the brows, sounding in the ears, prickings in the temples, the eyes in the morning do water or wax dim, the smelling is dull, the gums do swell. When thou feelest such tokens, forthwith purge the head with somewhat, not with vehement medicines but taking hyssop or *organum*, and the crops[4] of them boil with white or claret wine (half a pint), and therewith gargarise your mouth fasting until the phlegm be purged out of your head; this is the

---

i and forasmuch ... subtle] *O1 omits.*

1 *motes*] minute particles.
2 *Paul*] Paul of Aegina.
3 *cundites*] conduits, passages of the body.
4 *crops*] heads, top parts.

easiest medicine in dyscrasies of the head. It is also very wholesome to gargarise the mouth and breast with honey water whereunto mustard is put and mingled, but first the head must be rubbed with a warm cloth that the phlegm may easily come out of the head. And if these tokens be neglected, these manner of sicknesses do follow soon after: bleared eyes and humour letting the sight; clefts in the ears; swellings in the neck full of matter called the king's evil; corruption of the brain; poses or rheums; heaviness of the head; and toothache.

When the bulk[1] is like to suffer any sickness it is perceived by these tokens: all the body is in a sweat, the bulk most specially; the tongue waxeth thick; the spittle is either salt, or bitter, or choleric; the sides and shoulders do ache without any occasion; the patient gapeth often;[2] also there doth happen much waking; suffocations or lack of breath; thirst after sleep; the mind is vexed with heaviness; also the breast and arms are very cold and the hands do tremble. Against these things this remedy may be provided: after a moderate supper assay to vomit without any medicine; vomit is also profitable which meat doth follow. He that in such wise will vomit, let him eat hastily small radish roots, town cresses,[3] rocket, senvy,[4] or purslane, and drink after it a great quantity of warm water, and provoke himself to vomit. He that setteth little by the said tokens, let him fear these sicknesses following: the pleuresy, the sickness of the lungs, melancholy or madness, sharp fevers, the frenzy, the lethargy, inflammation with yexing.[5]

If any sickness be toward the belly they may be espied by these tokens: the belly is first wrapped together and in itself is troubled; all meats and drinks do seem bitter in taste; he feeleth heaviness in his knees; a stiffness in his loins; a weariness in all his body without any occasion; a sleepiness in his legs, with a little fever. When thou feelest these tokens, mollify the belly, not with medicine but with good order of diet, for it is best and most sure to use those things whereof lightly may ensure none annoyance; in the number of them are beets boiled in water of honey, garlic sodden, mallows, sorrel, mercury, and all things condite in honey. All these do expel the ordure of the belly, but if any of the said signs doth more and more increase, the liquor wherein the seed of *carthamus*,[6] called also *cnicus*, is boiled is a pleasant and sure medicine; small coleworts boiled in a good quantity of water, the liquor thereof in measure two pints, saving the third part of a pint, with honey and salt being drunken, shall profit much. Cicer[7] and the pulse called in Latin *ervum* (in English, I suppose, chits),[8] in water drunk fasting hath the same effect. To them which set little by the said tokens, these diseases do suddenly happen: flux of the belly, bloody flux, slipperiness of the bowels, pains in the gut, ache in huckle-bones,[9] the fever tertian, the gout, the apoplexy or palsy in the limbs, haemorrhoids, aching of joints.

---

1 *bulk*] chest, thorax.
2 *gapeth*] probably specifically meaning he yawns often.
3 *town cresses*] garden cress.
4 *senvy*] the mustard plant.
5 *yexing*] hiccuping.
6 carthamus] safflower or bastard saffron.
7 *cicer*] chickpea.
8 ervum *(in English, I suppose, chits)*] Chits means chiches, or chickpeas (*OED* chit, $n.^2$ 1.a.), however *ervum* is another kind of pulse (similar to vetch) called orobos.
9 *huckle-bones*] hip-bones (*OED* huckle, *n.* 1).

When the bladder is toward any sickness it is perceived by these tokens: fullness felt after little meat, breaking wind downward and upward, paleness of colour in all the body, heavy or troubleous sleeps, the urine pale and passing forth painfully, swellings about the cods[1] and privy members. When these tokens appear then is it expedient to have remedy of odoriferous things which do expel urine (which shall be done without any peril), with the roots of fennel and parsley steeped one or two days in good white wine, and to drink thereof fasting every morning three ounces and two drams, with the water of wild carrots or elecampane; which of these is next at hand, every of them have like effect. Also, water wherein the peason called in Latin *ciceres*[2] are steeped, being drunk with wine, is like commodious. He that neglecteth the said tokens, let him look for these sicknesses following: the dropsy, the greatness of the spleen, grief in the liver, the stone, ache of the back or pains in the reins, the difficulty of urine, fullness of the belly. In all these things that we have spoken of, we shall give to children most easy[3] medicines, to men those which be stronger in working.

This diet of Diocles, although at this time it seemeth not most pleasant nor according to the practise now used, yet being tempered with that which I have before remembered, something may be found in it which being experienced may be as commodious for the health of man's body as that diet which is more curious[4] or pleasant.

Chapter twelve: Of them in whose stomachs meat is corrupted

They in whom customably[5] meat is corrupted, let them, afore that they eat any meat, assay to vomit; drinking sweet wine, abstain from meat that engender botches,[6] inflammations, fumous ructations or vapours, and take such as nourish good juice, and choose them out which do mollify the belly and at sundry times take them. It is also good to take temperately that which looseth the belly, as the medicine called *picra* and to abstain from such things whereby ill juice is gathered and do engender sicknesses hard to be cured or never, as gouts, bone-ache, pains of the reins *et cetera*.

Chapter thirteen: Of the virtue of meats

Oribasius *de medicina simpli* [the title means "The Treatment of the Simple" and is presumably a reference to *The Power of the Simple*.]

He that is studious about the conservation of health, he needeth to know the virtue of meats. The meat which hath virtue to extenuate or make humours subtle, it openeth the pores and bringeth forth that which is fast in the flesh, it maketh that which is clammy subtle and doth extenuate or relent[7] that which is fat; it bringeth forth that which abideth long in the belly, but that which is eaten is a superfluity, watery and choleric, and at length maketh melancholy blood. Wherefore much using of them is prohibited, specially to them that are choleric, and only serveth for them that

---

1 *cods*] testicles.
2 *ciceres*] chickpeas.
3 *easy*] mild.
4 *curious*] fastidious.
5 *customably*] customarily, habitually.
6 *botches*] swellings, tumours, or boils.
7 *relent*] dissolve.

are replete with phlegm, crude or undigested humours, clammy or fat. The diet of fatting things doth nourish abundantly, so that the stomach and liver do digest well; meat of good juice maketh good blood but yet it stoppeth the liver and spleen. These do they[1] which make fat humours only: as the pulse called *lenticula* and they that are slimy, like mallows; some do make fat humours and be also slimy, as fishes with hard shells. Finally, the diet which doth extenuate and make lean is more sure for keeping of health than that which fatteth much. Nourishing meats would be therefore moderately used when a man perceiveth himself to have need thereof; it may be most surely used of them that be exercised temperately and can sleep when they list. They that cannot sleep by reason of exercise, let them eschew fattening meats; let none idle person attempt to use them. In the preservation of health sluggardy[2] is the greatest mischief; like as the temperate moving is good, so is the meat which between thick and thin is to man's health most convenient, which engendereth blood according to the competent constitution of man's body and therefore is to be chiefly used. Meat of ill juice is alway noyful, wherefore it ought to be eschewed. Likewise, the variety of meats is to be observed diligently, for it is a great thing to couple well together things of contrary virtues, for if they be not well digested that which is received may bring displeasure.

Chapter fourteen: A diet preservative in the time of pestilence
The bodies most apt to be infected are specially sanguine, next choleric, then phlegmatic; last melancholic, for in them the humour being cold and dry is most unapt to receive putrifaction, having also straight passages by the which venom must pass. The diet convenient for the time is to abstain from meats inflaming and opening the pores, also from the heat of the sun, from too much heat of fire or garments, from very hot herbs, and much use of tart things – except onions and chicory or radish with vinegar, for they do resist against venom – from wine very fumish, exercise incontinent after meals, from sweating, from all things that will cause oppilations and putrifaction, from things hot and moist where moisture hath the dominion in degree (specially being not sufficiently boiled), also from milk except it be in a little quantity and that with a little sugar. Fruit and herbs cold and dry, and therewith sour or somewhat bitter, are not prohibited; if ye eat figs, grapes, or sweet cherries, eat after them of an orange with salt. If ye eat things cold and moist, as cucumbers, melons, fish soft and fresh, or damsons, eat by and by after some fennel and orange with salt, drinking therewith a draught of good wine. Beware of mushrooms, much purslane, gourds, and all other things which will soon putrefy; notwithstanding I will not forbid eating of lettuce with a few mints or mixed with cinnamon. All things sour are commended as well in diet conservative as in that which is curative or healeth except where there is straitness of the breast[3] or weakness of the stomach. Then ought they to be tempered with sugar, salt, almond milk, cinnamon, pepper, fennel, saffron, eggs, and something that

Marsilio Ficino

---

1 *These do they*] these are they (i.e. the foods).
2 *sluggardy*] slothfulness.
3 *straitness of the breast*] tightness of the chest, shortness of breath.

is fat or unctious; capers are good to be used with vinegar. Cheese very fat, and salt is not commended, no more is coleworts or any kind of pulse, except chits;[1] great peason, rapes, nor spinach is good. Also, there be forbidden rocket and mustard; much wine; and eggs, except they be eaten with sorrel sauce. Vinegar or juice of oranges, parsley, and also parsnips be good; new wines be noyful. Let the meat be somewhat more than drink, but yet sustain not too much hunger nor thirst; beware of lechery, of a cloudy weather and close, eschew much resort or throng of people, winds comming from fens or moors, from sleep at noon.[2] Use with your meat this powder: sanders red, half an ounce; cinnamon, three drams and a half; saffron, half a dram. After your meat eat a little of coriander seed, well prepared. In the morning, at a temperate fire, comb your head backward, cleanse your body and head of all superfluities, use also moderate fricaces with sweet perfumes and odours, wash oftentimes your face and hands with pure vinegar mixed with rosewater; in cold weather mix it with mints, balm, rue, or mints and sometime cloves, in hot summer with roses or violets. Above all things use to take white wine good, white vinegar rosette,[3] water of roses, in equal portions; put thereunto a little setwall or of the rind of a citron and drink thereof a little, and oftentimes wash your hands and visage. Medicines preservative against the pestilence which be alway most ready are these: a fig with rue and a walnut eaten fasting; also treacle or mithridate, to old men a dram weight, to young men half a dram or a scruple, dissolved in vinegar and rose water or in water of tormentil;[4] scabious[5] or balm, if the plague be in summer. If it be in winter, put to the waters some white wine, also the pills commonly called *Pillule Rasis* (but indeed they were invented by Rufus)[6] are very excellent, specially if the aloe, which is in it be washed and thereunto added a little *bolus armenus*, and *terra sigilata*.[7] And if the person be of hot complexion a quantity of sorrel seed and red coral; this confectioned with syrup of citrons in cold complexions, or to old men, with white wine, use them every third day, one pill at a time, three hours or four afore dinner or supper. If ye take treacle or mithridate abstain from meat at the least six hours after. A piece of the root of setwall born in the mouth preserveth from infection, in likewise doth sorrel chewed fasting and the juice sucked down. To poor men Marsilius was wont to give a toast of bread steeped in vinegar with a piece of an onion or rue. All things which be cordial, that is to say which do in any wise comfort the heart, do resist pestilence; vehement hunger or heaviness be very pernicious. Other more exquisite[8] and costly preservatives I purposely pass over which Marsilius and other physcans do write of abundantly, forasmuch as I desire to be in this work compendious. One

---

1 *chits*] chiches, or chickpeas.
2 *sleep at noon*] Bullein also warns against sleeping at noon. In Shakespeare's *King Lear* the Fool's last words (perhaps ominously) are "And I'll go to bed at noon" (Shakespeare 1988, 3.6.43).
3 *vinegar rosette*] vinegar infused with the oil from rose petals.
4 *tormentil*] a herb with strongly astringent roots.
5 *scabious*] herbaceous plants of the genus Scabiosa; thought to help cure certain skin diseases.
6 Pillule Rasis] a pill containing purgative medicine that apparently originated with Galen but here according to modifications in the recipe made by Rasis (or Rufus, if Elyot is to be believed).
7 terra sigilata] a medicinal clay.
8 *exquisite*] carefully chosen.

thing I had almost forgotten, that there is no better preservative than to flee from the place corrupted betime,[1] and far off, and to let none approach you that hath made their abode where the plague is fervent. Moreover, receive not into your house any stuff that cometh out of a house where any person hath been infected, for it hath been seen that such stuff lying in a coffer fast shut by the space of two years after that the coffer hath been opened, they which have stand nigh to it have been infected and soon after have died. But here I alway except the power of God, which is wonderful and also merciful above man's reason or counsel, preserving or striking whom, when, and where it shall like, his majesty to whom be glory and praise everlasting. Amen.

Thus make I an end of this treatise, desiring them that shall take profit thereby to defend it against envious disdain, on whom I have set the adventure for the love that I bear to my country, requiring all honest physicans to remember that the intent of my labour was that men and women reading this work and observing the counsels therein should adapt thereby their bodies to receive more sure remedy by the medicines prepared by good physicians in dangerous sicknessess, they keeping good diet and informing diligently the same physicans of the manner of their affects, passions, and sensible tokens. And so shall the noble and most necessary science of physic, with the ministers thereof, escape the slander which they have of long time sustained and, according to the precept of the wise man, be worthily honoured forasmuch as the highest God did create the physician for man's necessity, and of the earth created medicine, and the wise man shall not abhor it. Thus fare ye well, gentle readers, and forget me not with your good report, and pray to God that I be never worse [i]occupied.

Londini in aedibus Thomae Bertheleti typis impress. Cum privilegio ad imprimendum solum.[2]

---

i occupied. Finis] O5, O6.

1 *betime*] in good time, early.
2 Londini ... Solum] "London, in the press of Thomas Berthelet, with the privilege for printing only".

A COMPENDIOUS REGIMENT, OR A DIETARY OF HEALTH

[i]*A Compendious Regiment, or* [ii]*a Dietary of Health,* [iii]made in Montpellier [iv]by [v]Andrew Boorde, of physic Doctor, [vi]newly corrected and imprinted with diverse additions. [vii]Dedicated to the armipotent[1] prince and valiant Lord Thomas Duke of Norfolk.[2]

[viii]*The preface, or the proem*

To the armipotent prince and valiant Lord Thomas Duke of Norfolk, Andrew Boorde, of physic doctor, doth surrender humile[3] commendation with immortal thanks.

After the time that I had travelled, for to have the notition[4] and practice of physic, in diverse regions and countries, and returned into England, and required to tarry, and to remain, and to continue with Sir Robert Drury, knight,[5] for many urgent causes, Your Grace hearing of me did send Sir John Garnyngham, now being knight, to me to come to Your Grace to have my counsel in physic for your infirmities. The message done, I with festination[6] and diligence did not prolong the time but did come to Your Grace according to my duty, the which was in the time when Lord Thomas Cardinal, Archbishop of York, was comanded to go to his see of York. And after my coming to you and feeling the pulses of your heart, the pulses of your brain, and the pulses of your liver, and that I had seen your urine and your egestion,[7] I durst not to enterprise or meddle without the counsel of Master Doctor Buttes,[8] the which did know not only your complexion and infirmity, but also he did know the usage of your diet and the imbecility[9] and strength of your body, with other qualities expedient

---

i A] hereafter foloweth a *Q1*; Here foloweth a *Q4*.   ii a] *Q3 omits*.
iii made in] Used at *Q3*.   iv by] compyled by *Q1, Q3*.
v Andrew Boorde, of physic Doctor] Doctour Lynacre, and other Doctours in Physycke *Q3*.
vi newly corrected and imprinted with diverse additions] *Q1, Q3 omit*.
vii Dedicated to ... Norfolk] *Q3, Q4 omit*.
viii The preface ... Jesus Christ. 1547] *Q1, Q3, Q4 omit; see Appendix 2 for Q1's alternative preface.*

---

1 *armipotent*] mighty in arms. Shakespeare uses the word in *Love's Labour's Lost, All's Well That Ends Well,* and *The Two Noble Kinsmen* (Shakespeare 1988, LLL 5.2.637, 644; AWW 4.3.239; TNK 5.1.53). As Susan Snyder noted, Shakespeare uses the word "in situations of heightened formality" (Shakespeare 1994, 183n239).

2 *Norfolk*] At this point in the copy text there is a picture of three bowls with round objects (perhaps fruit) in the centre one.

3 *humile*] humble.

4 *notition*] knowledge, information, intelligence.

5 *Sir Robert Drury, knight*] probably the lawyer and speaker of the House of Commons, b. before 1456, d. 1535 (Hyde 2004).

6 *festination*] haste, speed.

7 *egestion*] evacuation of the bowels.

8 *Master Doctor Buttes*] probably the physician William Butts. For his biography see Martin and Davies 2004.

9 *imbecility*] weakness.

and necessary to be known. But briefly, to conclude your recuperating or recovering your health, and for singular trust and high favour the which the king had to you was compocated[1] to be in the presence of his majesty, I then did pass over the seas again and did go to all the universities and great schools the which be approbated within the precinct of Christendom for to have the practice of physic. I, seeing many expedient things in diverse regions, at the last I did stay myself at Montpellier, which is the head university in all Europe for the practice of physic and surgery or chyrming.[2] I being there, and having a quotidial remembrance upon your bountiful goodness, did consult with many egregious Doctors of physic what manner that I might write the which might be acceptable for the conservation of the health of your body. The said doctors, knowing my zeal and true intention had to you, did advertise me to make a book of diet, not only for Your Grace but also for your noble posterity and for all men living, wherefore I do nominate this book, *The Dietary of Health*, the which doth pertract[3] how a man should order himself in all manner of causes pertaining to the health of his body. If Your Grace or any man will have further knowledge for diverse infirmities let him look in a book of my making named *The Breviary of Health*. And where I have dedicated this book to Your Grace and have not ornated it with eloquence and rhetoric terms, the which in all manner of books and writings is used these modernal[4] days, I do submit me to your bountiful goodness. And also diverse times in my writings I do write words of mirth; truly it is for no other intention but to make Your Grace merry, for mirth is one of the chiefest things of physic,[5] the which doth advertise every man to be merry and to beware of pensivefulness, trusting to your affluent goodness to take no displeasure with any of the contents of this book but to accept my good will and diligent labour. And furthermore, I do trust to your superabundant graciousness that you will consider the love and zeal the which I have to your prosperity and that I do it for a common weal,[6] the which I beseech Jesus Christ long to continue to his will and pleasure in this life and after this transitory life to remunerate you with celestial joy and eternal glory. From Montpellier, the first day of May, the year of our Lord Jesus Christ, 1547.

[i]Here followeth the table of the chapters[7]
The first chapter doth show where a man should situate or set his mansion place or house for the health of his body.

---

i *Here . . . chapters*] The table of this Booke Q3; The Table of the Chapters foloweth Q4.

1 *compocated*] not found elsewhere, meaning unclear.
2 *chyrming*] presumably related to chirurgery (= surgery).
3 *pertract*] treat of in narration, from the Latin *pertractāre* meaning to handle, to examine in detail, study carefully.
4 *modernal*] modern, of the present day.
5 *mirth is . . . physic*] William Bullein makes the same point in his *Government of Health* (pp. 252–4) and his *Regiment Against the Pleurisy* (Bullein 1562a, E4r–E4v) and so too does Thomas Elyot in his *Castle of Health* (the third book, chapter twenty-one). All are indebted to the medieval dietary *Regimen sanitatis Salerni* (De Mediolano 1607, A6r).
6 *weal*] welfare, well-being.
7 Here followeth the table of the chapters] The first seventeen chapters are not present in Q3, which begins with chapter eighteen and its discussion of boiled and roast meat; the table in Q3 reflects this difference.

The second chapter doth show a man how he should build his house and that the prospect be good for the conservation of health.

The third chapter doth show a man to build his house in a pure and ⁱa fresh air for to lengthen his life.

The fourth chapter doth show under what manner a man should build his house or mansion ⁱⁱin eschewing things that should shorten ⁱⁱⁱhis life.

The fifth chapter doth show how a man should order his house concerning the implements to comfort the spirits of man.

The sixth chapter doth show a man how he should order his house and household ⁱᵛand to live in quietness.

The seventh chapter doth show how the head of a house or a ᵛhousehold should exercise himself for the health of ᵛⁱthe soul and body.

The eighth chapter doth show how a man should order himself in sleeping and ᵛⁱⁱwatching and in his apparel-wearing.

The ninth chapter doth show that repletion or surfeiting doth much harm to nature and that abstinence is the chiefest medicine of all ᵛⁱⁱⁱmedicine.

The tenth chapter treateth of all manner of drinks, as of water, of wine, of ale, of beer, of cider, of mead, of metheglin, and of ⁱˣwhey.

The eleventh chapter treateth of bread.

The twelfth chapter ˣtreateth of pottage, of sew,¹ of stewpots, of gruel, of frumenty,² of pease pottage, of almond milk, of rice pottage, of caudles, of cullises, of ale-brews, of honeysops, and of all other manner of broths.

The thirteenth chapter treateth of white meat, as of eggs, butter, cheese, milk, cream, possets, ˣⁱof almond butter, and of bean-butter.

The fourteenth chapter treateth of fish.

The fifteenth chapter treateth of wild fowl, ˣⁱⁱof tame foul, and ˣⁱⁱⁱof birds.

The sixteenth chapter treateth of flesh, wild and domestical.

The seventeenth chapter treateth of particular things of fish and flesh.

The eighteenth chapter treateth of roast meat, of fried meat, of sodden or boiled meat, of broiled meat and of baken meat.

The nineteenth chapter treateth of roots.

The twentieth chapter treateth of ˣⁱᵛherbs.

The twenty-first chapter treateth of fruits.

The twenty-second chapter treateth of spices.

The twenty-third chapter showeth a diet for sanguine men.

The twenty-fourth chapter showeth a diet for phlegmatic men.

The twenty-fifth chapter showeth a diet for choleric men.

---

i a] *Q1 omits.*   ii in] *Q4 omits;* in *Q1.*   iii his] the *Q4;* his *Q1.*
iv and] *Q4 omits;* and *Q1.*   v household] howsholder *Q1.*   vi the] *his Q4;* the *Q1.*
vii watching] watche *Q4;* watchynge *Q1.*   viii medicine] medysons *Q1.*
ix whey] whaye. &c. *Q4;* whay *Q1.*   x treateth] *Q1 omits.*   xi of] and of *Q4;* of *Q1.*
xii of] and *Q4;* of *Q1.*   xiii of] *Q4 omits;* of *Q1.*
xiv herbs] certayne vsuall herbes *Q1; Q3.*

---

1 *sew*] stew, pottage.
2 *frumenty*] hulled wheat boiled in milk and seasoned with sugar, cinnamon etc.

The twenty-sixth chapter doth show a diet for [i]melancholy men.

The twenty-seventh chapter treateth of a diet and of an order to be used in the pestiferous time of the pestilence and the sweating-sickness.

The twenty-eighth chapter treateth of a diet for them the which be in an ague or a fever.

The twenty-ninth chapter treateth of a diet for them the which have the iliac or the colic and the stone.

The thirtieth chapter treateth of a diet for them the which have any of the kinds of the gouts.

The thirty-first chapter treateth of a diet for them the which have any [ii]kinds of leperhead.[1]

The thirty-second chapter treateth of a diet for them the which have any of the kinds of the falling-sickness.

The thirty-third chapter treateth of a diet for them the which have any pain in their head.

The thirty-fourth chapter treateth of a diet for them the which be in a consumption.

The thirty-fifth chapter treateth of a diet for them the which be asthmatic men, being short-winded or lacking breath.

The thirty-sixth chapter doth show a diet for them the which [iii]hath the palsy.

The thirty-seventh chapter doth show an order and a diet for them [iv]that be mad and out of their wit.

The thirty-eighth chapter treateth of a diet for them [v]the which have any kind of [vi]dropsy.

The thirty-ninth chapter treateth of a general diet for all manner of men [vii]or women being sick or whole.

The fortieth chapter doth show an order or a fashion[2] how a sick man [viii]shall be ordered in his sickness and how a sick man should be used that is likely to die.

[ix]Here endeth the table [x]and here followeth the *Dietary of Health*.[3]

The first chapter doth show where a man should situate or set his mansion place or house for the health of his body

What man of honour, or worship, or other estate the which doth pretend to build a house or any mansion place to inhabit himself, or else doth pretend to alter his house

---

i melancholy] Melancolycke Q4; melancoly Q1.
ii kinds of leperhead] of the kyndes of the lepored Q3, Q4; kyndes of lepored Q1.
iii hath] haue Q3, Q4; hath Q1.   iv that] the whiche Q3, Q4; ye Q1.
v the] Q1 *omits*; the Q4.   vi dropsy] the dropsy Q1, Q3.
vii or] and Q3, Q4; or Q1.   viii shall] shuld Q3; shulde Q4; shall Q1.
ix Here endeth the table] Thus endeth the Table of this Booke Q3; The ende of the table Q4; Here endeth the table Q1.
x and here followeth the *Dietary of Health*] Here foloweth the dyetary or the regyment of helth Q1; Q3 *omits*; Here foloweth the Dyetary of the Regyment of health Q4.

---

1 *leperhead*] leprosy.
2 *fashion*] method, way of doing things.
3 of Health] At this point in the copy text there is a picture featuring an oval shape in the centre with distorted oval shapes on either side and two swords at an angle in front of these shapes.

or to alter old building not only for his own proper commodity, wealth, and health but also for other men the which will resort to him, having also a respect to his posterity, first it is necessary and expedient for him to take heed what counsel God did give to Abraham. And after that to take heed what counsel God did give to Moses and to the Children of Israel, as it appeareth in the thirteenth chapter of Exodus, and the twentieth chapter of Numeri,[1] and the sixth chapter of Deuteronomy, and also in the book of Levites,[2] saying first to Abraham "Go thou forth of thy country and from thy cognation[3] or kindred and come thou into the country the which I will show to thee: a country abounding or plentiful of milk and honey".[4]

Here is to be noted that where there is plenty of milk there is plenty of pasture and no scarcity of water, and where there is plenty of honey there is no scarcity but plentifulness of woods, for there be more bees in woods, and so consequently abundance of honey, than there be bees or honey or ware[5] in the hives in gardens or orchards. Wherefore it appeareth that whosoever [i]will build a mansion place or a house, he must situate and set it there where he must be sure to have both water and wood, except for pleasure he will build a house in or by some city or great town the which be not destitute of such commodities. But he the which will dwell at pleasure and for profit and health of his body, he must dwell at elbow room, having water and wood annexed to his place or house, for if he be destituted of any of the principles, that is to say first of water, for to wash and to wring, to bake and to brew, and diverse other causes, specially for peril the which might fall by fire, [ii]were a great discommodious thing. And better it were to lack wood than to lack water, the premises considered, although that wood is a necessary thing, not only for fuel but also for other urgent causes, specially concerning building and reparations.

The second chapter doth show a man how he should build his house or mansion that the prospect be fair and good for the conservation of health

After that a man have chosen a convenient soil and place according to his mind and purpose to build his house or mansion on, he must have a forecast[6] in his mind that the prospect to and fro the place be pleasant, fair, and good to the eye, to behold the woods, the waters, the fields, the vales, the hills and the plain ground. And that everything be decent and fair to the eye, not only within the precinct of the place appointed to build a mansion or a house to see the [iii]commodities about it, but also it may be placable[7] to the eyes of all men, to see and to behold when they be a good distance off from the place that it [iv]do stand commodiously. For the commodious

---

i will] that wyll Q4; wyl Q1.   ii were] it were Q4; were Q1.
iii commodities] comodyte Q4; cōmodities Q1.   iv do] doth Q4; do Q1.

---

1 *Numeri*] Latin for Numbers, the fourth book of the Old Testament.
2 *the book of Levites*] Leviticus, the third book of the Old Testament.
3 *cognation*] ancestor, kindred.
4 *Go thou forth . . . milk and honey*] Leviticus 20.24, although not a direct quotation from Leviticus as suggested by Boorde.
5 *ware*] the goods produced by bees, that is, honey.
6 *forecast*] foresight of consequences and provision against them.
7 *placable*] pleasing, agreeable.

building of a place doth not only satisfy the mind of the inhabitor but also it doth comfort and rejoiceth a man's heart to see it, specially the pulchrous[1] prospect. For my conceit[2] is such that I had rather not to build a mansion or a house than to build one without a good ⁱprospect in it, to it, and from it. For and the eye be not ⁱⁱsatisfied, the mind can not be contended, and the mind cannot be contented, the heart cannot be pleased. If the heart and mind be not pleased, nature doth abhor, and if nature do abhor, mortification[3] of the vital ⁱⁱⁱand animal and spiritual powers do consequently follow.

The third chapter doth show a man to build his house in a pure and a fresh air to lengthen his life

There is nothing except poison that doth putrefy or doth corrupt the blood of man, and also doth mortify[4] the spirits of man, as doth a corrupted and a contagious air. For Galen ⁱᵛ*Terapentice nono*[5] sayeth, whether we will or will not, we must grant ᵛunto every man air, for without the air no man can live. The air cannot be too clean and pure, considering it ᵛⁱdoth compass us round about and we do receive it into us; we cannot be without it, for we live by it as the fish liveth by the water. Good air therefore is to be praised, for if the air be frisk,[6] pure, and clean about the mansion or house it doth conserve the life of man; it doth comfort the brain and ᵛⁱⁱthe powers natural, animal, and spiritual, engendering and making good blood ᵛⁱⁱⁱin the which consisteth the life of man. And, contrarily, evil and corrupt airs doth infect the blood, and doth engender many corrupt humours, and doth putrefy the brain, and doth corrupt the heart, and therefore it doth breed many diseases and infirmities through the which man's life is abbreviated and shortened. Many things doth infect, putrefy, and corrupteth the air, ⁱˣas the influence of sundry stars, and standing waters, stinking mists, and marshes, carrion lying long above the ground, much people in a small room lying uncleanly, and being filthy and sluttish. Wherefore he that doth pretend to build his mansion or house, he must provide that he do not situate his house nigh to any marsh or marsh-ground, ˣthat there be not nigh to the place stinking and putrified standing waters, pools, ponds, nor mires, but at least wise that such waters do stand upon a stony or a gravel ground mixed with clay and that some fresh spring have a recourse to nourish and to refresh the said standing waters. Also, there must be circumspection had that there be not about the house or mansion no stinking

---

i prospect] respecte *Q1*; prospecte *Q4*.   ii satisfied] *Q1* (satysfyed); satysfye *Q2*.
iii and] an *Q4*; and *Q1*.   iv *Terapentice*] terapentico *Q4*; terapentice *Q1*.
v unto] to *Q4*; vnto *Q1*.   vi doth] doth close and doth *Q4*; doth *Q1*.
vii the] *Q4 omits*; the *Q1*.   viii in] by *Q1*; in *Q4*.
ix as] The fyrst is *Q4*; as *Q1*.   x that] And that *Q4*; that *Q1*.

---

1 *pulchrous*] beauteous, fair.
2 *conceit*] conception, thought.
3 *mortification*] deadening or destruction.
4 *mortify*] deaden or destroy.
5 Terapentice nono] *Terapentice*, book nine; *Terapentice* is the translation from Greek into Latin of Galen's *De Methodo medendi* (*On The Therapeutic Method*) by Burdundio of Pisa.
6 *frisk*] full of life and spirit, brisk.

ditches, gutters, nor cannels,¹ nor corrupt dunghills nor sinks, except they be oft and diverse times mundified and made clean. Sweeping of houses and chambers ought not to be done as long as any honest man is within the precinct of the house, for the dust doth putrefy the air making it dense. Also, nigh to the place let neither ⁱflax nor hemp be watered, and beware of the snuff of candles and of the savour of apples for these things be contagious and infective. Also, misty and cloudy days, impetuous and vehement ⁱⁱwind, troublous and vaporous weather is not good to labour in it, to open the pores and let in infectious air. Furthermore, beware of pissing in draughts and permit no common pissing place be about the house or mansion, and let the common house or easement² be over some water or else elongated from the house. And beware of emptying of pisspots and pissing in chimneys³ so that all evil and contagious airs may be expelled and clean air kept unputrified. And of all things let the buttery, the cellar, the kitchen, the larder-house, with all other houses of offices be kept clean, that there be no filth in them but good and odiferous savours. And to expel and expulse all corrupt and contagious air look in the twenty-seventh chapter of this book.

The fourth chapter doth show under what manner and fashion⁴ a man should build his house or mansion in eschewing things ⁱⁱⁱthat shorteneth man's life
When a man doth begin to build his house or mansion place he must provide (sayeth Jesus Christ) before that he begin to build for all things necessary for the performation of it, lest that when he hath made his foundation and cannot finish his work that he hath begun every man will deride him, saying "this man did begin to build but he cannot finish or make an end of his purpose". For a man must consider the expense before he do begin to build, for there goeth to building many a nail, many pins, many lathes, and many tiles, or slates, or straws, beside other great charges, as timber, boards, lime, sand, stones, or brick, beside the workmanship and the implements. But a man the which have ⁱᵛpurveyed or hath in store to ᵛaccomplish his purpose, and hath chosen a good soil and place to situate his house or mansion, and that the prospect be good, and that the air be pure, frisky, and clean, then he that will build, let him make his foundation upon a gravelly ground mixed with clay, or else let him build upon a rock of stone, or else upon a hill or a hillside. And order and edify the house so that the principal and chief prospects may be east and west,

---

i flax nor hemp] hempe nor flaxe Q4; flaxe nor hempe Q1.   ii wind] wyndes Q1.
iii *that shorteneth man's life*] the whiche shulde shorten the lyfe of man Q4; that shortneth mans lyfe Q1.
iv purveyed] purnyd Q1; prouyded Q4.
v accomplish] Q1 *(accomplysshe)*; accomplysshed Q2.

---

1 *cannels*] A cannel was the gutter or surface watercourse in a street or by a road.
2 *common house or easement*] privy, toilet.
3 *pissing in chimneys*] In Shakespeare's *1 Henry 4* the Second Carrier complains about the poor state of the inn in which they have stayed, where they are compelled to urinate in the chimney: "Why, they will allow us ne'er a jordan, and then we leak in your chimney, and your chamber-lye breeds fleas like a loach" (Shakespeare 1988, 2.1.19–21).
4 *fashion*] method, way of doing things.

specially north-east, south-east, and south-west, for the meridial ⁱwind¹ of all winds is the most worst, for the south wind doth corrupt and doth make evil vapours. The east wind is temperate, fresh, and fragrant, the west wind is mutable, the north wind purgeth ⁱⁱill vapours, wherefore better it is of the two. Worst that the windows do open plain north than plain south, although that Jeremiah sayeth, from the north dependeth all evil,² and also it is written in Cantica Canticorum "rise by the north wind and come thou south wind and perfect my garden".³ Make the hall under such a fashion⁴ that the parlour be annexed to the head of the hall and the buttery and pantry be at the lower end of the hall, the cellar under the pantry, set somewhat abase,⁵ the kitchen set ⁱⁱⁱsomewhat abase from the buttery and pantry, coming with an entry by the wall of the buttery, the pantry house and the larder-house annexed to the kitchen. Then divide the loadings by the circuity of the quadrivial⁶ court and let the gatehouse be opposite or against the hall door, not directly but the hall door standing abase and the gatehouse in the middle of the front entrance into the place. Let the privy chamber be annexed to the ⁱᵛchamber of estate, with other chambers necessary for the building, so that many of the chambers may have a prospect into the chapel. If there be an outer court made, make it quadrivial,⁷ with houses of easements⁸ and but one stable for horses of pleasure. And see no filth nor dung be within the court, nor cast at the back side, but ᵛsee the dung to be carried far from the mansion. Also, the stables, and the slaughter house, a dairy, if any be kept, should be elongated the space of a quarter of a mile from the place. And also the bakehouse and brewhouse should be a distance from the place and from other building. When all the mansion is edified and built, if there be a moat made about it there should some fresh spring come to it, and diverse times the moat ought to be scoured and kept clean from mud and weeds; and in no wise let not the filth of the kitchen descend into the moat. Furthermore, it is a commodious and a pleasant thing to a mansion to have an orchard of sundry fruits, but it is more commodious to have a fair garden repleted with herbs of aromatic and redolent savours. In the garden may be a pool or two for fish, if the pools be clean kept. Also, a park repleted with deer and conies is a necessary and a pleasant thing to be annexed to a mansion; a dovehouse also is

---

i wind] *Q1 (wynde);* wyndes *Q2.*   ii ill] euyll *Q4;* yll *Q1.*
iii somewhat] *Q4 omits;* somwhat *Q1.*   iv chamber] great *Q4; Q1 omits.*
v see] *Q4 omits;* se *Q1.*

---

1 *meridial wind*] wind blowing from the South.
2 *Jeremiah . . . evil*] from the biblical Book of Jeremiah: "Out of the north an evil shall break forth" (1.14).
3 Cantica Canticorum . . . my garden] The text referred to is the biblical Song of Songs, also known as the Song of Solomon. The lines Boorde refers to are as follows: "Awake, O north wind; and come, thou south; blow upon my garden, that the spices thereof may flow out. Let my beloved come into his garden, and eat his pleasant fruits" (4.16).
4 *fashion*] in such a way.
5 *abase*] down, low; back.
6 *quadrivial*] quadrilateral.
7 *quadrivial*] quadrilateral.
8 *houses of easements*] privies, toilets.

a necessary thing about a mansion place. And among other things a pair of butts[1] is a decent thing about a mansion; and otherwhile for a great man necessary it is ⁱfor to pass his time with bowls in an alley. When all this is finished and the mansion replenished with implements, there must be a fire kept continually for a space to dry up the contagious moistures of the walls and the savour of the lime and sand. And after that a man may lie and dwell in the said mansion without taking any inconvenience of sickness.

The fifth chapter doth show how a man should order his house concerning the implements to comfort the spirits of man

When a man hath ⁱⁱbuilt his mansion and hath his houses necessary about the place, if he have not household stuff or implements the which be needful, but must borrow of his neighbours, he then is put to a shift and to a great after deal. For these men the which do brew in a bottle and bake in a wallet,[2] it will be long ere he can buy ⁱⁱⁱJack-a-salad.[3] Yet everything must have a beginning and every man must do after his possessions or ability. This notwithstanding, better it is not to set up a household or hospitality than to set up household lacking the performance of it, as now to ⁱᵛrun for malt and by and by for salt, now to send for bread and by and by to send for a sheep's head, and now to send for this, and now to send for that, and by and by he doth send he cannot tell for what. Such thing is no provision but it is a great abusion.[4] Thus a man shall lose his shirt and be put to a shift, his goods shall never increase and he shall not be in rest nor peace but ever in cark and care,[5] for his purse will ever be bare. Wherefore I do counsel every man to provide for himself as soon as he can, for if of implements he be destituted men will call him light-witted to set up a great house and he is not able to keep man nor mouse. Wherefore let every man look ere he leap, for many corns maketh a great heap.

---

i for to] to *Q4;* for to *Q1.*   ii built] buylded *Q4;* buylt *Q1.*
iii Jack-a-salad] Jack & salad *Q4;* Jacke a salet *Q1.*   iv run] come *Q4;* ron *Q1.*

---

1 *butts*] Given the context, Boorde is probably here referring to marks for archery practice rather than casks or barrels.

2 *brew . . . wallet*] that is, using small containers, which are unsuitable; a *wallet* is a bag.

3 *Jack-a-salad*] This appears to mean something of little value, not very much; Boorde is suggesting it will be a long time before such an irresponsible householder can buy anything, even something of little value, and little cost. A similar phrase is used by Humfrey Barwick who asks, "And again, was not Iack and Sallet [Jack and Salad] within our remembrance thought to be sufficient for arming of Souldiours [soldiers]?" (Barwick 1592, B2r). There might be a play on the word 'sallet', a piece of head-gear in medieval armour, as well as an early modern spelling of 'salad'. Complaints about the lack of money spent on arming soldiers going into battle were common in the early modern period because Elizabeth I was notoriously frugal in her funding of military campaigns.

4 *abusion*] a wrong or shameful act.

5 *cark and care*] a phrase denoting a troubled state of mind.

The sixth chapter doth show how a man should order his house and household and to live quietly

Whosoever he be that will keep a house, he must order the expenses of this house according to the rent of his lands. And if he have no lands, he must order his house after his lucre-winning or gains. For he that will spend more in his house than the rents of his lands or his gains doth attain to,[1] he shall fall to poverty and necessity will urge cause and compel him to sell his land or to waste his stock, as it is daily seen by experience of many men. Wherefore [i]he[2] the which will eschew such prodigality and inconvenience must divide his rents' portion and expenses whereby [ii]that he doth live into three equal portions or parts.

The first part must serve to provide for meat and drink and all other necessary things for the sustenation of the household.

The second portion or part must be reserved for apparel, not only for a man's own self but for all his household and for [iii]his servants' wages, deducting somewhat of this portion in alms-deed to poor neighbours and poor people, fulfilling [iv]the seven works of mercy.

The third portion or part must be reserved for urgent causes in time of need, as in sickness, reparation of houses, with many other quotidial expenses beside rewards and the charges of a man's last end. If a man do exceed this order he may soon fall in debt, the which is a dangerous thing many ways beside the bringing a man [v]to trouble. And he that is once behindhand and in trouble, he cannot be in quietness of mind, the which doth perturb the heart and so consequently doth shorten a man's life. Wherefore there is no wise man but [vi]he will eschew this inconvenience and will cast before what shall follow after, and in no wise to set up a household before he hath made provision to keep a house. For if a man shall buy everything that belongeth to the keeping of [vii]his house with his penny it will be long ere he be rich and long ere that he can keep a good house. But he is wise in my conceit[3] that will have, ere he do set up his household, two or three years' rent in his coffer. And if he have no lands, then he must provide for necessary things ere that he begin household lest [viii]that he repent himself after, through the which he [ix]do fall into pensivefulness and after that into sickness and diseases, living not quietly, whereby he shall abreviate his life.

---

i he] *this ed.;* they be Q2; they Q1.   ii that] Q4 *omits;* that Q1.
iii his] Q4 *omits;* his Q1.   iv the] other of the Q1.
v to trouble] Q4; to man trouble Q2; to trouble Q1.
vi he] Q4 *omits;* he Q1.   vii his] a Q4; his Q1.   viii that] Q4 *omits;* that Q1.
ix do] doth Q4; do Q1.

---

1 *attain to*] arrive at or reach a similar state.
2 *he the*] The sense is singular (see 'his' and 'he' later in the sentence). A cramped annotation of Q1 to change 'they' to 'he' might have been misunderstood by Q2's compositor as simply a call to insert 'be' after it.
3 *conceit*] conception, thought.

The seventh chapter doth show how the head of a house or a householder should exercise himself for the health of ⁱthe soul and body

After that a man hath provided all things necessary for his house and for his household, expedient it is for him to know how he should exercise himself both bodily and ghostly.[1] For there is no Catholic or Christian man living but he is bound in conscience to be more circumspect about the wealth of his soul than the health of his body. Our saviour Jesus Christ sayeth "what shall it profit ⁱⁱunto man if he get all the world and lose himself, and bring himself to a detriment?",[2] wherefore it appeareth that a man ought to be circumspect for the health and wealth of his soul. For he is bound so to live that night and day and at all hours he should be ready and when he is called for to depart out of this world he should not fear to die, saying the words with Saint Ambrose "I fear not to die because we have a good God".[3] When a man hath ⁱⁱⁱprepared for his soul and hath subdued sensuality and that he hath brought himself in a trade or a usage of a ghostly or a Catholic living in observing the commandments of God, then he must study to rule and to govern them the which be in his household or under his custody or dominion to see that they be not idle, for King Henry the Eighth said, when he was young, "idleness is chief mistress of vices all".[4] And also the head of a house must oversee that they which be under his tuition serve God the holy days as diligently, yea and more diligently, than to do their work the ferial[5] days, refraining them from vice and sin, compelling them to observe the commandments of God, specially to punish the swearers, for in all the world there is not such odible[6] swearing as is used in England, specially ⁱᵛamong youth and children, which is a detestable thing to hear it and no man doth go about to punish it. Such things reformed, then may a householder be glad, not ceasing to instruct them the which be ignorant but also he must continue in showing good example of living, then may he rejoice in God and be merry, the which mirth and rejoicing doth lengthen a man's life and doth expel sickness.

The eighth chapter doth show how a man should order himself in ᵛsleeping and in wearing his apparel

When a man hath exercised himself in the day time, as is rehearsed, he may sleep soundly and surely in God what chance so ever do fortune in the night. Moderate sleep is most praised for it doth make perfect digestion, it doth nourish the blood, and doth qualify the heat of the liver. It doth acuate,[7] quicken, and refresheth the

---

i *the*] his Q4; the Q1.   ii *unto*] to Q4; vnto Q1.
iii *prepared*] prouyded Q4; prepared Q1.   iv *among*] amonges Q4; amonge Q1.
v *sleeping*] slepynge and watchynge Q1; slepe and watche Q4.

---

1 *ghostly*] spiritually.

2 *What shall it profit . . . detriment*] The quotation is closest to that from the biblical book of Luke (9.25) but the idea is also present in Mark 8.36 and Matthew (16.26).

3 *I fear . . . good God*] Accounts of St Ambrose's life (based on the original biography by his secretary Paulinus of Milan) claim that these words were uttered by him as he approached death, having been urged to pray to God that his life be spared (Llewelyn Davies 1877, 97).

4 *idleness is . . . vices all*] a maxim that appears in Henry VIII's song 'Pastime with good company' in British Library Additional Manuscript 31922, folios 14v–15.

5 *ferial*] an ordinary weekday, not a holy day.

6 *odible*] hateful; horrible, odious.

7 *acuate*] sharpen.

memory, it doth restore nature, and doth quiet all the humours and pulses in man, and doth animate and doth comfort all the natural, and animal, and spiritual powers of man. And such moderate sleep is acceptable in the sight of God, the premises in the aforesaid chapter observed and kept. And, contrarily, immoderate sleep and sluggishness doth humect and maketh light the brain, it doth engender rheum and impostumes, it is evil for the palsy, whether it be universal or particular, it is evil for the falling-sickness called ⁱ*epilepsia, analepsia* and *catalepsia*,¹ apoplexia, soda,² with all other infirmities in the head for it induceth and causeth obliviousness, for it doth obfusk³ and doth obnebulate⁴ the memory and the quickness of wit. And shortly to conclude, it doth perturb the natural, and animal, and spiritual powers of man, and specially it doth instigate and lead a man to sin, and doth induce and infer brevity of life and, detestably, it displeaseth God. Our Lord Jesus Christ did not only bid or command his disciples to watch but did animate them and all others to do, saying "I say not only to you watch, but to all men I say watch", and to Peter he said "mightest not thou one hour watch with me?"⁵ Although these holy scriptures, with many other more the which I might ⁱⁱalligate,⁶ for me ⁱⁱⁱbe not greatly referred to this sense yet it may stand here with my purpose and matter without reprehension. These matters here need not ⁱᵛto be rehearsed, wherefore I do return to my purpose and do say that the moderation of sleep should be measured according to the natural complexion of man and in any wise to have a respect to the strength and the debility, to age and youth, and to sickness and health of man.

First, as concerning the natural complexion of man, ᵛas sanguine and choleric men, seven ᵛⁱhours is sufficient for them. And now considering the imbecility and weakness of nature, a phlegmatic man may sleep nine hours or more, ᵛⁱⁱmelancholy men may take their pleasure for they be ᵛⁱⁱⁱthe receptacle and the dregs of all the other humours.

Secondarily, youth and age would have temperance in sleeping.

Thirdly, strength may suffer a bounty in watch, the which debility and weakness cannot, as I will show by a familiar example. There were two men set at the dice together a day and a night and more. The weak man said to him "I can play no longer", the strong man said to him "fie on thee bench-whistler! wilt thou start away now?". The weak man, to satisfy the strong man's mind appetite and desire, playeth

---

i *epilepsia, analepsia and catalepsia*] *this ed.*; epilencia, analencia and cathalencia *Q2*.
ii alligate] *Q1, Q4*; allygated *Q2*.   iii be] althoughe they be *Q1*.
iv to] greatly to *Q4*; to *Q1*.   v as] *Q4 omits*; as *Q1*.
vi hours] howres of slepe *Q4*; hours *Q1*.
vii melancholy] Melancolycke *Q4*; melancholy *Q1*.   viii the] *Q1 omits*; the *Q4*.

1 epilepsia, analepsia and catalepsia] the three types of epilepsy identified by Galen, which were thought to originate variously in the brain, stomach, and other body parts.
2 *soda*] headache.
3 *obfusk*] obfuscate.
4 *obnebulate*] obscure, befog.
5 Our Lord . . . watch with me] The first quotation probably alludes to the biblical Book of Mark: "Take ye heed, watch and pray: for ye know not when the time is" (Mark 13.33); the second quotation is certainly from Mark, when Christ admonished Peter for falling asleep (14.37). See also Matthew 24.42 and 26.40.
6 *alligate*] connect, unite.

with his fellow through the which he doth kill himself. The strong man doth himself little pleasure, all things considered, the which I do pass over. Wherefore I will return to the sick man, which may sleep at all times when that he may get it, but if he may sleep at any time, best it is for him to refrain from sleep in the day and so take his natural rest at night when all things is or should be at rest and peace. But he must do as his infirmity will permit and suffice whole men of what age or complexion soever they be of should take their natural rest and sleep in the night and to eschew meridial sleep.[1] But [i]an need shall compel a man to sleep after his meat, let him make a pause and then let him stand, and lean, and sleep against a cupboard, or else let him sit upright in a chair and sleep. Sleeping after a full stomach doth engender diverse infirmities: it doth hurt the [ii]spleen, it relaxeth the sinews, it doth engender the dropsies and the gout and doth make man look evil-coloured. Beware of venerous acts before the first sleep,[2] and specially beware of such things after dinner or after a full stomach for it doth engender the cramp, [iii]the gout, and other displeasures. To bedward be you merry, or have merry company about you, so that to bedward no anger, nor heaviness, sorrow, nor pensivefulness do trouble or disquiet you. To bedward and also in the morning use to have a fire in your chamber to wash and consume the evil vapours within the chamber. I do advertise you not to stand nor to sit by the fire but stand or sit a good way off from the fire, taking the flavour of it,[3] for fire doth arefy[4] and doth dry up a man's blood and doth make stark the sinews and joints of man. In the night let the windows of your house, specially of your chamber, be closed. When you be in your bed lie a little while on your left side and sleep on your right side, and when you do wake of your first sleep make water if you feel your bladder charged, and then sleep on the left side and look as oft as you do wake so oft turn yourself in the bed from the one side to the other. To sleep grovelling upon the stomach and belly is not good unless the stomach be slow [iv]and tardy of digestion, but better it is to lay your hand or your bedfellow hand over your stomach than to lie grovelling. To sleep on the back upright is utterly to be abhorred; when that you do sleep let not your neck, neither your shoulders, neither your hands nor feet, nor no other place of your body lie bare undiscovered. Sleep not with an empty stomach nor sleep not after that you have eaten meat one hour or two after. In your bed lie with your head somewhat high lest that the meat which is in your stomach, through eructations or some other cause, ascend to the [v]orifice of the stomach. Let your nightcap be of scarlet and this I do advertise you: [vi]for to cause to be made a good thick quilt of cotton or else of pure flocks or of clean wool, and let the covering of it be of white fustian, and lay it on the feather bed that you do lie

---

i an] and Q4; an Q1. ii spleen] Q1, Q4; spen Q2.
iii the] and the Q4; the Q1. iv and] Q4 *omits*; and Q1.
v orifice] gryfe Q1; oryfe Q4. vi for] Q4 *omits*; for Q1.

---

1 *meridial*] in the middle of the day.
2 *the first sleep*] Segmented sleep was apparently common in the early modern period. It is thought this consisted of a first sleep, some time after dusk, followed by a period of wakefulness and activity or other of various degrees, and possibly including sex, before a second sleep (Ekirch 2001; Ekirch 2005).
3 *taking the flavour of it*] enjoying its warm smell.
4 *arefy*] dry up, wither.

on, and in your bed lie not too hot nor ⁱcold but in a temperance. Old ancient doctors of physic sayeth eight hours of sleep in summer and nine ⁱⁱhours of sleep in winter is sufficient for any man but I do think that sleep ought to be taken as the complexion of man is. When you do rise in the morning, rise with mirth and remember God. Let your hosen be brushed within and without and flavour the inside of them against the fire;[1] use linen socks or linen hosen next your legs. When you be out of your bed, stretch forth your legs and arms and your body, cough and spit, and then go to your stool and make your egestion,[2] and ⁱⁱⁱexonerate yourself at all times that nature would expel. For if you do make any restriction in keeping your egestion, or your urine, or ventosity it may put you to displeasure in breeding diverse infirmities. After you have evacuated your body and trussed your points[3] comb your head oft and so do diverse times in the day, and wash your hands and wrists, your face and eyes, and your teeth with cold water. And after that you be apparelled walk in your garden or park a thousand pace or two, and then great and noble men doth use to hear mass and other men that cannot do so but must apply their business doth serve God with some prayers, surrendering thanks to him for his manifold goodness with asking mercy for their offences. And before you go to your refection moderately exercise your body with some labour, or playing at the tennis, or casting bowl, or ⁱᵛpassing weights or plummets of lead in your hands, or some other thing to open your pores and to augment natural heat. At dinner and supper use not to drink of sundry drinks and eat not of diverse meats but feed of two or three dishes at the most. After that you have dined and supped, labour not by and by after but make a pause sitting or standing upright the space of an hour or more with some pastime, and drink not much after dinner. At your supper use light meats of digestion and refrain from gross meats. Go not ᵛunto bed with a full nor empty stomach, and after your supper make a pause ere you go to bed, and go to bed (as I said) with mirth. Furthermore, as concerning your apparel in winter, next your shirt ᵛⁱuse to wear a petticoat of scarlet, your doublet use at pleasure but I do advertise you to line your jacket under this fashion[4] or manner: dye you skins of white lamb and black lamb; and let your skinner cut both the sorts of the skins in small pieces, triangle-wise like half a quarel[5] of a glass window; and then sew up together a white piece and a black, like a whole quarrel of a glass window; and so sew up together quarrel-wise as much as will line your jacket. This fur for wholesomeness is praised above sables or any other fur; your external apparel use according to your honour. In summer use to wear a scarlet petticoat made of stammel or linsey-woolsey.[6] In winter and summer keep not your head

---

i cold] to cold Q4; cold Q1.　　ii hours of sleep] Q4 *omits*; houres of slepe Q1.
iii exonerate] Q1, Q4; exoncrate Q2.　　iv passing] *this ed.*; paysing Q2; paysyng Q1.
v unto] to Q4; vnto Q1.　　vi use] use you Q4; vse to Q1.

1 *flavour*] i.e. make them smell warm.
2 *egestion*] evacuation of the bowels.
3 *trussed your points*] tied your hose to your doublet (see *OED* point, *n.*¹ 23. a).
4 *under this fashion*] in this way.
5 *quarrel*] a small pane of glass in a latticed window.
6 *stammel or linsey-woolsey*] coarse woollen cloths; stammel was usually dyed red.

too hot nor bind it too straight, keep ever your neck warm; in summer keep your neck and face from the sun, use to wear gloves made of ⁱgoatskins, perfumed with ambergris. And beware of standing or lying on the ground in the reflection of the sun but be movable. If ⁱⁱyou shall common¹ or talk with any man stand not still in one place, if it be ⁱⁱⁱon the bare ground or grass or stones, but be movable in such places. Stand nor sit upon no stone ⁱᵛnor stones, stand nor sit long barehead under a vault of stone. Also, beware that you do not lie in old chambers which be not occupied, specially such chambers as mice, ᵛrats, and snails resorteth unto. Lie not in such chambers the which be deprived clean from the sun and open air nor lie in no low chamber except it be boarded. Beware that you take no cold on your feet and legs and, of all weather, beware that you do not ride nor go in great and impiteous winds.

The ninth chapter doth show that repletion or surfeiting doth much harm to nature and that abstinence is the chiefest medicine of all medicines
Galen, declaring Hippocrates' sentence upon eating too much meat, sayeth more meat than accordeth with nature is named repletion or a surfeit. Repletion or a surfeit is taken as well by gurgitations or too much drinking as it is taken by epulation,² or eating of crude meat, or eating more meat than doth suffice or can be truly digested. Or else repletion or a surfeit is when the stomach is farced,³ or stuffed, or repleted with too much drink and meat that the liver, which is the fire under the pot, is suppressed, that he cannot naturally nor truly decoct, defy, ᵛⁱnor digest the superabundance of meat and drink the which is in the pot or stomach. Wherefore diverse times these impediments doth follow: the tongue is deprived of his office to speak, the wits or senses be dull and obnebulated⁴ from reason. Sloth and ᵛⁱⁱsluggishness consequently followeth; the appetite is withdrawn; the head is light, and doth ache, and full of fantasies, and diverse times some be so sopited⁵ that the malt-worm⁶ playeth the devil so fast in the head that all the world runneth round about on wheels. Then both the principal members doth fail of their strength, yet the pulses be full of agility. Such repletion, specially such gurgitations doth engender diverse infirmities through the which brevity and shortness of life doth follow, for the wise man sayeth that surfeits do kill many men and temperance doth prolong the life. And also it is written Ecclesiasticus ᵛⁱⁱⁱ37 that there doth die many more by surfeit than there doth by the

---

i goatskins] goote skyn Q4; goote skynnes Q1.
ii you shall] thou shalt Q4; you shall Q1.   iii on] vpon Q4; on Q1.
iv nor] or Q4; nor Q1.   v rats] and rattes Q4; rattes Q1.   vi nor] this ed.; ne Q2.
vii sluggishness] Q1, Q4; slugyshene Q2.   viii 37] this ed.; 38 Q2.

---

1 *common*] communicate verbally.
2 *epulation*] feasting or indulging in dainty food.
3 *farced*] crammed, stuffed.
4 *obnebulated*] obscured, befogged.
5 *sopited*] made drowsy or dull.
6 *malt-worm*] the weevil that infested malt used in brewing; the term was also used to describe a heavy drinker.

sword[1] for, as I said, surfeiting engendereth many infirmities, as the dropsies, the gouts, leperhead,[2] saucefleme[3] and pimples in the face, vehement impressions, undigest humours, oppilations, fevers, and putrifactions. And also it doth perturbate the head, the eyes, the tongue and the stomach, with many other infirmities. For [i]as Galen sayeth, over-much repletion or surfeiting causeth strangulation and sudden death, for (as I said) the stomach is so enfarced[4] and the liver is so sore oppressed that natural heat and the powers be extincted, wherefore abstinence for this matter is the most best and the perfect medicine that can be. And in no wise eat no meat unto the time the stomach be evacuated of all [ii]ill humours by vomit or other convenient ways, for else crude and raw humours undigested will mutiply in the body to the detriment of man. Two meals a day is sufficient for a rest man[5] and a labourer may eat three times a day, and he that doth eat after liveth a beastly life. And he that doth eat more than once in a day, I advertise him that the first refection or meal be digested ere that he do eat the second refection or meal. For there is nothing more hurtful for man's body than to eat meat upon meat undigested, for the last refection or meal will let the digestion of the first refection or meal. Also, sundry meats of diverse operations eaten at one refection or meal is not laudable, nor it is not good to sit long at dinner and supper; an hour is sufficient to sit at dinner and not so long at supper. England hath a evil use in sitting long at dinner and at supper and Englishmen hath an evil use, for at the beginning at dinner and supper [iii]they will feed on gross meats and the best [iv]meat which be wholesome, and nutritive, and [v]light of digestion is kept for servants, for when the good meat doth come to the table through feeding upon gross meat the appetite is [vi]extinct. But man's mind is so avidious,[6] although he have [vii]eaten enough, when he seethe better meat come before him against his appetite he will eat, whereupon [viii]doth come repletion and surfeits.

The tenth chapter treateth of all manner of [ix]drink, as of water, of wine, of ale, of beer, of cider, of mead, of metheglin, and of whey
Water is one of the four elements of the which diverse liquors or drinks for man's sustenance be made of, taking their original and sustenance of it, as ale, beer, mead, and metheglin. Water is not wholesome sole by itself for an Englishman considering the contrary usage which is not concurrent with nature. Water is cold, slow, and slack of digestion. The best water is rainwater, sobeit that it be clean and purely taken.

---

i as] Q4 *omits;* as Q1.   ii ill] euyll Q4; yll Q1.   iii they] he Q1.
iv meat] meates Q1.   v light] lyeth Q1.
vi extinct] extynct whan ye good meet doth come to the table Q1.
vii eaten] Q4; eat Q2; eate Q1.   viii doth] do Q4; doth Q1.   ix *drink*] drynkes Q1.

---

1 *Ecclesiasticus . . . sword*] Boorde's abbreviation "Eccle." is probably a reference to the apocryphal biblical Book of Ecclesiasticus (there is no chapter 38 in the biblical book of Ecclesiastes). I cannot locate this proverbial saying in chapter 38 of Ecclesiasticus but chapter 37 does warn against surfeit bringing death to many (37.31).
2 *leperhead*] leprosy .
3 *saucefleme*] swelling and inflamation of the face, supposedly due to salt humours.
4 *enfarced*] stuffed.
5 *a rest man*] a man who is not much given to exertion, specifically one whose job does not involve physical labour.
6 *avidious*] avid or eager.

Next to it is running water, that which doth swiftly run from the East into the West upon stones or pebbles. The third water to be praised is river or brook water, the which is clear, running on pebbles and gravel. Standing waters the which be refreshed with a fresh spring is commendable but standing waters and well waters to the which the stone hath no reflection,[1] although they be lighter than other running waters be, yet they be not so commendable. And let every man beware of all waters the which be standing and be putrified with froth, [i]duckmeat,[2] and muddy, for if they bake, or brew, or dress meat with it, it shall engender many infirmities. The water the which every man ought to dress his meat withal, or shall use baking, or brewing, let it be running and put it in vessels that it may stand there two or three hours ere it be occupied, then strain the upper part through a thick linen cloth and cast the infernal part away. If any man do use to drink water with wine let it be purely strained, and then seethe it, and after it be cold let him put it to his wine, but better it is to drink with wine stilled waters, specially the water of strawberries, or the water of bugloss, [ii]or the water of borage, or the water of endive, or the water of chicory, or the water of sow-thistle and dandelion. And if any man be cumbered[3] with the stone or doth burn in the pudibund places,[4] use to drink with white wine the water of hawes and the water of milk. Look for this [iii]water in a book of my making named *The Breviary of Health*.[5]

[iv]Of wine

All manner of wines be made of grapes except raspis [v]the which is made of a berry.[6] Choose your wine after this sort: it must be fine, fair, and clear to the eye; it must be fragrant and redolent, having a good odour and flavour in the nose; it must sprinkle in the cup when it is drawn or put out of the pot into the cup; it must be cold and pleasant in the mouth and it must be strong and subtle of substance. And then, moderately drunken, it doth actuate and doth quicken a man's wits; it doth colour the heart; it doth scour the liver, specially if it be white wine; it doth rejoice all the powers of man and doth nourish them; it doth engender good blood; it doth comfort and doth nourish the brain and all the body and it resolveth[7] phlegm; it engendereth heat and it is good against heaviness and pencifulness; it is full of agility, wherefore it is medicinable, specially white wine, for it doth mundify and cleanse wounds and

---

i duckmeat] docknet *Q4*.   ii or the water of borage] *Q4*; *Q2 omits*.
iii water] *Q4*; mater *Q2*; matter *Q1*.   iv Of] *Q4 omits*; Of *Q1*.
v the] he *Q4*; the *Q1*.

1 *to the which ... reflection*] presumably meaning water which is dark or murky so that the stone will not be reflected in it.

2 *duckmeat*] duckweed, a green plant that floats on, and covers the surface of, still water. Q4's "docknet" may mean the same thing but it does not appear in *OED*.

3 *cumbered*] encumbered, hindered.

4 *pudibund places*] shameful places, that is, the private parts.

5 The Breviary of Health] This book, as its full title indicates, was intended to help alleviate "all maner of sycknesses and diseases the which may be in man, or woman" and was first published in 1547 (STC 3373.5).

6 *raspis, the which is made of a berry*] specifically raspberries.

7 *resolveth*] dissolves, disintegrates.

sores. Furthermore, the better the wine is, the better humours it doth engender. Wine must not be too new nor too old but high wines, as malmsey, may be kept long. And because wine is full of fumosity it is good therefore to allay it with water. ⁱWines high and hot¹ ⁱⁱof operation doth comfort old men and women, but there is no wine good for children and maids, for in High Almain² there is no maid shall drink no wine but still she shall drink water ⁱⁱⁱunto she be married. The usual drink there and in other High countries for youth is fountain water, for in every town is a fountain or a shallow well to the which all people that be young and servants hath a confluence and a recourse to drink. Mean wines, as wines of Gascony, French wines, and especially Rhenish wine³ that is fined, is good with meat, specially claret wine. It is not good to drink neither wine nor ale before a man doth eat somewhat, although there be old fantastical sayings to the contrary. Also, these hot wines: as malmsey, sack, alicant,⁴ bastard,⁵ tyre,⁶ osey,⁷ muscadel, caprycke,⁸ tent,⁹ roberdany,¹⁰ with other hot wines be not good to drink with meat but after meat and with oysters, with salads, with fruit, a draught or two may be suffered. Old men may drink, as I said, high wines at their pleasure. Furthermore, all sweet wines and gross wines doth make a man fat.

ⁱᵛOf ale

Ale is made of malt and water, and they the which do put any other thing to ale than is rehearsed, except yeast, barm,¹¹ or God's good, doth sophisticate their ale. Ale for an Englishman is a natural drink. Ale must have these properties: it must be fresh and clear, it must not be ropy nor smoky, nor it must have no weft nor tail.¹² Ale should not be drunk under five days old. New ale is unwholesome for all men, and sour ale and dead ale ᵛthe which doth stand a tilt is good for no man. Barley malt maketh better ale than oaten malt or any other corn doth; it doth engender gross humours but ᵛⁱyet it maketh a man strong.

---

i Wines] Q4 *omits*; wynes Q1.   ii of] Wynes of Q4; of Q1.
iii unto] vnto the tyme Q4; vnto Q1.   iv Of] Q4 *omits*; Of Q1.
v the] and ale the Q4; the Q1.   vi yet] Q4 *omits*; yette Q1.

---

1 *high and hot*] The word 'high' is presumably a reference to the altitude at which the grapes were grown; all wine was considered hot (heating the body), with white wine less hot than those of a darker hue.
2 *Almain*] Germany.
3 *Rhenish wine*] wine from the Rhineland.
4 *alicant*] wine made at Alicante in Spain.
5 *bastard*] a sweet Spanish wine available in two colours: white and brown, or, more specifically, light brown or tawny.
6 *tyre*] a strong, sweet wine.
7 *osey*] the name used to describe any of several wines from Lisbon in Portugal or the Auxois and Alsace areas of France; these wines were probably often sweet.
8 *caprycke*] presumably meaning wines from Caprycke in Belgium.
9 *tent*] a deep red Spanish wine with a low alcohol content.
10 *roberdany*] or 'Rob-Davy', probably a transmission error of 'Ribadavia', a town in the Galicia region of Spain where this wine is produced (*OED* Ribadavia, *n.*)
11 *barm*] froth that forms on top of fermenting malt liquors, which causes fermentation in other liquors.
12 *weft nor tail*] thread-like patterns that would indicate an inferior drink.

ⁱOf beer

Beer is made of malt, of hops, and water; it is a natural drink for a Dutchman.[1] And now, of late days, it is much used in England to the detriment of many Englishmen, specially it killeth them the which be troubled with colic, and the stone, and the ⁱⁱ"strangullion,"[2] for the drink is a bold drink. Yet it doth make a man fat and doth inflate the belly, as it doth appear by the Dutch men's faces and bellies. If the beer be well ⁱⁱⁱbrewed and fined it doth qualify the heat of the liver.

ⁱᵛOf cider

Cider is made of the juice of pears, or ᵛof the juice of apples, and otherwhile[3] cider is made of both. But the best cider is made of clean pears the which be dulcet.[4] But the best is not praised in physic, for cider is cold of operation and is full of ventosity, wherefore it doth engender evil humours, and doth swage[5] too much the natural heat of man, and doth let digestion, and doth hurt the stomach; but they the which be used to it, if it be drunk in harvest, it doth little harm.

ᵛⁱOf mead

Mead is made of honey and water boiled both together. If it be fined and pure it preserveth health, but it is not good for them the which have the iliac or the colic.

ᵛⁱⁱOf metheglin

Metheglin is made of honey, and water, and herbs boiled and sodden together. If it be fined and stale it is better in the regiment of health than mead.

ᵛⁱⁱⁱOf whey

Whey, if it be well-ordered, specially ⁱˣthe whey the which doth come of butter, is a temperate drink, and is moist, and it doth nourish. It doth cleanse the breast, and doth purge red colour, and ˣis good for saucefleme[6] faces.

ˣⁱOf posset ale

Posset ale is made with hot milk and cold ale. It is a temperate drink and is good for a hot liver and for hot fevers, specially if cold herbs be sodden in it.

---

i Of] Q4 *omits*; Of Q1.   ii strangullion] strayne coylyon Q4; strangulion Q1.
iii brewed and fined] serued and be fyned & not new Q1.
iv Of] Q4 *omits*; Of Q1.   v of] Q4 *omits*; of Q1.   vi Of] Q4 *omits*; Of Q1.
vii Of] Q4 *omits*; Of Q1.   viii Of] Q4 *omits*; Of Q1.   ix the] that Q1.
x is] *this ed.*; Q2 *omits*.   xi Of] Q4 *omits*; Of Q1.

---

1 *hops ... Dutchman*] Flemish immigrants brought new brewing practices to England; beer, made with hops, soon meant that traditional English ale was considered old-fashioned.

2 *strangullion*] inflammation or swelling of the glands of the throat, known as quinsy.

3 *otherwhile*] sometimes, now and then.

4 *dulcet*] sweet to the taste or smell.

5 *swage*] assuage.

6 *saucefleme*] swelling and inflamation of the face, supposedly due to salt humours

ⁱOf coyte¹

Coyte is a drink made of water in the which is laid a sour and a salt leaven three or four hours, then it is drunk. It is a usual drink in Picardy, in Flanders, in Holland, in Brabant,² and ⁱⁱin Zeeland.³ It doth but quench the thirst.⁴

To speak of a tisane, or of oxymel, or of aqua-vitae,⁵ or of hippocras,⁶ I do pass over at this time, for I do make mention of it in *The Breviary of Health*.

The eleventh chapter treateth of bread

Avicenna sayeth that bread made of wheat maketh a man fat, specially when the bread is made of new wheat, and it doth set a man in temperance. Bread made of fine flour without leaven is slow of digestion, but it doth nourish much if it be truly ordered and well baken. When the bread is leavened it is soon digested, as some old authors sayeth, but these days is proved the contrary by the ⁱⁱⁱstomach of men, for leaven is heavy and ponderous. Bread having too much bran in it is not laudable. In Rome and other high countries their loaves of bread be little bigger than a walnut, and many little loaves be joined together the which doth serve for great men, and it is saffroned; I praise it not. I do love manchet bread⁷ and great loaves the which be well moulded and thorough-baken, the ⁱᵛbran abstracted and abjected;⁸ and that is good for all ᵛages. ᵛⁱMaslin bread is made half of wheat and half of rye, and there is also maslin made half of rye and half of barley, and ᵛⁱⁱill people will put wheat and barley together. Bread made of these aforesaid grain or corns thus poached together may fill the gut, but it shall never do good to man, no more than horse-bread or bread made of beans and peason shall do, howbeit this matter doth go much by the education or the bringing up of the people the which have been nourished or nutrified with such bread. I do speak now in barleys or malts part to be eaten and also drunken. I suppose it is too much for one grain, for barley doth engender cold humours and peason and beans, and the sustenance coming from them repleteth a man with ventosity. But ᵛⁱⁱⁱand if a man have a lust or a sensual appetite to eat and drink of a grain beside malt or barley, let him eat and drink of it the which may be made of oats, for havercakes⁹ in Scotland is many a good lord and lord's dish, and if it will make good

---

i Of] *Q4 omits;* Of *Q1.*
ii in Zeeland. It doth but quench the thirst] Selonde *Q4;* Selande *Q1.*
iii stomach] stomackes *Q4;* stomacke *Q1.*   iv bran] *this ed.;* brande *Q2*
v ages] aches *Q4;* ages *Q1.*
vi Maslin] Breade made of Mestlynge or of Rye. Mestlynge *Q4;* Mestlyng *Q1.*
vii ill] euyll *Q4;* yll *Q1.*   viii and] *Q4 omits;* and *Q1.*

1 *coyte*] from the Old Flemish *kuyte*, meaning 'thin beer'.
2 *Brabant*] the Duchy of Brabant, a historic region in the Low Countries.
3 *Zeeland*] Boorde spells this word "Selande". He is probably referring to Zeeland, a province in the Netherlands, but he could be referring to Zealand, the largest island of Denmark.
4 *It doth but quench the thirst*] that is, it is not medicinal.
5 *aqua-vitae*] water of life (Latin); any form in which ardent spirits, such as whisky or brandy, have been drunk.
6 *hippocras*] a cordial drink made of wine flavoured with spices.
7 *manchet bread*] the finest wheaten bread.
8 *abstracted and abjected*] taken away, rejected.
9 *havercakes*] oatcakes.

havercakes consequently it will ⁱmake good drink or evil, everything as it is handled. For it is a common proverb, God may send a man good meat but the devil may send ⁱⁱevil cooks to destroy it. ⁱⁱⁱBut wives, and maids, and other brewers the which doth destroy malt the which should make good ale,[1] and they the which that doth not fill their pots, giving false measure, I would they were clacking their pots and tankards at Dimmingsdale.[2] And evil bakers, the which doth not make good bread of wheat, but will mingle other corn with wheat, or do not order and season it giving good weight, I would they might play bo-peep through a pillory,[3] for good bread doth comfort, confirm,[4] and ^{iv}doth stablish a man's heart. Beside the properties rehearsed, hot bread is unwholesome for any man for it doth lie in the stomach like a sponge, hastening undecoct[5] humours, yet the smell of new bread is comfortable to the head and to the heart.

Sodden bread, as symnels, and cracknels, and bread that saffron is in, is not laudable. Burnt bread, and hard crusts, and pasty crusts doth engender choler adust and melancholy humours, wherefore chip the upper crust of your bread.[6] And whoso doth use to eat the second crust after meat, it maketh a man lean and so doth wheaten bread, the which is full of ^vbran.

Bread the which is nutritive and praised in physic should have these properties: first it must ^{vi}not be new but a day and a night old, nor it is not good when it is past four or five days old, except the loaves be great, nor it must not be mouldy nor musty. It must be well ^{vii}moulded,[7] it must be ^{viii}thorough-baked, it must be light and not heavy, and it must be temperately salted. Old bread or stale bread doth dry up the blood or natural ^{ix}moisture of man, and it doth engender evil humours and is evil

---

i make] do make *Q1*; make *Q4*.   ii evil cooks] an euyll coke *Q1*.
iii But wives and maids . . . pillory] *Q1 omits*; see explanatory note for Q1's alternative passage.
iv doth] *Q4 omits*; doth *Q1*.   v bran] *this ed.*; brande *Q2*.
vi not] *Q4*; *Q2, Q1 omit*.   vii moulded] *Q1* (muldyd*)*; mylded *Q2*.
viii thorough-baked] *O6*; thorowe bake *Q2*.   ix moisture] moyst *Q4*; moyster *Q1*.

---

1 *wives and maids . . . good ale*] Women, known as ale-wives or brewsters, were the main producers of ale before men began to dominate production in the sixteenth century. Brewsters had a reputation for diluting their ale and other disreputable practices (Bennett 1996).

2 *I would . . . at Dimmingsdale*] Dimmingsdale is in North Staffordshire. Boorde here alludes to the invocation of witches in *Thersites*, an interlude written about 1537, probably by Nicholas Udall; it refers to the "wytches that walke in Dymminges dale / Clytteringe and clatteringe there youre pottes with ale" (Udall and Textor 1562, D2v).

3 *But wives and maids . . . pillory*] In Q1 this reads as follows: "wherefore gentyll bakers sophystycate not your breade made of pure whete, yf you do where euyl ale brewers and ale wyues for theyr euyl brewing & euyl measure, shuld clacke and ryng theyr tankardes at dym myls dale, I wold you shuld shake out the remnaunt of your sackes standyne in the tēmes [thames] up to the harde chynne and iii inches aboue, and whan you do come out of the water you myght shake your eares as a spanyell that veryly co[m]meth out of the water. Gentyll bakers make good breade for good breade."

4 *confirm*] strengthen, invigorate.

5 *undecoct*] undigested.

6 *chip . . . bread*] cut off the best bit of the bread (the upper crust) to eat, not the over-cooked or burnt bread at the bottom of the loaf. The phrase "upper crust" refers to the social elite and presumably means those who would have eaten the best bits of bread.

7 *moulded*] kneaded.

and tardy of digestion, wherefore there is no surfeit so evil as the surfeit of eating of evil bread.

The twelfth chapter treateth of pottage, of sew,¹ of stewpots, of gruel, of frumenty,² of pease pottage, of almond milk, of rice pottage, of caudles, of cullises, and of other broths

All manner of liquid things, as pottage, sew, and all other broths, doth replete a man that eateth them with ventosity. Pottage is not so much used in all Christendom as it is used in England. Pottage is made of the liquor in the which flesh is ⁱsodden in, with putting to chopped herbs and oatmeal and salt. The herbs with the which pottage is made withal, if they be pure, good, and clean, not ⁱⁱworm-eaten nor infected with the corrupt air descending upon them, doth comfort many men, the ventosity notwithstanding. But forasmuch as diverse times many parts of England is infected with the pestilence, through the corruption of the air the which doth infect the herbs, in such times it is not good to make ⁱⁱⁱany pottage nor to eat no pottage. In certain places beyond sea, whereas I have travelled in, in the pestilence time a general commandment hath been sent from the superiority to the commonality that no man should eat herbs in such infectious times.

ⁱᵛOf sew³ and stewpots

Sew and stewpots and gruel made with oatmeal, in the which no herbs be put in, can do little displeasure except ᵛit doth replete a man with ventosity but it relaxeth the belly.

ᵛⁱOf frumenty

Frumenty is made of wheat and ᵛⁱⁱmilk. It is hard of digestion but when it is digested it doth nourish and it doth ᵛⁱⁱⁱstrengthen a man. ⁱˣBut flesh sodded⁴ in milk is not commendable.

ˣOf pease pottage and bean pottage

Pease pottage and bean pottage doth replete a man with ventosity. Pease pottage is better than bean pottage for it is sooner digested and lesser of ventosity. They both be abstertive and do cleanse the body; they be competent of nutriment but bean-pottage doth increase gross humours.

---

i sodden] sod *Q4*; soden *Q1*.
ii worm-eaten] *Q4 (worme eaten)*; wanne eaten *Q2*; warme eaten *Q1*.
iii any] *Q4 omits*; any *Q1*.   iv Of] *Q4 omits*; Of *Q1*.
v it] that it *Q1*.   vi Of] *Q4 omits*; Of *Q1*.
vii milk] mylke, in the whiche yf flesh be soden, to eate it is not cōmendable, for *Q1*.
viii strengthen] *Q4*; strength *Q2, Q1*.   ix But . . . commendable] *Q1 omits*.
x Of] *Q4 omits*; Of *Q1*.

---

1 *sew*] stew, pottage.
2 *frumenty*] hulled-wheat boiled in milk and seasoned with sugar, cinnamon etc.
3 *sew*] stew, pottage.
4 *sodded*] soaked.

[i]Of almond milk and [ii]of rice pottage

Almond milk and rice pottage [iii]be hot and moist, it doth comfort the breast and it doth mollify the belly and provoketh urine. Rice pottage made with almond milk doth restore and doth comfort nature.

[iv]Of ale-brews, caudles, and cullises

Ale-brews, caudles, and cullises for weak men and [v]feeble stomachs, the which cannot eat solidate[1] meat, is suffered. But caudles made with hempseed and cullises made of shrimps doth comfort blood and nature.

[vi]Of honeysops and other broths

Honeysops and other broths, of what kind or substance so ever they be made of, they [vii]doth engender ventosity, wherefore they be not good nor wholesome for the colic, nor [viii]the iliac, nor other inflative impediments or sicknesses, specially if honey be in it, the sayings of Pliny, Galen, Avicenna, with other authors, notwithstanding. For in these days experience teacheth us contrary to their sayings and [ix]writings, for although the nature of man be not altered, yet it is weaker and nothing so strong now as when they lived [x]and did practise and making their books.

The thirteenth chapter treateth of white meat, as of eggs, butter, cheese, milk, and cream, et cetera

In England there is no eggs used to be eaten but hen eggs, wherefore I will first write and pertract[2] of hen eggs. The yolks of hen eggs be cordials, for it is temperately hot; the white of an egg is viscous, and cold, and slack of digestion, and doth not engender good blood. Wherefore whosoever that will eat an [xi]egg, let the egg be new and roast him rear and eat him or else poach him, for poached eggs be best at night and new rear, roasted eggs be good in the morning, sobeit they be tired[3] with a little salt and sugar that they be [xii]nutritive. In Turkey and other high Christian lands annexed to it [xiii]they use to seethe two or three bushels of eggs together hard, and pull off the shells, [xiv]and souse[4] them, and keep them to eat at all times; but hard eggs be slow and slack of digestion and doth nutrify the body grossly. Roasted eggs be better than sodden, fried eggs be naught; duck eggs and [xv]goose eggs I do not praise but pheasant eggs and partridge eggs physic doth singularly praise.

---

i Of] *Q4 omits*; Of *Q1*. ii of] *Q4 omits*; of *Q1*. iii be] *this ed.*; Almons be *Q2*.
iv Of] *Q4 omits*; of *Q1*. v feeble] fell *Q4*; feble *Q1*. vi Of] *Q4 omits*; Of *Q1*.
vii doth] do *Q4*; doth *Q1*. viii the] *Q4 omits*; the *Q1*.
ix writings] writing *Q4*; wrytyngz *Q1*.
x and did practise and making their books] &c. *Q1*. xi egg] Henne egge *Q4*; egge *Q1*.
xii nutritive] nutryue *Q1*. xiii they] *Q4 omits*; they *Q1*.
xiv and] *Q4 omits*; & *Q1*. xv goose] gese *Q1*.

---

1 solidate] solid.
2 pertract] treat of in narration, from the Latin *pertractare* meaning to handle, to examine in detail, study carefully.
3 tired] dressed; OED records this meaning in relation to venison (tire, *v.*[1] 4).
4 souse] pickle.

ⁱOf butter

Butter ⁱⁱmade of cream ⁱⁱⁱis moist of operation, it is good to eat in the morning before other meats. French men will eat it after meat, but eaten with other meat it doth not only nourish but it is good for the breast and lungs and also it ⁱᵛdoth relax and ᵛdoth mollify the belly. Dutch men doth eat it at all times in the day, the which I did not praise when I did dwell ᵛⁱamong them considering that butter is unctuous and everything that is unctuous is noisome to the stomach forasmuch as it maked lubrifaction.¹ And also, everything that is unctuous, that is to say butterish: oil, grease or fats, doth swim above in the brinks² of the stomach as the fatness doth swim about in a boiling pot. The excess of such natation³ or superfice⁴ will ascend to the ᵛⁱⁱorifice of the stomach and doth make executions, wherefore eating of much butter at one refection is not commendable, nor it is not good for them the which be in any ague or fever, for the ventosity of it doth ᵛⁱⁱⁱauge and augment the heat of the liver. A little portion is good for every man in the morning if it be new made.

ⁱˣOf cheese

Cheese is made of milk. ˣThere be four sorts of cheese, which ˣⁱis to say, green cheese, soft cheese, hard cheese ˣⁱⁱand spermyse. Green cheese is not called green by the reason of ˣⁱⁱⁱthe colour but for the newness of it, for the whey is not half pressed out of it and in operation it is cold and moist. Soft cheese, not too new nor too old, is best, for in operation it is hot and moist. Hard cheese is hot and dry and evil to digest. Spermyse is a cheese the which is made with curds and with the juice of herbs; to tell the nature of it I cannot, considering that every milk-wife⁵ may put many juices of herbs of sundry operation and vertue, one not agreeing with another. But and if they did know what they did gomble⁶ together without true compounding, and I knowing the herbs, then I could tell the operation of spermyse cheese. Yet beside these four natures of cheese there is a cheese called a ˣⁱᵛruen cheese⁷ the which, if it be well-ordered, doth pass all other cheeses (none excess taken). But take the best cheese of all cheese rehearsed, if a little do good and pleasure the overplus⁸ doth engender gross humours, for it is hard of digestion, it maketh a man costive, and it is not good for the stone. Cheese that is good ought not to be hard nor too soft but betwixt both,

---

i Of] *Q4 omits*; Of *Q1*.   ii made] is made *Q4*; made *Q1*.   iii is] and is *Q1*.
iv doth] *Q1 omits*; doth *Q4*.   v doth] *Q1 omits*.   vi among] amonges *Q4*; amonge *Q1*.
vii orifice] oryse *Q1*; oryfe *Q4*.   viii auge and] *Q4 omits*; auge and *Q1*.
ix Of] *Q4 omits*; Of *Q1*.   x There be] yet there is *Q1*.   xi is] *Q4*; be *Q2*.
xii and] or *Q4*; and *Q1*.   xiii the] *Q1 omits*.   xiv ruen] Ieueue *Q4*; rewene *Q1*.

---

1 *lubrifaction*] lubrication, that is, slippery or smooth.
2 *brinks*] brim, edge.
3 *natation*] that which swims or floats.
4 *superfice*] the surface of an object, the material forming this.
5 *milk-wife*] Women were the main producers of dairy produce.
6 *gomble*] compound (*OED* compounding, *n.*).
7 *ruen cheese*] a kind of soft cheese.
8 *overplus*] too much, an excessive amount.

it should not be tough nor brotel,[1] it ought not to be sweet nor sour, nor tart, nor too salt, nor too fresh. It must be of good savour and tallage,[2] [i]not full of eyes nor mites nor maggots. Yet in High Almain[3] the cheese the which is full of maggots is called there the best cheese, and they will eat the great maggot as fast as we do eat comfits.

[ii]Of milk

Milk of a woman[4] and the milk of a goat is a good restorative, wherefore these milks be good for them that be in a consumption; and for the great temperance the which is in them it doth nourish much.

Cow's milk and ewe's milk, so [iii]it be that the beasts be young and do go in good pasture, the milk is nutritive and doth humect and moisteth the members, and doth mundify and cleanse the entrails, and doth alleviate and mitigate the pain of the lungs and the breast. But it is not good for them the which have gurgulations in the belly nor it is not all the best for sanguine men, but it is very good for melancholy men and for old men and children, specially if it be sodden, adding to it a little sugar.

[iv]Of cream

Cream the which doth not stand long on the milk and sodden with a little sugar is nourishing. Clouted[5] cream and raw cream[6] put together is eaten more for a sensual appetite than for any good nourishment. Raw cream, undecocted,[7] eaten with strawberries or hurts,[8] is a rural man's banquet; I have known such banquets hath put men in jeopardy of their lives.[9]

Almond butter

Almond butter made with fine sugar, and good rose water, and eaten with the flowers of many violets is a commendable dish, specially in Lent when the violets be fragrant. It rejoiceth the heart, it doth comfort the brain, and doth qualify the heat of the liver.

---

i not] nor Q1.   ii Of] Q4 omits; Of Q1.
iii it be that] it be the Q1; be it the Q4.   iv Of] Q4 omits; Of Q1.

---

1 *brotel*] brittle, easily broken.
2 *tallage*] taste.
3 *Almain*] Germany.
4 *milk of a woman*] Boorde is typical of dietary authors in praising female breast milk as a medicinal drink for adults as well as children.
5 *clouted*] clotted.
6 *raw cream*] cream that forms naturally on the top of the milk, as opposed to that produced by heating milk.
7 *undecoted*] undigested.
8 *hurts*] hurtleberries; also known as whortleberries or bilberries.
9 *hath ... lives*] It seems to be the cream rather than the strawberries, or the foods combined, that Boorde is warning against since he praises strawberries later in his *Compendious Regiment* (the twenty-first chapter). However, Thomas Muffett in *Health's Improvement* warns against eating too many strawberries, noting that the Duke of Brunswick "is recorded to have burst a sunder ... with surfeiting upon them" (Muffett 1655, Gg3r).

Bean-butter

Bean-butter is used much in Lent in diverse countries. It is good for ploughmen to fill the paunch,[1] it doth engender gross humours, [i]it doth replete a man with ventosity.

The fourteenth chapter treateth of fish

Of all nations and countries England is best served of fish: not only of all manner of sea-fish, but also of fresh-water fish, and of all manner of sorts of [ii]salt fish.

[iii]Of sea-fish

Fishes of the sea, the which have scales or many fins, be more wholesome than the fresh-water fish the which be in standing waters. The [iv]elder a fish is, so much he is the better, sobeit that the fish be soft and not solidate.[2] If the fish be salt and solidate, the younger the fish is, the better it is to digest. But this is to understand that if the fish be never so solidate, it must have age but not overgrown, except it be a young porpoise,[3] the which kind of fish is neither praised in the Old Testament nor in physic.[4]

Fresh-water fish

The fish the which is in rivers and brooks be more wholesomer than they the which be in pools, ponds, or moats, or any other standing [v]water, for they doth labour and doth scour themself. Fish the which liveth and doth feed on the mud or else doth feed in the fen or moorish[5] ground doth savour of the mud, which is not so good as the fish that feedeth and doth scour themself on the stones, or gravel, or sand.

[vi]Of salt fish

[vii]Salt fish the which be powdered and salted with salt be not greatly to be praised, specially if a man do make his whole refection with it. The quality doth not hurt but the quantity, specially such salt fishes as will cleave to the fingers when a man doth eat it. And the skin of fishes be utterly to be abhorred for it doth engender viscous phlegm, and choler adust. All manner of fish is cold of nature and doth engender

---

i it] and Q4; it Q1. ii salt fish] salte fysshes Q4; salte fysshe Q1.
iii Of] Q4 omits; Of Q1. iv elder] older Q4; elder Q1.
v water] waters Q4; water Q1. vi Of salt fish] Salte fysshes Q4; Of salte fysshe Q1.
vii Salt fish] salte fysshes Q4; Salte fysshe Q1.

---

1 *paunch*] stomach.

2 *solidate*] solid, hard.

3 *porpoise*] As Ove Fossa noted, "Porpoise was a cherished dish in the finest medieval households both in France and England" (Fossa 1995, 81).

4 *the which kind ... in physic*] not a fish, of course, but a mammal related to whales and dolphins. Perhaps Boorde is referring to the biblical Pentateuch or five books of Moses (Genesis, Exodus, Leviticus, Numbers, and Deuteronomy) that dictate what Jews may eat. From the water anything that has fins and scales may be consumed (Leviticus 11.9: Deuteronomy 14.9) so fish like tuna, carp, salmon, and herring are permitted but shell-fish such as lobsters, oysters, shrimp, clams, and crabs are forbidden. Since the porpoise has fins (although finless porpoise also exist) and thus is allowed as a foodstuff, it is not clear why he thinks it is not praised.

5 *moorish*] boggy, marshy.

phlegm; it doth little nourish. Fish and flesh ought not to be eaten together at one meal.

The fifteenth chapter treateth of wild fowl and tame fowl [i]birds

Of all wild fowl the pheasant [ii]is most best, although that a partridge of all fowls is soonest digested, wherefore it is a restorative meat and doth comfort the brain, and the stomach, and doth augment carnal lust. A woodcock is a meat of good temperance, quails and plovers and lapwings doth[1] nourish but little for they doth engender melancholy humours, young turtle doves doth engender good blood. A crane is hard of digestion and doth engender evil blood; a young heronsew[2] is lighter of digestion than a crane. A bustard (well killed and ordered) is a nutritive meat, a bittern is not so hard of digestion as is an heronsew, a shoveler is lighter of digestion than a bittern. All these be noyful except they be well-ordered and dressed. A pheasant hen, a moorcock, and a moorhen (except they [iii]suit abroad)[3] they be nutritive. All manner of wild fowl the which liveth by the water, they be of discommendable[4] nourishment.

Of tame or domestical fowl

Of all tame fowl a capon is most best, for it is nutritive and is soon digested. A hen in winter is good and nutritive and so [iv]is a chicken in summer, specially cockerels and pullets[5] the which be untrodden.[6] The flesh of a cock is hard of digestion, but the broth [v]or jelly made of a cock is restorative. Pigeons be good for choleric and melancholy men; goose flesh and duck flesh is not praised except it be a young, green goose. Young peachicken[7] of half a year of age be praised; old peacocks be hard of digestion.

Of birds

All manner of small birds be good and light of digestion except sparrows, which be hard of digestion. Titmouses, coalmouses,[8] and wrens, the which doth eat spiders and poison, be not [vi]commendable. Of all small birds the lark is best, then [vii]praised the blackbird and the [viii]thrush. Rasis and Isaac praise the young stares,[9] but I do think because they be bitter in eating they should engender choler.

---

i birds] and byrdes Q4; byrdes Q1.   ii is] Q1; it Q2.
iii suit] be sutt Q1; do syt Q4.   iv is a] be Q4; is a Q1.   v or] of Q1; or a Q4.
vi commendable] cōmestyble Q4; cōmēdable Q1.   vii praised] is praysed Q1.
viii thrush] Thrusshes Q4; Thrusshe Q1.

---

1 *doth*] Boorde uses this form of the verb 'to do' even with plural subjects and his usage is not corrected here.
2 *heronsew*] a little or young heron.
3 *suit abroad*] have recourse to the open air; the sense is that the birds are free-range.
4 *discommendable*] inadvisable, not recommended.
5 *pullets*] young domestic hens.
6 *untrodden*] virginal.
7 *peachicken*] young peafowl (plural) (*OED* peachick, *n.* 1).
8 *titmouses, coalmouses*] both small birds.
9 *stares*] starlings.

The sixteenth chapter treateth of flesh of wild and tame beasts
Beef is good meat for an Englishman sobeit the beast be young and that it be not cow-flesh, for old beef and cow-flesh [i]doth engender melancholy and leprous humours. If it be moderately powdered, that the gross blood by salt may be exhausted, it doth make an Englishman strong, the education of him with it considered. Martinmas beef,[1] which is called hanged beef in the roof of the smokey house, is not laudable; it may fill the belly and cause a man to drink, but it is evil for the stone and evil of digestion and maketh no good juice. If a man have a piece hanging [ii]by his side and another in his belly, that the which doth hang by the side shall do [iii]him more good if a shower of rain do chance[2] that that the which is [iv]in his belly, the appetite of man's sensuality nothwithstanding.

[v]*Of veal*[3]
Veal is [vi]nutritive meat and doth nourish much a man for it is soon digested, whereupon many men doth hold opinion that it is the best flesh and the most nutritive meat that can be for man's sustenance.

[vii]*Of mutton and lamb*
Mutton of Rasis and Averroes is praised for a good meat, but Galen doth not laud it and surely I do not love it, considering that there [viii]is no beast that is so soon infected nor there doth happen so great murrain[4] and sickness to any quadruped beast as doth [ix]fall to the sheep. This notwithstanding, if the sheep be brought up in a good pasture, and fat and, do not flavour of the wool it is good for sick persons for it doth engender good blood.

Lamb's flesh is moist and phlegmatic, wherefore it is not all the best for old men except they be melancholy of complexion, nor [x]it is not good for phlegmatic men to feed too much of it [xi]for the flesh is waterish.

[xii]*Of pork, brawn, bacon, and pig*
Whereas Galen, with other ancient and approbate[5] doctors, doth praise pork, I dare not say the contrary against them, but this I am sure of, I did never love it. And in

---

i doth] do Q4; doth Q1.   ii by his side] besyde Q4; by his syde Q1.
iii him] a man Q4; hym Q1.   iv in his belly] within the bely Q4; in his bely Q1.
v Of veal] Veale Q4; Of veale Q1.   vi nutritive] a nutrytyue Q4; nutrytyue Q1.
vii Of] Q4 omits; Of Q1.   viii is] this ed.; it Q2.   ix fall] Q4 omits; fall Q1.
x it] Q4; bit Q2; it Q1.   xi for the flesh is waterish] doth hurte Q1; Q4 omits.
xii Of] Q4 omits; Of Q1.

1 *Martinmas*] salted beef; cattle were commonly slaughtered and salted for the winter on the feast of St Martin (11 November).
2 *that the which doth hang . . . do chance*] a man would be better off using the piece of beef as an impromptu umbrella than eating it.
3 *Of veal . . . man's sustenance*] In Q4 the section on veal appears between the section "Of mutton and lamb" and the section "Of pork, brawn, bacon, and pig".
4 *murrain*] infectious disease.
5 *approbate*] approved.

holy scripture it is not praised, for a swine is an unclean beast,[1] and doth lie [i]upon filthy and stinking soils, and with stercorous[2] matter diverse times [ii]doth feed [iii]in England. Yet [iv]High Almaine and other high countries, except Spain and other countries annexed to Spain, doth keep their swine clean and doth cause them once or twice a day to swim in great rivers like the water of Rhine, which is above Cologne. But Spaniards, with the other regions annexed to them, keep the swine more filthier than English persons doth. Furthermore, the Jew, the Saracen, the Turks, concerning their politic wit and learning in physic hath as much wisdom, reason, and knowledge to the [v]safety of their body as any Christian man hath. And [vi]many expert physicians I have known amongst them, yet they all lacked grace forasmuch as they do not know or knowledge Jesus Christ, as the holy scripture telleth us and them. They [vii]loveth not pork nor swine's flesh but doth vituperate[3] and doth abhor it, yet for all this they will [viii]eat adders, which is a kind of serpents, as well as any other Christian man dwelling in Rome and other high countries, for adders' flesh there is called flesh of the mountain. This notwithstanding, physic doth approbate adders' flesh good to be eaten, saying it doth make an old man young, as it appeareth by an hart eating an adder maketh him young again. But pork doth not so, for if it be of an old hog, not clean kept, it doth engender gross blood and doth humect too much the stomach; yet if the pork be young it is nutritive.

Bacon is good for carters and ploughmen, the which be ever labouring in the earth or dung, but and if they have the stone and use to eat it they shall sing "woe be [ix]the pie". Wherefore I do say that collops[4] and eggs is as wholesome for them as a tallow candle[5] is good for a horse-mouth or a piece of powdered beef is good for a blue-eyed mare. Yet sensual appetite must have a swinge,[6] [x]all these things [xi]notwithstanding.

[xii]Of brawn

Brawn is a usual meat in winter amongst Englishmen; it is hard of digestion. The brawn of a wild boar is much more better than the brawn of a tame boar; if a man eat neither of them both it shall never do him harm.

---

i upon] vpon, in Q4; vpon Q1.   ii doth] it doth Q4; doth Q1.
iii in] specyallye in Q4; in Q1.   iv High] Q4; in High Q2, Q1.
v safety] sanyte Q4; sauyte Q1.   vi many expert] noble Q1.
vii loveth] loue Q4; louyth Q1.   viii eat] rate Q1; eat Q4.
ix the pie] to the pie Q4; the pie Q1.   x all] at allQ4; all Q1.
xi notwithstanding] notwithstandynge, porke is conuertyble to mans flesshe Q1.
xii Of] Q4 omits; Of Q1.

---

1 *holy scripture ... unclean beast*] The Pentateuch, or five books of Moses (Genesis, Exodus, Leviticus, Numbers, and Deuteronomy), dictates that Jews may eat any animal that has cloven hooves and chews its cud (Leviticus 11.3; Deuteronomy 14.6), which does not include the pig because it has cloven hooves but does not ruminate and thus is considered unclean.
  2 *stercorous*] consisting of, or containing, faeces.
  3 *vituperate*] speak ill of, find fault with.
  4 *collops*] bacon.
  5 *tallow candle*] a candle made from animal fat.
  6 *swinge*] rule, authority, influence.

ⁱOf pigs¹

Pigs, specially sow pigs, is nutritive and made in a jelly it is ⁱⁱrestorative, sobeit the pig be flayed,² the skin ⁱⁱⁱtaken off, and then stewed with restoratives, as a cock is stewed to make a jelly. A young, fat pig in physic is singularly praised if it be well-ordered in the roasting, the skin not eaten.

^{iv}Of kid

Young kid's flesh is praised above all other flesh, as Avicenna, Rasis, and Averroes sayeth, for it is temperate and nutritive although it be somewhat dry; old kid is not praised.

Of wild beasts' flesh

I have gone round about Christendom, and overthwart³ Christendom, and a thousand or two and more miles out of Christendom, yet there is not so much pleasure for hart and hind, buck and doe, and for roebuck and doe⁴ as is in England. And although the flesh be dispraised in physic, I pray God to send me part of the flesh to eat, physic notwithstanding. The opinion of all old physicans was and is that venison is not good to eat, principally for two causes. The first cause is that ^vthe beast doth live in fear, for if he be a good woodman⁵ he shall never see no kind of deer but at the ten bite on the grass or browsing⁶ on the tree but he will lift up his head and look about him, the which cometh of timorousness, and timorousness doth bring in melancholy humours. Wherefore all physicans sayeth that venison, which is the second cause, doth engender choleric humours, and of truth it doth so, wherefore let them take the skin and let me have the flesh. I am sure it is a lord's dish and I am sure it is good for an Englishman, for it doth animate him to be as he is, which is strong and hardy. But I do advertise every man for all my words not to kill and so to eat of it except it be ^{vi}lawful, for it is a meat for great men, and great men do not set so much by the meat as they ^{vii}do by the pastime of killing of it.

^{viii}Of hares' flesh

A hare doth no harm ^{ix}nor displeasure to man if the flesh be not eaten, yet he maketh gentlemen good pastime.⁷ And better it is for the hounds or dogs to eat the hare after

---

i Of] *Q4 omits;* Of *Q1.*   ii restorative] a restorative *Q4;* restorative *Q1.*
iii taken] take *Q4;* taken *Q1.*   iv Of] *Q4 omits;* Of *Q1.*
v the beast] he the beast *Q4;* the beest *Q1.*   vi lawful] lefully *Q1.*
vii do] doth *Q4;* do *Q1.*   viii Of] *Q4 omits;* Of *Q1.*   ix nor] nor no *Q4;* nor *Q1.*

---

1 *Of pigs*] It is not clear why Boorde did not include this discussion of pigs (and the separate discussion of brawn) in the earlier section "Of pork, brawn, bacon, and pig".
2 *flayed*] skinned.
3 *overthwart*] across.
4 *hart and hind, . . . roebuck and doe*] male and female deer.
5 *woodman*] huntsman.
6 *at the ten bit . . . on the tree*] presumably meaning after the deer has taken ten bites from the grass or fed from the tree.
7 *he maketh gentlemen good pastime*] that is, in hunting.

they have killed [i]it than man should eat it, for it is not praised neither in the Old Testament, neither in physic, for the Bible sayeth the hare is an unclean beast.[1] And physic sayeth hares' flesh is dry and doth engender melancholy humours.

[ii]Of conies' flesh [iii]and rabbits

Conies' flesh is good but rabbits' flesh is best of all wild beasts for it is temperate, and doth nourish, and singularly praised in physic; for all things the which doth suck is nutritive.[2]

The seventeenth chapter doth treat of particular things of fish and flesh

The heads of fish and the fatness of fish, specially of salmon and conger, is not good for them the which be disposed to have rheumatic heads. And the heads of lampreys and lamperns, and the string the which is within them, is not good to eat. Refrain from eating of the [iv]skins of fish and flesh, and [v]burned meat, and brown meat[3] for it doth engender viscous humours, and choler, and melancholy, and doth make oppilations. The brains of any beast is not laudable except the brains of a kid, for it is evil of digestion, and doth hurt a man's appetite and the stomach, for it is cold and moist and viscous; a hot stomach may eat it but it doth engender gross humours. The brain of a woodcock, and of a snipe, and such like is comestible.[4] The fore-part of all manner of beasts and fowls be more hotter and lighter of digestion than the hinder parts be. The marrow of all beasts is hot and moist; it is nutritive if it be well digested, yet it doth molify the stomach and doth take away a man's appetite, wherefore let a man eat pepper with it. The blood of all beasts and fowls is not praised for it is hard of digestion. All the inwards of beasts and fowls – as the heart, the liver, the lungs, and tripes, and trillibubs,[5] with all the entrails – is hard of digestion and doth increase gross humours. The fatness of flesh is not so much nutritive as the leans of flesh; it is best when lean and fat is mixed one with another. The tongues of beasts be hard of digestion and of little nourishment. The stones of a cockerel and the stones of other beasts that hath not done their kind[6] be nutritive.

---

i it] it, as I sayd *Q1*.   ii Of] *Q4* omits; Of *Q1*.   iii and rabbits] *Q1* omits.
iv skins of fish and flesh] kynnes of fysshe, and flesshe *Q1*; skynnes of flesshe and fysshe *Q4*.
v burned] bornet *Q1*; burned *Q4*.

---

1 *for the Bible . . . beast*] The Pentateuch, or five books of Moses (Genesis, Exodus, Leviticus, Numbers, and Deuteronomy), dictates that Jews may eat any animal that has cloven hooves and chews its cud (Leviticus 11.3; Deuteronomy 14.6), which does not include the hare because it ruminates but has no cloven hooves and thus is considered unclean.

2 *all things . . . nutritive*] The term "rabbit" referred specifically to the animal's young, especially those still sucking from their mother.

3 *burned meat and brown meat*] in Q1's "bornet meate, and browne meate" the word "bornet" could mean "burnet", that is, "of a dark brown colour" (*OED* burnet, *adj.*); this word was perhaps changed to "borned", the Middle English spelling of "burned", in Q2 so as to avoid repetition of brown.

4 *comestible*] edible.

5 *trillibubs*] entrails; the repetition ("trillibubs, with all the entrails") is typical of Boorde and apparently for rhetorical effect.

6 *not done their kind*] not been used in copulation.

The eighteenth chapter treateth of roast meat, of fried meat, ⁱof sodden or boiled meat, of broiled meat, and of bake-meat

With us as Montpellier and other universities is used boiled meat at dinner and roast meat to supper. Why they should do so I cannot tell unless it be for a consuetude,[1] for boiled meat is lighter of digestion than roasted meat is; broiled meat is hard of digestion and evil for the stone; fryed meat is harder of digestion than broiled meat is and doth engender choler and melancholy; bake-meat,[2] which is called flesh that is buried, for it is buried in paste, is not praised in physic. All manner of flesh the which is inclined to humidity should be roasted and all flesh the which is inclined to dryness should be sodden or boiled. Fish may be sod, roasted, broiled and baken, every one after their kind, and use a fashion[3] of the country as the cook and the physician will agree and devise. For a good cook is half a physican, for the chief physic (the counsel of a physician except) doth come from the kitchen, wherefore the physician and the cook for sick men must consult together for the preparation of ⁱⁱmeat for sick men. For if the physican without the cook ⁱⁱⁱprepare any meat, except he be very expert, he will make a wearish[4] dish of meat the which the sick cannot not take.

The nineteenth chapter treateth of roots, and first of the roots ⁱᵛof borage and ᵛ*bugloss*

The roots of borage and bugloss, sodden tender and made in a succade, doth engender good blood and doth set a man in a temperance.

The roots of alexander[5] and elecampane

The roots of alexander, sodden tender and made in ᵛⁱa succade, is good for to destroy the stone in the reins of the back and bladder. The roots of elecampane, sodden tender and made in a succcade, is good for the breast, and for the lungs, and for all the internal members of man.

The roots of parsley and of fennel

The roots of parsley, sodden tender and made in a succade, is good for the stone and doth make a man to piss. The roots of fennel, sodden tender and made in a succade, is good for the lungs and for the sight.

---

i *of sodden or boiled meat, of broiled meat*] Q4 *(of soden or boyled meate, of bruled meate)*; Q2, Q1 *omit*.
ii *meat*] meates Q3, Q4; meate Q1.   iii *prepare*] proper Q3.
iv *of*] Q1 *omits*; of Q4.   v *bugloss*] of bugloss Q1.   vi *a*] Q3 *omits*.

1 *consuetude*] custom, habit.
2 *bake-meat*] a pie, as in *Hamlet*: "The funeral baked meats / Did coldly furnish forth the marriage tables" (Shakespeare 1988, 1.2.179–80).
3 *fashion*] method, way of doing things.
4 *wearish*] lacking in flavour, tastless.
5 *alexander*] horse-parsley.

The roots of turnips and parsnips

Turnips boiled and eaten with flesh augmenteth the seed of man; if they be eaten raw, moderately, it doth provoke a good appetite. Parsnips sodden and eaten doth increase nature; they be nutritive and doth expel urine.

Radish roots and carrots

Radish roots [i]doth break wind and doth provoke a man to make water, but they be not good for them the which hath the gout. Carrots sodden and eaten doth auge and increase nature and doth cause a man to make water.

The roots of rapes

Rape roots, if they be well boiled, they do nourish, if they be moderately eaten; [ii]immoderately eaten they [iii]doth engender ventosity and doth annoy the stomach.

[iv]Of onions

Onions doth provoke a man to venerous acts and [v]to somnolence,[1] and if a man drink sundry drinks it doth rectify and reform the [vi]variety of the operation of them. They maketh a man's appetite good and putteth away fastidiousness.[2]

[vii]Of leeks

Leeks doth open the breast and doth provoke a man to make water, but they doth make and increase evil blood.

[viii]Of garlic

Garlic of all roots is used and most praised in Lombardy and other countries annexed to it, for it doth open the breast and it doth kill all manner of worms in a man's belly, which be to say lumbrici, ascarides[3] and cucurbitini, which is to say long worms, small little long worms, which will tickle in the fundament, and square worms. [ix]It also heateth the body and dissolveth gross winds.

The twentieth chapter treateth [x]of herbs, and first of borage and bugloss

Borage doth comfort the heart, and doth engender good blood, and cause a man to be merry, and doth set a man in [xi]temperance; and so doth bugloss, for he is taken of more vigour, and strength, and efficacy.

---

i doth break] breketh Q3. ii immoderately] immedyatly Q3.
iii doth] do Q4.   iv Of] Q3, Q4 omit; Of Q1.   v to] Q3 omits.
vi variety] nature Q3.   vii Of] Q3, Q4 omit; Of Q1.
viii Of] Q3, Q4 omit; Of Q1.   ix It also heateth] also it heleth Q3.
x of] of vsuall Q1; Of certayne vsuall Q3, Q4.
xi temperance] a temperaunce Q3; a temporaunce Q4; temperance Q1.

---

1 *somnolence*] an inclination to sleep, drowsiness.
2 *putteth away fastidiousness*] stop him from being over-disgusted or over-squeamish.
3 *ascarides*] thread-worms.

Of artichokes and rocket

There is nothing used to be eaten of artichokes but the head of them. When they be almost ripe they must be sodden tender in the broth of ⁱbeef and after eat them at dinner; they doth increase nature and doth provoke a man to venerous acts. Rocket doth increase the seed of man and doth stimulate the flesh and doth help to digestion.

Of chicory and endive

Chicory doth keep the stomach and the head in temperance and doth qualify choler. Endive is good for them the which hath hot stomachs and dry.

Of white beets and purslane

White ⁱⁱbeets be good for the liver and for the spleen and be abstertive. Purslane doth extinct the ardour of lasciviousness and doth mitigate great heat in all the inward parts of man.

Of thyme and parsley

Thyme breaketh the stone; it doth dissolve winds and causeth a man to make water. Parsley is good to break the stone and causeth a man to piss; it is good for the stomach and doth cause a man to have a ⁱⁱⁱsweet breath.

Of lettuce and sorrel

Lettuce doth extinct venerous acts, yet it doth increase milk in ⁱᵛa woman's breast; it is good for a hot stomach and doth provoke sleep and doth increase blood and doth set the blood in a temperance. Sorrel is good for a hot liver and good for the stomach.

Of pennyroyal and hyssop

Pennyroyal doth purge melancholy, and doth comfort the stomach and the spirits of man. Hyssop cleanseth viscous phlegm, and is good for the breast and for the lungs.

Of rosemary and roses

Rosemary is good for ᵛthe palsey, and for the falling-sickness, and for the cough, and good against cold. Roses be a cordial, and doth comfort the heart and the brain.

Of fennel and anis[1]

These herbs be seldom used, but their seeds be greatly occupied.[2] Fennel-seed is used to break ᵛⁱwind[3] and good against poison. Aniseed is good to cleanse the bladder and

---

i beef] beefe, or with beefe Q_3, Q_4; beef Q_1.   ii beets] Q_1, Q_3 (beetes); beeten Q_2.
iii sweet] sote Q_3.   iv a woman's breast] women brestes Q_3.
v the palsey] palses Q_1; the palses Q_3.   vi wind] vryne Q_4.

---

1 *anis*] aniseed.
2 *occupied*] used.
3 *to break wind*] Q_4's "vryne" instead of "wind" is possible; there is a reference to those who "breake wind, or urine" in scene one of Shackerley Marmion's play *Holland's Leaguer* (Marmion 1632, B2r).

the reins of the back, and doth provoke urine, and maketh one to have a ⁱsweet breath.

Of sage and mandragora

Sage is good to help a woman to ⁱⁱconception and doth provoke urine. Mandragora doth help a woman to conception and doth provoke a man to ⁱⁱⁱsleep.

Of all herbs in general

There is no herb nor weed but God have given virtue to them to help man. But forasmuch as Pliny, Macer, and Dioscorides (with many other old ancient and approbate doctors) hath written and pertracted[1] of their virtues, I therefore now will write no further of ⁱᵛherbs but will speak of other matters that shall be more necessary.

The twenty-first chapter treateth of fruits, and first of figs

Avicenna sayeth that figs doth nourish more than any other fruit. They doth nourish marvellously when they be eaten with blanched almonds; they be also good roasted and stewed; they do cleanse the breast and the lungs, and they do open the oppilations of the liver and the spleen; they doth restore a man to venerous acts, for they doth auge and increase the seed of generation, and also they do provoke a man to sweat, wherefore they do engender lice.

Of great raisins

Great raisins be nutritive, specially if the stones be pulled out, and they do make the stomach firm and stable, and they do provoke a man to have a good appetite if a few of them be eaten before meat.

Of small raisins of Corans[2]

Small raisins of Corans be good for the reins of the back and they do provoke urine, howebeit they be not all the best for the spleen for they make oppilation.

Of grapes

Grapes sweet and new be nutritive and doth stimulate the flesh; and they do comfort the stomach and the liver and doth avoid oppilations, howebeit ᵛthey do replete the stomach with ventosity.

Of peaches, of medlars, and services[3]

Peaches doth molify the belly and be cold, medlars taken superfluous doth engender melancholy, and services be in man of like operation.

---

i sweet] soote Q1; sote or a swete Q3; swete Q4.   ii conception] conceyue Q3.
iii sleep] sleep well Q3.   iv herbs] herbe Q3.   v they] it Q1, Q3.

---

1 *pertracted*] treated of in narration, from the Latin *pertractare* meaning to handle, to examine in detail, study carefully.
2 *raisins of Corans*] raisins of Corinth or currants.
3 *services*] small, round or pear-shaped fruits from the service tree, eaten when over-ripe.

Of strawberries, cherries, and hurts[1]

Strawberries be praised above all berries, for they do qualify the heat of the liver and doth engender good blood eaten with sugar. Cherries doth molify the belly and be cold; hurts be of a grosser substance, wherefore they be not for them the which be of a clean diet.

Of nuts great and small

The walnut and [i]the bannut[2] be of one operation: they be tardy and slow of digestion. Yet they doth comfort the brain if the pith or skin be pilled[3] off, and then they be nutritive. Filberts be better than hazelnuts; if they be new, and taken from the tree and the skin or the pith pulled off, they be nutritive and doth increase fatness. If they be old they should be eaten with great [ii]raisins, but new nuts be far better than old nuts, for old nuts be choleric, and they be evil for the head, and evil for old men, [iii]and they doth engender the palsy to the tongue, yet they be good against venom and immoderately taken or eaten doth engender corruptions, as boils, blains[4] and such putrifaction.

Of peason and beans

Peason the which be young be nutritive, howbeit they doth replete a man with ventosity. Beans be not so much to be praised as peason for they be full of ventosity although[5] the skins or husks be ablated[6] or cast away; yet they be strong meat and doth provoke venerous acts.

Of pears and apples

Pears the which be mellow, and doulce,[7] and not stony doth increase fatness, engendering waterish blood, and they be full of ventosity. But wardens roasted, stewed, or baken be nutritive and doth comfort the stomach, specially if they be eaten with comfits. Apples be good after a frost have taken [iv]them [v]or they the which be of good odour and mellow. They should be eaten with sugar, or comfits, or with fennel seed, or aniseeds because of their ventosity; they doth comfort then the stomach and doth make good digestion, specially if they be roasted or baken.

---

i the] Q4 *omits*.   ii raisins] myseris Q3.   iii and] For & Q3.
iv them] them or whan they be olde, specyally red apples Q1; them, or whan they be olde specially red appulles Q3.
v or] and Q1.

---

1 *hurts*] hurtleberries; also known as whortleberries or bilberries.
2 *bannut*] filbert.
3 *pilled*] peeled.
4 *blains*] inflammatory swellings or sores, often ulcerated; blisters.
5 *although*] even if.
6 *ablated*] removed.
7 *doulce*] sweet.

Of pomegranates and quinces

Pomegranates be nutritive and good for the stomach. Quinces baken, the core pulled out, doth molify the belly, and doth help digestion, and doth preserve a man from drunkenship.[1]

Of dates and melons

Dates moderately eaten be nutritive but they doth cause oppilations of the liver and of the spleen. Melons doth engender evil humours.

Of gourds, of cucumbers, and pepons

Gourds be evil of nourishment, cucumbers restraineth venerousness, or lasiviousness, or luxuriousness. Pepons be in manner of like operation but the pepons [i]engendereth evil humours.

Of almonds and chestens[2]

Almonds causeth a man to piss; they do molify the belly, and doth purge the lungs, and six or seven eaten before meat preserveth a man from drunkenship.[3] Chestens doth nourish the body strongly and doth make a man fat if they be through-roasted and the husks abjected,[4] yet they doth replete a man with ventosity or wind.

Of prunes and damsons

Prunes be not greatly praised but in the way of medicine, for they be cold and moist. And damsons be of the said nature, for the one is old and dried and the other be taken from the tree. Six or seven damsons eaten before dinner be good to provoke a man's appetite; they doth mollify the belly and be abstertive. The skin and the stones must be ablated,[5] and cast away, and not used.

Of olives and capers

Olives condited and eaten at the beginning of [ii]refection doth corroborate[6] the stomach and provoketh appetite. Capers doth purge phlegm and doth make a man to have an appetite.

Of oranges

Oranges doth make a man to have a good appetite, and so doth the rinds if they be in succade, and they doth comfort the stomach; the juice is a good sauce [iii]and doth provoke an appetite.

---

i engendereth] ingenderyng Q1; ingenderynge Q3.
ii refection] a refection Q3, Q4; refectyon Q1.
iii and doth] to Q3, Q4; and dothe Q1.

---

1 *drunkenship*] drunkenness.
2 *chestens*] chestnuts.
3 *drunkenship*] drunkenness.
4 *abjected*] rejected.
5 *ablated*] removed.
6 *corroborate*] strengthen.

The twenty-second chapter treateth of spices, and first of ginger
Ginger doth heat the stomach and helpeth digestion. Green ginger,[1] eaten in the morning fasting, doth actuate and quicken the remembrance.

Of pepper
There be three sundry kinds of pepper, which be to say white pepper, black pepper, and long pepper.[2] All kinds of peppers ⁱdo heat the body, and doth dissolve phlegm and wind, and doth help digestion, and maketh a man to make water. Black pepper doth make a man lean.

Of cloves and ⁱⁱmaces
Cloves doth comfort the sinews, and doth dissolve and doth consume superfluous humours, ⁱⁱⁱand restoreth nature. Maces is a cordial, and doth help the colic, and is good against the bloody flux and laxes.[3]

Of grains[4] and saffron
Grains be good for the stomach, and the head, and be good for women to drink. Saffron doth comfort the heart and the stomach, but he is too hot for the liver.

Of nutmeg and cinammon
Nutmegs be good for them the which have cold in their head, and doth comfort the sight, and the brain, and the mouth of the stomach, and is good for the spleen. Cinnamon is a cordial, wherefore the Hebrician[5] doth say "why doth a man die and can get cinammon to eat?",[6] yet it doth stop[7] and is good to restrain fluxes or laxes.[8]

Of licorice
Licorice is good to cleanse, and to open the lungs and the breast, and doth loose phlegm.

---

i do] to *Q1, Q3*; doth *Q4*.   ii maces] mace *Q1*.   iii and] *Q3, Q4*; *Q2, Q1* omit.

1 *Green ginger*] the fresh root of ginger, often in preserve.
2 *long pepper*] *Piper longum*, sometimes called Indian long pepper, is a relative of *Piper nigrum* from which black and white pepper is derived; it tastes similar to black pepper but is hotter. From the medieval period onwards the round black pepper became more commonly used in European cooking than the long pepper familiar to the ancients.
3 *laxes*] looseness of the bowels, diarrhoea.
4 *grains*] possibly "grains of paradise" or cardamom (see Bullein).
5 *the Hebrician*] the Hebrew scholar; it is not clear to which particular one Boorde refers.
6 *why doth . . . eat*] In his Government of Health Bullein, citing the *Regimen sanitatis Salerni*, asks the same of sage (pp. 257–8).
7 *stop*] bind.
8 *laxes*] looseness of the bowels, diarrhoea.

The twenty-third chapter showeth a diet for sanguine men
Sanguine men be hot and moist of complexion, wherefore they must be circumspect in eating of their meat considering that the purer the complexion is, the sooner it may be corrupted and the blood may be the sooner infected. Wherefore they must abstain to eat inordinately fruits, and herbs, and roots: as garlic, onions, and leeks. They must refrain from eating of old flesh, and eschew the usage of eating of [i]the brains of beasts, and from eating the udder of kine.[1] They must use moderate sleep and moderate diet or else they will be too fat and gross. Fish of muddy waters be not good for them; and if blood do abound, cleanse it with stufes[2] or by phlebotomy.[3]

The twenty-fourth chapter showeth a diet for phlegmatic men
Phlegmatic men be cold and moist, wherefore they must abstain from meats the which is cold and also they must refrain from eating viscous meat, [ii]specially from all meats the which doth engender phlegmatic humours, as fish, fruit, and white meat. Also, to eschew the usage of eating of crude herbs, [iii]special to refrain from meat the which is hard and slow of digestion (as it appeareth in the properties of meats [iv]above rehearsed) and [v]to beware not to dwell nigh to waterish and moorish[4] ground. [vi]These things be good for phlegmatic persons moderately taken: onions, garlic, pepper, ginger, and all meats the which be hot and dry, and sauces the which be sour. These things following doth purge phlegm: polypody, nettle, elder, agaric,[5] ireos, maidenhair, and stechados.[6]

The twenty-fifth chapter showeth a diet for choleric men
Choler is hot and dry, wherefore choleric men must abstain from eating hot spices, and to refrain from drinking of wine, and eating of choleric meat; howbeit, choleric men may eat grosser meat than any other [vii]complexions, except their education have been to the contrary. Choleric men should not be long fasting. These things following do purge choler: fumitory, centaury, wormwood, wild hops, violets, mercury, manna, rhubarb, eupatory,[7] tamarinds, and the whey of butter.

---

i the] Q3 *omits*.   ii specially] & specially Q3.
iii special] specyallye Q4; specyall Q1.   iv above] afore Q3.
v to] Q4 *omits*; to Q1.   vi These] This Q3.
vii complexions] of complexions Q1; of the complexions Q3, Q4.

---

1 *the udder of kine*] udders from cows. Apparently not an unusual dish at the time; in Jonson's *Bartholomew Fair* Ursula admonishes Knockem for spreading a rumour that she had died from "a surfeit of bottle ale and tripes" to which he replies, "No, 'twas better meat, Urs: cow's udders, cow's udders!" (Jonson 1960, 2.3.14–16).
2 *stufes*] hot air-baths.
3 *phlebotomy*] bloodletting.
4 *moorish*] boggy, marshy.
5 *agaric*] a type of fungus that grows on trees.
6 *stechados*] French lavender.
7 *eupatory*] hemp agrimony but also the name given to liverwort.

The twenty-sixth chapter treateth of a dietary for melancholy men
Melancholy is cold and dry, wherefore melancholy men must refrain from fried meat, and meat the which is over-salt, and from meat ⁱthe which is sour, and hard of digestion, and from all meat the which is ⁱⁱburnet¹ and dry. They must abstain from immoderate thirst, and from drinking of hot wines and gross wine (as red wine), and use these things: cow-milk, almond milk, yolks of new eggs. Boiled meat is better for melancholy men than roasted meat. All meat the which will be soon digested, and all ⁱⁱⁱmeats the which doth engender good blood, and meats the which be temperately hot be good for melancholy men and so be all herbs the which be hot and moist. These things following doth purge melancholy: ⁱᵛquickbeam, sene,² stechados,³ hart's-tongue,⁴ maidenhair, puliol mountain,⁵ borage, *organum*, sugar, and white wine.

The twenty-seventh chapter treateth of a diet and of an order to be used in the pestiferous time of the pestilence and sweating-sickness
When the plagues of the pestilence or the sweating-sickness is in a town or country, ᵛwith us at Montpellier and all other high regions and countries that I have dwelt in, the people flee from the contagious and infectious air, ᵛⁱpreservatives with other ᵛⁱⁱcounsel of physic notwithstanding. In lower and other base countries, houses the which be infected in town or city be closed up, both doors and windows, and the inhabitors shall not come abroad, neither to church, nor to market, nor to any house or company for infecting other the which be clean without infection. A man cannot be too ware⁶ nor cannot keep him self too well from this sickness, for it is so vehement and so parlous⁷ that the sickness is taken with the savour of man's clothes the which hath infected the infectious house, for the infection will lie and hang long in clothes, and I have known that when the straw and rushes hath been cast out of a house infected the hogs the which did lie in it died of the pestilence. Wherefore in such infectious time it is good for every man that will not fly from the contagious air to use daily, specially in the morning and evening, to burn juniper, or rosemary, or rushes, or bay-leaves, or majoram, or frankensense, ᵛⁱⁱⁱor benzoin.⁸ Or else make this

---

i the which] yᵗ Q1; that Q3.   ii burnet] burned Q3, Q4; burnet Q1.
iii meats] meate Q3.   iv quickbeam] Q3, Q4 (quyckebeme); Seene, quekbeme Q2.
v with us] Q3 omits.
vi preservatives] preseruatyue Q3; preseruacions Q4; preseruatyues Q1.
vii counsel] counsayles Q4; counceyll Q1.   viii or] Q1 omits; or Q4.

---

1 *burnet*] of a dark brown colour.
2 *sene*] senna.
3 *stechados*] French lavender.
4 *hart's-tongue*] a type of fern.
5 *puliol mountain*] probably wild thyme.
6 *ware*] aware, cautious.
7 *parlous*] dangerous, capable of harming.
8 *benzoin*] a dry and brittle substance from the *Styrax benzoin* tree; it is often called gum Benjamin or gum benjoin. Popular since the Middle Ages, it smells rather like camphor and is supposed to be a disinfectant.

powder: take of *storax calamite*¹ half an ounce, of frankensense an ounce, of the wood of aloes the weight of six and mix all these together. Then cast half a spoonful of this in a chafing² dish of coals and set it to fume abroad in the chambers, and the hall, and other houses; and you will put to this powder a little labdanum³ it is so much the better. Or else make a pomander ⁱafter this manner: take of labdanum three drams, of the wood of aloes one dram, of ambergris two drams, and a half of nutmegs, of *storax calamite*⁴ of each a dram and a half, confect all ⁱⁱthese together with rose water and make a ball. And this aforesaid pomander doth not only expel contagious ⁱⁱⁱairs but also it doth comfort the brain, as Barthelmew of Montagnaue⁵ sayeth, and other modernal⁶ doctors doth afirm the same. Whosoever ⁱᵛthat is infected with the pestilence, let him look in ᵛmy *Breviary of Health* for a remedy. But let him use this diet: let the chamber be kept close, and keep a continual fire in the chamber of clear-burning ᵛⁱwood or charcoal without smoke. Beware of taking any cold, use temperate meats and drink, and beware of wine, beer, and cider. Use to eat stewed or baken ᵛⁱⁱwardens if they can be gotten, if not eat stewed or baken pears with comfits. Use no gross meats, but those the which be light of digestion.

The twenty-eighth chapter showeth of a diet the which be in any fever or ague
I do advertise every man that hath a fever or an ague not to eat no meat six hours before his course doth take him, and in no wise as long as the ague doth endure to put off ᵛⁱⁱⁱshirt nor doublet, nor to rise out of the bed but when need shall require, and in any wise not to ⁱˣgo nor to take ˣany open air. For such provision may be had that, at uttermost at the third course, he shall be delivered of the fever using the medicines the which be in ˣⁱthe *Breviary of Health*. And let every man beware of casting their hands and arms at any time out of the bed, in or out of their agony, or to sprawl with the legs out of the bed. ˣⁱⁱGood it is for the space of three courses to wear continually gloves, and not to wash the hands, and to use such a diet in meat and drink as is rehearsed in the pestilence.⁷

---

    i after] *Q3;* under *Q2.*   ii these] this *Q3, Q4;* these *Q1.*
    iii airs] ayre *Q1;* ayres *Q4.*   iv that] *Q3 omits.*
    v my *Breviary*] this boke of dyetory *Q3.*
    vi wood or charcoal] asshe wode or cole *Q3;* wood or cole *Q4;* wodde, or chare cole *Q1.*
    vii wardens ... baken] *Q3 omits.*   viii shirt] the sherte *Q3;* the shert *Q4;* shertte *Q1.*
    ix go] hop *Q3.*   x any] yᵉ *Q3;* the *Q4;* any *Q1.*
    xi the *Breviary of Health*] this dyetary of helth *Q3.*   xii Good] and good *Q3.*

---

    1 storax calamite] *storax* is a fragrant gum-resin (*OED* storax, *n.* 1); *storax calamite* is the name given to the substance when dried.
    2 *chafing*] inflaming, burning, hot.
    3 *labdanum*] ladanum, a gum-resin derived from plants of the cistus family that was used in perfumes and fumigation.
    4 storax calamite] *storax* is a fragrant gum-resin (*OED* storax, *n.* 1); *storax calamite* is the name given to the substance when dried.
    5 *Barthelmew of Montagnaue*] Probably Bartholomeus Anglicus.
    6 *modernal*] modern, of the present day.
    7 *drink as is rehearsed in the pestilence*] as is advised in the previous chapter on what diet to use in the time of pestilence.

The twenty-ninth chapter treateth of a diet for them the which have the iliac or the colic and the stone

The iliac and the colic be engendered of ventosity, the which is intrused[1] or enclosed in two guts, the one is called ilia and the other is called colon. For [i]these two infirmities a man must beware of cold, and good it is not to be long fasting, and necessary it is to be laxative and not in no wise to be constipate. And these things following be not good for them the which have these aforesaid infirmities: [ii]hot bread nor new ale. They must abstain also from drinking of beer, of cider, and red wine, and cinnamon. Also refrain from all meats that honey is in, eschew eating of cold herbs, use not to eat beans, peason, nor pottage. Beware of the usage of fruits and of all things the which doth engender wind. For the stone, abstain from drinking of new ale, beware of beer, and of red wine and hot wine, refrain from eating [iii]of red herring, Martinmas beef,[2] and bacon, and salt fish, and salt meats. And beware of going cold about the middle, specially about the reins of the back. And make no restriction of wind, and water, nor [iv]egestion[3] that nature would expel.

The thirtieth chapter treateth of a diet for them the which have any kinds of the [v]gout

They the which be infected with the gout, or any kind of it, I do advertise them not to sit long bolling and bibbing,[4] dicing and carding, in forgetting themself to exonerate[5] the bladder and the belly when need shall require. And also to beware that the legs hang not without some stay nor that the boots or shoes be not over-strait.[6] Whosoever hath the gout must refrain from drinking of new ale, and let him abstain from drinking of beer, and red wine. Also, he must not eat new bread, eggs, fresh salmon, eels, fresh herring, pilchards, oysters, and all shell-fish. Also, he must eschew the eating of fresh beef, of goose, [vi]of duck, and of pigeons. Beware of taking cold in the [vii]legs, or riding, or going wetshod.[7] Beware of venerous acts after refection or after or upon a full stomach, and refrain from all things that doth engender evil humours and be inflative.[8]

---

i these] the Q3.   ii hot bread] new bred, stale bred Q1; stale breede. new ale Q3.
iii of red herring] Q3 *omits*.   iv egestion] seege Q1, Q3.
v gout] gowtes Q3, Q4; gowte Q1.   vi of] or Q3.
vii legs] legge Q1; legges Q4.

---

1 *intrused*] having a form as if pushed or thrust inwards.

2 *Martinmas beef*] salted beef; cattle were commonly slaughtered and salted for the winter on the feast of St Martin (11 November).

3 *egestion*] discharge or emptying out; perhaps specifically here referring to the evacuation of the bowels.

4 *bolling and bibbing*] boozing, to quaff the bowl and drink frequently. It seems that Boorde is here alluding to the Old Testament Book of Micah (2.11) from the Coverdale Bible, which is cited by OED in its definition of boll (*v.* 2): "They might sit bebbinge and bollynge".

5 *exonerate*] relieve of its load.

6 *over-strait*] too tight.

7 *wetshod*] with wet shoes.

8 *inflative*] tend to inflate or cause bloating.

The thirty-first chapter treateth of a diet for them the which have any of the [i]*kinds of leperhead*[1]

He that is infected with any of the four kinds of the leperhead must refrain from all manner of wines, and from new drinks, and strong ale. Then let him beware of rioting and surfeiting. And let him abstain [ii]from eating of spices, and dates, and from tripes and puddings and all inwards of beasts. Fish, and eggs, and milk is not good for leperous persons and they must abstain from eating of fresh beef and from eating of goose, duck, and from waterfowl, and pigeons. And in no wise [iii]eat no venison nor hare-flesh and such like.

The thirty-second chapter treateth of a diet for them the which have any of the [iv]*kinds of the falling-sickness*

Whosoever he be that have any of the kinds of the falling-sickness must abstain from eating of white [v]meats, specially of milk; he must refrain from drinking of wine, new ale, and strong ale. Also, they should not eat the fatness of fish nor the heads of fish, the which doth engender rheum. Shell-fish, eels, salmon, herring, and viscous fishes be not good for epilentic[2] men. Also, they must refrain from eating of garlic, onions, leeks, [vi]chibols,[3] and all vaporous meats the which doth hurt the head. Venison, hare-flesh, beef, beans, and peason be not good for epilentic men. And if [vii]they know that they be infected with [viii]this great sickness, they should not resort where [ix]there is great resort of company, which is [x]in church, in sessions, and marketplaces on market days. If they do, the sickness will infect them more there than in any other place or at any other time. They must beware they do not sit too nigh the fire, for the fire will overcome them and will induce the sickness. They must beware of lying [xi]hot in their bed or [xii]to labour extremely, for such things causeth the grief to come the ofter.

The [xiii]*thirty-third chapter treateth of a diet* [xiv]*for them the which have any pain in* [xv]*the head*

Many [xvi]sicknesses, or infirmities, and impediments may be in a man's head, wherefore whosoever have any impediments in the head must not keep the head too hot nor too cold but in a temperance and to beware of engendering of rheum, which is the cause of many infirmities. There is nothing that doth engender rheum so much as doth the fatness of fish, and the heads of fish, and surfeits, and taking cold in the feet, and taking cold in the nape of the neck or head. Also, they the which have any

---

i *kinds*] kynde Q3. ii from] for Q3, Q4; from Q1. iii eat no] to eate Q3.
iv *kinds*] kynde Q3. v meats] Q3 *(meates)*; meate Q2. vi chibols] Q3 *omits*.
vii they know] Q3 *omits*. viii this] these Q3, Q4; this Q1. ix there is] any Q3.
x in] Q1 *omits*; in Q4. xi hot] to hote Q3, Q4; hote Q1. xii to] Q3 *omits*.
xiii *thirty-third*] Q4 *(xxxiii)*; 34 Q2. xiv for them] Q1, Q3 *omit*; for them Q4.
xv *the*] theyr Q3, Q4; the Q1. xvi sicknesses] O6; sycknes Q2.

---

1 *leperhead*] leprosy.
2 *epilentic*] epileptic.
3 *chibols*] A species of the genus *Allium* that was also known as as stone leek, rock onion, and Welsh onion; in appearance intermediate between the onion and the leek and now little cultivated in Britain.

infirmity in the head must restrain of immoderate sleep, specially after meat; also, they must abstain from drinking of wine and use not to drink ale and beer the which is over strong. Vociferation, hallowing, crying and high-singing is not good for the head. All things the which is vaporous or doth fume is not good for the head and all things the which is of evil savour as carrion, sinks,¹ ⁱwide draughts, piss bowls,² snuff of candles, dunghills, stinking cannels,³ and stinking standing waters, and stinking marshes, with such contagious airs doth hurt the head and the brain and the memory. All odiferous savours be good for the head, and the brain, and ⁱⁱthe memory.

The thirty-fourth chapter treateth of a diet for them the which be in a consumption

Whosoever he be that is in a consumption must abstain from all sour and tart things as vinegar and alegar⁴ and such like. And also he must abstain from eating of gross meats, the which be hard ⁱⁱⁱand slow of digestion, and use cordials, and restoratives, and nutritive meats. ⁱᵛAll meats and drinks the which is sweet and that sugar is in be nutritive, wherefore sweet wines be good for them the which be in ᵛconsumptions, moderately taken. And sour wine, sour ale, ᵛⁱand sour ᵛⁱⁱbeer is good for no man for it doth fret away nature. And let them beware that be in ᵛⁱⁱⁱa consumption of fried meat, of broiled meat, and ⁱˣburnt meat the which is over-roasted; and in any wise let them beware of anger and pensivefulness. These things following be good for them the which be in ˣconsumptions: a pig or a cock stewed and made in a jelly, cockerels stewed, goat-milk and sugar, almond milk in the which rice is sodden, and rabbit stewed, ˣⁱand new laid eggs, and rear yolks of eggs, and rice sodden in almond milk.

The thirty-fifth chapter treateth of a diet for them the which be asthmatic men, being short-winded or lacking breath

Shortness of wind cometh diverse times of impediments in the lungs and straitness⁵ ˣⁱⁱof the breast oppilated through viscous phlegm, and otherwhile when the head is stuffed with rheum called the pose⁶ letteth the breath of his natural course. Wherefore he that hath shortness of breath must abstain from eating of nuts, specially if they be old; and cheese and milk is not good for them, no more is fish, and fruit, and raw

---

i wide draughts] Q3 *(wededraughtes)*; wynkraughtes Q2.   ii the] for the Q3.
iii and slow] Q3 omits.   iv All meats] Q3 omits.
v consumptions] consūpcion Q1; consumpcions Q4.   vi and] Q1, Q3; Q2 omits.
vii beer] Q3, Q4 *(beere)*; breade Q2; brede Q1.   viii a] Q1 omits; a Q4.
ix burnt] Q3 *(brent)*; bronte Q2, Q1; burned Q4.
x consumptions] consumpcion Q3; Q4 cōsumpcion; cōsumpcions Q1.
xi and new laid eggs, and rear yolks of eggs, and rice sodden in almond milk] &c. Q1.
xii of the breast] in the breastes Q4; of the brest Q1.

---

1 *sinks*] a pool or pit for the receipt of waste water, sewage, filth.
2 *piss bowls*] bowls or pots for holding urine.
3 *cannels*] a cannel was the gutter or surface watercourse in a street or by a road.
4 *alegar*] sour ale or vinegar made from ale.
5 *straitness*] tightness.
6 *the pose*] a cold in the head; catarrh.

ͥor crude herbs. Also, all manner of meat the which is hard of digestion is not good for them. They must restrain from eating of fish, specially from eating fish the which will cleave to the fingers and be viscous and slimy, and in any wise beware of the skins of fish and all manner of meat the which doth engender phlegm. Also, they must beware of cold, and when any house is a-sweeping[1] to go out of the house for a space into a clear air. The dust also that riseth in the street through the vehemence of the wind or other wise is not good for them. And smoke is evil for them and so is all thing that is stopping,[2] wherefore necessary it is for them to be laxative ⁱⁱand to be in a clean and pure air.

The thirty-sixth chapter treateth of a diet for them the which have the palsy
They the which have the palsy universal or particular[3] must beware of anger, hastiness, and testiness;[4] and must beware of fear, for through anger or fear diverse times the palsy do come to ⁱⁱⁱman. Also, they must beware of drunkenness and eating of nuts, which things be evil for the palsy of the tongue. Coldness, and contagious and stinking, ⁱᵛfilthy, airs be evil for the palsy. And let every man beware ᵛof lying upon the bare ground or upon the bare stones, for it is evil for the palsy. The savour of castory[5] and the savour of a fox is good against the palsy.

The thirty-seventh chapter doth show an order and a diet for them the which be mad and out of their wit
There is no man the which have any of the kinds of madness but they ought to be kept in safeguard for diverse inconvenience that may fall, as it appeared of late days of a lunatic man named ᵛⁱMichel, the which went many ᵛⁱⁱyears at liberty and at last he did kill his wife, and his wife's sister, and his own self. Wherefore I do advertise every man the which is mad, or lunatic, or frantic, or demoniac to be kept in safeguard in some close house or chamber where there is little light[6] and that he have a keeper the which the madman do fear. And see that the mad-man have no knife, nor shears, nor other edge-tool, nor that he have no girdle, except it be a weak list of cloth,[7] for hurting or killing himself.[8] Also, the chamber or the house that the madman is in, let there be no painted cloths, nor painted walls, nor pictures of man, ᵛⁱⁱⁱnor woman, or fowl, or beast, for such things maketh them full of fantasies. Let the mad person's

---

i or] *Q3 omits.*   ii and to be in a clean and pure air] *Q1, Q3 omit.*
iii man] a man *Q1, Q3.*   iv filthy] and fylthy *Q3*; & fylthy *Q4*; fylthy *Q1.*
v of] *O5, O6*; on *Q2.*   vi Michel] Antony a Physycion *Q3.*
vii years at] times at his *Q3.*   viii nor] or *Q3, Q4*; or *Q1.*

---

1 *a-sweeping*] being swept.
2 *stopping*] binding.
3 *the palsy universal or particular*] affecting the entire body or only a specific part of the body.
4 *testiness*] being testy or petulant.
5 *castory*] a strong-smelling substance obtained from two sacs in the inguinal region of the beaver.
6 *kept in safeguard ... little light*] this is similar to the situation the "mad" Malvolio experiences at the hands of Feste, as Sir Topas the curate, in *Twelfth Night* (Shakespeare 1988, 4.2).
7 *a weak list of cloth*] presumably a cloth with a weak border or hem (*OED* list, *n.*3. I.) so that it would rip if a man tried to hang himself with it.
8 *for hurting of killing himself*] in order to avoid the risk of him hurting or killing himself.

head be shaven once a month, let them drink no wine, nor strong ale, nor strong beer, but moderate drink, and let them have three times in a day warm suppings and ⁱa little warm meat. And use few words to them except it be for reprehension or gentle reformation, and if[1] they have any wit or perserverance to ⁱⁱunderstand what reprehension or reformation is.

The thirty-eighth chapter treateth of a diet for them the which have any of the kinds of the dropsies

Saint Bede sayeth the more a man doth drink that hath the dropsy the more he is a thirst, for although the sickness doth come by superabundance of water yet the liver is dry, whether it be alchytes, hyposarca, leucoflegmancia, or the tympany.[2] They that hath any of these four kinds of the dropsies must refrain from all things the which be constipate and costive, and use all things the which be laxative. Nuts, and dry almonds, and hard cheese ⁱⁱⁱis poison to them; ⁱᵛa tisane and posset ale made with cold herbs doth comfort them. Whosoever he be the which will have a remedy for any of these four kinds of the ᵛdropsies and will know a declaration of these infirmities ᵛⁱand ᵛⁱⁱall other sicknesses ᵛⁱⁱⁱlet him look in a book of my making named *The Breviary of Health*, for in this book I do speak but of diets and how a man should order his mansion place and himself and his household with such like things for the conservation of health.

The thirty-ninth chapter treateth of a general diet for all manner of men and women being sick or whole

There is no man nor woman the which have any respect to themself that can be a better physician for their own safeguard than their own self can be, to consider what thing the which doth them good and to refrain from such things that doth them hurt or harm. And let every man beware of care, sorrow, thought, pensivefulness, and of inward anger. Beware of surfeits and use not ⁱˣto much venerous acts. Break not the usual custom of sleep in the night. A merry heart and mind the which is in rest and quietness, without ˣadversity, causeth a man to live ˣⁱlong and to look youngly

---

i a] *Q3; Q2, Q1 omit;* a *Q4.*
ii understand . . . is] vnderstande *Q1;* vnderstandynge *Q3.*
iii is] *Q4 omits;* is *Q1.*
iv a tisane . . . conservation of health] *Q4 omits;* A ptysane. . . . conseruacion of helth *Q1.*
v dropsies] Idropysey *Q3.*
vi and all . . . conservation of health] *Q4 omits;* and all . . . conservation of health *Q1.*
vii all] *Q3 omits.*
viii let him look . . . of health] do as this dyetory do teache you *Q3; Q4 omits;* let him look . . . of health *Q1.*
ix to] so *Q1;* to *Q4.*
x adversity] aduersyte, and to moche worldly busynes *Q1;* aduersyte, and to moche worldlye busynes *Q3.*
xi long] longer *Q3.*

---

1 *and if*] that is if.
2 *alchytes . . . tympany*] all kinds of dropsy, although a tympany is specifically a morbid swelling or tumour in the abdomen without the accumulation of fluid.

although he be aged. Care and sorrow bringeth in age and death, ⁱwherefore let every man be merry and if he cannot, let him resort to merry company to break of his perplexatives.¹ Furthermore, I do advertise every man to wash their hands oft every day, and diverse times to comb their head ⁱⁱevery day, and to plunge the eyes in cold water in the morning. Moreover, I do counsel every man to keep the breast and the stomach warm, and to keep the feet from wet, and otherwhile to wash them, and that they be not kept too hot nor too cold but indifferently. Also, to keep the head and the neck in a moderate temperance, not too hot nor too cold, and in any wise to beware not to meddle too much with the venerous acts, for that will cause a man to look agedly and also causeth a man to have a brief or a short life. ⁱⁱⁱAll other matters pertaining to any particular diet you shall ⁱᵛhave in the diets above in this book rehearsed.

The fortieth chapter doth show an order or a fashion how a sick man should be ordered and how a sick man should be used that is likely to die

Whosoever that is sore sick, it is uncertain to man whether he shall live or die, wherefore it is necessary for him that is sick to have two or three good keepers the which at all times must be diligent and not sleepish, sluggish, ᵛnor sluttish, and not to weep and wail about a sick man, nor to use many words, nor that there be no great resort to common² and talk, for it is a business ᵛⁱa whole man to answer many men, ᵛⁱⁱspecially women, that shall come to him. They the which cometh to any sick person ought to have few words or none, except certain persons the which be of counsel of the testament making,³ the which wise men be not to seek of such matters in their sickness, for wisdom would that every man should prepare for such things in health. And if any man for charity will visit any person, let him advertise the sick to make everything even between God, and the world, and his conscience, and to receive the rights of holy church like a Catholic man. And to follow the council of both physicians, which is to say the physician of the soul and the physician of the body – that is to say the spiritual council of his ᵛⁱⁱⁱghostly father and the bodily council of his physician – concerning the receipts of his medicines to recover health. For Saint Augustine sayeth he that doth not ⁱˣthe commandment of his physician doth kill himself. Furthermore, about a sick person should be redolent ˣsavours, and the

---

i wherefore] where *Q1*; wherfore *Q4*.
ii every day, and to plunge] & euery day to plonge *Q3*.
iii All] Also *Q4*; All *Q1*.
iv have in the diets above] haue it afore *Q3*; haue it in the dyettes aboue *Q4*; haue in the dyetes aboue *Q1*.
v nor] *Q1* omits; nor *Q4*.   vi a] for a *Q3, Q4*; a *Q1*.
vii specially] and specially *Q3*.   viii ghostly father] curate *Q3*.
ix the commandment] obserue the Cōmaundement *Q3*; obserue the cōmaundements *Q4*; the commandment *Q1*.
x savours] *Q3* (sauoures); sauour *Q2*; sauour *Q1*; sauours *Q4*.

---

1 *perplexatives*] things which perplex.
2 *common*] verbal communication.
3 *testament making*] drawing up a will.

chamber should be replenished with herbs and flowers of odiferous savour.¹ And certain times it is good ⁱto use some perfumes to stand in the middle of the chamber. And in any wise let not many men, ⁱⁱand specially women, be together at one time in the chamber, not only for babbling but specially for their ⁱⁱⁱbreaths. And the keepers should see at all times that the sick persons drink be pure, fresh, and stale² and that it be a little warmed, turned out of the cold. If the sick men were sicker and sicker, that there is ⁱᵛlittle hope or amendment but signs of death, then no man ought to move to him any worldly matters or business but to speak of ghostly and godly matters, and to read the Passion of Christ, and to say the psalms of the Passion, and ᵛto hold a cross or a picture of the Passion of Christ before the eyes of the sick person. And let not the keepers forget to give the sick man ᵛⁱin such agony warm drink with a spoon, with a spoonful of a caudle or a cullis. And then let every man endeavour himself to prayer, that the sick person may finish his life Catholicly, in the faith of Jesus Christ, and ᵛⁱⁱso depart out of this miserable world; I do beseech the Father, the son, and the Holy Ghost, through the mercy of Jesus Christ's Passion that I and all creatures living may do so. ᵛⁱⁱⁱAmen.³

Imprinted at London in Fleet Street at the sign of the George, next to Saint Dunstone's Church by William Powell. In the year of Our Lord, M.CCCCC.LXVII.⁴

---

i to use some perfumes] to be vsed a lytell of some perfume Q_1, Q_3.
ii and] Q_4 *omits*; and Q_1.   iii breaths] hote breathes Q_4; brethes Q_1.
iv little] lykely Q_4; lykle Q_1.
v to hold . . . sick person] byd the sycke man remembre how christe suffred death & passyon for hym Q_3.
vi in] yᵉ is in Q_3; that is in Q_4; in Q_1.   vii so] so to Q_3, Q_4; so Q_1.
viii Amen] Amen. Thus endeth this dyetory Q_3.

---

1 *odiferous savour*] sweet-smelling.
2 *stale*] not in the modern perjorative sense meaning not fresh but rather a reference to alcoholic drink that has stood long enough to be clear, that is freed from dregs or lees, and thus considered old and strong.
3 *Amen*] At this point Q3 contains additional material (two and a half pages) not present in the other editions advising what quanities of particular medicines ought to be used.
4 MCCCCCLXVII] 1567; apparently an error since this edition was actually printed in 1547.

A NEW BOOK OF PHYSIC CALLED
THE GOVERNMENT OF HEALTH

A New Book [i]of Physic called *The Government of Health* wherein [ii]be uttered many notable rules for man's preservation, with sundry simples and other matters, no less fruitful than profitable, [iii]collected out of many approved authors, reduced into the form of a dialogue for the better understanding of the unlearned, whereunto is added a sovereign regiment against the pestilence.

By William Bullein.

Imprinted at London by John Day, dwelling over Aldergate, beneath Saint Martin's.

Cum privilegio ad imprimendum solum.[1]

To the right worshipful Sir Thomas Hilton, knight, Baron of Hilton, and Captain of the King and Queens' majesties castle of Tynemouth, William Bullein wisheth increase of worship and health.[2]

Quintus Curtius, the famous writer of the great battles that King Alexander, the son of Philip of Madedon, had against the most noble and rich king of the Medes and Persians, called Darius (right worshipful sir), declareth that when one Philip,[3] the physician unto the said King Alexander and his most trusty subject. By sudden chance the King fell sore sick, to the great heaviness of all his royal army, at which time with all speed this physician did prepare a medicine most excellent for his sovereign lord, whom he so dearly loved, to this end, that the great virtue thereof might prevent his present sickness and imminent danger. But malicious spite, that wretched enemy, which never sleepeth but watcheth ever to bring virtue and good fame to destruction, immediately before this gentle Philip did present himself unto the king with his medicine, letters were sent to the King Alexander contending that the said Philip was corrupted so with money from King Darius that he had put most deadly poison and uncurable venom into Alexander's medicine.[4] The King perusing the letters kept them secret until he had drunk his medicine and immediately he took his physician by the hand and delivered him the letters that he might read them, having in him so great confidence that he did in no manner of case mistrust him. The cause why I have alleged this most worthy prince King Alexander and his excellent physician Philip is

---

i of Physic called] Entituled O1.   ii be] is O1.   iii collected] *this ed.*; collect O2.

1 Cum privilegio ad imprimendum solum] "With the privilege for printing only". Following this statement, the copy text has a picture of the coat of arms of Thomas Hilton with his initials below it.

2 *To the right worshipful ... health*] See the Introduction on Bullein, p. 28.

3 *when one Philip*] the sense is 'there was one called Philip'.

4 *But malicious spite ... medicine*] Bullein had good reason to be antagonistic towards those who defame physicians since he had been accused of poisoning Sir Thomas Hilton, his patron, by Hilton's brother (see Introduction on Bullein, p. 29).

to declare the great trust in the one and the fidelity in the other, not forgetting the shameless conditions of the flattering parasites which ever walketh with two faces in one hood bearing fire in the one hand and water in the other: sowers of discord, reapers of mischief, which be always enemies unto the disciples of Philip whose venomous stings cannot hurt them which ever have in store the precious jewel of patience and arm themselves to do good to every good man for the preservation of their lives by the true rules of the government of health,[1] which here I am bold to present unto your worship. For whereas there lacketh government in a commonwealth the people do eftsoons fall into ruin; the ships that lack good governance oftentimes be cast away upon sands and rocks. And therefore there is nothing under heaven that hath life but if it lack good government it will quickly fall into utter decay. For like as the creator of all things [i]hath informed the bodies of all men into the goodliest shapes of every living thing that every was, or ever shall be, even so he hath ordained for man herbs, fruits, roots, seeds, plants, gums, oils, precious stones, beasts, fowls, fishes, for the preservation of health to be moderately used with discretion, which preserveth the body in good estate, without whose virtues the bodies cannot live for they be the nourishers of life. But misusing or abusing them bringeth to the body many diseases, as rheums, catarrhs, dropsies, impostumes, gouts, fluxes, oppilations, vertigoes, blindness, ruptures, frenzies, with many more noisome diseases, which come through the corruption of meats and ill air. For what availeth riches, honours, costly buildings, fair apparel, with all the pomp of this world, and to be honoured of the people, and in the mean time to be eaten with worms in the breast or in the belly, consumed with agues, tormented with gouts, soreness, bone-ache, etc.? Well, I think an whole Codrus[2] is better than a sick Midas,[3] and seeing that to possess health is better than to govern gold, insomuch that health maketh men more happier, stronger, and quieter than all manner of riches, lacking health. As example: great princes, noble men of great substance, when they be wrapped and enclosed with many and sundry sicknesses and in daily dangers of death, in their extreme pains and passions they do more greatly covet one drop of health than a whole ton of gold, crying out for the help and counsel of the physician whom Jesus Sirach in his goodly book[4] did counsel all wise men to honour, and whom the almighty God did create and ordain for the infirmity of mankind, and also for his help, and that no wise man should despise them. Therefore, yet again (most worthy knight) I shall most humbly desire you to [ii]accept the good will of him which wisheth the years of

Codrus

Midas

Capitulum 38

---

i hath informed] haue formed O1.   ii accept] except O1, O3.

1 *the disciples of Philip ... health*] physicians and self-appointed experts in medicine, like Bullein himself.

2 *Cordus*] according to Greek legend, the last King of Athens who famously disguised himself as a peasant and sacrificed his life for his country. It is possible that Bullein refers to Valerius Cordus, the sixteenth-century German physician and botanist since reference to the physician would allow comparison between health (Cordus) and wealth (Midas) even if comparison between two kings is perhaps more likely.

3 *Midas*] King Midas, whose touch turned everything to gold and who thus represents the wealthy man.

4 *Jesus Sirach in his goodly book*] the apocryphal Biblical book Ecclesiasticus.

your prosperous life and health to be equal to Nestor, Arganton, and Galen, whose lives were long, healthful, and happy.¹ And thus wishing the daily increase of your worship with continual health to God's pleasure, whoever be your guide and governor. Amen. Your worship's always to command.

William Bullein.

<blockquote>

Nestor

Arganton

Galen

</blockquote>

Cursed be Bacchus, the father of drunkenness,²
Founder of ⁱloathsome lust and lechery,
Thy servants twain be intemperance³ and idleness,
Which gentle diet and soberness do defy,
But soberness doth live when gluttony doth die,
Though banquets do abound, eyes for to please,
Overcharging the stomach bringeth small ease.

The abundance of wine and lust of meat,
Feasting in the day and riot in the night,
Inflameth the body with unnatural heat,
Corrupteth the blood and abateth⁴ the sight,
The sinews will relax, the arteries have no might,
Apoplexia and vertigo will never from the start,
Until the vital blood be killed in the heart.

Oh happy is poverty, with good governance,
Which of fine food hath no great plenty,
Nature is sufficed with things sufficience,
But poisoned with floods of superfluity,
Consider your food in the time of poverty,
Example ⁱⁱof Diogenes, sitting in his tun,⁵
ⁱⁱⁱHe was pleased with ⁱᵛthe beams of the sun.

Beasts and fowls of nature ravenous,
In fields and forests seek their adventure,
Upon their preys devouring most odious,
Consuming by gluttony many a creature,
Yet each of them according to their nature,
Can purge their crudity with casting venomous,
Man, through repletion, is in danger perilous.

---

i loathsome] lothelie *O1*.   ii of] to *O1*.   iii He] *O1 omits*.
iv the beams] reflection *O1*.

1 *Nestor, Arganton, and Galen ... long, healthful, and happy*] Nestor was the ancient Greek King of Pylos who returned safely from the Trojan War, although he was too old to actually do any fighting; Arganto was the last King of ancient Tartessos, or Tartessus. Like Galen, they were reputed to have lived long lives.
2 *Bacchus, the father of drunkenness*] the Roman god of wine.
3 *intemperance*] Temperance (the middle way between excess and lack) is one of the Christian virtues celebrated by Edmund Spenser in Book Two of his epic poem *The Faerie Queene*.
4 *abateth*] destroys.
5 *Diogenes, sitting in his tun*] Diogenes the Cynic, who denounced material goods and lived in a tun, a large cask used to hold wine.

Man's nature doth weaken as this world doth waste,
As things engendered, corrupting by time,
Your life is present, but death maketh haste,
ⁱShortened by surfeit, I tell you in rhyme,
Example of the epicures, rottened into slime,
As God's word and stories, the truth ⁱⁱdo tell,
That unsatiate gluttons shall fast in hell.

Truly to wise men this is the chief medicine,
Moderate diet, with temperate travail,
Good air in sweet fields, when the sun doth shine,
Flying ⁱⁱⁱstinking mists, that the life will expel,
Digestion of stomach, they shall feel full well,
And to shake off anger and passions of the mind,
Thus quietness of conscience ^{iv}happy men shall find.

We know each one, and see by experience,
That men shall waste and physic fade,
What is man when he is in most excellence?
Soon fallen to dust and sleepeth still in shade,
^vLeaves, flowers, and fruits ^{vi}grow in summer most glad,
But from their branches (as it is daily seen),
^{vii}They fall down with wind, when they are fresh and green.

Sun, moon, and stars, with heavenly influence,
The earth do garnish with flowers fresh of hue,
The trees spring with fruit of their benevolence,
Rain nourisheth sweet fields with silver drops new,
The lily, ^{viii}the red rose, ^{ix}the flowers pale and blue,
The corn and cattle and ^xall things temporal,
Be not these God's gifts for these our lives mortal?

^{xi}To know these creatures is a gift ^{xii}excellent,
Complexions hot or cold, moist or dry,
And to what nature they be convenient,
Hippocrates and Galen in their time did try,
Dioscorides and Avicen, with Pliny would not lie,
Aristotle the philosopher[1] in learning most excellent,
So be many men now in this life present.

To them I bend my knee with due reverence,
As one unworthy their footsteps for to kiss,
Lacking no good will, confessing my negligence,
Though many will judge my intent amiss,

---

i Shortened] Festinate *O1*.   ii do] to *O1*.   iii stinking] stinging *O1*.
iv happy men] the happy man *O1*.   v Leaves, flowers] Flowers, leaues *O1*.
vi grow] groweth *O1*.   vii They fall] Are beaten *O1*.   viii the] *O1 omits*.
ix the] and *O1*.   x all things] eeurything *O1*.   xi To] But to *O1*.
xii excellent] most excellent *O1*.

---

1 *Aristotle the philosopher*] cited by Bullein not only for his philosophical views but also his views on medicine.

Pouring water in the sea, where aye plenty is,
But of your worship to whom I present this gift,
[i]Accept (I pray you) such a simple shift.

[ii]And read you this government, short I [iii]shall it make,
Between one called John and Humphrey, the wise,
When you are at leisure in your hand it take,
Though it lack eloquence, yet do it not despise,[1]
I [iv]recite no authors using to make lies,[2]
[v]I submit myself still unto the learned judge,[3]
[vi]I force not if the ignorant [vii]at this my travail grudge.

Esse cupis sanus? Sit tibi parca manus,
Pone gule metas, etas ut sit tibi [viii]*longa.*[4]

[ix]This book to praise I will not be curious,[5]
Let the wise reader with judgement discuss,[6]
The sun need no candle to give it more light,
The eagle requireth none to teach him his flight,
Each fruits have their taste, and witness forth bring,
From what trees they came and had their growing.
So is this work a sign of a zeal,
Worthy to be praised, to readers I appeal.
The beginning, scope, and end of the counsel,
Health to prefer and sickness to expel,
Such matter digesting as thee do offend,
Applying good medicines those evils to amend,
With herbs that doth bind or else be expulsive,
Vicious humours to correct and outdrive.
God blessed the earth from whence these things grow,
And willeth his people their natures to know,
But ignorance hereof engendreth distain
In them that lack learning and ignorant would remain.
Other have such delicate and curious conditions
When no cause constrains, then they cry for physcians,
As though they should never once taste of their grave,

---

i Accept (I pray you) such] Except it better thē nothing to make *O1*.
ii And read you] I pray you red *O1*.   iii shall] wil *O1*.
iv recite no authors using to make] will assite no authour, which haue writen *O1*.
v I submit myself still] And stil wil submitte my self *O1*.
vi I force not if] And forse not of *O1*.   vii at this] whiche at *O1*.
viii *longa*] longa. FINIS *O1*.   ix This book to praise ... FINIS. quod R. B.] *O1 omits*.

---

1 *Though it lack eloquence . . .*] Extreme modesty about one's writing, even to the extent of denigrating it, was a common practice in the early modern period.
2 *I recite no authors using to make lies*] I do not cite authors who tell lies.
3 *the learned judge*] this could be the intelligent reader, or his patron (Thomas Hilton), or God himself.
4 Esse ... longa] Latin: "If you wish to be healthy, you need a sparing hand, / Put limits on gluttony, so that you may have a long life".
5 *curious*] fastidious, overly concerned (i.e. to praise).
6 *discuss*] examine, decide.

Whose days were prescribed when God life them gave.
All flesh is like grass, that withereth with wind,
As earth came from earth, so shall it to that kind.
In the mean season refuse not to take
The virtuous physicians for remedies' sake,
Which can supplant pain and health set in place,
So shalt thou live quietly and finish thy race.
At last, when death comes, whereto thou must trust,
Call to God for grace, let death do his worst.
                                    FINIS. quod R. B.[1]

To the gentle reader

Here I do present unto thee (gentle reader) a simple government of health, beseeching thee most heartily for to accept it as one unfeignedly that greatly do covet the good estate and happy health of mankind, which by daily casualties, surfeits, and age do decay and fall into many grievous and painful sicknesses, for which cause, although perhaps I cannot in all points answer to thy request in this little government, yet I shall desire thee to accept me among the fellowship of botchers,[2] which do help to repair things that fall into ruin or decay. Even so be the practisers of physic no makers of men, but when men do decay through sickness then the counsel of the physician and the virtue of medicine is not to be refused but most lovingly to be embraced as a chief friend in the time of adversity. If thou readest this little book and observe [i]the rules therein, I trust it will pay as much as it doth promise. And because I am a young man[3] I would not presume to take such a matter in hand, although the words be few, but did conciliate and gather things together which of myself I have practised and also read and noted in the works of Hippocrates, Galen, Avicenna, Pliny, Haly Abbas, [ii]Avenzoar, Rasis, Dioscorides, Leonhart Fuchs, Conrad Gesner, *et cetera*. And thus I leave thee to the company of this my little book, wishing thee health, and all them that shall read it.

A table for this Book of the Government of Health[4]
A

Against frenzy	p. 286
Age provided for	p. 230
Ague is caused	p. 283
Agues burning	p. 259

---

i the rules therein] it O1.   ii Avenzoar] Wenzoar O1.

1 R. B.] probably William's brother, Richard Bullein. See Introduction on Bullein (pp. 28–9). Following these initials the copy text has a picture of William Bullein.

2 *accept me among the fellowship of botchers*] As earlier in the text, when Bullein claims his work lacks eloquence, this is an example of the extreme modesty towards one's writing that was common in the early modern period.

3 *because I am a young man*] Bullein was probably forty-three in 1558, when the first and second editions of his *Government of Health* were published.

4 *A Table of Health*] In O2 the table is broadly alphabetical, although (as for Elyot) alphabetization is incomplete and is here corrected. In the first edition of Bullein's work (O1) the table lists the various foods and themes in the order in which they appear and is shorter than in O2.

Air corrupt hurteth — p. 245
Air may corrupt — p. 245
Airs made sweet — p. 246
Airs observed — p. 246
Ale and beer — p. 292
Ale and beer surfeiteth — p. 292
Ale sweet — p. 292
Ale wholesome for whom? — p. 292
Almonds — p. 274
Almonds before meat — p. 293
Almonds diverse — p. 293
Aloes — p. 296
Anatomy — p. 233
Anger is described — p. 253
Aniseeds — p. 255

B

Barberries — p. 276
Baths — p. 239
Baths, after bathing, what ointments? — p. 239
Beer and ale — p. 292
Beer brewed clean — p. 292
Bees: an example — p. 288
Biting of a dog: what plaster? — p. 261
Blackbirds — p. 283
Blood purged — p. 296
Bloody flux — pp. 255, 277
Boar's flesh — p. 278
Boiled meats — p. 277
Boxing: when? — p. 239
Brain and memory holpen — p. 281
Brain: what doth comfort it? — p. 281
Bread — p. 292
Bread mean baken — p. 292
Bread of a day old — p. 293
Bread of barley — p. 293
Bread sodden — p. 293
Breath stinking — p. 274
Breath that is sweet — p. 262
Bruised: what is good for them? — p. 259

C

Calamus odoratus[1] — p. 295
Capers — pp. 236, 276

---

1 *calamus oderatus*] sweet calamus; referred to as a "principal spice" in the Bible (Exodus 30.23).

Cassia fistula	p. 295
Chamomile	p. 257
Cheese and butter	p. 290
Cherries	p. 275
Chestnuts	p. 294
Chickens	p. 281
Chickenweed[1]	p. 256
Child dead: to deliver it	pp. 257, 263, 265, 267
Children should well be brought up	p. 230
Choler hot in the stomach	p. 263
Choleric men	p. 243
Choleric signs	p. 251
Choler purged	p. 271
Cinnamon	p. 295
Cloves	p. 294
Clyster	p. 239
Cock that is old	p. 281
Colic holpen	p. 262
Colour like lead	p. 250
Colours many	p. 251
Combing of the head	p. 240
Complexions described	p. 226
Complexions of man	p. 244
Compounded creatures	p. 228
Conies	p. 280
Contents in urine	p. 251
Coughs holpen	p. 280
Crabs	p. 285
Cramp holpen	p. 298
Crayfish	p. 285
Crudity: what?	p. 251

D

Dandelion	p. 259
Death: what sign?	p. 251
Decoction or syrup	p. 234
Devils incarnate	p. 253
Diet	p. 252
Dieting	p. 242
Dieting the sick	p. 243
Diet well used	p. 242
Digestion	p. 277
Digestion holpen	p. 247
Digestion stronger in winter	p. 280

---

1 *Chickenweed*] chickweed.

Dragon the herb — p. 264
Drink wholesome — p. 283
Dropsy — pp. 235, 255
Drunkenness: a preservative against it — p. 280

E

Eating considered — p. 240
Eggs — p. 290
Eggs: a mean to stop the flux — p. 290
Eggs fried — p. 290
Eggs new laid — p. 290
Elements described — p. 227
Elements felt — p. 228
Emperici[1] — p. 224
Epicures' desire — p. 221
Epinyctidas[2] — p. 260
Exercise before meat — p. 247
Exercise causeth — p. 247
Exercise moderate — p. 246
Eyes: a medicine — p. 277
Eyes bloody — p. 280
Eyes watery — p. 296

F

Falling-sickness — pp. 256, 266
Fennel — p. 262
Feverfew — p. 263
Figs and herb-grace — p. 274
Filberts — p. 294
Filipendula[3] — p. 264
Fish: diverse sorts — p. 284
Fish eaten: labour not soon after it — p. 285
Fish fat — p. 285
Fish feeding — p. 285
Fish in fens — p. 284
Fish in rivers — p. 284
Fish of the sea — p. 284
Fish unscaled — p. 285
Fish: what choice? — p. 285
Fish white scaled — p. 285
Flesh and fish together may hurt — p. 241

---

1 Emperici] the Empiricists who favoured medical symptoms and causes in diagnosis and treatment over the theoretical speculation that was favoured by the Dogmatists (see below).

2 Epinyctidas] pustules, which erupt at night.

3 *Filipendula*] several flowering plants in the rose family; the most well-known species are meadowsweet and drop-wort.

Flesh of lambs and wethers	p. 279
Flux	p. 277
Flux stopped: how?	pp. 263, 272, 298
Fowls great	p. 282
Frication wholesome	p. 240
Fruits of banquets	p. 222

G

Galangal	p. 294
Garlic	p. 260
Geese of the Basse	p. 282
Gelded beasts best	p. 277
Ginger	p. 295
Gluttony rewarded	p. 222
Good things to provoke urine	p. 272
Gout holpen	p. 287
Grapes	p. 275
Green sickness	p. 298

H

Haemorrhoids: the cause	p. 296
Hair kept from falling	p. 261
Hairs cut	p. 240
Hands washed with cold water	p. 240
Hares	p. 280
Harvest	p. 228
Head purged	p. 268
Hearing holpen	p. 285
Heart glad	p. 297
Heart: what comfort?	p. 267
Heat burning: cooled with a plaster	p. 263
Heliogabalus' court	p. 221
Herb-grace and figs	p. 274
Herbs engender melancholy	p. 270
Honey clarified	p. 288
Honey new, laxative	p. 288
Honey praised	p. 288
Hops	p. 292
Horehound, comfort the hearing	p. 258
Hothouses	p. 239
House: what situation?	p. 246
Humours coined[1]	p. 227
Humours natural	p. 231
Hyssop	p. 262

---

1 *coined*] this word looks like "roined" in O2 but "coined" makes better sense, meaning 'made' or 'produced'.

I

Idleness the ¹mother of mischief	p. 247
Ire: a grievous passion	p. 253

J

Jaundice yellow	p. 256

K

King's evil	p. 258

L

Labour is made easy with use	p. 247
Labour soon after eating fish: hurteth	p. 285
Lamb's flesh	p. 279
Larks	p. 283
Leprosy	p. 234
Lilies	p. 265
Lily that is white	p. 265
Liverwort	p. 268
Lodging: clean kept	p. 248
Lodgings: fit for all persons	p. 249
Lust of the flesh	p. 261

M

Maidenhair	p. 269
Man born naked	p. 232
Man's body considered	p. 226
*Manus Christi*¹	p. 289
Many practisers	p. 240
Meats and medicine	pp. 228, 238
Meats of diverse sorts hurt man's body	p. 242
Meats salt unwholesome	p. 249
Medlar	p. 276
Megrim holpen	p. 298
Melancholy	pp. 227, 243
Melancholy caused of herbs	p. 270
Melancholy purged	p. 271
Melliot	p. 269
Members: what?	p. 232
Merry-Man	p. 252

---

i mother of mischief] *O1, O3, O4*; mother *O2*.

1 Manus Christi] Latin for 'hand of Christ': refined sugar and rose water boiled together until the sugar hardens, after which ground-up pearls or other precious stones are added; other flowers or spices might be used for this compound. Bullein provides a recipe for *manus christi* in his *Bulwark of Defence* (Bullein 1579, Ccc2r).

Middle vein	p. 237
Milk, ^i^how it may be used	p. 290
Milk new	p. 289
Milk not good for	p. 289
Milk of goats	p. 289
Milk of sheep	p. 289
Milk of women	p. 289
Mind troubled	p. 253
Mints	p. 261
Moist	p. 229
Morphew holpen	p. 284
Morphew white	p. 295
Mouse-ear[1]	p. 256
Muscles and gland's flesh	p. 233
Mustard	p. 266
Mutton tender	p. 279

N

Names of herbs	p. 223
Neezing	p. 239
Neezing: how?	p. 273
Nutmegs	p. 294

O

Oil in urine	p. 250
Oil-Olives	p. 286
Oily excrements	p. 251
Onions	p. 260
Opinions diverse	p. 222
Oysters	p. 285

P

Palsy	pp. 235, 257, 266
Part called by the ^ii^name of the whole	p. 233
Peaches	p. 274
Pears	p. 274
Periotides[2]	p. 250
Pestilence: ^iii^a preservative from	p. 280
Pestilence holpen	p. 274
Phlegm purged	p. 271

---

i how it] *O3; O2 omits.*   ii name of the whole] *O1; O2 omits.*
iii preservative from] *this ed.;* a preser. *O2.*

---

1 *Mouse-ear*] Pilosella officinarum, a type of hawkweed.
2 *Periotides*] possibly peritonitis.

Physic divided   p. 225
Physic: God author   p. 223
Physicians   p. 245
Physic is defined   p. 223
Physic is praised   p. 223
Physic: what some say   p. 222
Pigeons roasted best   p. 282
Place: most wholesome   p. 245
Plantain   p. 256
Pleasant people   p. 246
Polypody   p. 258
Pottage comfortable   p. 269
Prayer unto God, help   p. 246
Prunes sweet   p. 276
Pruning of birds   p. 240
Puddings of swine   p. 278
Pulial Royal[1]   p. 266
Purge: ¡best time to   p. 238
Purgers of choler   p. 271
Purgers of melancholy   p. 271
Purgers of phlegm   p. 271
Purging the head   p. 268
Purslane   p. 263

Q

Quietness is praised   p. 252
Quinces raw hurt   p. 275
Quinces wholesome   p. 275

R

Rabbits   p. 281
Raisins   p. 276
Raw herbs   p. 299
Repletion   p. 234
Rhubarb   p. 296
Rice   p. 293
Roots sodden nourish   p. 269
Rosemary   p. 265
Rue good against poison   p. 259

---

i best time to] *O1*; *O2 omits.*

1 *Pulial Royal*] pennyroyal; as Walter Skeat pointed out, "pennyroyal" is a corruption of the old name for the herb from the Latin puleium regium, "a name given to the plant from its supposed efficacy against fleas" from pulex and regius, latin for "flea" and "royal" (Skeat 1993, "Penny-royal").

S

Saffron	p. 297
Saffron in England	p. 297
Sage	p. 257
Sage good for old ⁱpeople	p. 258
Salad oil	p. 286
Salt	p. 287
Salt meats not wholesome	p. 249
Sanguine	p. 243
Savory	p. 267
Saxifrage	p. 267
Seed increased	p. 261
Setwall	p. 295
Sick folk: what?	p. 243
Signs	pp. 228, 234
Signs deadly	p. 251
Signs of crudity	p. 251
Sleep after dinner	p. 248
Sleep and waking	p. 248
Sleep at noon: be ⁱⁱill for the plague and memory	p. 299
Sleep eight hours	p. 300
Sleep on the right	p. 248
Sleeps in fields	p. 249
Sleep sound: how?	p. 248
Sleep: what thing doth cause it?	pp. 260, 265, 267
Sores of the pestilence: plaster to break them	p. 265
Sores that be rotten	p. 257
Sorrel leaves good	p. 256
Soul departeth	p. 241
Spinach	p. 259
Staunching of blood	p. 262
Stinging of serpents	p. 259
Stomach pained	p. 263
Stone, the disease	p. 249
Stone (the disease) to break	pp. 263, 268
Stone (the disease) what pain?	p. 249
Stone (the disease) what remedy?	p. 249
Stools soft and hard	p. 252
Stop the flux: how?	p. 263
Suppositories	p. 239
Swelling	p. 275
Swine described	p. 278
Swine's flesh abhorred of Mahomites[1]	p. 278

i people] *this ed.*; O2 *omits.*   ii ill for the plague and memory] O3; O2 *omits.*

1 *Mahomites*] Muslims.

Syrups and drinks   p. 243
Syrups or decoctions   p. 234

T

Theriaca excellent   p. 235
Throat pained   p. 287
Throats that is stopped   p. 234
Thyme the herb   p. 267
Time for all things   p. 237
Tokens dangerous   p. 245
Toothache   p. 298
Tripes of swine   p. 278

U

Urine circles noted   p. 250
Urine hath four things to be noted   p. 249
Urine like fleshy broth   p. 250
Urine of golden colour   p. 250
Urine that is green   p. 250
Urine that is grey   p. 250
Urines to provoke   p. 272
Urine white and thick   p. 250
Urine white and thin   p. 250
Use maketh labour ⁱeasy   p. 247

V

Verbena   p. 258
Vinegar   p. 287
Violets   p. 265
Voice clear   p. 283
Vomiting customary   p. 239
Vomits, what stoppeth?   p. 261

W

Walnuts   p. 293
Washing of hands in cold water   p. 240
Water corrupt   p. 286
Water hot unwholesome   p. 240
Water of ice and snow   p. 287
Water that is salt   p. 287
Water: which is best?   p. 286
Wether's flesh   p. 279
Whey wholesome: when?   p. 289
White lily   p. 265

---

i easy] *O1*; *O2 omits.*

Wind that is short	p. 235
Wine-bibbers, have a glass to look in	p. 291
Wine is best: when?	p. 291
Wine that is claret	p. 291
Wine that is red	p. 291
Wine that is white	p. 291
Winter	p. 228
Wormwood	p. 255

The End of the Table.

JOHN   Of all the pleasures and pastimes methinks there is none like unto good cheer. What should man do but pass away the time with good fellows and make merry? Seeing we have but a time to live, cast away care. Wherefore is meat and bellies ordained but the one to serve the other? The flesh that we daily increase is our own. Abstinence and fasting is a mighty enemy and nothing pleasant to me, and be used of very few that love themselves but only of beggars and covetous sparers, which do spare much and spend little. *The epicure desireth to live altogether in belly-cheer*

HUMPHREY   I know well your goodly expense of time. Iwis,[1] it is no marvel, although you make your belly your God and boast of it, you see that all lusty revellers and continual banquet makers come to great estimation. As example: to Varius Heliogabalus,[2] which was daily fed with many hundred fishes and fowls, and was accompanied with many brothels, bawds, harlots, and gluttons. And thus it doth appear by your abhorring virtue, that of right you might have claimed a great office in Heliogabalus' court if you had been[3] in those days, but you have an infinite number of your conversation in these days, the more pity. *Heliogabalus' court fit for belly gods*

JOHN   What, good sir, I require not your counsel. I pray you, be your own carver and give me leave to serve my fantasy. I will not charge you, you are very ancient and grave and I am but young. We be no matches.[4]

HUMPHREY   Good counsel is a treasure to wise men but a very trifle to a fool. If thou hadst seen those things which I have seen I know thou wouldst not be such a man nor thus spend thy time.

JOHN   What hast thou seen that I have not seen?

---

1 *Iwis*] certainly; truly.
2 *Varius Heliogabalus*] Roman emperor with a reputation for decadent self-indulgence. His extravagant feasts are alluded to by Jonson in Volpone's wooing of Celia in *Volpone* 3.7.201–4 and in the fantasies of Epicure Mamon in *The Alchemist* 2.2.75–7 (Jonson 1983, 200n201ff; Jonson 1967, 56n75–7).
3 *if you had been*] if you had lived.
4 *we be no matches*] i.e. John's youth gives him precedence.

The just reward of belly gods

HUMPHREY I have seen many notable and grievous plagues which have fallen upon greedy gluttons, as wasting their substance, deforming their bodies, shortening their pleasant days. And in this point to conclude with thee, whereas gluttony remaineth from thence is moderate diet banished. And those bellies that follow the lust of the eyes (in meats) in youth shall lack the health of all their bodies in age if they live so long.

JOHN Methinks thou canst give good counsel, thou seemest to be seen[1] in physic. I pray thee, is it so great hurt to delight in plenty of banquets?

Fruits of inordinate banquets [Fruits] The frutes O1.]

HUMPHREY Sir, if it will please you to be somewhat attentive, I will tell you. It is the very grain whereof cometh stinking vomits, saucy faces, dropsies, vertigo, palsies, obstructions, blindness, fluxes, apoplexies, catarrhs, and rheums, *et cetera*.

JOHN Is it true, that you have said to me?

HUMPHREY Would to God daily experience did not try it. I do perfectly know it. And once thou shalt be a witness thereof if thou come to age.

JOHN Then I beseech thee, gentle friend Humphrey, declare to me why there is such division among physicians.

Variety of opinions [opinions] opinions amōg mē O1.]

HUMPHREY Thou seest among the theologians there is much variety and yet but one truth. Dioscorides be soon known of musicians, and the physicians be not ignorant of the general natures of things. No division is, although it do so appear, for regents, place, age, time, and the present state of man's nature must be observed and not the old rules in all points.[2] For man's nature is sore altered and changed into a viler sort than it was wont to be.

An objection against physic

JOHN Some do report that men of great estimation say what needeth physic it is but an invention only for money? We see (say they) who liveth so well as they which never knew physic, and so evil as these ⁱapothecaries do mean?[3]

HUMPHREY Many men be more rich than wise and more esteemed for titles of their honours and worships than for any other virtue or cunning. Such men in some points be more ingrateful[4] to natural remedies than dogs, which can elect or chose

---

i apothecaries do mean] pothicary men O1.

1 *seen*] well versed.

2 *the physicians be not ignorant ... in all points*] i.e. physicians ought not simply to follow written authorities but should observe the general condition of man's nature.

3 *so evil ... do mean*] either the apothecaries live evil lives or they intend evil to other men and perhaps suggesting both. Bullein also criticizes apothecaries in his *Bulwark of Defence*, advising "make your medicines your selfe, and trust not so mutch the Apothecaries" (Bullein 1579, Ee1v).

4 *ingrateful*] ungrateful.

their vomiting grass or birds which can choose gravel or stones for their casting.[1] But to conclude with thee in this matter, Pliny, the great clerk,[2] have a thousand reasons to prove them foolish that will object against physic. And the author of all things[3] did well foresee and know what was good for man's nature when he stretched out so large a compass round about the earth with the noble planets and signs, and their courses, influences and heavenly qualities, and garnished the earth with fruits, herbs, flowers, leaves, grains, oils, gums, stones for man's comfort and help and ordained the physician for to help man. Thus the almighty have done, sayeth Solomon. And in recompense, God hath not appointed the physicians to be railed upon or despised, but honoured and rewarded, yea, esteemed of princes. And seeing [i]good nature and wise men be on my side, I force not of other men's fantasies, with whom neither [ii]good wisdom, nor [iii]good nature is guide.

God the author of physic

The inestimable goodness of God ordained herbs for the health of man

Solomon

Ecclesiastes 36

JOHN   Why is physic of such great authority or hath it been in estimation among old fathers? May that be proved of thy part?

HUMPHREY   [iv]Yes, that I can.

JOHN   If thou canst bring in any reverent fathers that loved physic, I will not despise but greatly esteem it and desire counsel in demanding of a few questions.

HUMPHREY   Physic hath been in so high an estimation that the Gentiles all consent it came from the immortal gods. The Hebrews did well know it, as Moses in the most ancient book called Genesis *primo*[4] doth describe the work of the almighty God of herbs, fruits, and plants, that Adam might teach the virtues of them to his children. Jesus Sirach, which was endued with the spirit of God, have left a laud[5] behind him greatly commending physic amongst the divines of the Hebrews, Mercury amongst the Egyptians. Ovid doth greatly commend Apollo, the inventor of herbs; when they were almost out of memory, he revived their virtues and taught their nature to others that followed him. After that came in Aesculapius,[6] which did many most excellent cures, and Chiron, the instructor of Achilles, whose name can never die as long as the herb centaury groweth upon the earth, which is called

The praise and excellency of physic

Moses

Adam

Jesus Sirach capitulum 38

Diodoro, Test. Ovid Metamorphoses [*Diodoro, Test*] Presumably Diodorus, perhaps his *Testimonia*.]

Chiron Centaurus

---

i good] God, O3.   ii good] God, O3.   iii good] O3 *omits*.
iv Yes, that I can] That I can proue O3.

---

1 *vomiting grass ... casting*] to 'cast' means to vomit. Some animals chew grass to provoke vomit, which eases digestive problems; it seems that some birds consume stones to help digest their food.
2 *clerk*] scholar.
3 *the author of all things*] God.
4 *primo*] the first, that is the first book of the Bible, which is Genesis.
5 *laud*] praise.
6 *Aesculapius*] or Asclepius, the Greek god of medicine, thought to be based on a historical figure.

Podalirius

Machaon

Hippocrates

Galen

after his name.¹ Podalirius and Machaon² were two brethren in the time of the battle of Troy, which were excellent physicians, and be greatly commended of Homer, who was more excellent than Hippocrates in the Isle of Cos, whose works will never die for he brought in physic and digested it into fair books for man's great health.³ Then came Galen, not unknown to all wise and learned physicians. I could rehearse here many more but this shall suffice to prove physic to be of great authority among old fathers.

JOHN   I pray thee, friend Humphrey, what is physic? I would be glad to learn some of thy knowledge, for thou hast a good order in talking and seem to be grounded of authority. Therefore I am sorry that I have contended with thee. I pray thee be not angry with my former talk.

Hippocrates in hb. defla. [hb. defla.] Presumably his *On Airs, Waters, and Places.*]

The definition of physic.

Theoricha

Hippocrates in *primo* aphorism

HUMPHREY   Hippocrates in his book of winds or blasts sayeth that physic or medicine is but a putting to the body which it lacketh or taking from the body things superfluous. And although our life be short, yet the art of physic is long⁴ because great numbers of things be in it and requireth much study, labour, and practice. And, first of all, it requireth much contemplation or knowledge in studying good books, which is called *theoricha*. Secondly, the very effect of contemplation or study is *practica* or *activa*,⁵ which is doing of the things that learning have taught, as repairing, amending, or preserving the bodies of men, women, and children, *et cetera*.

JOHN   It seemeth to be a goodly science

Herodotus

Emperici

Philinus

HUMPHREY   Herodotus sayeth they greatly err that call it a science, for it is an excellent art in doing of notable things and science is but to know things. There is also in this excellent art sundry sects of physicians, some be called *Emperici*,⁶ who suppose that only experience doeth suffice and so by use and experience do take in hand to heal diseases, not knowing the cause of the said disease or sickness. Philinus⁷ was one of that sect at the first

---

1 *Chiron ... name*] in Greek mythology a centaur who had great knowledge of medicine; he was said to have taught Aesculapius as well as Achilles.

2 *Podalirius and Machaon*] sons of the God Aesculapius.

3 *Homer ... health*] there is information on how to treat injuries sustained in battle in Homer's *Iliad* and *Odyssey*.

4 *although long*] a Latin translation of *Ars longa, vita brevis* meaning "art is long, / life is short!" from the first aphorism by Hippocrates.

5 theoricha ... practica *or* activa] theory and practice; *practica* was the term used to describe the focus on particular diseases and their remedies, as opposed to general principles such as humoral theory.

6 Emperici] the Empiricists who favoured medical symptoms and causes in diagnosis and treatment over the theoretical speculation that was favoured by the Dogmatists (see below).

7 *Philinus*] Philinus of Cos.

beginning, then followed Serapion, and after that the Apollonius,¹ and then came Glaucias, Menodotus,² Sextus,³ *et cetera*. Another kind of physicians be called *Methodici*,⁴ which neither observe time, place, age, state nor condition, and think them things of small profit, but only their respect is to their disease. They love not long study in physic and are greatly deceived because they would build without foundation and have the fruits before they have planted the trees. These men's cures be but by chance medley; one Sirus⁵ began this, which received certain rules of Asclepiades.⁶ The chief and best sect of physicians called *Dogmatici*;⁷ these be the wise men which set not the cart before the horse nor the roots of the trees upward. They do prudently consider the change of man's nature, the dwelling place, the alteration of the air, the time of the year, the custom of people, the manners of diseases, the fashion of men's diet.⁸ And this they will prove by true arguments and reasons and will be very careful for their patients. The disciples of those men be the best scholars, therefore I counsel thee John to love well Hippocrates, the prince of physicians, which began the best manner to give rules to all the lovers of physic. Of this writeth Galen, much lauding⁹ Hippocrates and his followers, and in these days Leonart Fuchs, Matheolus,¹⁰ *et cetera*.

Serapion
Apollonius
Methodici

Asclepiades
Dogmatici

Hippocrates

JOHN Seeing thou has spoken of sundry parts of physicians, I pray thee what parts be there of physic?

HUMPHREY Truly there be five things to be noted in physic, as five principal parts, as Galen sayeth in *liber De elementis*. The first is to consider the nature of man's body. The second is to keep the body in health and to defend it from sickness and infirmities. The third is to know all the causes, rules, and seeds whereof the sickeness doth grow. The fourth is crisis¹¹ or judgement of the disease of things present, past, and to come. The fifth is the best and most excellent, for it showeth the manner of healing, dieting, fashion,¹² order, and way to

Galen *De elementis*,
De temperamentis,
De facultatibus
naturalibus

Physic divided into
five parts

---

1 *Apollonius*] Apollonius Antiochenus.
2 *Menodotus*] Menodotus of Nichomedia.
3 *Sextus*] Sextus Empiricus.
4 Methodici] the Methodics rejected the views of the Empiricists and the Dogmatists, believing that disease was the consequence of a tenseness or looseness of the body resulting in constriction or flux.
5 *Sirus*] This could be St Cyrus, who practised medicine, but is more likely a reference to Themison of Laodicea.
6 *Asclepiades*] Asclepiades of Bithynia.
7 Dogmatici] the Dogmatists or Rationalists who, unlike the Empiricists, were committed to thoretical principles and the application of natural philosophy to medicine.
8 *the fashion of men's diet*] their customary diet.
9 *lauding*] praising.
10 *Matheolus*] presumably Matheolus Perusinus.
11 *crisis*] the point in the progress of a disease where the patient will either recover or die.
12 *fashion*] customary or usual way of behaving.

help the sick body and preserve the same as long as man doth remain in the state of life.

JOHN   Thou hast spoken of the parts of physic, what is the form, manner of distribution thereof?

HUMPHREY   It is distributed in three forms: one is natural, another unnatural, the third against nature. The first is by those things whereof the body is compact,[1] constituted, or made, as Galen sayeth in his third book of his *Tempramentis*, chapter 4. The second is called not natural, as meats or things to preserve the body in health; they be not called unnatural because they be against the body, but because the rash taking or gluttonous using of them may bring many things to the utter destruction of the body. The third be things against nature, which doth corrupt the body or poison nature whereof Galen writeth.

Galen, liber 3, De temperamentis, capitulum 4
Galen in liber 2, Therapeutic Method

JOHN   Now thou has taught me short rules of the parts and forms physical, I pray thee show me some pretty rules of the complexions of men and that I may aptly know them with their properties, elements, temperaments, and humours.

HUMPHREY   Upon my lute some time, to recreate myself, I join with my simple harmony many plain verses. Among all other, one small song of the four complexions. Wilt thou hear it? Take that chair and sit down and I will teach thee my song.

JOHN   I thank thee.

The description of the sanguines [sanguines] sanguene persons O1.]	HUMPHREY	The bodies where heat and moisture dwell, Be sanguine folks, as Galen tell, With visage fair and cheeks rose ruddy, The sleeps is much, and dreams be bloody, Pulse great and full, with digestion fine, Pleasantly concocting flesh and wine, Excrements abundant, with anger short, Laughing very much and finding sport, Urine gross, with colour red, Pleasant folks at board and bed.
The description of the phlegmatic [phlegmatic] fleumatike persons O1.]		Where cold with moisture prevaileth much, Phlegmatic folks be always such, Fatness, softness, here plain and right, Narrow veins and colour white, Dull of wit, no heart too bold, Pulse very slow, digestion cold, Sleeping over much, urine gross and pale, Spittle white and thick, thus ends this tale.
The description of the choleric		Choler is hot and dry as fire, Leanness of limbs and puffed with ire, Costive bellies, with little sleep, Dreams of fire or wounds deep,

---

1 *compact*] made up.

Sallow coloured[1] or tawny red,
Feeding on salt meats[2] and crusts of bread,
Voice sharp and quickness of wit,
Urine yellow and saltness of spit,
Pulses swift and very strong,
Cruel countenance, not angry long.
Melancholy is cold and very dry,   *The description of*
As here in rhyme his signs will try,   *melancholy*
Hair plain and very thin,
A lean wretch with hardness of skin,
Choler whitely or like to lead,
Much watch, and dreams of dread,
And stiff in foolish fantasy,
Digestion slow, and long angry,
Fearful of mind, with watery spittle,
Seldom laughing, and pulse little,
Urine watery and very thin,
The cold earth to him is kin.

JOHN   This is a good song, and I will learn it, for though it seem not very pleasant yet I preceive it is profitable.[3] Now thou has spoken of the signs of the four complexions, I pray thee teach me shortly how to know the elements.

HUMPHREY   They be the four beginners, unmingled and untempered, from whose mixtures every corporal thing hath his substance.   *Hippocrates; De elementis; Avicenna in Cantica*

JOHN   What be the parts? I pray thee, tell me.

HUMPHREY   Four: the one is earth, the heaviest matter and grossest, which is cold and dry and melancholy; and the other is water, which is lighter and more subtle than the earth and of nature is cold, moist, and phlegmatic. Then is air more purer and lighter than water and, if it be not altered with any other strange cause, it is hot, and moist, and sanguine. Then fire is most light, pure and clear, a clarifier and a cleanser of all the other elements when they are corrupted, and is of his own nature hot, dry, and choleric. And of these four elements both man, beast, fish, fowl, herb, stone, metal have their proper working, not of one of the elements alone, but of all, some more and some less, according to their natures. Hippocrates sayeth after the soul is gone from the body, the body doth return to the first matter whereof it was made. And, to conclude, all things that be made upon the earth shall return unto the earth again in time.

The description of the 4 elements

Galen in liber 8 decr. [decr.] Possibly a reference to De diebus decretoriis.]

Hippocrates in lib. de. na. [O1; O2 omits.] [lib. de. na.] Presumably liber De natura humana.]

---

1 *Sallow coloured*] brownish-yellow.

2 *salt meats*] salted meats, here "meat" is used specifically in the sense of animal flesh rather than the more general sense of 'food'.

3 *though ... profitable*] a variation on the common saying that something is 'pleasant and profitable'; John is apparently suggesting that Humprey's song is not very good.

JOHN Why might not men, beasts, fish or fowl, herb or tree, be of one element as well as of four? I pray you tell me.

<small>Creatures are compounded of more elements than one</small>

HUMPHREY No, for as Aristotle sayeth, *Deus et natura nihil agunt frustra*: God and nature hath done nothing in vain. And if anything upon the earth sensible were of one element, no sickness could hurt it, nor disease corrupt it, but everything living upon the earth seeing it hath had beginning must needs have ending, to whom these four complexions doth belong, if they do greatly abound or diminish, or withdraw their virtues with quantities or qualities.

JOHN May a man see any of the elements?

HUMPHREY The thing which men do see be none of the four elements, not earth but earthy, not water but watery, not air but airy, not fire but fiery. But the things

<small>Elements felt and not seen</small>

which man do feel be the four elements, as earth, air, fire, and water. And these be the uttermost simples of complexions, diversely and specially, alone of themselves, or mingled with other, taking sundry and diverse effects, manners, conditions, forms, and qualities, both in man and beast, and every living thing, sensible and insensible.

JOHN What is the complexions of the four quarters of the year, and names of the signs?

<small>Hipocrates in *liber De natura humana*</small>

HUMPHREY The springtime, when blood doth increase; summer, when red choler doeth rule; harvest, when choler adust or melancholy doth reign; winter, when phlegm doth abound in

<small>Winter, Spring, Summer, Harvest</small>

full strength. It is called winter from the twelfth day of December unto the tenth day of March, this season is cold and moist; it is called springtime from the twelfth day of March and endeth about the twelfth day of June; summer beginneth about the twelfth day of June and endeth about the twelfth day of September; autumn or harvest beginneth about the thirteenth day of September and endeth about the eleventh day of

<small>Of the twelve signs [O1 omits.]</small>

December. Capricorn, Aquarius, and Pisces be winter signs; Aires, Taurus, and Gemini be signs for the spring; Cancer, Leo, and Virgo be the figures for summer; Libra, Scorpio, and Sagittarius be the signs for harvest. And the sun goeth through all these twelve signs in twelve months; and the moon goeth twelve times through each of the foresaid signs once in the year, and do take sundry effects in man, beasts, and fruits in the said signs, hot or cold, moist or dry.

JOHN What be the complexions of medicines?

<small>Avicenna in *pri Cantica*</small>

HUMPHREY Those things that overcometh and govern the body, as purgations, expulsives, *et cetera*, these be called medicines; and those things that nourisheth and augmenteth the body be called meats. For the complexions of meats and medicines be

<small>Meats and medicine be known by tasting</small>

known by their tastes, as coldness, hotness, moistness, dryness, bitterness, saltness, sweetness, fatness, sharpness, styptic, and clammy. And because thy request is to have prescribed unto thee but only a little government of health, I will show unto thee another of my little songs in plain metre how thou shalt know meats and medicines by their tastes.

JOHN   That is my chief desire; I will hear thee, say on.

HUMPHREY   Cold quencheth the choler's pride,   Cold, Moist
Moist humecteth that which is dried,
The flowing moisture, ⁱby proof I try,
Is wasted of humours hot and dry.
The subtle food that is piercing quick,
The clammy meats maketh it thick,
Bitter things cleanse, and wipeth oft,
And expel phlegm, and maketh soft.
Salt drieth and resolveth¹ phlegm tough,   Salt
Fat nourisheth and make subtle enough,   Bitter, Clammy,
Styptic or rough taste on the tongue   Styptic, Sweet [O1
Bindeth and comforteth appetite long.   omits.]
Sweet things in cleansing is very good
It dissolveth much, nourisheth blood.
These things well used, nature will please,
But abusing them beastly bringeth disease.

JOHN   In good faith, methinks thou sayest well, for there appear perfect reasons in these thy pretty rules. Now thou hast declared unto me the signs of complexions of men, with the way and apt knowledge of meats by their tastes, I would fain learn shortly the temperaments and complexions of mankind.

HUMPHREY   There was never no discreet nor wise physician that either feared God, or pitied mankind, or loved his own honesty would take in hand either to prescribe diet or to minister medicine to anybody before he well did consider and wisely weigh with himself the temperament, mixture, or complexion of mankind. First, whether he were hot or cold, moist or dry, fat or lean, or indifferent between them both, tempered by health, or distempered by sickness, as the extremities of hotness, coldness, moistness, and dryness. Therefore   Avicenna in *pri* tract
John, these things may not be forgotten. You must note also the   *Cantica*. Galen *liber*
four ages of mankind, and first the tender state of children, which   1, *capitulum 2; liber*
beginneth at the birth and so continueth until fifteen years next   1, *capitulum 3; liber*
after their said birth. Their temperaments, or complexions, be hot   4, *capitulum ultimo*
and moist,² very like unto the seed whereof they be procreated.   *De simplicium*
Then, next unto childhood or innocent age, youth, which is the   *medicamentorum*
second part of life, beginneth to reign; his temperament or com-   *facultatibus [liber 1,*
plexion hath rather more fiery heat than perfect natural heat and   *capitulum 3] li. 2.*
this second age continueth for ten years (as Galen sayeth well). In   cap 3 O1.]
this two first states of life let all natural fathers and mothers bring   Galen *liber* 5
up their youth³ ⁱⁱset ⁱⁱⁱGod before their eyes, for ⁱᵛthey have   *Aphorisms*,
         comment 9

i by] O3; be O2.   ii set] virtuously set O3.   iii God] yᵉ fear of God O3.
iv they] parents O3.

---

1 *resolveth*] dissolves, disintegrates.
2 *hot and moist*] i.e. sanguine.
3 *bring up their youth*] i.e. bringing up the young.

An exhortation for bringing up of youth [exhortation for] ernest brief exhortacion for ye O1.]

no small charge committed unto them that must give account to God how they have brought up their children. And they that in these years do spare correction truly be grievous enemies unto their children, and at last shall be recompensed with shame when they shall see misfortune and wretchedness fall upon the fruits of their own seeds. For men have small profit of their corn which be choked and overcome with thistles, briars, and brakes,[1] which were not weeded in time, much less of their children, which have received neither correction nor honest learning in due season. If the keepers of gardens be careful over their late sown seeds and tender herbs, which are in danger to be destroyed of every frost, what should good fathers and mothers do for their children whose temper[2] and youthful years be carried away and overcome of every foolish fantasy? And it is no marvel, but this shall suffice for the wise and small profit the fools. But to my matter which I took in hand, I will return unto the third age of mankind, which is called the lusty state of life and beginneth at twenty-five years and continueth unto thirty-five. This age is hot and dry, and very choleric (as Galen

Galen in liber De simplicium medicamentorum facultatibus

sayeth). This part of life is subject to many burning and extreme fevers and hot ulcers, therefore it is necessary to know this temperament or complexion, which is called choleric, as plainly may appear by age, strength, diet, urine, *et cetera*. This is the best time for mankind to travail in, with goodly exercise in science, art, and profitable travels in his vocation, putting in practice the virtues which he hath learned in youth, for this is the summer part of life, wherein all goodly fruits do flourish in every good occupation. This is the very harvest, to gather precious

The best time to provide for age

corn and fruit of their labours against the cold storms and cloudy days of their aged winter, wherein the body shall be weak, and the eyes' sight decay, and the hands tremble. And therefore it is not comely to see the state of age without rest, which in the time of youth did honestly travail. For there is a grace given to many creatures unreasonable, both beasts and fowls, to make provision beforehand what is then to be required of men reasonable, as followeth in these verses:

> The bird in time her nest can make,
> The bee will build his house full fine,
> The crane with stone in foot will wake,
> The cony will carve under the mine,
> The squirrel in trees her nuts can keep,
> Against cold winter to seed and sleep,
> And should not man well foresee,
> In youth to know his old degree.

Then from thirty-five, or few years following, the lusty branches of youth begin to abate: his pleasant leaves, flowers, and fruit by little and little will decay; raw humours, cramps, dropsies, quartans, melancholy will then draw near. The riots, surfeits, sore labours, bearing of extreme burdens, wrestlings, acts venerous, with the

---

1 *brakes*] bracken or thickets.
2 *temper*] due proportion or mixture of humours or qualities.

abuse of youth, will then spring forth to the detriment of age and sudden decay of life, in especial of drunkards.

JOHN What be the places of blood, choler, phlegm and melancholy; natural or unnatural? Thou hast not made a particular distinction of their proper places, but generally thou hast spoken well in thy tongue.

HUMPHREY There are also other descriptions of the four humours very necessary to be known, and their places whereas they dwell within the body. And first of blood: as Galen sayeth in his first book of affected places, blood (sayeth he) that is in the pluses doth greatly differ from the blood of the veins, for the blood of the pulses is thinner, yellower and hotter and this blood may be called the governor of life. The spring and fountain of the blood general is in the liver, which serveth every vein of blood, and this blood in colour is very red. Phlegm is white and is engendered in the stomach and at length, by the virtue of natural heat, pure phlegm is turned into blood. There be also watery, slimy, glassy, gross, salt, sour, thick, hard, binding, and extreme cold phlegms, which indeed be unnatural, that be engendered through surfeits, coldness, or idleness bringing to the body many noisome diseases. There is also choler, which is yellow, whose place in the body is the gall,[1] which cometh of the cleansing or purifying of blood, and this choler is clear, hot, and dry, and the comforter of decoction. Green choler, or choler mingled with phlegm, be unnatural. Melancholy natural in the spleen is nothing but the six degrees or heavy residents of the blood. The natural melancholy is known by his blackness, the unnatural cometh of the burning of choler and is lighter and hotter, brown of colour, sour of taste, and putteth the body in great danger, as madness, black jaundice, continual fevers, and sudden deadly diseases. Therefore, my friend John, remember this short description of humours, as the words of Galen and Avicenna say. *The four humours natural and unnatural are described*

Avicenna in liber *Cantica*

JOHN Thus I have heard the several placing of the four complexions of blood, choler, phlegm, and melancholy; and is there any distinct hotness, coldness, moistness, and dryness in any other creature besides man? Tell me.

HUMPHREY Not only in man, but in beasts, fish, fowl, serpents, trees, herbs, metals, and everything sensible and insensible according to their natures; and be equally mingled or tempered together, which is called mean temperance, or else exceedeth in degrees, which is called intemperance. Hot and moist may be compounded together, so may cold and dry, hot and dry, cold and moist. Example: a choleric man, hot and dry; a phlegmatic man, cold and moist, *et cetera*. Of herbs, as hyssop and rue, hot and dry; purslane and cucumbers, cold and moist, *et cetera*. But temperaments or complexions of men, beasts, and trees, be some hotter, some colder, according to their natures. As a lion is hotter than a choleric man, pepper is hotter than cloves. And though there be degrees in more hotness or more coldness, yet they are called but hot or cold, as men after labour or travail they will say they are hot, *Galen in* liber 4 De temperamentis

---

1 *the gall*] the gall-bladder.

but the fire, which people warm them at, is hotter. Also, there be things repugnant to temperaments, as moist and dryness together, heat and coldness together, as fire to be cold, or the water of his own nature to be hot, which water *per accidens*[1] of the fire is made hot and fire quenched by the water. And everything exceeding greatly with distemperance, or wanting temperance or complexion, do eftsoons come to an end, and men by extreme sicknesses, surfeits, or wounds, or, finally, age, lacking natural virtue. Of heat and moistness of trees and herbs, from whom juice and sap is withdrawn, these things of necessity must needs die and come to corruption, as Galen and Aristotle sayeth.

<small>Galen in *liber* 4 De temperamentis; Aristotle *De generatione et corruptione*</small>

JOHN   Whether be men or women of colder complexion?

<small>Avicenna</small>

HUMPHREY   Avicenna sayeth: like as men be hot and dry so be women cold and moist.

JOHN   Yea, but Lucian sayeth they be perilous hot of their tongues and full of venom. Though I am no physician yet can I make a description of that member, for I am oftentimes stinged with it. I would to God they had been wormed when they were young, but when they are old they are past all cure. But the best medicine that I have is a gentle herb called rue, which I am never without great store.

<small>Whether this be true let the married judge</small>

HUMPHREY   Mankind was born naked to this end: that he might clothe himself with other creatures, which he brought not into this world with him, as cloth, leather, harness made of iron, for his defence, because he is the chief creature. But horses of nature have hard hooves, lions sharp teeth, porcupines sharp pricks, which is their continual and natural armour, as things ever prepared to debate and strife, and by no art can scant be tamed. The rose, as pleasantly as she doth appear and as sweet as she doth smell, spring [2]not further without a great number of sharp pricks. Therefore it is tolerable for men to bear with them whom nature hath sealed and marked for his own with that humour most choleric. Digress from this thy communication and let us talk of things more profitable, for indeed this is pleasant to no man.

<small>All things bringeth his apparel with him saving man</small>

JOHN   Seeing thou wilt not describe me this particular members of which we have spoken, I would be glad to know the parts of mankind, with a description of his members.

HUMPHREY   Members be simple and also compound. The simples be ten in number: the cartilages, the gristles, the bones, veins and sinews, arteries, pannicles,[3] ligaments, cords, and the skin. Members compounded be those that be joined and built together of simple members, as the hands, face, feet, liver, and heart, and so compounded members be made of simple. Some of the compounded members be called

<small>A definition of members</small>

---

1 per accidens] Latin: by accident.
2 *spring*] Bullein sometimes uses the plural form of a verb (*spring*) with a singular subject (*rose*) as do many early modern writers.
3 *pannicles*] membranes.

principals: as the heart, from whence the arteries springs; the brain, from whence the sinews springs; the liver, which is the well of the blood, from whence the veins do spring; and the stones of generation, from whence the seed of life do spring.[1] But those compounded members that be principal be all the other members except the simple, as the nose, the ears, the eyes, the face, the neck, the arms and legs. And the brains and chief substance of our flesh be compounded members of sinews, and covered with pannicles,[2] which be of a sinewy nature, but that sinews give feeling to all the whole body, even as the arteries giveth spiritual blood from the heart to every member. The whole body is covered with films and skins. Out the head springeth hard matter issuing from the places called the pores, to purge vapours and smoke from the brain, which ascended out of the stomach into the head and is cleansed through *pia mater*, called the tender covering of the brain or spirits animal. And therefore as some parts of the body being divided in sunder be each like unto the other, and yet called by the name of the whole – as for example when the bones be broken in sunder, or the flesh cut into diverse pieces, or the blood poured into sundry vessels – a piece of flesh is still called flesh, a fragment of a bone is called a bone, and a drop of blood is called blood; even so, an hand, arm, vein, or such like unseparate parts being divided into pieces or called by the name of pieces, and not by the name of the whole part (as is before). But, my friend John, to make a large description of anatomy it were too long for me but, shortly, I will say something. And first of the definition thereof, is what the body of a dead man or woman is: cut and opened, and the members divided, or for the want of dead bodies to read good books, as Galen, Avicenna, *et cetera*. And it behoveth them that cutteth a dead corpse to note four things: first the nutramental members, as the liver with the veins; the second is the members spiritual, as the heart with the arteries; the third is the animal members, as the head, brains, and sinews; the fourth, and last be extremities of the body, as arms, legs, skin, hair, *et cetera*. Of these said members, with the bones, is all the body compounded. And like as every tree and herb have their roots in the earth and their branches springeth upward, even so the roots of mankind have the beginning in the brain, and the sinew[3] and branches groweth downward, in the which brain dwelleth the virtues of imagination, fantasy, memory, *et cetera*. And these animal virtues be placed, as it were, heavenly above all the members, communicating their heavenly influences down unto the heart, as to a prince or chief ruler within the body, which giveth life to every part thereof. Thou shalt consider that the heart was the first that received life from the spirits and shall be the last that shall die. Note also that as there be noble senses given to the body, as seeing, hearing, smelling,

Muscles and gland's flesh [In the original text this marginal note also appears in the paragraph above that discusses the rose, which is apparently an error.]

A part is called by the name of the whole and not the whole by the part

What anatomy is

Four things considered in the body of man

Example

---

1 *stones ... seeds of life*] the testicles from which sperm is produced.

2 *pannicles*] membranes.

3 *sinew*] See earlier note on 'spring' (above); here Bullein uses the singular form of the verb with a plural subject ('branches').

tasting, feeling, even so nature hath four principal virtues: first, attractive; the second retentive; the third digestive; the fourth expulsive. Attractive is that by which every part of the body draweth the food of life, and serveth the virtue digestive. And the retentive do hold the meat until it be ready to be altered and changed. Digestive do alter and maketh the food like unto the thing that it nourisheth, as phlegm, blood, *et cetera*. Expulsive do separate them from the other, the good from the bad. Thou oughtest also most chiefly to learn the knowledge of the veins, and for what sickness they must be opened, and what medicines, either in syrups or pills, thou must use. And first mark this figure of the anatomy here present before thee, with the heavenly signs, because I have not painted at large the several parts of the said anatomy.[1] The middle vein of the forehead is good to be opened against megrim, forgetfulness, and passions of the head. And they that be let blood of this or any other vein must first have their head purged with *Pillule Cochie Rasis*[2] or some purgation, but first use things to extenuate matter, as syrup of bugloss, *et cetera*.

<small>Take syrups or decoction of roots or herbs before you receive purgations [O1 omits.]</small>

Against leprosy and deafness let blood the two veins behind the ears and use the said pills, or else *Pillule Aurea Nicholai*,[3] or *Arabice*,[4] or *Confeccio Hameth Minor*.[5]

<small>Leprosy [O1 omits.]</small>

Against repletion, or too much blood, or blood in the eyes flowing in the head, open the temples' veins called arteries, for they be ever beating, and use to purge with *Pillule Artritice Nicholai*[6] or *Puluis ad Epithama Hepatis*.[7]

<small>Repletion [O1 omits.]</small>

Against squinance, stopping the throat,[8] and stopping of the breath, let blood the veins under the tongue; and for this use *Philoniūmaius Nicholai*,[9] and gargarisms, *Pillule Bechie*,[10] and *Oxymel Simplex*.

<small>Stopping in the throat [O1 omits.]</small>

---

1 *anatomy*] At this point in the copy text there is a picture of the human body labelled with astrological signs.

2 Pillule Cochie Rasis] a pill containing purgative medicine that apparently originated with Galen but here according to modifications in the recipe made by Rasis.

3 Pillule Aurea Nicholai] a pill containing an antidote derived from gold (hence "Aurea"), presumably created by the Byzantine physician Nicholas Myrepsos.

4 Arabice] "the pill of Arabica" or "the Arabic pill", containing a number of ingredients including aloes, that is described in the *Pharmacopoeia Londinensis* (Culpepper 1653, Ll2v).

5 Confeccio Hameth Minor] confection of Hamech, a medicinal preparation used as a purge; Bullein provides a recipe for *Confeccio Hameth* in his *Bulwark of Defence* (Bullein 1579, Aaa3v).

6 Pillule Artritice Nicholai] presumably similar to *Pilulae Arthriticae* or pills for the arthritic following the instructions of Nicholas Myrepsos; Bullein provides a recipe for *Pilulae Arthriticae* in his *Bulwark of Defence* (Bullein 1579, Ddd3v).

7 Puluis ad Epithama Hepatis] apparently a powder applied externally to the surface of the body (a fomentation) to aid the liver.

8 *stopping the throat*] obstructions in the throat.

9 Philoniūmaius Nicholai] presumably some preparation following the instructions of Nicholas Myrepsos but it is not clear which one.

10 Pillule Bechie] Instructions are given for making "Trochisci Bechici", also a kind of pill made from sugar, liquorice and other ingredients, in the *Pharmacopoeia Londinensis* (Culpepper 1653, Mm1v).

Veins called originals open not without great counsel of a learned physician or cunning surgeon; they be in the neck and have a great course of blood that governeth the head and the whole body.

Veins [*O1* omits.]

Against short wind, and evil blood approaching to the heart, and spitting blood, open the vein called ⁱ*Cordiaca*, or heart vein, in the arm. Use things to extenuate, as *Aromaticum*,¹ *Chariophillatum Mesue*,² *Serapium ex Absinthii*³ in cold time; *Serapium Boraginis*, hot time, and *Pillule Stomochi*.⁴

Short wind [*O1* omits.]

Against palsy, yellow jaundice, burning heats, and apostimations of the liver, open the liver vein upon the right arm; take *Serapium ex Endive, Diamargariton frigid Avicenni*.⁵

Palsy [*O1* omits.]

Against dropsy open the vein between the belly and the branch,⁶ the right side against the said dropsy and the left side against the passions of the milt, but be not rash, unless you have the counsel of one well seen in the anatomy; use *Pillule Hiere cum Agarico*.⁷

Dropsy

Against the stopping the secret terms or fluxions of women, or helping the haemorrhoids, and purging sores, open the vein called Sophane under the ankle; ⁱⁱuse *Theriaca Andromaci, Pillule Mastichine Petri d'Abano*.⁸

Helping the haemorrhoids

Theriaca is an excellent treacle

Within twenty hours after one is infected with the pestilence coming suddenly, open the vein between the rest of the foot and the great toe; use *Serapium Cichorii*⁹ and *Pillule Pestilentialis Ruffi*.¹⁰

---

i *Cordiaca*] *O1*; Dordiaca *O2*.   ii use *Theriaca*] this ed.; *Theriaca O2*.

---

1 Aromaticum] "of sweet spices" (Latin).

2 Chariophillatum Mesue] a preparation devised by the physician Mesue, probably clove water.

3 Serapium ex Absinthii] essence of wormwood.

4 Pillule Stomochi] a pill for the stomach; instructions on how to make them are given in the *Pharmacopoeia Londinensis* (Culpepper 1653, Ll1v).

5 Diamargariton frigid Avicenni] pearls in cold water, following instructions by Avicenna; ground-up pearls were often used as medicine, for example in *manus christi*, and were thought to strengthen the heart.

6 *branch*] arm.

7 pillule Hiere cum Agarico] pills of *hiera picra* with agaric. *Hiera picra* was a purgative drug made from canella (cinnamon, or cassia bark), aloes, and other ingredients (*OED* hiera picra, *n*). Agaric was the name given to a type of fungus growing on trees, especially the larch; Bullein presumably intends the female variety since it was cathartic and the male variety styptic (*OED* agaric, A. *n*. 1). Information on how to make *hiera picra* is given in the *Pharmacopoeia Londinensis* (Culpepper 1653, Ll1r).

8 Pillule Mastichin, Pietro d'Abano] mastic pills of Pietro d'Abano; these were purgative pills made from mastic, a gum or resin from tree-bark (*OED* mastic, *n*. 1).

9 Serapium Cichorii] probably a reference to Egyptian chicory (after the God Serapis) or saccharum chicory.

10 Pillule pestilentialis Ruffi] pills for the pestilence according to Rufus of Ephesus; instructions for making these pills are given in the *Pharmacopoeia Londinensis* (Culpepper 1653, Ll1v).

Against stinking breath open the vein between the lip and the chin; use for this *Catharicum Imperialie Nicholaus Alexandrinus*.[1]

Against the toothache open the vein in the roof of the mouth and first purge with *Pillule Cochie Rasis*[2] or with pills of mastic.[3]

Use to eat capers and take *Pillule Jude Haly* or *Pilule de Lapide Lazule* [Jude Haly is possibly Haly Abbas, although he was not Jewish; *Lapide Lazule* refers to the semi-precious blue-coloured stone lapis lazuli.]

Miracle helpeth but no medicine in this case

Against quartans, tertians, and pains of the left side, open the spleen-vein, commonly called the low vein, with a wide cut and not deep, for surgeons nicely pricking or opening veins with little scarifications, doth let out good pure blood and still retain gross, cold, and dry, earthly matter, to the great hurt of their patients. And albeit many more veins might here be spoken of, and their utilities, yet this shall well suffice, by God's grace, to keep all people in health that upon just cause have these veins opened, except old men, women with child, and children under fourteen years of age, or men after diverse agues, for bloodletting will then engender perilous palsies, as very excellent physicians have well declared. And after one be infected with the pestilence twenty-four hours, before he have received medicine or bloodletting, miracle helpeth him, but truly, no medicine have virtue to do it.

JOHN This same figure, although it appeareth in many books, yet very few do understand it in all points, such be the secret works of nature. And whereas thou hast well spoken of some veins and apt medicines for the body, I would fain see the true form and shape of the bones.

HUMPHREY Oh John, it were a long time to declare the singular members with the compounds, as Galen do in his book of the parts and bones.[4] It requireth only one work, but I have taken in hand to teach thee but a government of health. Notwithstanding, at thy request, I will ^i^show unto thee a proportion of the bones, no less true than new, which is the very timber or posts whereupon our frail flesh is builded, beginning in our mothers' wombs and ending in earth, the mother of all things. And as the noble prince Avicenna affirmeth, the number of all the bones be 244, beside sisamina[5] and os laude.[6]

---

i show unto thee a proportion] briefly rehearse the number O4.

---

1 Catharicum Imperialie Nicholaus Alexandrinus] an electuary; Nicholaus Alexandrinus is another name for Nicholas Myrepsos, after Alexandria where he used to visit and perhaps also lived.

2 Pillule Cochie Rasis] a pill containing purgative medicine that originated with Galen but here according to modifications in the recipe made by Rasis.

3 *mastic*] a gum or resin from tree-bark.

4 *in his book of the parts and bones*] a reference to his work *De ossibus* (*Of the Bones*) and perhaps also *De usu partium corporis humani* (*Of the Uses of the Different Parts of the Human Body*).

5 *sisamina*] sesamoid bones, which are small bones and cartilage that form in tendons (Lewis 1988, "Sisamina"); see also *OED* sesamoid *n*.

6 *os laude*] an apocryphal bone. Following these words the copy text has a picture of a skeleton leaning on a spade; the picture appears to have been copied from Vesalius' *De humani corporis fabrica* (Vesalius 1543, 163).

JOHN Thou hast spoken of the opening of veins, and medicines convenient to cleanse the blood, with the figure of the bones, but thou has not spoken of convenient time when to let blood nor of the state or age of them whose veins should be opened. Therefore, I would be glad to learn not only time of bloodletting but also of purging the belly, vomits, bathings, neezings, and rubbing of the body, *et cetera*.

HUMPHREY Everything hath his time convenient and must be done with sober discretion and not with rash ignorance, which killeth an infinite number. Therefore the cause must be known and the time observed, as Galen writeth in the commentary of the *Aphorisms* of Hippocrates.[1] Many bodies be extinguished by sudden death in whom is extreme fullness or abundance, for abundance of blood or any other humour (sayeth Aristotle) is the cause of many sicknesses, and those men that useth much gluttony in winter shall be apt to receive many diseases in the springtime. Therefore when the body have extreme heat, fullness of veins, flushing with sudden redness in the face, gross and red urine, and such burning heat in the night that let the sleep, *et cetera*, then it is time to evacuate the body with some purgation, bloodletting, or abstinence as the strength and age of the patient will serve. For many diseases be helped by discreet bloodletting, as pleurisies, hot fevers, frenzies, repletion, or surfeits taken with over-much eating or drinking. As Galen sayeth, the letting of blood dryeth up the superfluous moisture of the belly, helpeth memory, purgeth the bladder, quieteth the brain, warmeth the marrow, openeth the organs of hearing, helpeth digestion, induceth sleep, *et cetera*. Unto this agreeth Rasis, saying it helpeth greatly against leprosies, squinances, apoplexies, pestilences, *et cetera*. But old men, children, or women with child ought not to be let blood, nor also those people that dwell in cold regions may not be let blood because the blood is the chief warmer of nature. The people that dwell in hot regions, if they let blood it will dry their bodies, for blood is the chief moisture of nature. Therefore is the heat of summer and the coldness of winter forbidden to open veins or let blood, except for a stripe[2] or sudden chance. As Rasis sayeth, the spring of the year is the chief time to let blood in the right arm or right foot, in the vein called median, which vein must be opened, as well at other times, in the beginning of sicknesses, as hot fevers and pleurises, *et cetera*, as basilica[3] should be opened in the midst or toward the end of a sicknesss. Purgation ought to be ministered with great discretion and not rashly to be taken for every trifle; as thou hast heard me speak of bloodletting, so,

Time for all things

Hippocrates in 1, *Aphorisms* 3

Aristotle in *pri problemata* 59; Avicenna in 2 *pri* doc. 2 *capitulum* 6 [*problemata* 59] prob. 56 O1.]

Galen in *liber de flobothomia* [de flobothomia] of phlebotomy. Galen wrote several books on bloodletting.]

Rasis in 4 *Almansorem*, *capitulum* 15 [*capitulum* 15] cap. 14 O1.]

Rasis in 4 *Almansorem*, *capitulum* 14

Middle vein [Middle] the midle O1.]

---

1 Aphorisms *of Hippocrates*] one of the earliest collections of aphorisms, written 400 BCE.
2 *stripe*] a stroke of divine judgement.
3 *basilica*] the basilic vein, which is in the arm.

Hippocrates in 3 *pri* doct. a *capitulum*. [*doct.*] possibly indicating 'doctrine'. It is not clear which work by Hippocrates is being referred to here.]	observe the selfsame rules in purgation as time, person, quality, or quantity. For Hippocrates sayeth, without doubt it is needful to purge the superfluity of the body. As, if blood abound to take things to purge blood; if phlegm be superfluous then take things to cleanse his superfluity; if choler be too ardent hot, use things to extinguish; if melancholy be too extreme, then taste things to bring him into a mean. And not to purge one humour with the
Usurpation in medicine is ill [is ill] be euill *O1*.]	medicines of another, but to take them in due order and aptness for the said humours, as Valerius Cordus, Mesue, and Nicholas[1] teacheth the manner of making of the most excellent purgations
Best in the morning to let blood, evil toward night [Best in the morning] In the mornyng is beste *O1*.]	with their quantities. And, as in bloodletting, sleep must be avoided for eight or twelve hours after them. So, when your purgations be taken, air is to be avoided and to be kept close[2] for two or three days or more, as the malice of the disease or power of the purgations be. And the counsel of Rasis must be followed, which sayeth oftentimes to take purgations or laxative medicines
Rasis 4 *Almansorem*, *capitulum* 15	doth make the body weak and apt to the fever ethic[3] and specially in very lean or weak persons. They that be very fat have small guts and veins, purgations be very noisome unto them; but strong bodies having large vessels may sustain purgations without any hurt. But strong purgations, either in pills or potions, if they anything do exceed be very hurtful, therefore the doses or quantites may not exceed. And also, they must be made as pleasant as art
Meats and medicine grieveth not except pills before supper	can do them, unless they offend the stomach. Hippocrates giveth counsel that men should not mingle medicines with meat, but to take them three or four hours before meat or else so long after, unless they be pills called *Ante Cibum*,[4] which may be taken at the beginning of supper, or else *Pilli Chochi*, a little before sleep,
Time to purge	two hours after supper. The best time of purgations is in the springtime, as the doctors doth affirm; the apt days and signs are commonly known in the English almanacs, calculated into English
Digges, Cunningham	as in the writings of master Leonard Digges and of William Cunningham, a learned student both in astronomy and physic,[5] with many more good men that taketh pains to profit the

---

1 *Nicholas*] presumably the Byzantine physician Nicholas Myrepsos.

2 *kept close*] kept indoors.

3 *fever ethic*] common fever. In the poem *Willoughby His Avisa* (probably written by Henry Willoughby under the pseudonym Hadrian Dorrell) Willoughby relates how the first sight of Avisa has caused him him to be "sodenly infected with the contagion of a fantasticall fit" and he complains "I haue the feauer Ethicke right, / I burne within, consume without" (Dorrell 1594, L1v–L2v, canto 44).

4 *Ante Cibum*] before food (Latin).

5 *William Cunningham ... and physic*] Presumably this is the same William Cunningham praised by Bullein in *Bulwark of Defence*, where he is described as "learned in Artes and in Sciences, Natural and moral. A father in phisicke, whose Learninge gaue liberty to the ignoraunt" (Bullein 1579, Aa4r).

commonwealth. There is another manner of purging of the body by vomit for it cleanseth from the midriff upward if they have large breasts and be choleric persons. It is good against dropsies and leprosies and better in summer than in winter (as Hippocrates sayeth), and wholesomer one hour before supper than at any other time, and not to be used as a custom, for the custom of vomits hurteth greatly the head, and eyes, and make the stomach so feeble that it will scant bear any meats or drinks but eftsoons cast them up again. They which have narrow throats and breasts and long necks, vomits be neither apt nor good for them. And Avicenna sayeth that vomits ought to be twice in the month for the conservation of health but that which is more doth hurt the body. There is another kind of the cleansing of the body by sweating, as with hot drinks, warm clothes, perfumes made of olibanum, brimstone,[1] nitre,[2] *et cetera*. There is also baths and sweating in hothouses for the pox, scurf,[3] scabs, haemorrhoids, piles, which hothouses hath the virtue of helping the said diseases. But if any that be of an whole, temperate complexion do sweat in dry hothouses, it doth them much harm, as hindering their eyesights, decaying their teeth, hurting memory. The best bathing is in a great vessel or a little close place with the evaporation of diverse sweatherbs well sodden in water, which have virtue to open the pores softly, letting out feeble and gross vapours, which lieth between the skin and the flesh. This kind of bathing is good in the time of pestilence or fever quartan. In the end of the baths it is good to anoint the body with some sweet oil, to mollify and make soft the sinews. And thus to conclude of bathing, it is very wholesome so that it be not done upon an empty stomach, palsies may come thereby or to take sudden cold after it. There followeth another purgation called neezing or sternutation, which is beneficial for the body if it be used upon an empty stomach. Twice or thrice in a morning with a leaf of betony put into thy nose, it helpeth memory, good against oppilation, stopping, and obstructions. Suppositories be good for weak people or children, made with *hiera picra* and honey, made in the length of a finger. Scarifying or boxing (as Galen sayeth) applied unto the extreme parts, as the legs and the arms, doth great help unto the body in drawing watery humour away from the body; but boxing is not good for the breast, applied thereto in hot fevers is dangerous. Clysters made according to art[4] be good for them which be too weak to take purgations. The manner of the said clysters, because they be

Vomits and their profits

Hippocrates, sent. in 4 Aphorisms [*sent.*] presumably sententia; probably the fourth aphorism in section 4 of *Aphorisms.*]

Custom to vomit weakeneth the stomach

Avicenna in 4 pri capitulum 13

Of baths and their properties

The discommodity of common hothouses

To use ointment after bathings is good

To bathe upon an empty stomach is perilous

Of neezing

Of suppositories

Boxing doth much good to the body

I will speak more of clysters in my book of healthful medicine.

---

1 *brimstone*] sulphur.
2 *nitre*] potassium nitrate or saltpetre.
3 *scurf*] a skin condition, especially of the head, causing scaly skin and inflammation.
4 *according to art*] skilfully.

not here to be spoken of at large, I intend by God's grace to set forth in my next book of healthful medicines.[1] Purgations venerous there be so many practitioners thereof that I need to write no rules but this: that [i]effection,[2] lust, and fantasy have banished charity, temperance, and honesty.

Many practitioners of acts venerous

JOHN   Plain people in the country, as carters, threshers, ditchers, colliers, and ploughmen use seldom times to wash their hands, as appeareth by their filthiness, and as very few times comb their heads, as it is seen by flocks,[3] nits, grease, feathers, straw, and such like, which hangeth in their hairs. Whether is washing or combing things to decorate or garnish the body or else to bring health to the same?

HUMPHREY   Thou seeest that the deer, horse, or cow will use friction or rubbing themselves against trees, both for their ease and health. Birds and hawks after their bathing will prune and rouse themselves upon their branches and perks,[4] and all for health. What should man do, which is reasonable, but to keep himself clean and often to wash the hands, which is a thing most comfortable to cool the heat of the liver, if it be done often. The hands be also the instruments to the mouth and eyes, with many other things commonly to serve the body. To wash the hands in cold water is very wholesome for the stomach and liver, but to wash with hot water engendereth rheums, worms, and corruption in the stomach because it pulleth away natural heat unto the warmed place which is washed. Frication, or rubbing the body, is good to be done a-mornings after the purgation of the belly, with warm clothes from the head to the breast, then to the belly, from the belly to the thighs, legs, and so forth, so that it be done [ii]downward; and in dry folks to be rubbed with the oil of camomile. Combing of the head is good a-mornings and doth comfort memory; it is evil at night and opens the pores. The cutting of the hair, and the paring of the nails, clean-keeping of the ears, and teeth be not only things comely and honest, but also wholesome rules of physic, for [iii]they be superfluous things of the excrements.

Beasts and birds use frictions and pruning themselves

The profit which cometh in washing the hands with cold water

Hot water is unwholesome to wash hands in

Frication wholesome for the body [wholesome] is wholesome O1.]

Combing the head

Cutting of hair and paring of nails [of nails] of nayles be comly for men O1.]

JOHN   The chief thing that I had thought to have demanded, and the very mark that I would have thee to shoot at, is to tell me something of dieting myself with meat and drink, in health and sickness.

A consideration to be had in eating and drinking

HUMPHREY   There is to be considered in eating and drinking the time of hunger or custom, the place of eating and drinking, whether it be cold or hot, also the time of the year, whether it be winter or summer. Also, the age or complexion of the eater and

---

i effection] affection O4.   ii downward] downward, it is good. O1.   iii they] to O1.

1 *my next book of healthful medicines*] Bullein's *Bulwark of Defence*, first published in 1562.
2 *effection*] fabrication (*OED* fabrication, 1. a.).
3 *flocks*] tufts of wool or cotton; this would presumably come from the animals they tend.
4 *perks*] perches.

whether he be whole or sick. Also the things which be eaten, whether they be fish or flesh, fruits or herbs. Note also the complexions and temperaments of the said meats, hot or cold, dry or moist, and most chiefly, mark the quantity and so forth. And like as lamps do consume oil, which is put into them for the preservation of the light, although it cannot continue for ever, so is the natural heat which is within us preserved by humidity and moistness of blood and phlegm, whose chief engenderer be good meats and drinks. As Avicenna sayeth, *De ethica*,[1] when natural heat is quenched in the body, then of necessity the soul must depart from the body, for the workman cannot work when his instrument is gone. So the spirits of life can have no exercise in the body when there is no natural heat to work upon. Without meat (sayeth Galen) it is not possible for any man to live, either whole or sick. And thus to conclude, no vital thing liveth without refection and sustenance, whether it be animal reasonable or animal sensible, without reason, or any vital thing insensible, both man, beast, fish, and worm, tree, or herb. All these things be [i]nourished with the influence or substance of the four elements or any of them.

<small>A cause why the soul departeth from the body</small>

JOHN Well, Humphrey, thou knowest [ii]well my complexion and disorder of my diet; what remedy for me, that have lived like a rioter?

HUMPHREY I know it well thou art phlegmatic and therefore it is long ere thy meat is digested. When thou dost eat fish and flesh together it doth corrupt in the stomach and stink; even so doth hard cheese, and cold fruits, and old powdered meats, and raw herbs engender evil humours. So, the diversity of quality and quantity of diverse meats doth bring much pain to the stomach and doth engender many diseases, as thou mayst read in the first book of Galen: *De juvamentis memborum*[2] chapter 4. And the Prince[3] himself sayeth in 3 *pri*, [iii]*doc.* 2,[4] *capitulum* 7, saying nothing is more hurtful than diverse meats to be joined together, for while as the last is [iv]received, the first beginneth to digest. And when the table is garnished with diverse meats, some roasted, some fried and baken, some warm, some cold, some fish, some flesh, with sundry fruits and salads of diverse herbs to please thine eye,

<small>To eat both fish and flesh together hurteth the phlegmatic</small>

<small>Galen</small>

<small>Hippocrates</small>

---

i nourished] newtrified *O1*.   ii well] *O4 omits*.   iii doc.] doct. *O4*.
iv received] receauing *O1*.

1 De ethica] perhaps a reference to the first book of Avicenna's *Canon of Medicine*, which is on general medical principles.
2 De juvamentis memborum] A twelfth-century Latin version of an Arabic translation of Galen's *De usu partium*. The translation is a shorter and simplified version of Galen's text and thus is quite different from the original. It was popular in the early modern period and indeed more successful than Galen's original (Carlino 1999, 10n5).
3 the Prince] Hippocrates.
4 3 pri, *doc.* 2] it is not clear which work by Hippocrates is here being referred to here; "doc.2" perhaps indicates "doctrine 2", as "doct. 2" in O4 would suggest.

remember with thyself that the sight of them all is better than the feeding of them all. Consider with thyself thou art a man and no beast, therefore be temperate in thy feeding and remember the wise words of Solomon: be not greedy (sayeth he) in every eating and be not hasty upon all meats, for excess of meats bringeth sickness,[1] and gluttony cometh at the last into an immeasurable heat.[2] Through surfeit have many one perished, but he that dieteth himself temperately prolongeth his life. Therefore gross fish, lambs' flesh, the inmeats[3] of beasts, raw herbs, pigs' brains, and all slimy meats be evil for thee, but late suppers is worst of all, [i]specially if they be long, for it causeth painful nights to follow. But Galen sayeth in his book [ii]*De euchymia*,[4] the meats which be without all blame be those which be between subtle and gross: good bread of clean wheat, flesh of capons or hens, pheasants and partridges, pigeons and turtle-doves, blackbirds, and small field birds, roasted veal or boiled mutton; these do engender good blood sayeth Galen. Note also that any other meat that thou dost eat at supper, although it seem repugnant to a phlegmatic stomach, if thou sleep well after it and feel no pain thou mayst use it as a meat necessary. And when thou canst not sleep well, if the default came through meat, mark that meat or drink, although it appear pleasant, refuse it as an enemy. And whereas thou has used evil diet as a custom in abusing time, quantity, and quality, by little and little bring thyself into good order and to time, both for thy breakfasts, dinner, and supper. Provided alway to eat good things but not many things. For like as repletion or abundance of meat is an enemy unto the body and [iii]soul and bringeth sudden death, so is emptiness a shorter of time, a weaker of the brain, a hinderer of memory, an increaser of wind, choler, and melancholy,[5] and oftentimes to many bringeth sudden death also except nature have something to work upon. As I did tell thee before, use some light things at breakfast, of perfect digestion. Within four hours after that receive thy dinner, observing the good order of diet, drinking wine or beer oftentimes, and little at once, eschewing great draughts of drink, which is used amongst beasts. And mingle thy meat with mirth, which is ever the best dish at the board,[6] and be thankful to God. And so leave

Margin notes:
To feed of diverse sorts of meats corrupteth the body. Ecclesiasticus 37
Good diet prolongeth life
[Good] A good O1.]
What kinds of meats doth cause good blood
What hurt cometh of an empty stomach when ye go to bed
An order of dieting

---

i specially] But specially O1; and O4.   ii *De euchymia*] De ethimia O1; Dieuchymia O3.
iii soul] the soul O1.

1 *Solomon ... sickness*] It was thought by some that Solomon was the author of Ecclesiastes. It seems that Bullein here confuses Ecclesiastes with Ecclesiasticus, written by Jesus Sirach, which warns that an excess of meats causes sickeness (37:30).
2 *heat*] perhaps a reference to the heat of hell-fire.
3 *inmeats*] entrails.
4 De euchymia] O2 has "Diechimia", which is presumably *De euchymia et cacochymia: seu de malisbonusque succis generandis*.
5 *So is emptiness ... melancholy*] Excessive fasting was regarded with suspicion because associated with Catholic monastic orders.
6 *board*] table, as in the modern "bed and board".

with an appetite, passing the time wisely between dinner and supper with exercise, labour, study or pastime, unto the end of six hours, and then begin thy supper, provided that it be shorter than thy dinner, eating thy meat ⁱby little and little, for greedy and sudden eating is hurtful to nature, as Galen sayeth in his dietary. Note also that thou mayst eat more meat in winter than in summer because thy natural heat is enclosed within thy body in winter but universally spread in summer. Also, choleric men may as lightly digest beef, bacon, venison, *et cetera*, with as much speed and little hurt as the phlegmatic man may eat rabbit, chicken, and partridge, *et cetera*. But the melancholy man, through the coldness of the stomach, ⁱⁱhath not that strength in the stomach as he hath promptness in will; to eat things warm and moist be good for him. The sanguine man is not so swift in this digestion as the hot and choleric man is but, notwithstanding, he hath good digestion through the humidity and warmness of blood and coveteth to eat sweet things, which greatly augment the blood. Therefore sharp sauces made with vinegar, onions, and barberries be wholesome; purslane, sorrel, small fishes that feedeth upon the stones in fair running waters, cucumbers and pure French wine, partly delayed¹ with water, be good for the said sanguine men, to keep them from much increase of flesh.

Galen. metrite [metrite] French for "womb".]

Choleric [O1 omits.]

The melancholy

The Sanguine

JOHN Thou hast showed unto me a very discreet and wholesome order of diet particular to myself, and partly to other complexions, but what rule or pretty government is for sick folks?

HUMPHREY They that be suddenly vexed with sharp sickness must have thin diets, with water, gruel thin, mutton or ⁱⁱⁱchickens, pottage without any fat or thickness, violet leaves, endive leaves, and such like cooling herbs, and let their drinks be made of tisanes. Thus do to them that have hot, sharp sicknesses occasioned of choler; and also cold syrups of endive, violets, sugar, water, and vinegar sodden together be very wholesome. But if sicknesses be long of continuance their diet must be the thicker and their meats made the stronger, specially if their diseases be cold: with the flesh of cocks, capons, temperate wine, stewed broth; with wholesome herbs as bugloss, borage, basil, parsley, and ⁱᵛfennel roots; with some maces, dates, damask prunes,² raisins of the sun ³and such like; syrups of hyssop and citron, provided that they neither take meat nor medicine immediately before or soon after their fits, posset ale⁴ with clarified herbs excepted, which they may take for their comfort according to the estate of

An order for the dieting of such as be sick of sharp fevers

Of syrups and drinks

---

i by] be O1.   ii hath] haue O1.   iii chickens, pottage] chicken pottage O4.
iv fennel] fyncle O1.

---

1 *delayed*] diluted.
2 *damask prunes*] dried damsons.
3 *raisins of the sun*] sun-dried grapes.
4 *posset ale*] ale to which hot milk, sugar, spices or other ingredients were added; a drink often given to the sick and infirm.

their disease. Such as be sick must have meat contrary to their complexion: for they that be cold must have hot meat and medicines; and they that be dry must have moist things; but they that be hot must have cold things, for the ardent heat of the fire is quenched with the moistness of the water and so the quantity of one quality overcometh the quality of another. And, indeed, physic sayeth the bodies that be hot must be fed with things like, as they that be moist with moist things to preserve their moistness, they that be hot with hot things to preserve their heat, and such like. But when they do exceed in heat, cold, moist or dry, then let the qualities of moistness be tempered with dryness and the coldness with warmness. For like as man delighteth in things of like, as the choleric man choleric things, even so do beasts, and fruits, as the coloquintida,[1] which is bitter, delighteth in bitter ground, hot spices delight to grow in hot ground, and every fruit and herb doth delight in the thing that is of like, even so doth man in his food. But in all things let him beware of distemperance, surfeits, or repletion, rear suppers and drunkenness.

As the complexion is, so man requireth

The 3rd doctrine, the 7th chapter. Moderate walk after meat profiteth

Galen n. 6. de accedeti & morbo, 1 capitulum [de accedeti & morbo] Presumably a reference to Galen's *De causis morborum* (*Of the Causes of Diseases*).]

Avicenna in 13 theo. 3 tracte. 3 capitulum [*theo. 3 tracte. 3*] perhaps a reference to tract 3 of the thirteenth theory.]

To help digestion by diverse ways

Hippocrates in secundo prim. doc. 3 capitulum 6 Hec sig. na declarant [*Hec sig. na declarant*] It is not clear what Bullein means here.]

JOHN But if a man feeleth great grief after meats or drinks, what way is there then for to help him?

HUMPHREY Use walking up and down and perhaps that will digest, as Avicenna sayeth. And Rasis sayeth to walk a hundred paces after meat is wholesome for it comforteth digestion, provoketh urine, and giveth one power and strength of stomach to eat his supper. But the counsel of Galen must here be observed, which sayeth there is no meat but it will corrupt or stink if the body be cast into a sudden heat by strong travail soon after meat, which corruption of digestion is the mother of all diseases and the beginner of all infirmities, as Avicenna reporteth. And if you see this will not help to digest your engorged, full stomach, then provoke yourself to sleep lying upon your right side, leaning toward your breast and belly, laying your warm hand upon your breast. As Averroes sayeth, the power of digestion is made strong when a man sleepeth, for natural heat that is drawn inwardly with warmness or heat hath power to digest. But if sleep ease you not, provoke vomit or fast it out; and this is the counsel of many learned men. For it is no marvel although many meats corrupt one man, which be of sundry and diverse workings in the stomach, liver, and veins, for the qualities do hinder nature as much as the quantities. And take heed these signs and evil tokens, be not found in ⌞you⌟: the pains of all your members, with idleness and weariness to go or move your body, sudden great blushing or

---

i you] youth O4.

---

1 *coloquintida*] an especially bitter apple; its bitterness is mentioned by Iago in *Othello* (Shakespeare 1988, 1.3.348–9).

readiness in your face, veins swelled and puffed up, red urine, and gross skin extended or stretched out with fullness like a blown bladder, full pulses, small desire to meat, ill rest and grief in sleep, seeming in sleep to bear some intolerable burden or dreaming to be speechless. These be the evil and dangerous tokens of repletion and of this I give you warning, for it hath slain as many by abundance as hunger hath killed through scarcity.

<small>Dangerous tokens [*O1* omits.]</small>

JOHN   I have heard say that wholesome air is a great comfort to man's nature, but corrupt air doth much harm. I shall require you therefore to tell me of the good and the bad air that I may learn to use the good and refuse the bad.

HUMPHREY   Galen in *liber De sectis*[1] sayeth a wise physician ought to know the natures of men, of waters, of air, of regions, and dwellings generally. Particularly to thyself, being a natural English man of birth and education, this land is very temperate, howbeit our dwellings in this land be variable, as fens, marishes,[2] woods, heaths, valleys, plains and rocky places, and near the seaside. But the said Galen giveth counsel in his regiment of health, saying a good air, which is pure and wholesome is that which is not troubled in standing ⁱwater pools. Therefore marish grounds, and places where hemp and flax is rotten, and dead carrions be cast, or multitudes of people dwelling together, or houses environed with standing waters whereinto jakes[3] or sinks have issues, or wallowing[4] of swine, or carrion unburied, or foul houses, or such like places, be dangerous, corrupt the blood, which is worse than infection of meat.[5] For the prince[6] sayeth that all places of concavities, as cellars, vaults, holes of minerals where metals be digged, or houses or walls joined together whereas the sun with reflection beateth in with sudden heat, whose absence bringeth cold, ⁱⁱthese airs are distempered. But pleasant clear airs, sweet gardens, goodly hills in days temperate when one may see far off, these be ⁱⁱⁱgood. There be certain stars called infortunates in their exaltation, whose influence bringeth corruption to creatures, rot and pestilence to men and beasts, poisoning waters and killing of fish, blasting of fruit in trees and corn in fields, infecting men with diverse diseases, fevers, palsies, dropsies,

<small>Physicians ought to have a perfect knowledge [*O1* omits.]

Note which be the most wholesome airs to dwell in

What airs corrupteth the blood

Corrupt air bringeth sundry diseases</small>

---

i water pools] waters, pooles *O1*.   ii these airs are] This aire is *O1*.
iii good] good also *O1*.

---

1 liber De sectis] his book *De sectis* (*On Sects*), which described contemporary schools of medicine.
2 *marishes*] marshes; Bullein consistently uses the obsolete "marish" instead of "marsh", which apparently is also a dialectal variant.
3 *jakes*] toilets.
4 *wallowing*] rolling about in dirt
5 *infection of meat*] i.e. consuming infected food.
6 *the prince*] Hippocrates.

Fervent prayer unto God doth mitigate his wrath

Sweet air to be made in the time of sickness

frenzies, falling-sicknesses, and leprosies. Against these said influences all Christian men must pray to God to be their defence, for they be God's instruments to punish the earth. Example we have of mortal pestilence, horrible fevers, and sweating-sickness and of late a general fever that this land is often plagued withal. Then [i]make a fire in every chimney within thy house and [ii]burn sweet perfumes to purge this foul air. And now, in conclusion, to answer thy question for the health of dwelling, Avicenna sayeth to dwell upon hills is cold, and in valleys comprised with hills is hot; upon a hillside against the north is cold and dry; toward the west, gross moist; very subtle towards the east; and clear and warm towards the south. And Rasis sayeth in his first book *Afforien*,[1] a man dwelling near the sea-side or greater waters cannot live long nor cannot be without weakness of members or blindness; but the best building of a house is upon a dry ground, and a hill towards the west side, and south-west doors, and windows open towards the east and north-east, having near unto the said house sweet springs of running waters from stony or chalky ground, which is both pleasant and profitable to the house. For Hippocrates sayeth in his book of air and water,[2] the second chapter, cities and towns [iii]placed toward the east be more surer than towns builded towards the north, for temperate air, or wind, and sickness be less. And in the said book Avicenna greatly commendeth pleasant rivers running towards the rising of the sun, the dwellers in such places (sayeth he) be fair and well-favoured, smooth-skinned, clear and sharp voices. And [iv]this shall suffice at this time, what and where good and pleasant dwelling is. Note also that thou must observe air [v]as thou [vi]dost meat: [vii]cold sicknesses, warm air; dry sicknesses, moist air. And so in the contraries to them that be sick and they that be whole: air of like quality is most wholesome. They that have long sicknesses, change of air is a great help, both in fevers, dropsies, falling-sicknesses, and rheums.

What situation is best for a house [What situation is] Situació *O1*.]

Pleasant people

Airs are to be observed in sickness as in health [*O1* omits.]

JOHN I have found very much disquietness in my body when my servants and labouring family have felt ease and yet we are partakers of one air.

Moderate exercise a sovereign thing

HUMPHREY The cause why thy labouring servants in the field at plough, pastures, or wood have such good health is exercise and labour; and [viii]disquietness cometh partly of idleness and lack of travail, which moderately used is a thing most sovereign to nature.

---

i make] one must make *O1*.   ii burn] perfume *O3*.
iii placed] which is placed *O1*; which are placed *O4*.
iv this shall] thus to conclude with thee this shall *O1*.   v as] in sickenes as *O1*, *O3*.
vi dost] must do *O1*.   vii cold sicknesses] in sickenes, colde sicknessis *O1*.
viii disquietness] thy disquietness *O1*.

---

1 Afforien] possibly a reference to Rasis' *The Book of Aphorisms*.
2 *his book of air and water*] Entitled *On Airs, Waters, and Places*.

JOHN   I pray thee, tell me something of exercise.

HUMPHREY   The well-learned man Fulgentius sayeth that exercise is a file and chafer of the heat natural, which chaseth away sleep and consumeth [i]superfluity, strength of the natural virtues, redeeming of time, enemy unto idleness, due unto young men, joy of old men; and, to say the truth, he which doth abstain from exercise shall lack the joys of health and quietness, both of body and mind. And Galen sayeth in his regiment of health, if we will keep perfect health we must begin [ii]of labours and moderate travail, and then to our meat and drink, and so forth to sleep. And this is the cause why falconers, shooters, hunters, [iii]ploughmen and gardeners, *et cetera*, have so good digestion and strength of body. Who be stronger-armed men than smiths because of the exercise of their arms;[1] stronger-bodied than carpenters, which lift great blocks; and masons, which breaketh great stones? Not only in their youth, but such men will take marvellous travails in age, which to idle people seemeth very painful, but unto themselves that travail no pain but pleasure because of custom. These people can digest gross meats, eating them with much pleasure and sleeping soundly after them, whereas the idle multitude in cities and noble men's houses, great numbers for lack of exercise do [iv]love meats of light digestion and dainty dishes, marry[2] indeed they may be very profitable to physicians. But if travail be one of the best preservers of health [v]then is idleness the destroyer of life; as Averroes sayeth and Hippocrates [vi]sayeth, every contrary is removed and helped by his contrary, as health helpeth sickness, exercise putteth away idleness, *et cetera*. But every light moving or soft walking may not be called an exercise (as Galen sayeth), therefore tennis, dancing, running, wrestling, riding upon great horses, ordained as well for the state of men's health as for pleasure, [vii]where it is now converted rather to the hurt of many than the profit of few. Exercise doth occupy every part of the body, quicken the spirits, purge the excrements both by the reins and guts; therefore it must be used before meat, for if strong exercise be used immediately after meat it conveyeth corruption to each part of the body because the meat is not digested. But when thou seest thy water after meat appeareth somewhat citrine or yellow, then mayst thou begin exercise for digestion is then well.

Fulgentius in liber *2*
[liber 2] It is not clear which of Fulgentius' works is being referred to here.]

What profit cometh of exercise

Use maketh labour easy

Aphorisms

Idleness the mother of all mischief

Exercise before meat

---

i superfluity] superfluous O*1*, O*3*.   ii of labours] w labors O*3*; at labour O*4*.
iii ploughmen] and ploughmen O*1*.   iv love] abhorre O*1*.
v then] so O*1*.   vi sayeth] saying O*1*.   vii where] wherunto O*1*.

1 *Who be stronger-armed men than smiths ... arms*] There is a medical dimension to their strength since blacksmiths commonly extracted teeth and set bones in the early modern period (Porter 1987, 21).
2 *marry*] variant of Mary and a reference to the mother of Jesus, which was used for emphasis or in oaths.

Little travail for the sick [O1 omits.]

But sick folks, lean persons, young children, women with child may not much travail. The exercise of dice, cards, fighting, drinking, knavish railing, of bawdry, and such like rather may be called an exercise of devils than of men. And thus I conclude with Solomon, *quam pretiosus sit sanitas thesaruus*.[1]

JOHN   After painful labour and exercise or disquietness of the mind there was never thing that hath done me so much comfort as sleep hath done.

Avicenna in *Cantica*
Of sleep and waking

Tully in *libro De senectute*

Aristotle in *libro De somno et vigilia*

The chief cause of perfect sleep [O1 omits.]

sleep after dinner not healthful

HUMPHREY   Avicenna sayeth that sleep is the rest and quietness of the powers of the soul, of movings, and of senses, without the which man cannot live. And truly, sleep is nothing else but an image or brother to death (as Tully[2] sayeth). And if, by imagination, thou didst perceive sleeping and waking weighed in the balance together, there thou should see them equal in weight, for Aristotle sayeth that man doth sleep as much as he doth wake. But this is to be considered in sleep, that natural heat is drawn inwardly and digestion made perfect, the spirits quieted, and all the body comforted, if the true order of sleep be observed in six points. First, a quiet mind without the which either there is no sleep or else dreadful dreams, tormenting the spirits. Secondly, the time of sleep, which is the night, or time of most quiet silence, for the day sleeps be not good, most chiefly soon after dinner, except to sick persons or young children, in ⁱtheir times convenient.

Thirdly, the manner of sleep, that is to eschew the lying on the back, which bringeth many grievous passions, and killeth the sleeper with sudden death. To lie upon the

Sleep on the right side is best

Gal. sen. 1. terap. *capitulum* 6 [*capitulum* 6] ca. 6 O1.] [Probably chap. 6 of *Terapentice*, Burdundio of Pisa's Latin trans. of Galen's *Methodus medendi*.]

Such as have the ague must beware of sleep [O1 omits.]

Thy lodging must be kept clean

left side is very evil in the first sleep but tolerable in the second; but the most surest way to make the digestion perfect is to lie upon the right side with one of the hands upon the breast. Fourthly, sleep hath the quantity, which must be mean, for superfluous sleep maketh the spirits gross and dull and decayeth memory; six or eight hours will suffice nature. For like as much watch dryeth the body and is perilous for falling-sickness, and blindness, even so too much sleep is as perilous, for extremes be ever ill. Fifthly, in the time of cold fevers the patient must not sleep until the trembling fit be past, for then the hot fit that followeth will be extremer than any other fit and hard to help. Note furthermore, that those bodies that be full of hot inflammations sleep not well, therefore they must use things to extenuate and to make cold, as tisanes and cold syrups, or gentle purging from the belly and liver, or, finally, to have the median vein opened according to time, state, and age. Sixthly, the chamber must be considered, that it be clean, sweet,

---

i their] O3; there O2.

---

1 quam pretiosus sit sanitas thesaruus] "how precious is the treasure of health" (Latin).
2 *Tully*] Marcus Tullius Cicero, the Roman philosopher and orator.

comely; clothes fit for the time of the year and the age of the people; and to keep the head warm is very wholesome, for in sleep, natural heat is drawn into the body, for the brain of nature is cold and moist. Windows in the south part of the chamber be not good; it is best for them which have cold rheums, dropsies, *et cetera*, to lie in close lofts, and for dry bodies to lie in low chambers, and in the time of the pestilence often to shift chambers is healthful. Lying upon the ground, in gardens under trees, or near unto stinking privies be hurtful to the body.¹ And this shall suffice for thine information of sleep, provided that thou dost not long retain thine urine for fear of the stone and pain in thy reins.

<small>Lodgings fit for all persons [*O1* omits.]</small>

<small>Sleepers in fields in harvest shall be in danger of quartans in winter</small>

JOHN   There is nothing which I more fear than the stone, for my father was sore vexed therewith. What shall I mark in mine urine?

HUMPHREY   Among all mortal diseases the stone is the greatest: a preventer of time, a deformer of man and the chief weakener of the body, and a grievous enemy to the commonwealth. How many noblemen and worshipful personages hath it slain in this realm? Many one, which cometh of hot wines, spices, long banquets, repletions, fullness, costiveness, warm-keeping of the back, salt meats, *et cetera*. The remedy whereof is in all points contrary to these causes: small² wines; temperate beer or ale; no spices, but wholesome herbs, as thyme, parsley, saxifrage, ⁱfennel-roots, chicory-roots, *et cetera*. Light meals, most chiefly the supper, no baken nor roasted thing but only sodden meats, and oftentimes to relax the belly with *cassia fistula*, new drawn from the cane, ⁱⁱVenice turpentine³ by pills, with sugar, and to eschew salt meats, and not to keep the back warm. The stone is often found in young children, which cometh of the ⁱⁱⁱparents, which stones be engendered as I have said, besides ⁱᵛof milk, fruits, herbs, salt fish, and flesh, hard cheese, *et cetera*. Now, mark well this lesson following, for thine urine.

<small>The pain of the stone [*O1* omits.]</small>

<small>The cause of the stone</small>

<small>Remedies for the stone</small>

<small>Salt meats not wholesome [*O1* omits.]</small>

JOHN   That shall I gladly, read but softly and I ᵛshall write thy words.

HUMPHREY   First in urine four things mark,
            Thus said Actuarius the good clerk,⁴

<small>Four things noted in urine</small>

---

i fennel-roots, chicory-roots] *this ed.*; fennel-roots, Cicuri-roots *O2*; *O1* omits.
ii Venice turpentine by pills] *O1* omits.
iii parents] parents, and oftentimes in old folke *O1*.   iv of] *O1* omits.
v shall] wyll *O1*.

---

1 *Lying upon the ground ... hurtful to the body*] Bullein also warns against lying on the ground in gardens or fields in his *Regiment Against the Pleurisy* (Bullein 1562a, B4r); "privies" are toilets, the word possibly relating to the privet hedges that would have concealed areas for this purpose (*OED* privet 1. 4. note).

2 *small*] weak; more commonly used of beer.

3 *Venice turpentine*] fluid obtained by the distillation of resin from certain trees (*OED* venice 2. c.).

4 *Actuarius the good clerk*] Johannes Actuarius, who wrote a treatise on urine, with "good clerk" meaning good scholar.

	Colour, regions, and contents therein,
	Substance gross, thick or thin,
	A fair, light, an urinal pure,
	Then of thy sight thou shalt be sure.
Golden urine	Colour of bright gold or gilt,
	Is health of liver, heart, and milt.
Red urine	Red as cherry or saffron dry,
	Excess of meat in him I spy.
Green urine	Colour green or like dark red wine,
	Or resembling the liver of a swine,
	Is adustion with fiery heat,
	Surfeiting the liver and stinking sweat.
Colour like lead	Leady colour or black as ink,
	Death draweth near as I do think,
	Except the terms, which women have,
	Purging black choler, which many do save.[1]
Grey urine [*O1 omits*.]	Colour grey as horn or clear as water,
	Is lack of digestion sayeth mine author,
Urine like flesh-broth [*O1 omits*.]	Urine like flesh-broth is very good,
	Beginneth digestion and nourish blood.
	Subcitrine[2] and yellow be urine next best,
	Bread and flesh will well digest.
White and thick urine	The urine that is white and thick,
	Is ever called Phlegmatic.
White and thin urine	Melancholy water is white and thin,
	The red and gross is sanguine.
Yellow urine	Yellow and thin, spring from the gall,[3]
	Wherein ⁱcholer ruleth all.
	The swelling liver and brains bloody
Circles are to be noted	Causes circle thick with colour ruddy,
	But when circles be thin and red,
	Choler green the right side of the head.
	If leaden circles swim on the brink,
	It is falling-sickness, as I do think.
Oil in urine	When oil in urine doth appear,
	Resolutio pinguis[4] draweth near,
	When oil appeareth in fevers hot,
	Dissolving the body causeth a blot,
Periotides is tertian or quartan	But of Periotides[5] thou felt'st no pains,
	This oil prognostic consuming reins.
	The gravel red declareth for ever,
	In dry-backed men double tertian fever.

i *choler*] holler *O1*.

---

1 *save*] retain.
2 *subcitrine*] yellowish-green colour.
3 *gall*] gallbladder.
4 Resolutio pinguis] the resolution of a fat.
5 *Periotides*] possibly peritonitis.

When golden gravel appeareth alone,	Of gravel in urine
It hurt the reins but is no stone.	
When gravel is of colour white,	
Stone in the bladder worketh spite.	
Contents like small threads or hairs,	Contents in urine be
Through heat or dryness the body wears.	the chief things to
Consumption, scab, smallpox, and lust,	know diseases
Is when many hairs be mingled with dust.	
In the bottom of veins or vessels great,	
Lieth stopping matter, like bran of wheat.	
Wherein contents are like scales of fish,	
As appeareth in the chamber dish,	
These signify fevers and ethics old,[1]	
Or scabs, which the bladder doth enfold.	
White froth swimming cometh of ¹wind,	
The yellow froth is of jaunders kind.[2]	
Thus of urine I do conclude,	
With words of truth but metre rude.	

Here is also a little of the signes of the excrements of the belly:

Our filthy dung and fex[3] most vile,	Many colours in
The dregs of nature's food,	one stool is evil
When they be diverse coloured made	
The signs be never good.	
If the siege be like unto the meat,	Signs of crudity and
New drawn into the maw,[4]	wind
Or fleeting[5] with phlegm or burbles great[6]	
The body is windy and raw.	
The yellow doth from choler come,	Choleric signs
The green is burnt adust,	
The black and leady[7] be deadly signs	Signs deadly
That flesh will turn to dust.	
The excrement that is in the jakes cast,	Oily excrements
If it have oil or fat,	signify consumption
Consumption of body then begin,	except the cause be
The chiefest sign is that.	of fat meats

---

i wind] wine O4.

---

1 *ethics old*] common fevers.
2 *jaunders kind*] indicating jaundice.
3 *fex*] sediment, waste, excrement.
4 *maw*] stomach.
5 *fleeting*] floating.
6 *burbles great*] big bubbles.
7 *leady*] lead-like.

Stools soft and hard	The privy[1] soft, well compact,[2]
	Made in the accustomed time,
	Is ever good, and the hard is ill,
	And thus I end my rhyme.

JOHN   Once I fell into a great sickness, and hitherto I am scant recovered of it the surfeit was so great. But counsel was given me that I should not stay myself upon the opinion of any one physician but rather upon three. Then, said I, to retain three at once requireth great charge, for those men to whom lives be committed ought liberal rewards to be given. Then, said my friend, they are good gentlemen and no great takers. What be their names? said I; he answered, saying the first be called Doctor Diet, the second Doctor Quiet, the third Doctor Merry-Man. I did write their names, but yet I could not speak with them.[3]

Diet; Quiet; Merryman

HUMPHREY   Hitherunto I have said something that shall well suffice for thee to know Doctor Diet; as for Quiet and Merry-Man, they lie in no physician's hands to give but only in God's. For small it helpeth to any man to have honour, riches, fame, conning,[4] *et cetera*, and in the meantime to want quietness and mirth, which be the chief friends, tenderest [i]nourishers, wholesomest physicians, most pleasant musicians, and friendliest companions to nature. Pleasant birds singing in the branches be more happier than [ii]ravening cormorants and greedy hawks, which with pains enchaseth their preys. The quiet lambs be ever happier in their kind than the greedy, ravening foxes, wolves, and lions, which never cease vexing themselves to kill living things for their food. The poor oyster lurking under the rock or sand, which is never removed of strong ebbs nor floods, is farther from travail and continual pains than the horrible whale, most fearful to fishes. The low shrubs or bushes growing near to the ground be ever in more safeguard than the lusty, high, flourishing trees, spread with pleasant branches, which be subject to every strong wind. The poor boats in harbour be in less peril than the [iii]fickle, rich ships tossed up and down on the cruel floods. What shall I say? But this, that the miserable ragged begger called Irus[5] was more happier in his poverty with quietness and mirth than was the gluttonous beast and monstrous man, King Sardanapalus, with all his golden glory, court of ruffians and courtesans,

It were better to lack riches than to want quietness and mirth

Many apt similitudes or metaphors

---

i nourishers] nouryshes O1; nourses O4.   ii ravening] O1, O3, O4; raueringe O2.
iii fickle, rich] rich fickle O4.

---

1 *privy*] in this context, stool; excrement.

2 *compact*] made up, specifically solid, dense.

3 *Doctor Diet ... Merry-Man*] These three "doctors" also appear in Harington's translation of the medieval text the *Regimen sanitatis Salerni* (De Mediolano 1607, A6r) and are mentioned again by Bullein in his *Regiment Against the Pleurisy* (Bullein 1562a, C6v).

4 *conning*] learning.

5 *Irus*] the nickname given to Arnaeus, a beggar in Homer's *Odyssey* (after Iris, messenger of the Gods) because of his willingness to run errands (Homer 1919, 2: book 18, lines 1–7, p. 197).

which came to an end most shameful.¹ Diogenes (I warrant you) was not inferior to Alexander in the state of happiness, and hath left as great a fame behind him, saving that Alexander was a more cruel murderer than Diogenes a chaste liver.² Indeed, the poor, silly shepherd doth pleasantly pipe to his sheep when mighty princes do ⁱsigh among their subjects and break many sleeps in golden beds, when bakers in bags and brewers in bottles do snort upon hard straw, fearing no sudden mishap.³ The great pains and secret griefs⁴ that disquieted minds do daily sustain be not much unlike unto the infernal torments that the wicked do feel. Physic unto an extreme, troubled mind (say what they list)⁵ helpeth as little as to apply a plaster to the breast or head of a dead body to revocate⁶ the spirits of life or soul again. The sickness of the body must have medicine, the passions of the mind must have good counsel. What pleasure hath a condemned man in music or a dead man in physic? Nothing at all, God knoweth. Oh, how many men have been cast away by thought, and most for loss of estimation, and some of other affections of the mind, as inordinate love, or coveting things that they cannot get, or obtaining those things that they cannot keep, or ire of other men's prosperity or good hap. As Tully⁷ sayeth, ⁱⁱand Ovid (as fine in poetry as Apelles⁸ was in painting) describeth, this vile passion of ire with a pale face, lean body, scowling look, gnashing teeth, ⁱⁱⁱvenomous tongue, choleric stomach; ⁱᵛingrateful,⁹ seldom smiling but at mischief, outward appearing (as it were) quiet, inwardly the serpent gnaweth, freteth, and devoureth, *et cetera*. These men be devils incarnate, beginning hell in this life, most enemies to themselves. And if they

marginalia:
The pleasure of poor men

The torments of the mind

Thought hath killed many [Through thought many are killed *O1*.]

Ire is a grievous passion

Tully in *Tusculanae quaestiones liber 3*; Ovid in *liber 2 Metamamorphoses*.

The description of Ire [*O1* omits.]

Devils incarnate

A good face in a glass

---

i sigh] fight *O1*.   ii and] *O1 omits*.   iii venomous] venym *O1*.
iv ingrateful] tounge full of poyson, ingratefull *O1*.

---

1 *King Sardanapalus ... end most shameful*] the wanton and gluttonous last king of Assyria who, rather than face capture by his enemies, burnt himself to death in his palace along with his eunuchs and concubines (Diodorus 1933, 1: book 2, chapters 23–7).
2 *Diogenes ... liver*] the Greek philosopher Diogenes of Sinope, also known as Diogenes the Cynic. Plutarch, amongst others, tells of a meeting between Diogenes and Alexander the Great: when Alexander asks Diogenes if he wants anything, he answers "stand a little out of my sun" (Plutarch 1919, 7:259). The anecdote reveals the philosopher's disregard for wealth and power.
3 *poor silly shepherd ... mishap*] the notion that wealthy princes suffered more than their poor subjects was traditional; the point comes up in Shakespeare's *Henry V* when King Henry proclaims: "Not all these, laid in bed majestical, / Can sleep so soundly as the wretched slave / Who with a body filled and vacant mind / Gets him to rest, crammed with distressful bread" (Shakespeare 1988, 4.1.264–7).
4 *griefs*] grief usually means physical pain but here the sense is apparently psychological.
5 *list*] like
6 *revocate*] recall, call back.
7 *Tully*] Marcus Tullius Cicero, the Roman philosopher and orator.
8 *Apelles*] a celebrated painter from ancient Greece; Pliny the Elder considered him superior to all other artists (Pliny 1952, 9: book 35, chapter 36, sections 79–81).
9 *ingrateful*] ungrateful.

[behold](themselves in a glass[1] in the time of their tempests, should not their countenances be more fearful to themselves than their ire hurful to others? Yes, and perhaps make them staring mad in seeing such a devil's image. Therefore let wise men be of this mind: first, [ii]that they would have no man to be ireful against them or distain them, even so let them do to others; secondly, let them think it is better to be spited then pitied,[2] for every prosperous felicity hath his enemy waiting upon him. The fool hateth the wise, the wise man pitieth the fool, [iii]the wretch envieth the worthy man, and so forth; only except adversity and extreme misery, all prosperous men have enemies. Let this suffice, and consider what Galen sayeth, that immoderate, ireful motions cast the body into a choleric heat whereof come fevers and all hot diseases dangerous to the body. Of this writeth Petrus De Apono: the passion of the mind, called dread or fear, is when the blood and spirits be drawn inwardly, and maketh the outward parts pale and trembling. To this ([iv]besides pitiful experience) Haly Abbas, Galen, and Aristotle do witness the same. The sudden passion of joy or gladness is clean contrary to fear, for the heart sendeth forth the spiritual blood, which in weak persons the heart can never recover again but death incontinent (as Galen sayeth). And as we may see by experience in the meeting of men and their wives, children and their parents, which either by prison or banishment were without all hope ever to see each other, and in joy of meeting the dilating and spreading of the heart-blood hath cast the body into swooning. And thus, my friend John, I do conclude upon certain affections of the mind, wishing Doctor Diet, Quiet, and Merry-Man to help thee what thou shalt need. For mirth is beloved of musicians, pleasant birds, and fishes, as the dolphin.[3] What is mirth honestly used? An image of heaven, a great lordship to a poor man, a preserver of nature.[4] And Solomon sayeth: *Non est oblectatio super cordis gaudium*,[5] *et cetera*. And yet I say:

Marginalia:

Better to be spited than pitied in some cases

Galen *De regimine sanitatis*, liber 1

In come. 32. septi. problem [Perhaps this means comment 32, problem 17.]

Haly in 5. theo. *capitulum ultimo*; Ga. i. qui. de acc. & morbo.c. 6.; Aristotle. 10 *problems* [*de acc. & morbo. c. 6*] Presumably a reference to Galen's *De causis morborum*, chapter 6.]

Hudson [it is not clear who or what is being referred to here.]

Ecclesiasticus, *capitulum* 30

---

i behold] did behold *O1*.   ii that] to thinke that *O1*.
iii the wretch] wel couit rather to be spyted then pittied, the wrech *O1*.
iv besides] *O4*; by sides *O1*, *O3*.

---

1 glass] mirror.

2 it is better to be spited then pitied] Given the context, it is likely that Bullein means, rather, £it is better to be pitied than spited", that is, it is better that people feel sorry for a man than that they hate and envy him.

3 dolphin] Mistakenly, the dolphin was thought to be a fish rather than a mammal by the early moderns.

4 mirth ... a preserver of nature] Bullein makes the same point when concluding his *Regiment Against the Pleurisy* (Bullein 1562a, E4r–E4v).

5 Non est... gaudium] "There is no pleasure above the joy of the heart" (Ecclesiasticus 30.15). Bullein apparently confuses Ecclesiastes, which some thought Solomon had written, with Ecclesiasticus.

The ireful man is ever a thrall,
The joyful mind is happiest of all,
Zeal burn like flames of fire,
When honest mirth hath his desire.
Love well mirth but wrath despise,
This is the counsel of all the wise.

JOHN [i]Humphrey, I think thee for thy great pains. Sure, I purpose to follow thy counsel, but if thou wouldst show me the operation of certain simples, [ii]I will, if it be in my power, recompense thy pains. And first, what is wormwood?

HUMPHREY [iii]*Absinthium*[1] is a common [iv]herb. It is of diverse kinds, as *Ponticum*, *Romanum*,[2] *et cetera*. It is hot in the first and dry in the second degree, and it is very bitter, and being dried keepeth clothes from worms and moths, and the syrup thereof, eaten before wine, preserveth men from drunkenness. If it be sodden in vinegar it will help the sores that breeds in the ears, being laid warm upon. It is to be drunk against *apoplexia*; and *ofthalmia*, which is a sickness of the eye, is greatly helped with [v]wormwood if it be stamped and made luke warm with rosewater and layed upon the eye and covered with a clean-picked[3] walnut shell. The syrup helpeth the bloody flux, it doth help a cold stomach if it be drunk ten days together; every morning two spoonful of the syrup is good against the dropsy, every day drunk two ounces fasting. And thus, sayeth Avicenna: figs; cockle; wormwood; nitre,[4] stamped together and made in a plaster, is good against the disease of the spleen and also killeth worms in the belly. Used in the foresaid manner, one dram of the powder may be drunk at once in wine. It hath many more goodly virtues.

<small>The virtues of wormwood</small>

<small>Bloody flux [*O1* omits.]</small>

<small>Dropsy [*O1* omits.]</small>

<small>Avicenna *liber* 2, Sim. 2 [*Sim.* 2] Possibly "simple 2".]</small>

JOHN What be the properties of aniseeds?

HUMPHREY It is much like unto fennel seed and is called Roman fennel, that is warm, and sweet, and hot in the second, and dry in the third degree; the new seeds is the best. It engendereth vital seed, openeth the stopping of the reins and matrix, being drunk with tisanes, or clean, temperate wine.

<small>Gal. de. sim. [Presumably a reference to Galen's *De simplicium medicamentorum facultatibus*.]</small>

---

i Humphrey ... operation] I wold very fayne knowe the nature of *O1*.
ii I will, if it be in my power, recompence thy pains,] *O1* omits.
iii *Absinthium* is] *O1* omits.   iv herb] knowen herb *O1*.
v wormwood] the wormwood *O1*.

---

1 Absinthium] artenisia absinthium or wormwood.
2 Ponticum, Romanum] Pontic wormwood or Roman wormwood; both varieties of wormwood were often referred to as wormwood gentle.
3 *clean-picked*] cleaned and made bare by use of a pick or toothpick (*OED* picked *ppl. a.* 1).
4 *nitre*] potassium nitrate or saltpetre.

JOHN   What thinkest thou of mouse-ear?[1]

A remedy for the falling-sickness [O1 omits.]

HUMPHREY   An herb commonly known, cold and moist in the first degree. As Galen sayeth, [i]a decoction of this herb sodden in water with sugar is good against the falling-sickness, being oftentimes drunk; and put a leaf thereof into the nose it will provoke sternutation or neezing, which wonderfully doth cleanse the veins.

JOHN   I would fain know what is chickenweed?[2]

To draw phlegm out of the head [O1 omits.]

toothache [O1 omits.]

HUMPHREY   Almost every ignorant woman doth know this herb, but there be of it diverse kinds. [ii]They be very good to keep wounds from impostumations,[3] stamped and applied unto them, and draweth corruption out of wounds, and sodden with vinegar doth draw phlegm out of the head if it be often warm. Put it into the mouth and spit it out again, in this same manner it helpeth the teeth, and sodden in wine and so drunk, it will clean the reins of the back.

JOHN   What is sorrel, might I know of thee the property thereof?

The properties of sorrel

Yellow jaundice [O1 omits].

Sorrel leaves good against the pestilence [O1 omits.]

HUMPHREY   Thy cook doth right well know it, and all they that make green sauce,[4] but that description I leave to Dioscorides and Leonhart Fuchs, not only in this herb but in all other, and to tell thee the virtue I will. It is cold and dry in the second degree, it also stoppeth.[5] It is like endive in property because it overcometh choler and is much commended; it helpeth the yellow jaundice if it be drunk with small wine or ale and also quencheth burning fevers. To eat of the leaves every morning in a pestilence is most wholesome if they be eaten fasting. This herb doth Dioscorides, Galen, and Avicenna greatly commend, besides the great learned men of this time.

JOHN   What is plantain or waybread?

The properties of plantain

HUMPHREY   The greater plantain is the better, it hath seven great veins, it is cold and dry; the [iii]seeds drunk with red wine, [iv]or the roots sodden therein, stoppeth the bloody flux. [v]Likewise the roots [vi]and leaves being sodden with [vii]fair water, [viii]or with

---

i a] the *O1*.   ii They be ... warm] *marginal note*: The operation of chiekinwede] *O1*.
iii seeds] seede of it *O1*.   iv or the roots sodden therein] *O1 omits*.
v Likewise] *O1 omits*.
vi and leaves] and leaves sodden and dronke in wyne, stoppeth the bloudy flix: the rootes *O1*.
vii fair] sweat *O1*.
viii or with borage-water and sugar] and with Sugar or borage water *O1*.

---

1   *mouse-ear*] *Pilosella officinarum*, a type of hawkweed.
2   *chickenweed*] chickweed
3   *to keep wounds from impostumations*] to prevent wounds from festering.
4   *green sauce*] a sauce made with green herbs.
5   *stoppeth*] i.e. prevents the abnormal flowing of bodily fluids.

borage-water and sugar, given to him that hath an ague, either tertian or quartan, two hours afore his fit ⁱhelpeth prove this, for thus have I helped many. It is very comfortable for children that have great fluxes and agues, and is a friend unto the liver. This herb is greatly praised of the ⁱⁱlearned writers.

<small>To help the ague [O1 omits.]</small>

JOHN   What is chamomile, and the preparation thereof?

HUMPHREY   This herb is very hot, it is drunk against cold winds and raw matter being in the guts. The Egyptians did suppose it would help all cold agues and did consecrate it to the sun, as Galen sayeth. Also, if it be tempered and strained into white wine and drunk of women having the child dead within the body, it will cause present deliverance. It doth mightily cleanse the bladder and is excellent to be sodden in water to wash the feet. The oil is precious as is declared hereafter.

<small>A help for dead children [To what purpose camomeil serueth O1.]</small>

JOHN   Hops be well beloved of the beer-brewers. ⁱⁱⁱWhat do the physicians say ⁱᵛof them?

HUMPHREY   There be which doth cool, be called *lupilum*;[1] those that we have be hot and dry, bitter, sour, hot, sayeth old herbals. ᵛAnd Fuchs sayeth they cleanse phlegm, and choler, and the water between the skin and flesh. The syrups will cleanse gross, raw phlegm from the guts, and is good against ᵛⁱobstructions. If the juice be dropped in the ear it taketh the stink away of rotten sores; the roots will help the liver and spleen, being sodden and drunk. The beer is very good for phlegmatic men.

<small>A help for rotten sores [O1 omits.]</small>

JOHN   What is sage? For that I love well.

HUMPHREY   There be two kinds of sage; they be herbs of health and therefore they be called *salvia*.[2] This herb is hot and dry and provoketh urine, cleaneth the matrix, stoppeth the blood in a wound. If it be put in a pig[3] it dryeth the humours that would engender phlegm. It is good against the palsy; oftentimes eaten or sodden in wine it will help and cleanse itch, scabs, and filth from the pudent and secret members.[4] Aetius[5] doth greatly commend this herb and the excellent regiment of Salerno,[6] where it sayeth *cur moritur homo, cui salvia crescit in horto* (enquiring

<small>The wonderful gifts given to sage [The wonderful gifts] A wonderful gift O1.]

Palsy [O1 omits.]</small>

---

i helpeth] *O1 omits*.   ii learned writers] Doctours *O1*.   iii What] howe *O1*.
iv of] to *O1*.   v And Fuchs sayeth] *marginal note*: Fucchi *O1*.
vi obstructions] obstructions sodden *O1*.

---

1   lupilum] From the Latin for the common hop, *humulus lupulus*; some hops are more bitter than others.
2   salvia] sage (Latin).
3   *put in a pig*] presumably inserted into the dead animal's body when cooking it whole.
4   *pudent ... members*] sexual organs
5   *Aetius*] Aetius Amidenus, a Byzantine physician and medical author.
6   *regiment of Salerno*] The *Regimen sanitatis Salernitanum* that emerged from the Italian medieval medical school at Salerno.

An. in. 3. 1. capitulum. sing. [Possibly 'Am' intended, meaning a work by Aetius Amidenus.]	why men do die that have sage growing in gardens). But truly, neither physic, herb, nor cunning can make man immortal, but assuredly sage is wholesome for old folks, to be put into their meats for it cleanseth phlegm from the sinews, which phlegm will relax the sinews. The wine of sage drunk upon an empty stomach is wholesome for phlegmatic persons or them which have the falling-sickness or dropsy.
Sage good for old people [*O1* omits.]	

JOHN   What is polypody, that groweth upon the oak tree?

Of polypody

HUMPHREY   If this herb be sodden with beets and mallows in the broth of a hen and drunk it will loose the belly and cleanse phlegm. The root of this herb, being dry and beaten into fine powder and drawn into the nostrils, helpeth a disease called polypus.[1]

JOHN   I have heard talk of horehound, I would fain hear of his working.

What diseases horehound helpeth

HUMPHREY   It is an herb hot and dry; if it be sodden with fair water, sugar or honey, and strain it, this drink doth cleanse the stomach from stinking phlegm. It is an excellent herb for women to cleanse their month-terms. The water of this is good to help them which have a moist rheum falling from the head upon the lungs, being often drunk, but it is hurtful to the bladder and reins. The syrup thereof doth cleanse the king's evil, and also, put into the ears doth greatly comfort the hearing if the ears be troubled. And stamped with honey and applied into the eyes it cleanseth the sight.

Horehound helpeth the ears [*O1* omits.]

JOHN   What is verbena?

Of verbena and his properties

HUMPHREY   It is called the holy herb; it dryeth and bindeth. If it be sodden with vinegar it helpeth a disease called Saint Antony's fire[2] oftentimes washing the pained place. The leaves of verbena, and roses, and fresh swine's grease stamped together will cease pain and grief in every wound and will keep wounds from corruption. It is good for people that have the tertian or quartans agues, and thus sayeth Dioscorides. Moreover, he sayeth the weight of a dram of this herb, with three halfpennies' weight of olibanum, and put in nine ounces of old wine, tempered together and drunk forty days of this quantity fasting, it will help a disease called the king's evil or pain in the throat.

To keep wounds from corruption [*O1* omits.]

Dioscorides

To help the king's evil [*O1* omits.]

JOHN   What is rue or herb-grace?

HUMPHREY   I tell thee, this herb is very hot and bitter and doth burn because of his hotness in the third degree. If a little of this rue be stamped and sodden with wine

---

1 *polypus*] nasal polyp; a fleshy growth within the nasal passage.
2 *Saint Antony's fire*] A bacterial infection causing inflammation of the skin, especially on the face.

and drunk, it is an excellent medicine against poison and pestilence. With roses and vinegar and rue, stamped together and put in a forehead cloth or biggen,[1] applied unto the temples of the head or forehead do cease grievous pains in the head. And in like manner it healeth the bitings of serpents or dogs, stamped with vinegar. Many nice[2] people cannot abide it, crying "fie, it stinks". The seed of this herb, beaten in powder, and put in fresh, clarified butter[3] and pitch,[4] melted together, is good for them to drink that are bruised.

Rue good against poison

Bitings of dogs and serpents [O1 omits.]

For them that are bruised [O1 omits.]

JOHN   What is burnet?

HUMPHREY   It is of the nature of five-finger:[5] dry and binding and not moist, as many say. Stamp it and put it to the eyes, doth take away the dropping, and pricking,[6] and doth heal wounds, and is good to drink for the tertian ague.

The properties of burnet

JOHN   What is dandelion?

HUMPHREY   It is temperate, cold, and dry; with roses and vinegar tempered together it helpeth the head in hot diseases. The sow-thistle, called *soncus*, hath the same virtue and so hath ⁱchicory. If they be sodden, they loose the belly and quencheth heat, which burneth in the stomach, and defendeth the head from hot, smoking vapours, and purgeth yellow choler, and rebateth venerous and fleshly heat, and is good to be sodden and drunk in hot, burning agues. Though this herb ⁱⁱcommonly known and counted of many as a vile weed, yet it is reported of Dioscorides to be an excellent herb.

The virtue of dandelion

Burning agues [O1 omits.]

JOHN   What is spinach?

HUMPHREY   An herb much used in meat; cold and moist in the first degree. It mollifyeth and maketh soft the belly; it is good for them that be hot and dry and evil for phlegmatic men.

JOHN   What be cucumbers?

HUMPHREY   They be (truly) in the second degree very moist and cold. ⁱⁱⁱThe seeds be good to be given in hot sicknesses; the powder of the said seeds, drunk in clean wine, is good against diverse passions of the heart. This fruit will cause one to make water well; the root dried in powder, thereof drunken in water and honey, provoketh vomit. If they be moderately eaten

To provoke vomit [O1 omits.]

---

i chicory] Suckery O1.   ii commonly] be commonly O1.
iii The seeds ... vomit] *marginal note:* For what purposes cōcōber serueth O1.

---

1 *biggen*] a hood or cap, perhaps specifically a nightcap.
2 *nice*] fastidious or delicate and suggesting also foolish.
3 *clarified butter*] butter that has been heated in order to remove its milk solids.
4 *pitch*] distilled turpentine or tar.
5 *five-finger*] the cinquefoil or a similar species of five-leaved plant.
6 *pricking*] pain or smarting.

Epinyctidas they bring good blood. Tempered with honey and anoint the eyes, that helpeth a disease called *epinyctidas*,[1] which troubleth men with strange sights in the nights. The best of this fruit is which beareth the best seeds; the savour of [i]them is not wholesome. Melons, [ii]citruls,[2] pumpions, and this kind of pepons[3] or great apples be much used in England, and is more common than profitable because they use to eat them raw. Englishmen, being born in a temperate region, inclining to cold, may not without hurt eat raw herbs, roots, and fruits plentiful, as many men which be born far in the south parts of the world, which be most hot of stomach. Therefore, [iii]eat these fruits boiled or baken with honey, pepper, and fennel seeds or such like. There be another hot kind of bitter cucumbers, which do purge.

JOHN   What is garlic? [iv]Some call it the poor men's treacle, but what say you?

The properties of garlic and his operation

HUMPHREY   Garlic is very hot and dry in the [v]fourth degree. It troubles the stomach, it is hurtful to the eyes and head, it increaseth dryness, but it will provoke urine and is good to be laid upon the biting of a snake or adder. It is good for the haemorrhoids, applied to the sore place, being first stamped. If it be sodden the stink is taken from it, but the virtue remaineth to be eaten against the coughs and pains in the lungs; it cutteth and consumeth corrupt phlegm and bringeth sleep. It is not good for hot men, [vi]and women with child, or nurses giving milk to children.[4] But [vii](as thou sayest) Galen calleth it the common people's treacle. If sanguine men do eat much of it, it will make them to have red faces, but it is a special remedy against poison.

Good for sleep

JOHN   What [viii]be onions?

Of onions and their properties [The diuersitie of Onions and their properties O1.]

HUMPHREY   They do make thin the blood and bring sleep; they be not good for choleric men. The long onion[5] is more vehementer than the round, and the red more than the white, the dry more than the green,[6] and the raw more than the sodden or preserved in salt, although they cause sleep very painful and troublous.

Hot in the third degree, [ix]but they warm [x]and cleanse the stomach, [xi]bring good colour [xii]to the face, and help the green sickness, provoke urine,

---

i them] that O1.   ii citruls] *this ed.*; citrons O2.   iii eat] lette them eat O1.
iv Some call it ... what say you?] O1 *omits.*   v fourth] third O3.
vi and] nor O1.   vii (as thou sayest)] O1 *omits.*   viii be] is O1.
ix but they] and O1.   x and] in the stomacke O1.   xi bring] and bring O1.
xii to the face] O1 *omits.*

---

1 epinyctidas] pustules, which erupt at night.
2 *citruls*] yellow-coloured water-melons and pumpkins, from the Latin *citrus*.
3 *pumpions ... pepons*] Bullein uses two words, pumpion and pepon, for pumpkins (*Cucurbita Pepo*).
4 *nurses ... children*] specifically wet-nurses, lactating women who were hired to breast-feed other people's children.
5 *long onion*] an onion with a partially developed root bulb and long green neck such as the spring onion, also termed scallion.
6 *green*] raw.

openeth the haemorrhoids if they be sodden in vinegar and laid warm to them. Peel off the rind and cut it at both ends and cast it into fair, warm water and let it lie an hour or two and then slice it, this takes away the vehement sharpness of it. Rue, salt, honey, and one onion stamped together is a goodly plaster to lay upon the biting of a dog. Leeks[1] purge the blood in March, and paineth the head, and be not greatly praised for their ill juice, ⁱsayeth Dioscorides; the head being annointed with the juice thereof keepeth hair from falling. There is much variety of this onion amongst writers, sayeth Pliny, but this shall suffice. A plaster for biting of a dog [*O1* omits.]
To keep hair from falling [*O1* omits.]

JOHN   What is lettuce?

HUMPHREY   It doth mightily increase milk in women's breasts,[2] and therefore is called lettuce, as Martial[3] sayeth: The properties of lettuce

> First shall be given to the virtue and power,
> To increase milk in the breasts every hour.[4]

Lettuce is an herb cold and moist and is comfortable for a hot stomach, bringeth sleep, mollifyeth the belly. The drier it be eaten, the better it is, I mean if it be not much washed in water; adding clean salad oil, sugar, and vinegar to it, it abateth carnal lust and much use of it dulleth the sight. The seed is precious against hot diseases, drunk with tisanes. There is an herb called rocket gentle[5] ⁱⁱthat partly smelleth like a fox, which is very hot; an increaser of seed, ⁱⁱⁱthis herb must always be eaten with lettuce. The root thereof sodden in water will draw broken bones and will help the cough in young children. To abate carnal lust [*O1* omits.]
An increaser of seed [*O1* omits.]

JOHN   What be mints?

HUMPHREY   Mints be of two kinds: garden and wild mints. They be hot unto the third and ⁱᵛdoth dry in the second degree. Garden mints is best: the powder of this with the juice of pomegranates stoppeth vomits, helpeth sighing, cleanseth hot choler. Three branches of this sodden with wine doth help repletion, drunk fasting. This juice, tempered with good treacle and eaten of children a-mornings, will kill worms, and stamped with salt, The properties of mints
Stopping of vomits [*O1* omits.]
To kill worms [*O1* omits.]

---

i sayeth] *Adoge* sayeth *O1*.   ii that] which *O1*.
iii this] whiche *O1*.   iv doth] dooeth *O1*.

---

1 *Leeks*] a member of the onion family.

2 *increase milk ... breasts*] According to the *OED* "letuse", the Middle English spelling for lettuce, is connected, via Old French, with *lac*, the latin word for milk and this refers to the milky juice of the plant (*OED* lettuce).

3 *Martial*] the English name for the Latin poet Martial Valerius Martialis.

4 *First ... hour*] These lines are presented as prose in the first edition of Bullein's text (*O1*). They sound like one of Martial's *Epigrams*, or part of an epigram, translated into English, but I have been unable to locate these lines in his work.

5 *rocket gentle*] also known as wintercress or yellow rocket.

To help the colic [*O1* omits.]
To stop blood [*O1* omits.]
To make sweet breath

apply it to the biting of a dog, it will heal it. It is wholesome sod[1] with windy meats and sodden in posset ale with fennel it helpeth colic;[2] it increaseth vital seed. It is not best for choleric complexions, but good for phlegmatic and indifferent for melancholy, and it will stop blood, stamped and applied to the place. The juice of mints is best to mingle in medicine against poison. The powder of mints is good in pottage to help digestion and to make sweet breath.

JOHN   What is [i]fennel?

The properties of fennel

HUMPHREY   It hath power to warm in the third degree, and dry, and maketh sweet the breath. The seed eaten oftentimes upon an empty stomach doth help the eyesight; the roots clean washed be very wholesome in pottage and is good in tisanes. The green

To break the stone [*O1* omits.]

or red tufts growing upon the stalks, sodden in wine, pottage, or ale, helpeth the bladder, reins, and breaketh the stone, increaseth milk in women's breasts, and seed of generation.[3] It is good to use endive or such like with it because it is very hot. And [iii]it is good in barber's baths[4] [iii]and washing water [iv]with balm, savory.[5] It is good to wash one's feet to bedward;[6] the syrup is very wholesome, it helpeth a phlegmatic stomach.

JOHN   What is hyssop?

The operation of hyssop [*O1* omits.]

HUMPHREY   An herb commonly known growing in gardens and hot in the third degree; it hath virtues to make humours thin and warm. Sodden with figs, rue, and honey, in clean water and drunk it greatly helpeth the sickness in the lungs, old cough and rotten humours [v]dripping upon the lungs. Sodden with erius[7] and grains of paradise called the cardamom it mightily purgeth and bringeth good colour. Figs, salt nitrum,[8] and hyssop stamped together and applied to the spleen helpeth it much and taketh away the water that runneth between the skin and the flesh. Sodden with oxymel it cleanseth phlegm.

To help rotten humours [*O1* omits.]

To help the spleen [*O1* omits.]

---

i fennel] Finkle *O1*.   ii it is] *O1 omits*.   iii and] *O1 omits*.
iv with] and with *O1*.   v dripping] droppinge *O1*

---

1 *sod*] boiled; Bullein usually uses the word 'sodden'.
2 *colic*] pains in the abdomen, often due to excess wind.
3 *seed of generation*] sperm.
4 *barber's baths*] Presumably equivalent to the barber's basin, which was a round metal dish with a broad edge and a semicircular opening for the customer's neck so their chin could reach into the bowl (*OED* barber, *n.* C2)
5 *balm, savory*] i.e. balm and savory.
6 *to bedward*] before going to bed.
7 *erius*] It is unclear which substance Bullein is referring to here; it is possible that he meant "verius" meaning verjuice.
8 *salt nitrum*] potassium nitrate or saltpetre.

JOHN What is sention [i]or groundsel?

HUMPHREY It is of a mixed temperament. It cooleth and partly cleanseth if it be chopped and sodden in water; and drink it with your pottage, it will heal the grief of the stomach and purge it from hot choler. [ii]His down,[1] with saffron and cold water, stamped and put in the eyes, it will dry the running drops; and stamped plasterwise,[2] it helpeth many grievous wounds.

Hot choler in the stomach [O1 omits.]

To help the eyes [O1 omits.]

JOHN What is purslane?

HUMPHREY Cold in the third and moist in the second. If it be stamped with steeped barley it maketh a goodly plaster to cool the head, eyes, and liver in ague's burning heat. To eat of it stoppeth fluxes, and quencheth choler, and extinguish venerous lust, and greatly helpeth the reins and bladder; and will kill round worms in the belly, and comfort the matrix against much phlegm, and the juice is good to drink in hot fevers. It may be preserved with salt and then it is very good with roasted meats. Pliny sayeth it is supposed to make the sight blunt and weak, further he sayeth that in Spain a great nobleman whom he did know did hang this purslane root in a thread commonly about his neck, which was [iii]troubled of a long sickness and was healed.

A plaster to cool the burning heat [The operation of purleine O1.]

To stop the flux [O1 omits.]

Purslane good against fevers [O1 omits.]

JOHN What is mugwort?

HUMPHREY [iv]Mugwort, and feverfew, and tansy be very hot and dry in the second degree. Mugwort, spurge, and oil of almonds, tempered plasterwise and applied cold to the sick, pained stomach will bring health. It is good in baths (sayeth Galen), it is wholesome for women, it cleanseth and warmeth and comforteth and breaketh the stone. Pliny sayeth it is good against serpents and wholesome for travelling men: if they carry it, it comforteth them from [v]worms. Tansy doth mightily cast worms from children. Drunk with wine, a cold plaster stamped and laid upon the belly of a woman whose child is dead win[3] her, it will separate the dead child from the living mother, causing her to neeze with betony leaves.[4]

A plaster for a pained stomach [O1 omits.]

Breaking the stone [O1 omits.]

killing worms in children [O1 omits.]

A present help for the delivery of a dead child [O1 omits.]

i or groundsel] *O1 omits.*   ii His down] *This done O3.*
iii troubled] *muche troubled O1.*
iv Mugwort ... health] *marginal note: The operation of Mugworte O1.*
v worms] *O1; werines O2.*

1 *His down*] possibly a reference to soft, downy hairs on the flower heads or leaves; alternatively, Bullein might mean 'This done', as in O3.
2 *stamped plasterwise*] crushed in a mortar with a pestle so as to make a medicine for topical application.
3 *win*] dwelling, residing in (her womb).
4 *neeze*] this usually involves cleaning the nasal passage but here Bullein apparently suggests that the betony leaves be inserted into the vagina.

JOHN There is an herb commonly used, to the great relief of many, called cabbage. Is it so good as it is reported of?

The operation of cabbage

To bind the belly [O1 omits.]

Aristotle 3 perprob.; Avicenna 2 Cantica; Rasis 3 Almansorem [perprob.] possibly a reference to Aristotle's work Problemata.]

HUMPHREY Cabbage is of two properties: of binding the belly and making laxative. The juice of cabbages lightly boiled in fresh beef-broth is laxative, but the substance of this herb is hard of digestion; but if it be twice sodden the broth of it will also bind the belly if it be tempered with alum.[1] This herb hath virtue to cleanse a new red leprosy, laid upon the sore place in the manner of a plaster. But to conclude of this herb, the broth of it hath virtue to preserve from drunkenness (as Aristotle, Rasis, and Avicenna doth report) eaten before drinking-time.

JOHN What is filipendula?[2]

Of filipendula

HUMPHREY It is an herb hot and dry. If it be sodden in white wine and drunk it dryeth up windy places in the guts and cleanseth the reins in the back and bladder.

JOHN What is agrimony?

The operation of agrimony

HUMPHREY Dioscorides sayeth that if this herb with swine's grease be stamped together and laid upon an old, rotten sore, being hot it hath virtue to heal it. The seed of this herb drunk with wine is good against the biting of serpents, stopping of the liver,[3] and bloody flux.

JOHN Some men say that the herb dragon[4] is of great virtue.

The virtue of dragon

The savour of dragon evil for women with child [O1 omits.]

HUMPHREY The juice of it (sayeth Dioscorides) dripped into the eye doth cleanse it and giveth much insight unto the eyes of them which have dark sights. The water of this herb hath virtue against the pestilence[5] if it be drunk blood-warm with Venice treacle.[6] The savour of this herb is hurtful to a woman newly conceived with child. Pliny sayeth that whoso beareth this herb upon them, no venomous serpent will do them harm. This herb is hot and dry.

---

1 *alum*] a mineral salt.

2 *filipendula*] several flowering plants in the rose family; the most well-known species are meadowsweet and drop-wort.

3 *stopping of the liver*] an obstruction in the liver, which it was believed would prevent blood flowing properly from the liver through the body.

4 *dragon*] gum-dragon, also called adragant or tragacanth.

5 *The water ... pestilence*] In Francis Beaumont's play *The Knight of the Burning Pestle* Rafe, a Citizen, asks his wife the following question: "But what brave spirit could be content to sit in his shop with a flappet of wood and a blue apron before him, selling mithridatum and dragon's water to visited houses, that might pursue feats of arms, and through his noble achievements procure such a famous history to be written of his heroic prowess?" (Beaumont 2002, 1.248–53).

6 *Venice treacle*] An electuary (medicinal conserve or thick paste) comprising many ingredients and reputedly devised by the Greek physician Andromachus the Elder.

JOHN   There is a very sweet flower called a violet. Is it so profitable as it is pleasant?

HUMPHREY   Simeon Sethi reporteth that it doth help against hot inflammations of the guts, head, and stomach if the cause be of burning choler, either the water, syrup, or conserve of the said violets, either eaten or drunk in the time of any hot passion; but undoubtedly it offendeth the heart because of the coldness. The savour of the flowers be pleasant; the oil that is made of this herb have virtue to bring quiet sleeps to them which have grievous hot pain in the head.

The virtue of violets [violets] violet O1.]

To cause sleep [O1 omits.]

JOHN   What is the virtue of the pleasant, white lily?

HUMPHREY   Dioscorides sayeth that the oil of lilies doth mollify the sinewes and the mouth of the matrix.[1] The juice of lilies, vinegar, and honey sodden in a brazen[2] vessel doth make an ointment to heal both new and old wounds. If the root be roasted and stamped with roses it maketh a healing plaster against burning of fire;[3] the same root roasted hath virtue to break a pestilence sore applied hot unto the sore place and is dry in the first degree. The oil of waterlilies be moist, sufferent[4] against all hot diseases to anoint the ardent[5] places, and doth reconcile quiet sleep if the forehead be anointed therewith.

Of white lily and of his operation

A plaster to break the pestilence sore [O1 omits.]

JOHN   In the time of the pestilence my wife maketh me a medicine of an herb called centaury. Doth she well or not?

HUMPHREY   Pliny sayeth that the syrup of this herb drunk with a little vinegar and salt doth cleanse the body. The leaves and flowers be of great virtue to be sodden and drunk against all raw humours of gross phlegm, watery or windy. It doth cleanse cruent or bloody matter within the bodies of men or women; the powder of this herb is good in pessaries for women, causing the dead child to depart from the mother, and is wholesome against the pestilence in the time of winter, and is hot and dry.

The virtue of centaury [The] Of yᵉ O1.]

Dead child [O1 omits.]

JOHN   We beautify and make pleasant our windows with rosemary, using it for small other purposes.[6]

HUMPHREY   Rosemary is an herb of great virtue, hot and dry. Sodden in wine and drunk before meat it doth heal the king's evil or pains in the throat, as Dioscorides and Galen sayeth. The

Of rosemary

---

1 *mouth of the matrix*] neck of the womb.
2 *brazen*] brass.
3 *burning of fire*] i.e. burns caused by fire.
4 *sufferent*] effective; the word means "patient" and apparently the sense here is that the oil patiently works against the heat.
5 *ardent*] hot, burning.
6 *using ... purposes*] i.e. it is not used for much else.

savour of it doth comfort the brain and heart; the flowers of rosemary is an excellent cordial called anthos[1] [i]and be good after fevers or for melancholy men.

JOHN   Is pulial royal[2] an herb of any value, or a weed of contemption?

The operation of pulial royal

HUMPHREY   It is an herb of much virtue and profit; hot and dry in the third degree. Dioscordes sayeth if this herb be sodden with honey and aloes and drunk it will cleanse the liver and purge the blood; most chiefly it helpeth the lungs. Simeon Sethi sayeth if women drink it with white wine it will provoke and cleanse the terms menstrual; and is a very wholesome pot-herb.

JOHN   What sayest thou unto mustard?

The operation of mustard [mustard] muster *O1*.]

Palsy [*O1 omits*.]

Falling-sickness [*O1 omits*.]

HUMPHREY   Pliny doth greatly laud[3] it, saying that there is nothing that doth pierce more swiftlier into the brain that it doth. Honey, vinegar, and mustard, tempered together is an excellent gargarism to purge the head, teeth, and throat. Mustard is good against all the diseases of the stomach or lungs, wind, phlegm, and rawness of the guts, and conduceth meat into the body, provoketh urine, helpeth the palsy, wasteth the quartan,[4] drieth up moist rheums applied plasterwise unto the head. Honey and mustard helpeth the cough and is good for them that have the falling-sickness, notwithstanding the common use of mustard is an enemy to the eye. Many more virtues have I read of mustard, but the occasion of time hath unhappily prevented not only my large description in this but also in many other [ii]simples.

JOHN   They say that bugloss is very wholesome.

The virtues of bugloss

HUMPHREY   It is an herb most temperate between hot and cold. Of an excellent virtue: a comforterer of the hart, a purger of melancholy, a quieter of the frenzy, a purger of the urine, wholesome to be drunk in wine but most effectual in syrup. Dioscorides and Galen doth greatly commend this herb and that doth daily experience well prove.

JOHN   What is thy mind of sweet basil?

---

i and be good after fevers or for melancholy men] *O1 omits*.
ii simples] simples, whyche heareafter, I entende largely to wryte vpon if, it please God to permit me *O1*.

---

1 *anthos*] from the Greek for flower and specifically applied to rosemary.
2 *pulial royal*] pennyroyal; as Walter Skeat pointed out, "pennyroyal" is a corruption of the old name for the herb from the Latin *puleium regium*, "a name given to the plant from its supposed efficacy against fleas" from *pulex* and *regius*, latin for "flea" and "royal" (Skeat 1993, "Penny-royal").
3 *laud*] praise.
4 *wasteth the quartan*] rids the body of a fever that occurs every fourth day.

HUMPHREY   This herb is warm in the second degree, having the virtue of moisture. And if it be sodden in wine with spikenard and drunk it is good against dropsies, winds, phlegm, coldness of the heart, hardness of the stomach. The savour of basil doth comfort the brain and heart; the use of this herb in meats doth decay the sight.

The virtues of basil

Comforts of the brain and heart [O1 omits.]

JOHN   The plain people of the country will say that those flowers which be pleasant in smelling be oftentimes unwholesome in working. The rose is pleasant in sense, what is it in virtue?

HUMPHREY   It hath an odour most pleasant and hath virtue to cool and bind. The water is good to make *manus christi*[1] and many other goodly cordials. Roses and vinegar applied unto the forehead do bring sleep; conserve of roses have virtue to quench burning choler and to stay the rage of a hot fever. Oil of roses, vinegar, and the white of an egg beaten together doth not only quench *sacra ignis*[2] but also bring a mad man into quietness if ⁱhis forehead be well annointed therewith after the receipt of pills of cochie.[3] In the time of pestilence there is nothing more comfortable than the savour of roses.

The virtue of roses

To cause sleep [O1 omits.]

To help a mad man into quietness [O1 omits.]

JOHN   What sayest thou of savory?

HUMPHREY   It is hot and dry in the third degree. If the green herb be sodden in water or white wine and drunk, these be his virtues: to make ⁱⁱthe liver soft, to cleanse dropsies, cold coughs, cleanseth women's diseases, and separateth the dead child from the mother (as Dioscorides and Galen sayeth). Also, germander is not much unlike the virtue of this herb.

The virtue of savory

Dead child [O1 omits.]

JOHN   ⁱⁱⁱHumphrey, but for troubling of ⁱᵛthee I would be glad to know ᵛthy mind of thyme and ᵛⁱso of a few of other herbs.

HUMPHREY   It is vehement of heat, with dryness in the third degree. Dioscorides sayeth if it be drunk with vinegar and salt it purgeth phlegm. Sodden with honey or mead it hath virtue to cleanse the lungs, breast, matrix, reins, and bladder, and killeth worms.

The virtue of thyme

JOHN   What sayest thou of parsley and saxifrage?

---

i his] this O3.   ii the] O1; O2 omits.   iii Humphrey] O1 omits.
iv thee] you O1.   v thy] youre O1.   vi so of] O1 omits.

---

1 *manus christi*] Latin for 'hand of Christ': refined sugar and rose water boiled together until the sugar hardens, after which ground-up pearls or other precious stones are added; other flowers or spices might be used for this compound. Bullein provides a recipe for *manus christi* in his *Bulwark of Defence* (Bullein 1579, Ccc2r).

2 *sacra ignis*] holy fire or St Antony's fire, a bacterial infection causing inflammation of the skin, especially on the face.

3 *pills of cochie*] pills containing purgative medicine.

Breaking the stone [O1 omits.]	HUMPHREY ⁱThey have virtue to break the stone. Parsley is hot in the second degree and dry in the middest of the third. The seed drunk with white wine provoketh the menstrual terms, as Dioscorides sayeth; also, smallage¹ hath the like virtue.

JOHN   What is thy judgement of liverwort?

The virtue of liverwort	HUMPHREY It hath virtue to cleanse and cool. Dioscorides sayeth it doth heal the wounds of the liver and quencheth the extreme heat thereof. Tempered with honey and eaten doth help a disease called *regius morbus*² and pains of the throat and lungs.

JOHN   What is betony?

The virtue of betony	HUMPHREY They be of diverse kinds. Leonhart Fuchs doth call the sweet gillyflowers by the names of betony, but the one seemeth to talk of that which is commonly known of the people called the
To kill worms [O1 omits.]	land-Betony, which hath the virtue to kill worms within the belly, and helpeth the quartan, cleanseth the matrix, and hath the virtue to heal the body ⁱⁱwithin if it be bruised.³ It is of great effect if

it be sodden with wormwood in white wine to purge phlegm; ⁱⁱⁱis hot in the first degree ⁱᵛand dry in the second.

JOHN   I have heard small commendations of beets.

The virtue of beets	HUMPHREY They be of two kinds and be both praise-worthy; Simeon Sethi writeth that they be hot and dry in the third degree. The white beet is the best: they have virtue to cleanse, as nitre⁴
Purging the head [O1 omits.]	hath, but hath evil juice. The juice of this herb with honey applied into the nose do purge the head; it is an wholesome herb in pottage if it be well sodden or else it is noisome to the stomach. If it be

parboiled and eaten with vinegar it is good against the stopping of the liver.⁵ Notwithstanding, the juice of this herb do stop⁶ the belly being simply taken.

JOHN   What is maidenhair?

---

i They ... the stone] *marginal note*: The vertue of persly & saxifrage O1.
ii within if it be bruised.] within. If it be brused O1.
iii is] and is O1.   iv and] O1 omits.

---

1 *smallage*] wild celery or water parsley.
2 *regius morbus*] the regal disease or king's evil (scrofula).
3 *if it be bruised*] It is possible that Bullein here refers to the body being bruised within, although he might mean that the plant should be bruised (i.e. crushed), which is the meaning apparent from the punctuation of O1, as detailed in the collation note.
4 *nitre*] potassium nitrate or saltpetre.
5 *stopping of the liver*] an obstruction in the liver, which it was believed would prevent blood flowing properly from the liver through the body.
6 *stop*] bind.

HUMPHREY   It is an herb between hot and dry. If it be sodden in wine it breaketh the stone; it cleanseth the matrix, bringeth down the seconds[1] as Dioscorides and Galen sayeth. The best doth grow upon hard rocks.

The virtue of maidenhair

JOHN   What is melliot?

HUMPHREY   It hath virtue to ripe, and is more hotter than cold. Melliot, flax-seed, rose leaves, camphor, and woman's milk tempered together doth make a goodly medicine against the hot inflammation of the eyes. If this herb be drunk with wine it doth mollify the hardness of the stomach and liver. The most excellent plaster against the pains of the spleen doth Mesue describe, which is made of melliot.

The virtue of melliot

To help the spleen [O1 omits.]

JOHN   Be pease and beans anything beneficial to nature?

HUMPHREY   Beans be more grosser and fuller of wind than pease be and maketh evil matter except they be well sodden and buttered and so eaten with the whitest and sweetest onions that may be gotten because they be hard of digestion. Howbeit they do make fat and partly cleanse yet they are not to be compared with tender, white peason well sodden and buttered or else made in pottage with garden mints and gross pepper, which hath virtue to cleanse the reins of the back and bladder. [i]Lentils be of the same virtue; barley, being clean-hulled and sodden with milk, clean water, and sugar maketh a very comfortable and wholesome pottage for hot choleric persons or young people. And of this is much used in the north parts of England and is called big kele.

The operation of pease and beans

A comfortable pottage [O1 omits.]

JOHN   What be the virtues of [ii]leeks and roots of radish, turnips, parsnips, rapes or navews?

HUMPHREY   Leeks be evil (engender painful sleep) but eaten with honey then they purge blood. But roots eaten raw breedeth ill juice, therefore being first sodden and the water cast away and then sodden with fat mutton or tender, fat beef these roots nourisheth much. Rapes and navews be windy; turnips causeth one to spit easily that have corrupt stomachs, but maketh raw juice. Carrots do expulse wind; radish roots provoke urine, but be very evil for phlegmatic persons having grief in their bones or joints and must be eaten in the beginning of the meal (as Galen sayeth); but many do use them in the end of meals and find ease as Sir Thomas Elyot, that worthy knight and learned man, reporteth in

Leeks and their properties

Roots sodden nourisheth [Of the vertues of radish with other rotes O1.]

Galen *De alimentorum facultatibus*

---

i Lentils ... virtue] *marginal note*: But lintels and tares be melancholy *O1*.
ii leeks] the leeks *O1*.

---

1 *the seconds*] the secundine or afterbirth.

his ⁱgood book called *The Castle of Health*.¹ And thus I do conclude of those herbs and roots that I have written upon, admonishing thee that herbs and roots be all windy engenderers of melancholy and engrossers of the blood except lettuce, borage, and purslane. Therefore, the gross binding together and seething of herbs in broths and pottage be more wholesomer than the fine chopping of them. Thus, John, I have declared unto thee the virtues of certain herbs, which if thou wilt follow and observe my rules in them, I doubt not but thou shalt receive much profit thereby. I would have also taught you some pretty ways for distillation of waters but am prevented therein, and I am glad thereof for as much as thou shalt see very shortly both *Thesaurus* Euonymus and Ulstad, which be excellent learned men in that science wherein I am sure thou wilt much delight.² For I ensure thee, the like books never were set forth in our mother tongue with the lively fashion³ of the furnaces and also of the stillatories.⁴

_{Herbs engender melancholy}

_{Ulstad, *Thesaurus*, Euonymus}

JOHN ⁱⁱThen seeing thou wilt go no further with me in declaration of the properties of herbs, I pray thee, think not the time too long, but tell me ⁱⁱⁱwhich of these will digest and purge choler, phlegm, and melancholy, provoke sternutation and stop ⁱᵛfluxes.

HUMPHREY

> ᵛ**Digesters of choler**
> Endive
> Purslane
> Poppy
> Sorrel
> Mercury
> Liverwort
> Whey
> Tisanes
> Tamarinds

---

i good] *O4 omits.*   ii Then seeing ... tell me] *O1 omits.*
iii which of these] what *O1.*   iv fluxes.] Flixes, tel me? *O1.*
v Digesters of] Things to digest *O1.*

---

1 his good ... Health] Bullein also praises Elyot in his *Bulwarke of Defence*, referring to he "who hath planted such fruitful trees that his graftes do grow in each place in this our common wealth, and his Castel of health, cannot decay" (Bullein 1579, Aa4r).

2 Thesaurus ... *much delight*] Conrad Gesner (under the pseudonym Euonymus Philiatri) and Philipp Ulstad both wrote works on distillation. Bullein seems to be aware of the English translation of Gesner's work by Peter Morwyng, published in 1559, a year after the first edition of *The Government of Health* (1558); it is possible, as Catherine Cole Mambretti suggests, that he had seen Morwyng's translation in manuscript (Mambretti 1974, 290). As Mambretti also points out, no English translation of Ulstadt's work is known (Mambretti 1974, 296n31).

3 *fashion*] style.

4 *stillatories*] still-houses.

The four cold seeds of gourdes and cucumbers
Sanders
Buttermilk or the milk which cometh of the pressing of the cheese

Purgers of choler
Manna 6 drams
Rhubarb 2 drams or 3 but put into infusion from 5 to 7
Pills of aloes
Wild hops
Syrup of wormwood
Syrup of fumitory
Diaprunes[1]

[i]Digesters of phlegm
Puliol[2]
Mints
Betony
Agrimony
Mugwort
Honey
Pepper
Hyssop
Pimpernel
Juniper berries
Neppe[3]
Fennel
Parsley roots
Smallage[4]

Purgers of phlegm
A garlic infused from 2 to 5 drams [ii]siccus[5]
The myrobalans[6] of all the kinds
Polypody of the oak
Centaury
Horehound
Maidenhair

Good purgers of melancholy
Helleborus niger[7]

---

i Digesters] The digester O1.   ii siccus] *this ed.*; Sticaus O2.

1 *Diaprunes*] a medicinal preparation made of prunes and other ingredients.
2 *Puliol*] either of two aromatic herbs from the same family: penny-royal and wild thyme.
3 *Neppe*] catmint.
4 *Smallage*] wild celery or water parsley.
5 *siccus*] dried (Latin), referring back to the garlic. O2's reading of "Sticaus" appears to be an error.
6 *myrobalans*] the plum-like astringent fruits from tropical trees.
7 Helleborus niger] black hellebore.

Capers
Lapis lazuli[1]
Senna of Alexander
Borage
Hart's tongue
Honey sodden in sweet wine
Savory
Thyme
Trusses of capers, of coloquintida, and of wormwood

Good things to provoke urine
Parsley
Thyme
Saxifrage
Cassia fistula
Rams
Radish
The flesh of an hare
Pills of [i]*térébenthine*[2]
Maidenhair
The berries of eglantine
Brome seed

Comforters for the brain to smell upon
Roses
Violets
Gillyflowers in summer, but in winter cloves
[ii]Spikenard
Musk
Ambergris

Things good to stop flux
Cinnabar called dragon's blood
Sloes or their decoction
Cinnamon
Bole armeniac
Red wine
Plaintain
Olibanum
Hard eggs
Hard cheese scraped in red wine and drink

---

i *térébenthine*] *this ed.*; Tiriabenthen O2.   ii Spikenard] *this ed.*; Spike O2.

1 *Lapis Lazuli*] a semi-precious stone of intense blue colour.
2 térébenthine] turpentine (French).

Things good to provoke sternutation or neezing
Betony leaves,
Primrose roots moderately used
Helleborus albus[1] and ginger

Good comforters for the heart
Musk
Ambergris
Roses
Pearls
Maces
Diamuschi dulcis diamber[2]
The flowers of rosemary and
Nutmegs
Spiknard
Galangal

JOHN [ii]Well thou has satisfied me of this matter, which I hope I will not forget, but [iii]would to God thou wouldst tell me [iv]the virtue of dates and figs [v]and other necessary fruits commonly used.

HUMPHREY Serapion sayeth that the dates which be preserved with sugar be good. The crude raw date doth calefy[3] the body and doth convert quickly into choler; it is not good for the heads of the hot people, ill for the throat, and stoppeth the liver, and maketh the teeth rotten. But if they be clean pilled[4] and the inward rind taken away they do greatly nourish and restore being sodden in stewed broth. They be of diverse kinds in quantity and quality but generally hot and moist in the second degree. Figs (as Hippocrates sayeth) the best be white, the second be red, the third be black. The ripest be the best and amongst all fruits doth most nourish, provoketh sweat because it doth purge the superfluity of humours through the skin; it doth engender lice. They be hot in the first degree and the new figs be moist in the second. The seeds

[marginal notes:] Rasis in 3 *Almansorem*; Halia in. 5 Theori, Ra. Moy[.]ses [*Halia in.* 5 *Theori, Ra. Moy[.]ses*] Perhaps a reference to Haly Abbas's theory 5; it is not clear what "Ra. Moy[.]ses" refers to but the indistinguishable character could be a line-ending hyphen giving the name Moyses.]

Hippocrates 2 can. *capitulum* 208 [*can* possibly short for "canon" and thus a reference to the *Hippocratic Canon*.]

---

i good] *O1 omits.*   ii Well ... tell me] *O1 omits.*
iii would ... dates and figs] *marginal note*: Of figges and dates *O1*.
iv the virtue] What be the vertue *O1*.   v and other ... used] *O1 omits.*

---

1 Helleborus albus] white hellebore.
2 Diamuschi dulcis diamber] a sweet stomachic and cordial containing ambergris, musk and other aromatics (*OED* diamber). Bullein provides a recipe for "that most worthy and excellent Cordiall *Diamuscum dulce*" in his *Bulwark of Defence* (Bullein 1579, Ccc6v). In Thomas Middleton's *A Mad World My Masters* the fake doctor, Penitent Brothel, offers to cure the courtesan who is pretending to be sick with a "precious cordial" containing a number of ingredients including coral and unicorn's horn "finely contunded and mixed in a stone or glass mortar with the spirit of diamber" (Middleton 2007, 3.2.57, 67–8).
3 *calefy*] heat.
4 *pilled*] peeled.

Almonds [*O1* omits.]	and the skin of the fig be not greatly commended. Figs and almonds eaten of a fasting stomach be very wholesome to make the way
Figs and herb-grace to be eaten together [*O1* omits.]	of good digestion but best if they be eaten with nuts. Figs and herb-grace stamped together be very wholesome to be eaten against the pestilence. Roasted figs beaten together and hot applied
To help a pestilence sore [*O1* omits.]	upon the pestilence sore doth draw, mollify, and make ripe the sore. And to the lungs, liver, and stomach, figs be very comfortable
Galen *De alimentorum facultatibus*	(as Galen sayeth).

JOHN   What be pears?

	HUMPHREY They be of diverse kinds, heavier than apples, not
The operation of pears	good until they be very ripe unless they be tenderly roasted or baken and eaten after meals. There is a kind of pears growing in
Blackfriars pear	the city of Norwich called the Blackfriars pear: very delicious and pleasant and no less profitable unto a hot stomach, as I heard it

reported by a right worshipful physician of the same city called Doctor Mansfield, which said he thought those pears without all comparison were the best that grew in any place of England.

JOHN   What sayest thou of apples?

The operation of apples	HUMPHREY Apples be very cold and windy, hard to digest, engenderers of evil blood, hurtful to phlegmatic people. Good to choleric stomachs if they be through ripe, but best if they be

roasted or baken and eaten with gross pepper to bedward.[1] They be of many kinds:

	as ⁱthe costard, the green-coat, the pippin, the queen apple, and so forth. The distilled water of apples, camphor, vinegar, and milk is a good
A medicine for the small pox	medicine to anoint the faces of children that have the smallpox when the said pox be ripe to keep ⁱⁱthem from ⁱⁱⁱpits[2] provided that the said children have given them in their milk saffron

or *mithridatum* to expel the venom and keep them from the air during the said sickness.

JOHN   What be peaches?

The operation of peaches	HUMPHREY The leaves be hot, for if they be stamped in plasterwise[3] and applied unto the belly they kill worms. The fruit is cold and very good to the stomach; they be good to be eaten of
Against stinking breath [*O1* omits.]	them that have stinking breaths of hot causes, eaten of an empty stomach, ⁱᵛwhich is Galen's counsel, which sayeth if they be eaten after meat they do corrupt both in themselves and the meats

---

i the] *O1*; *O2* omits.   ii them] their faces *O1*.   iii pits] eres *O1*.
iv which is Galen's counsel] *O1*; as the counsell of Galen *O2*.

---

1 *to bedward*] before going to bed.
2 *pits*] marks or scars.
3 *stamped in plasterwise*] crushed in a mortar with a pestle so as to make a medicine for topical application.

lately eaten and they be binders of the belly. But quinces be most comfortable after meat for they do enclose the stomach, and letteth vapours ^i ascend into the brain, and stoppeth vomits.¹ They be wholesome for sick folks that be swelled in their bodies: eaten with the gross powders of galangal, spikenard, calamus,² and ginger, may be eaten before meat of the said sick patients as well as ^ii after. But much use of them be not so profitable as delectable to the eaters ^iii thereof.

Quinces wholesome [O1 omits.]

Swelling [O1 omits.]

JOHN What be quinces?³

HUMPHREY If thy stomach be very hot or moist or thy belly laxative then quinces be good to be eaten before meat, being roasted or eaten cold, and in this case the tarter be the better; and pomegranates be of the same virtue, as Isaac sayeth. But eaten after meat they do enclose the stomach and moist the belly. They ought not to be used in common meats⁴ (the custom of them hurteth the sinews) but in the way of medicine they be excellent, and the cores being taken out and preserved in honey or kept their mucilage⁵ then they may long continue to the use of roasting or baking for they be perilous to the stomach eaten raw. But preserved they do mightily prevail against drunkenness; they be cold in the first degree and dry in the beginning of the second.

The operation of quinces

Isaac in perticudie [perticudie] presumably Isaac's Diaetae particulares.]

Quinces raw hurteth [O1 omits.]

JOHN What be cherries?

The tart cherries undoubtedly be more wholesomer than the sweet and eaten before meat do mollify the belly, prepare digestion, and they be most excellent against hot burning choler. They be good also after meat and be of many kinds: as black, red, and pale. The red cherry, partly tart, is best; Galen and Rasis greatly commend this fruit. In the country⁶ of Kent be growing great plenty of this fruit; so are there in a town near unto Norwich called Ketteringham. This fruit is cold and moist in the first degree.

The operation of cherries

Galen De alimentorum facultatibus; Rasis liber 23 capitulum

JOHN What be the virtues of grapes, raisins, prunes, barberries, oranges, and medlars?

HUMPHREY Hippocrates sayeth that the white grapes be better than the black, and wholesomer when they are two or three days gathered from the vine than presently pulled from it, and if they

The goodness of grapes

---

i ascend] to ascend O1.   ii after] after meat O1.   iii thereof] of them O1.

---

1 *But quinces ... after meat*] Bullein is disagreeing with Galen here.
2 *calamus*] a reed or cane; possibly a reference to the native sweet flag or sweet rush.
3 *quinces*] Quinces are apparently confused with peaches by Humphrey in the section preceding but they actually belong to the same family as apples and pears.
4 *used in common meats*] i.e. as an everyday food.
5 *mucilage*] pulp from the fruit.
6 *country*] county.

Galen *De alimentorum facultatibus* 2; Rasis in 4 *Almansorem* 20 *capitulum*	be sweet they be partly nutrative and warm the body. And unto this agreeth Galen and Rasis, ⁱwhich seemeth to commend sweet grapes above dates, saying although they be not so warm yet they do not stop the body or make oppilation as dates do. They be wholesome to be eaten before meat, even as nuts be good after fish. Toward the south and south-east parts of the world there

be many growing in diverse regions whereof the wines be made; the farther from us,

Blaxhall in Suffolk — the hotter wine. There be very good grapes growing here in England in many places, as partly I have seen at Blaxhall in Suffolk where sometime I was near kinsman unto the chiefest house of

Raisins [*O1* omits.] that town.¹ Raisins of the sun be very wholesome and comfort digestion, but the stones and rinds would be refused and then they be good for the spleen and liver, so be alicant.² Rasis doth much commend them, but undoubtedly the small raisins be hurtful to

Sweet prunes be laxative but tart prunes be binding — the spleen. Prunes or damsons have virtue to relax the belly if they be sweet and ripe; ⁱⁱthey do nourish very little but quench choler. Grapes, rasins and prunes, plums and sloes, if they be sour be all

Oxiacantha called the barberry — binders of the belly, and so is the barberry called *oxiacantha*,³ and oranges, except the said oranges be condited with sugar and then they be good coolers against hot choler whose rinds be hot and

Mespila called the medlar — dry of nature. The fruit called the medlar is used for a medicine and not for meat, and must be taken before meat, provoketh urine, and of nature is styptic.

JOHN   What be capers and olives?

The operation of capers — HUMPHREY   Fresh capers be hot and dry in the second degree, and eaten before meats do greatly comfort digestion, and be the best things for the spleen or to cleanse melancholy that can be taken. Preserved olives in salt, eaten at the beginning of meals, do greatly fortify the stomach and relaxeth the belly, cleanseth the liver, and be hot and dry in the second degree.

JOHN   I beseech thee, show me ⁱⁱⁱthy opinion of the natures of some ⁱᵛkinds of flesh. ᵛFirst, of the properties of beef.

Simeon Sethi — HUMPHREY   I will not undertake to show mine opinion to thy request, but I will declare the minds of some wise and learned men and first of Simeon Sethi, which sayeth that the flesh of oxen that be young do much nourish, and make them strong that be fed with them, but it bringeth melancholy and melancholious diseases. It is cold and dry

---

i which] *O1* omits.   ii they] but they *O1*.   iii thy] the *O1*.
iv kinds] kind *O1*.   v First] and first *O1*.

---

1 *Blaxhall ... that town*] See the Introduction on Bullein, p. 28.
2 *alicant*] a wine from Alicante in Spain.
3 *oxiacantha*] an alkaloid obtained from the root of the barberry (*OED* oxyacanthin).

of nature, and hard to digest except it be of choleric persons, but being tenderly sodden it nourisheth. Much beef, customably[1] eaten of idle persons and nice[2] folks that labour not, bringeth many diseases (as Rasis sayeth). And Avicenna sayeth that the flesh of oxen or kine[3] be very gross, engendering ill juice in the body whereof oftentimes come to scabs, cankers, biles; but unto hot, strong, choleric stomachs it is tolerable and may be used as we have the daily experience thereof. The broth wherein the beef hath been sodden is good to be supped half a pint every morning against the flux of the belly and running forth of yellow choler if the said broth be tempered with salt. Mustard, vinegar, or garlic, *et cetera*, be commonly used for the sauces to digest beef withal, for the said sauces do not only help digestion but also defendeth the body from sundry inconveniences and diverse sicknesses as dropsies, quartans, leprosies, and such like. The gall[4] of an ox or a cow distilled in the month of June and kept in a close glass doth help to cleanse the eyes from spots if you put a drop of this water with a feather into thy eyes when ye go to bed. The milt of a bull dried and the powder thereof drunk with red wine will stop the bloody flux. Light powdered young beef is better than either fresh or much powdered in specially those cattle that be fed in fair and dry pastures and not in stinking fens. The great, learned man Gesner in his description of beasts doth write more of the virtues of bulls, oxen, kine and calves than any other hath done.[5] And thus to conclude, the flesh of the male beasts is more better than the female, and the gelded beasts be more commodious to nature than any of them, and the young flesh more commendable than the old for it is more moist and a friend to the blood (as Haly Abbas sayeth). Roasted flesh doth nourish the body much for it is warm and moist, baken meats be very dry, clean boiled meats with wholesome herbs and fruits be excellent to comfort the body if they be nutrimental flesh. Calves' flesh do greatly nourish and make good blood.

Rasis in liber 2, capitulum 3; *Avicenna in* 2 liber pri, capitulum 15

To help the flux [flixe *O1*.]

Digestion

A medicine for the eyes

To stop the bloody flux [*O1 omits.*]

Conrad Gesner

Gelded beasts best [*O1 omits.*]

Haly in. 5, The. *capitulum*. 4 [5, The. capitulum 4] possibly a reference to theory 5, chapter 4.]

Boiled meats comforteth the body [*O1 omits.*]

JOHN Thou hast said well of beef, but what goodness may be reported of pork? I think very little or nothing.

HUMPHREY There be many goodly commodities in the flesh of boars, gelded swine, and pigs, for they be good for man's nature.

---

i the] *O1 omits.*

1 *customably*] customarily, habitually.
2 *nice*] fastidious or delicate and suggesting also foolish.
3 *kine*] cows.
4 *gall*] secrection of the liver, bile.
5 *Gesner ... description of beasts*] Conrad Gesner's *Historiae Animalium*.

The description of swine	JOHN For man's nature? That is marvel. For how can those be good for man's nature which be so vile of their own nature? Their foul feeding of most stinking filth and carrion, the noisome wallowing in the mire and dirt, the eating of their own pigs, and oftentimes pulling children out of the cradle for their dinners if the good wife be not at home. Who is able to behold such noisome spirits or hellhounds? Did not almighty God command the Jews to eat none of them? and the Mahomites[1] at this day will kill that man that eateth of their flesh. Why should we then commend them? for they are most vile.
Florida corona [a dietary by Antonio Gazio.]	HUMPHREY All the ancient and wisest physicians that ever were in this world did all consent that, of all flesh, the flesh of young, gelded swine, partly salted or powdered, was ever a meat
Isaac; Galen in sec. comp *capitulum* 2 [*sec. comp.* *capitulum* 2] it is not clear which work by Galen is referred to here.]	of the best: nourishing, moister, and colder than other flesh, for Isaac sayeth it is a flesh very moist, except it be the flesh of lambs, as Galen reporteth.[2] Yet it is not good to every complexion, nor ito every age, but unto youth and middle age.[3] Whereas thou hast spoken against the vile nature of swine, calling them unreasonable, thou dost use more words than wit, for there is no beast
Beasts want reason [want] haue no *O1*.]	that may be called reasonable but man only. And whereas God did prohibit the Jews to eat swine's flesh, it was a figure,[4] to abstain from unclean things, which I leave to the theologians.
Why the Mahomites abhor swine's flesh [*O1* omits.]	The Mahomites[5] abhor swine's flesh because their drunk, false prophet and pseudo apostle was torn and rent in pieces with swine, being drunken and fallen in the mire.[6] So, the one must
puddings of swine	give credence to time and to learned physicians. The blood of swine doth nourish much, as it is seen in puddings[7] made with great oatmeal, sweet suet, and fennel or aniseeds. Pigs be very moist, therefore sage, pepper, and salt do dry up the superfluous humours of them when they be roasted; they be not wholesome to be eaten before they be three weeks old. The tripes and guts
Tripes of swine [Of swine *O1*.]	be wholesomer and doth nourish better than any other beast's iiguts. Bacon is very hard of digestion, and much discommended,[8] and is hurtful. Only unto a hot, choleric, labouring body, the
Boar's flesh [*O1* omits.]	flesh of a boar is more wholesomer than the flesh of any sow. The brains of a boar and his stones or any part of them stamped

---

i to] *O1* omits.   ii guts] guts, or in meats *O1*; or in-meats *O4*.

1 *Mahomites*] Muslims.
2 *swine ... lambs*] pork is colder than all meats, with the exception of lamb.
3 *unto youth and middle-age*] i.e. it ought not to be eaten after middle age.
4 *a figure*] used to illustrate only and not meant to be taken literally.
5 *Mahomites*] Muslims.
6 *The Mahomites ... fallen in the mire*] This refers to the Christian medieval legend that claimed that Muhammad, whilst in a drunken state, was eaten by a herd of swine (Setton 1992, 1).
7 *puddings*] The stomach or one of the entrails of an animal mixed with ingredients to bind it and then seasoned; pudding might also be the stuffing that was cooked inside the body of an animal.
8 *discommended*] advised against, not recommended.

together and laid warm upon a pestilence sore in the manner of a plaster, it will break it incontinent. Swine's grease is very cold, and good to anoint burning hot places of the body or a disease called Saint Antony's fire.[1] And thus much have I spoken of swine.

JOHN   I pray you, tell me of the flesh of the rams, wethers, and lambs, and how profitable they are to man's nature.

HUMPHREY   Simeon Sethi sayeth lamb's flesh is partly warm but superfluous moist,[2] and evil for phlegmatic persons, and doth much harm to them that have the dropsy, bone-ache, or a disease called *epiolus*,[3] which is spitting of phlegm like glass. Therefore, if lambs flesh were sodden, as it is roasted, it would bring many diseases unto the body, without[4] it were sodden with wine and some hot groceries,[5] herbs, or roots. When a wether is two years old, which is fed upon a good ground, the flesh thereof shall be temperate and nourish much. Hippocrates sayeth that the lamb of a year old doth nourish much; Galen seemeth not greatly to commend mutton, but that which is tender, sweet, and not old is very profitable, as experiences and custom doth daily teach us. The dung, tallow,[6] and wool be very profitable in medicines, as Pliny sayeth and Conrad Gesner, *De animalibus*,[7] and Galen in his third book, *De alimentorum facultatibus*.

JOHN   What is the flesh of goats or kids?

HUMPHREY   They be beasts very hurful unto young trees and plants, but Simeon Sethi sayeth that kid's flesh is ⁱeasy of digestion; in health and sickness they be very good meat. They be dry of nature. Hippocrates sayeth it behoveth the conservers and keepers of health to study that his meat be such as the flesh of kids, young calves that be sucking, and lambs of one year old, for they be good for them that be sick or have evil complexions. Haly Abbas doth say that the flesh of kids do engender good blood and is not so phlegmatic, watery, and moist as the flesh of lambs. They remain kids for six months and afterward cometh into a grosser and hotter nature and be called goats. The flesh of them that be gelded[8] is

A plaster for a pestilence sore [A playster *O1*.]

The flesh of lambs sodden hurteth [*O1* omits.]

The flesh of wethers [*O1* omits.]

Hippocrates in [.] pri. doc. *capitulum* 15 [*pri. doc*] possibly 'first doctrine' in unnamed Hippocrates' work. Character before "pri." unclear.]

Tender mutton

De alimentorum facultatibus, liber tertio 3

in ter. 12. doc. secū. *capitulum* 7 [it is not clear which work is being referred to here.]

Haly in quincte theori. *capitulum* 2 [*quincte theori*] presumably this means the fifth theory.]

---

i easy of] of easy *O1*.

1 *Saint Antony's fire*] a bacterial infection causing inflamation of the skin, especially on the face.
2 *superfluous moist*] with a superfluity of moisture, that is, overly moist.
3 *epiolus*] not otherwise known as a disease.
4 *without*] unless.
5 *groceries*] all goods consumed in the household that were not sold by specialist tradesmen (for example fishmongers), specifically spices, dried fruits, and sugar (*OED* grocer 2. a.).
6 *tallow*] fat.
7 De animalibus] This is the title of Aristotle's study of the internal workings of animals; Bullein presumably means Gesner's work *Historiae animalium*.
8 *gelded*] castrated.

A medicine for drunkards [*O1* omits.]	wholesome to eat, the lungs of them eaten before a man do drink doth defend him that day from drunkenness, as I have read in the reports of learned men. But the flesh of the old he or male goats
A good medicine to be preserved from the pestilence [A good medicine *O1*.]	be ill and engender the agues or fevers. If the urine of goats be distilled in May with sorrel, the water distilled is not hurtful nor noisome, but whosoever use to drink thereof two drams morn and evening, it will preserve him from the pestilence. The milk of goats I will describe in the proper place.

JOHN What ⁱbe the fleshes of red and fallow deer?

	HUMPHREY More pleasant to some than profitable to many,
Hippocrates; Simeon Sethi	as appeareth once a year in the corn field, the more it is to be lamented.¹ Hippocrates and Simeon Sethi do plainly affirm the flesh of them to engender evil juice, and melancholy, cold diseases,
Rasis *Ad almansorem, capitulum* 3	and quartans. The flesh of winter deer doth less hurt the body than that which is eaten in summer, for in winter man's digestion is more stronger and the inward parts of the body warmer and
Digestion stronger in winter than in summer [*O1* omits.]	may easier consume gross meats than in summer, as we see by experience. In cold weather and frosts healthful people be most hungriest. The lungs of a deer sodden in barley water and taken forth and stamped with penedice² and honey of equal quantity to
To help coughs [*O1* omits.]	the said lungs and eaten a-mornings doth greatly help old coughs and dryness in the lungs. There be many goodly virtues of their horns, bones, blood, and tallow.³

JOHN What ⁱⁱbe the properties of hares' and conies' flesh?

Avicenna in 2 *Cantica capitulum* 146	HUMPHREY Avicenna sayeth the flesh of hares ⁱⁱⁱis hot and dry, ⁱᵛengenderer of melancholy, not praised in physic for meat but rather for medicine. For, indeed, if a hare be dried in the month of March in an oven or furnace and beaten into powder and kept
To break the stone [*O1* omits.]	close and drunk a-mornings in beer, ale, or white wine it will break the stone in the bladder if the patient be not old. If children's gums
A medicine for bloody eyes	be anointed with the brains of an hare their teeth will easily come forth and grow. The gall⁴ of an hare mingled with clean honey
Hares [*O1* omits.]	doth cleanse watery eyes or red bloody eyes. The flesh of hares must be tenderly roasted, and well larded, and spiced because of
Conies [*O1* omits.]	the grossness, but it is better sodden. The flesh of conies are better

---

i be] is *O1*.   ii be] is *O1*.   iii is] be *O1*.   iv engenderer] ingenderers *O1*.

1 *More pleasant ... lamented*] Humphrey is perhaps complaining that the deer eat the farmer's corn, which John later complains conies will do.

2 *penedice*] plural of penide derived from the Old French with Italian influence (*OED* penide *n.*); a penide is a piece or stick of boiled sugar.

3 *tallow*] fat.

4 *gall*] secrection of the liver, bile.

than hares' flesh and easier of digestion, but rabbits be wholesomer. And thus, to conclude of conies, experience teacheth us that they are good if they be cold and dry of nature, and small mention is made of them among the ancient physicians (as Galen sayeth). I need not to speak very long of every kind of beasts as some of the beasts that be in Iberia, like little hares, which be called conies.[1]

Rabbits [*O1 omits.*]

Galen in 3 *De alimentorum facultatibus, capitulum* 1

JOHN [i]If some that knew not conies (which were seen in the nature of many other beasts) [ii]had dwelt in diverse places of England, they should have known them right well and perhaps received of them as small pleasure as many husbandmen[2] have found [iii]by them in their corn. Now, thou has well satisfied me of the four-footed beasts which commonly English men feed upon. Now, I pray thee, tell me some of the virtues of fowls, and first of cocks, capons, and hens.

HUMPHREY Chickens [iv]or hens, sayeth Avenzoar, [v]be most commended and most laudable[3] of any flesh, and nourisheth good blood; it is light of digestion and doth comfort the appetite. Cock chickens be better than hens, the capon is better than the cock; they do augment good blood and seed, as Rasis reporteth and experience proveth, in men both whole and sick. An old cock which is well beaten after his feathers be pulled off until he be all bloody, and then cut off his head, and draw him,[4] and seethe him in a close pot with fair water and white wine, fennel roots, borage roots, violet, plantain, succory and buglos leaves, dates, prunes, great raisins, maces and sugar, and put in the marrow of a calf, and sanders, this is a most excellent broth to them that be sick, weak, or consumed. The brains of hens, capons, or chickens be wholesome to eat, to comfort the brain and memory. And thus to conclude, these foresaid fowls be better for idle folks that labour not than for them that use exercise or travail, to whom gross meats are more profitable.

Chickens [*O1 omits.*]

Avenzoar *liber pri*

Rasis in *liber* 4 Afforism

Old cock [*O1 omits.*]

To help consumed bodies [*O1 omits.*]

To comfort the brain and memory [*O1 omits.*]

JOHN What [vi]be the properties of geese?

HUMPHREY Wild geese and tame, their flesh [vii]is very gross and hard of digestion (as Avicenna sayeth). The flesh of great fowls and of geese be slow and hard of digestion; for their humidity, they do breed fevers quickly, but their goslings or young geese,

Avicenna in. 2 cano. *capitulum* 46 [*cano.*] probably Avicenna's *Canon of Medicine.*]

---

i If some that knew not] If the olde and ignoraunte menne of *O1*.
ii had dwelt] that hadde dwelt *O1*.   iii by them] profit by them *O1*.   iv or] of *O1*.
v be] is *O1*.   vi be] is *O1*.   vii is] be *O1*.

---

1 little hares ... conies] Bullein seems to think a cony is a small hare when it is actually an adult rabbit, as noted in the glossary (Appendix 4).
2 husbandmen] farmers.
3 laudable] praiseworthy.
4 draw him] pull or tear it into pieces.

Galen in 3 *De alimentorum facultatibus* [in 3 *De alimentorum facultatibus*] in *lib.* 3 *de. alimen O1.*]	being fat, are good and much commended in meats. And Galen sayeth that the flesh of fowls be better than the flesh of beasts. But undoubtedly, goose, mallard, peacock, swan, and every fowl having a long neck be all hard of digestion and of no good complexions. But if geese be well roasted and stuffed with salt, sage, pepper, and onions they will not hurt the eaters thereof. There be great geese in Scotland, which breedeth upon a place called the Basse.[1] There be also barnacles which have a strange generation, as Gesner sayeth, and as the people of the north parts of Scotland knoweth, and because it should seem incredible to many I will give none occasion to any, either to mock or to marvel.[2] And thus I give warning to them which love their health, to have these foresaid fowls somewhat powdered or stopped with salt[3] all the night before they be roasted.
Of great fowls	
The geese of the Basse [O1 omits.]	
Conrad Gesner [*Gesnerus* O1.]	

JOHN   I pray thee tell me of the flesh of ducks.

Hippocrates in 2 can. *capitulum* 46 [*can.*] possibly 'canon', meaning Hippocrates'.]	HUMPHREY They be the hottest of all domestical or yard fowls and unclean of feeding. Notwithstanding, though it be hard of digestion and marvellous hot, yet it doth greatly nourish the body and maketh it fat. Hippocrates sayeth that they that be fed in puddles and foul places be hurtful but they that be fed in houses, pens, or coups be nutritive, but yet gross, as Isaac sayeth.
Isaac in 16. 8. *capitulum* 16	

JOHN   What be pigeons, turtles[4] or doves?

Avicenna in *Cantica* [in *Cantica*] in can. de ca. *O1.*]	HUMPHREY The flesh of turtles be marvellous good and equal to the best, as Avicenna sayeth. They be best when they be young, and wholesome for phlegmatic people. Simeon Sethi sayeth the house dove is hotter than the field dove and doth engender gross blood. The common eating of them is ill for choleric persons with red faces, for fear of leprosy. Therefore cut off the feet, wings, and head of your pigeons or doves, for their blood is that which is so venomous; they be best in the springtime and harvest. And Isaac sayeth because they are so lightly converted into choler, they did command in the old time that they should be eaten with sharp vinegar, purslane, cucumbers, or citron. Roasted pigeons be best. The blood that cometh out of the right wing, dropped into one's eye, doth mightily help the eye if it swelleth or pricketh.[5] And thus much have I spoken of pigeons or doves.
Isaac in *liber dieta capitulum* 16 [*liber dieta*] presumably Isaac's *Diaetae particulares.*]	
Roasted pigeons best	
To help the pricking of the eye [O1 omits.]	

---

1 *the Basse*] possibly the Bass Rock in the Firth of Forth, Scotland.

2 *barnacles ... marvel*] Bullein will not repeat the belief that barnacle geese grew from barnacles or shells on the barnacle tree in order to avoid mockery; he discusses this belief in his *Bulwarke of Defence* (Bullein 1579, B6r). It is also mentioned by John Gerard in his *Herbal*, where he refers to "the Goose tree, Barnacle tree, or the tree bearing Geese" (Gerard 1633, 5R6r).

3 *powdered or stopped with salt*] seasoned or stuffed with salt.

4 *turtles*] turtle-doves.

5 *pricketh*] feels pain or irritation.

JOHN   What is the flesh of peacocks?

HUMPHREY   Simeon Sethi sayeth it is a raw flesh and hard of digestion unless it be very fat, but if it be fat it helpeth the pleurisy. Haly Abbas sayeth that both swans, cranes, peacocks and any great fowls must, after they be killed, be hanged up by the necks two or three days with a stone weighing at their feet, as the weather will serve, and then dressed and eaten, provided that good wine be drunken after them. [margin: Simeon Sethi / Haly in 5 Retho. capitulum 23 [5 Retho.] It is not clear to what this refers.]

JOHN   What is the flesh of cranes?

HUMPHREY   Simeon Sethi sayeth their flesh is hot and dry; the young be good but the old increase melancholy. They do engender seed of generation[1] and being tenderly roasted do help to clear the voice and cleanse the pipe of the lungs. [margin: Simeon Sethi [O1 omits.] / To clear the voice [O1 omits.]]

JOHN   What is ⁱswan's flesh?

HUMPHREY   Every gross fowl is choleric, hard of digestion. The cygnets be better than the old swans; if their galantines[2] be well made it helpeth to digest their flesh.

JOHN   What is the flesh of herons, bitterns, and shovelers?

HUMPHREY   These fowls be fishers and be very raw and phlegmatic, like unto the meat whereof they are fed. The young be best and ought to be eaten with pepper, cinnamon, sugar, and ginger, and to drink wine after them for good digestion, and thus do for all water fowls.

JOHN   What be partridges, pheasants, quails, larks, sparrows, plover, and blackbirds?

HUMPHREY   Partridges doth bind the belly and do nourish much; the cocks be better than the hen birds, they do dry up phlegm and corruption in the stomach. Pheasants ⁱⁱbe the best of all flesh, for his sweetness is equal unto the capon or partridge but he is somewhat dryer. And Rasis sayeth pheasant's flesh is good for them that have the fever ethic,[3] for it is not only a meat but a medicine and doth cleanse corrupt ⁱⁱⁱhumours in the stomach. Quails, although they be eaten of many, yet they are not to be commended for they do engender agues and be evil for the falling [margin: Avicenna; Rasis in 3 Almansorem, capitulum 10 / Rasis in liber 4 Aphorisms / Engenders of agues [O1 omits.]]

---

i swan's flesh] swan O1.   ii be] is O1.   iii humours in] humers it O1.

---

1 *seed of generation*] sperm.
2 *galatines*] sauces to accompany flesh or fish.
3 *fever ethic*] common fever. In the poem *Willoughby His Avisa* (probably written by Henry Willoughby under the pseudonym Hadrian Dorrell) Willoughby relates how the first sight of Avisa has caused him to be "sodenly infected with the contagion of a fantasticall fit" and he complains, "I haue the feauer Ethicke right, / I burne within, consume without" (Dorrell 1594, L1v; L2v, canto 44).

sickness; for as Conciliatur[1] sayeth, of all fowls that be used for meats it is the worst. Dioscorides sayeth [i]larks roasted be wholesome to be eaten of them that be troubled with the colic. Blackbirds taken at the time of frost be wholesome and good of digestion. The dung of blackbirds, tempered with vinegar and applied to any place that hath the black morphew or black leprosy, oftentimes annointed with a sponge, doth help them. The flesh of plover doth engender melancholy. Sparrows be hot and provoke venus or lust; Pliny doth describe their properties, the brains be the best part of them. Woodcocks be of good digestion and temperate to feed upon. All small birds of the field, as robin redbreast,[2] linnets, finches, red sparrows, goldwings, and such like, if they be fat they be marvellous good and do greatly comfort nature, either roasted or boiled. And thus do I conclude with thee of birds.

Dioscorides

To help the morphew

Pliny liber 2, capitulum 36 [Pliny actually refers to the lechery of sparrows in book 10, chapter 36 of his Natural History.]

JOHN   I heartily thank thee, gentle Master Humphrey for thy painstaking in [ii]uttering these thy rules unto me concerning the proper use of beasts and fowls in meats. I would be glad to know the virtues of some fishes.

Aristotle in Problemata

HUMPHREY   In many islands of this world near adjacent unto the ocean-seas the people live there most chiefly by fish and be right strong and sound people of complexion; as Aristotle sayeth, "*Consuetudo est taquam altera natura*": "Custom is like unto another nature". But because I speak of fish I will divide them in three parts: first of the fishes of the sea, secondly the fish of fresh running rivers, thirdly of the fishes in pools and standing waters. The sea hath many gross and fat fishes, which be noisome to the stomach, but the smaller kind of fishes that feed about rocks and clear, stony places be more drier and less of moistness than the fresh-water fish and doth engender less phlegm and wind by the reason of their salt feeding; as Galen sayeth, they be the best fishes that feed in the pure sea and chiefest of all fishes for the use of mankind. But Haly Abbas sayeth new fish lately taken is cold and moist and phlegmatic, but least of all the sea-fish: fish that swimmeth in fresh, clear rivers or stony places. Whereas the water is sweet, being fishes that bear scales be marvellous good. If they feed near unto places where much filth is daily cast out, there the [iii]fishes be very corrupt and unwholesome, as the said Haly Abbas sayeth. Fish that feedeth in fens, marishes,[3] ditches, and muddy pools be very [iv]unwholesome and do corrupt the blood;

Fish divided into three parts

Of sea-fish

Galen De sanitate tuenda

Haly in quin, the. capitulum 25 [quin, the.] perhaps quincte, the 5th theory.]

Fish in rivers

Fish in fens [O1 omits.]

---

i larks] that Larkes *O1*.   ii uttering] *O1 omits*.   iii fishes] fishe *O1*.
iv unwholesome] *O1, O3;* wholesome *O2*.

---

1 *Conciliatur*] It is not clear to whom Bullein refers.
2 *robin redbreast*] The notion that it was bad luck to kill this bird presumably came later.
3 *marishes*] marshes.

they be gross and slimy, corrupt and windy. But those fishes that be fed in fair ponds ⁱwhereunto running waters may ensue, and whereas sweet herbs, roots, weeds that grow about the banks do feed the fish, those fishes be wholesome. Galen sayeth fish that is white, scaled, hard, as perches, chevins,¹ ruffs, carps, breams, roaches, trouts, *et cetera*, be all good. But unscaled fishes, as eels, tenches, lampreys,² and such like, be dangerous unless they be well baken, ⁱⁱand roasted, and eaten with pepper, ginger, and vinegar. And note this, that it is not wholesome travailing or labouring immediately after the eating of fish, for it doth greatly corrupt the stomach and (as Galen sayeth) the nourishments of flesh is better than the nourishments of fish. And thus much generally I have spoken of fish. *[margin: Best feeding for fish; Fish white, scaled [O1 omits.]; Fish unscaled [O1 omits.]; To labour soon after the eating of fish is hurtful; Galen]*

JOHN ⁱⁱⁱThus it seemeth by thy words that great fishes that be devourers in ⁱᵛthe sea, as seal, ᵛporpoise, and such like, be unwholesome and that the smaller fishes, as codlings, whitings, plaices, smelts, butts, soles, pike, perch, bream, roach, carp, and such as feed in clean, stony waters, thou sayest they be wholesome. Eels, lampreys, and other muddy fishes, thou dost not greatly commend. There be some kinds of fish soft and ᵛⁱsome be hard, which be the best? *[margin: Fat fish be gross food [Oyle fat, fishe be gross e fode O1.]]*

HUMPHREY If fish be soft the eldest fish is the ᵛⁱⁱbest, if fish be hard the youngest is best, for it is either soft or hard. Of hard fish take the smallest, of soft fish take the greatest, provided that your fish be not very slimy, and thus sayeth Avicenna in his book of fishes. *[margin: The election of fish; Avicenna, capitulum de piscibus]*

JOHN I pray thee, tell me some thing of shell-fishes.

HUMPHREY Crayfishes and crabs be very good fishes. The meat of them doth help the lungs but they be hurtful for the bladder; yet they will engender seed³ if crabs of the fresh-water be sodden in pure green oil-olive.⁴ This oil dropped into the ear lukewarm doth heal hot, burning obstructions and stopping matter that hindreth the hearing. As for limpets, cockles, scallops, as Galen sayeth, they be hard of digestion; mussels and oysters *[margin: Crayfishes and crabs; Crabs [O1 omits.]; To help hearing [O1 omits.]; Galen in libra De alimentorum facultatibus; Oysters [O1 omits.]]*

---

i whereunto] wherein two *O1*. ii and] or *O1*. iii Thus] And thus *O1*.
iv the] *O1 omits*. v porpoise] and Porpos *O1*. vi some be] *O1 omits*.
vii best] be best *O1*.

---

1 *chevins*] chubs, which are river-fish of the carp family.
2 *unscaled fishes ... lampreys*] King Henry I and King John reputedly died after eating an excess of lamprey; in Shakespeare's *King John* the fish is not mentioned and and Hubert announces, "The King, I fear, is poisoned by a monk" (Shakespeare 1988, 5.6.24).
3 *seed*] sperm.
4 *oil-olive*] olive oil.

Oil olives best [*O1* omits.]	would be¹ well boiled, roasted, or baken with onions, wine, butter, sugar, ginger, and pepper, or else they be very windy and phlegmatic. Choleric stomachs may well digest raw oysters but they have cast many one away.²
Salad oils wholesome [*O1* omits.]	JOHN What is the virtue of oil?
Averroes commendeth oil in *quinto de ovis* [quinto de ovis] apparently "the fifth book, on sheep".]	HUMPHREY Green oil of olives is the mother of all oils, which doth draw into her own nature the virtues of herbs, buds, flowers, fruits, and roots. Sweet salad oil is wholesome to digest cold herbs and salads tempered with sharp vinegar and sugar. New oil doth moist and warm the stomach, but old oil corrupteth the stomach, and cleaveth to the lungs, and maketh one hoarse. Oil of roses and sharp vinegar tempered together is good to annoint the foreheads of them that be troubled with extreme heat or frenzy so that bugloss be sodden in their posset ale or else drink the syrups of endive or bugloss. There be many goodly virtues in compounded oils, both to ⁱmake hot and also to cool the body when it is extreme hot, as the great learned man John Mesue hath described in his *Antidotarii*.³
Oil of roses [*O1* omits.]	
Against frenzy [*O1* omits.]	
Galli. 3. de uic. in. aui li..1. fen. 2 [possibly referring to Galen's *De victu attenuante* and pointing the reader towards *liber* 1, fen 2 in Avicenna's *Canon of Medicine*.]	
	JOHN Wilt thou be so good as to tell me the properties of water?
What kind of water is best	HUMPHREY Water is one of the four elements, more lighter than earth, heavier than fire and air. But this water which is here amongst us in rivers, ponds, springs, floods, and seas be no pure water for they be mingled with sundry airs, corruptions, grossness, and saltness. Notwithstanding, in all our meats and drinks water is used and amongst all living creatures cannot be forborn;⁴ both man, beast, fish, fowl, herb, and grass ⁱⁱuse it. And (as Avicenna sayeth) the clay-water is pure, for clay cleanseth the water and is better than the water that runneth over gravel or stones, so that it be pure clay, void of corruption. Also, waters running toward the east be pure, coming out of hard, stony rocks, and a pint of this water is lighter than a pint of the standing water of wells or pools. The lighter the water, the better it is. Also, waters that ⁱⁱⁱis put in wine, *et cetera*, ought first to be sodden ⁱᵛere it be occupied cold, and so the fire doth cleanse it from corruption. Standing waters and water running near unto cities and towns, or marish ground,⁵ woods, and fens be ever full of corruption because there
Avicenna *liber* 1, fen 3 *De dispositionibus aquarum*. [De dispositionibus aquarum] From dispositions of water.]	
The lighter water best [*O1* omits.]	
Corrupt waters [*O1* omits.]	

---

i make hot] calify and to *O1*.   ii use it] *O1* omits.   iii is] are *O4*.
iv ere] or *O1*.

---

1 *would be*] should be.
2 *they have cast many one away*] Either the choleric person has thrown away raw oysters (that is, not eaten them) or, more likely, raw oysters have killed ("cast away") many a choleric person.
3 *Mesue ... Antidotarii*] Mesue's *Antidotarium sive grabadin medicamentorum*.
4 *forborn*] avoided or dispensed with.
5 *marish ground*] marsh ground.

is so much filth in them of carrions and rotten dung, *et cetera*. The higher ^(i)the water doth fall, ^(ii)the better water it is. Ice and snow waters be very gross and be hurtful to the bodies of men and beasts. To drink cold water is evil, for it will stop the body and engender melancholy.¹ Salt-water helpeth a man from scabs, itch, and moist humours. It killeth lice and wasteth blood between the skin and the flesh but it is most hurtful to the stomach; but the vapour and smoke of it is good for them that have the dropsy.

<small>Ice and snow-waters [*O1* omits.]
Salt-water [*O1* omits.]</small>

JOHN What is vinegar?

HUMPHREY Vinegar is cold and dry and is hurtful for them that be melancholy. But when it is drunk or poured upon an outward wound, ^(iii)it stoppeth the blood. It also killeth hot apostumations of *Erysipelas*;² it is an enemy to the sinews. Vinegar and brimstone³ sodden together is good for the gout, to wash it withal. Vinegar tempered with oil-olive or oil of roses and sodden with unwashed wool helpeth a disease called soda in the head,⁴ applied warm unto the ^(iv)place. It is good in sauce for all warm and moist men. Vinegar with clean, clarified honey, penides,⁵ and fair water sodden together doth greatly help the pains in the throat or lungs, or stopping the wind, and quencheth hot diseases. And sharp vinegar mingled with salt and put upon the biting of a dog doth heal it; and against poison it is excellent, chiefly to drink a little thereof against the pestilence in a morning.

<small>The properties of vinegar

To help gout [*O1* omits.]

Pain in the throat [*O1* omits.]
Biting of a dog [*O1* omits.]</small>

JOHN What is the virtue of our common salt?

HUMPHREY Rasis sayeth salt is hot and dry; Dioscorides sayeth salt hath virtue to stop, to scour, and mundify, and of that mind is Oribasius, saying salt is compounded of matter abstersive and styptic, which matters be both binding and drying moist humours. And is good to powder fat flesh, both beef and pork and other fat meat, for it hath virtue to dry up superfluous humours, as water and blood, *et cetera*. But it is not good for lean bodies or hot complexioned people, for the much use of it maketh the body choleric appear aged and to be angry. The very use of it

<small>Rasis in. 3 *Almansorem, capitulum* 17

The virtue of salt

Much eating of salt hurteth [*O1* omits.]</small>

---

i the] it *O1*.   ii the better water it is] then the water is *O1*.   iii it] *O1* omits.
iv place] place it dothe helpe hoate diseases in the hed called soda *O1*.

---

1 *To drink cold water ... melancholy*] In his *Regiment Against Pleurisy* Bullein claims the disease is mainly caused by bad diet, as when "poore people, for want of clere Ale, Bere, or Wine, are forced to drinke colde water" (Bullein 1562a, B3r).

2 *apostumations of* Erysipelas] abscesses caused by the bacterial infection also known as St Antony's fire; *erysipelas* is Greek for red skin, a symptom of the disease.

3 *brimstone*] sulphur.

4 *a disease called soda in the head*] a headache.

5 *penides*] pieces or sticks of boiled sugar, similar to barley-sugar.

Averroes in 5 Simeon Sethi	is only to season meats but not to be meat. Much good salt is made here in England, as at Wich,¹ Holland in Lincolnshire, and in the Shields near unto Newcastle.

JOHN   What is honey or the virtue thereof?

HUMPHREY   Averroes sayeth honey is hot and dry in the second degree, and doth cleanse very much, and is a medicinable meat, most chiefliest for old men and women for it doth warm them and convert them into good blood. It is not good for choleric persons because of the heat and dryness. They do greatly err that say honey is hot and moist, but if it be clarified from his wax and dross and kept in a close vessel there is nothing that is liquid upon the earth than remaineth longer. And this precious jewel, honey, hath ever been more praised above sugar, for it will conserve and keep any fruit, herb, root or any other thing that is put into it over an exceeding long time. Marvellous is the work of God in honey, being a heavenly dew that falleth upon flowers and leaves (as Avicenna sayeth) and is neither the juice of leaves nor fruit but only the heavenly dew, whereunto the bees come in due time and gather the said honey and lay it up in store in their curious builded houses whereas they dwell together in most goodly order. Oh bees, bees, how happier are you than many wretched men, which dwell never together in unity and peace but in continual discord and disquietness; as Virgil sayeth, "*En quo discordia cives, perduxerit miseros*": "Behold, ⁱwhither ⁱⁱhath brought wretched citizens".² But now, to make an end of the most excellent virtues of honey: it is good in the meats of them which be phlegmatic; honey newly taken out of the combs ⁱⁱⁱis partly laxative, but clarified honey doth bind, and dry up phlegm and keepeth the bodies of phlegmatic and old persons from corruption. The best honey is gathered in the springtime, the second in summer, but that which is gathered in winter is ill and hurtful. One part of honey and some part of water sodden together until the froth be all scummed³ off, and then is cold, kept in a close stone pot, this drink (sayeth Galen) is wholesome for summer, cleanseth the lungs, and preserved the body in health. *Oxymel Simplex* and compositum⁴ be made with honey and so be many more things which be of great

Side notes:
- Honey a precious jewel [*O1* omits.]
- Honey an heavenly dew. Avicenna in 2 Cano. *capitulum* 504 [Avicenna ... 504] *O1* omits.] [*Cano.*] Probably Avicenna's *Canon of Medicine*.]
- Bees be an example unto us, both for love and working in the commonwealth. [Bees ... example] god hath ordeyned yᵉ Bees to bee an example *O1*.]
- Virgil
- New honey laxative [*O1* omits.]
- Clarified honey doth bind [*O1* omits.]
- An healthful drink for the summer [*O1* omits.]
- Galen *De sanitate tuenda Libra* 4
- Sugar [*O1* omits.]
- Haly Abbas in 5 theo. *capitulum*. 27 [5 *theo.*] Possibly a reference to theory 5.]

---

i whither] what *O1*.
ii hath brought wretched citizens] wretched citizins haue broughte forth *O1*.
iii is] be *O1*.

---

1 *Wich*] Droitwich in Worcestershire, which was formerly called "Wich"; the word was used locally to mean salt-works and occurs in the names of other salt-making towns in England such as Middlewich, Nantwich, Northwich in Cheshire.
2 *as Virgil sayeth ... citizens*] from Virgil's *Eclogues* 1:68–9.
3 *scummed*] skimmed.
4 *compostium*] compound.

virtue. Sugar, which is called *mel* cane (honey of the reed)[1] being clean, and not full of gross panele,[2] doth cleanse and is not so hot as bees' honey, and doth agree with the stomachs of choleric persons. Haly Abbas sayeth it moveth not the stomach to dryness and that the clean white sugar (not ⁱill mingled)[3] doth nourish more than honey. Of rose water, pearls, and sugar is made a goodly comforter for the heart, called *manus christi*.[4]

_{To make *manus christi* [O1 omits.]}
_{Simeon Sethi}

JOHN   What is the property of milk?

HUMPHREY   Simeon Sethi sayeth that milk is of three parts: whey, curds, and cream. Whey is wholesome to drink in summer, specially of choleric persons; it cleanseth the body. Milk of fat beasts doth nourish more than the lean beasts, and the milk of young beasts is better than of the old, and the new milk is wholesomer than that which hath stand in the air (as Rasis sayeth). And also, those beasts that feed in dry pastures amongst sweet herbs, grass, and flowers, having convenient water, their milk is very good. Milk in the beginning of summer is very wholesome; in winter it is unwholesome for phlegmatic persons or them which have corrupt and foul stomachs, for if the milk be sour it doth engender the stone in the reins or bladder. Cow's milk is the thickest milk and unctuous[5] or full of butter, but the best milk that helpeth against consumptions is woman's milk.[6] The next is goat's milk, which goat's milk rather nourisheth too much if it be taken commonly.[7] Sheep's milk is not very pleasant to the stomach; and note this, that milk is not wholesome to them which have pains in the head or teeth. But the people that be brought up with milk be fair-coloured and healthful bodies. Isaac sayeth if honey and a little salt be sodden in the milk then it is wholesome and is not windy nor phlegmatic. If mints, borage leaves, rosemary

Whey wholesome in summer [O1 omits.]

Milk [O1 omits.]

New milk [O1 omits.]

Rasis in. 3 *Almansorem, capitulum* 15

Milk not good for foul stomachs

Woman's milk [Hip. in. *li. de air. et aqua* O1.]

Goat's milk [O1 omits.]

Sheep's milk [O1 omits.]

For whom milk is not wholesome [O1 omits.]

---

i   ill mingled] adulbrated O1.

1   mel *cane (honey of the reed)*] sugar cane.

2   panele] brown, unpurified sugar from the Antilles.

3   *ill-mingled*] badly mixed or adulterated, which is apparently what is meant by "adulbrated" in O1.

4   manus christi] Latin for 'hand of Christ': refined sugar and rosewater boiled together until the sugar hardens, after which ground-up pearls or other precious stones are added; other flowers or spices might be used for this compound. Bullein provides a recipe for *manus christi* in his *Bulwark of Defence* (Bullein 1579, Ccc2r).

5   unctuous] high in fat, rich.

6   *woman's milk*] Human breast-milk was ordinarily considered healthy for consumption by adults in the period.

7   *nourisheth too much*] Bullein may be suggesting that too much of this milk will make a person fat.

How milk may be used [*O1* omits.]	flowers, honeysuckles, and a little sugar be layed in a basin and covered with a fine linen cloth, and milk the said basinful through
Galen *De alimentorum facultatibus*	the cloth, and let it stand all night,[1] this is pleasant to drink in the morning upon an empty stomach two hours before any other meat; it cleanseth the rage of hot burning [i]choler.

JOHN   What is butter?

The operation of butter and cheese	HUMPHREY Butter is hot and moist; fresh butter is used in many medicines. New made butter, meanly salted, is good with bread, flesh, and fish; it helpeth the lungs and purgeth the dryness of the throat and helpeth coughs, most chiefly if it be mingled with honey or sugar. It is good for young children when their teeth do
Buttermilk nourisheth [*O1* omits.]	grow or ache. Buttermilk, if ye crumb new white bread into it and sup it [ii]of, there is no milk nourisheth so much, goat's milk excepted. Cheese, if it be new it is indifferently well commended,
Isaac in doc. *capitulum* 15; Avicenna in *secundo capitulo* 128 [*doc.*] possibly indicating "doctrine".]	but hard, salt cheese doth dry the body and engendereth the stone, as Isaac and Avicenna say, and many other [iii]learned men more do discommend[2] it than praise it. When pots or stones be broken, if hard cheese be steeped in water, and made soft, and ground upon a painter's stone it will join the broken pots or stones together
An occasion of the stone [*O1* omits.]	again. By this, I gather the cheese will engender the stone before any other meats. Therefore cheese should be made in summer when the cream is not taken from the milk. And betony, saxifrage, and parsley chopped together be wholesome to be mingled amongst the curds. And thus I conclude with Haly Abbas that old cheese is unwholesome.

JOHN   [iv]Tell me somewhat of eggs.

HUMPHREY   Galen sayeth in his book of simples that [v]the eggs is no part of the fowls but a portion of the thing from whence it came. Simeon Sethi, writing of the diversity of eggs, sayeth the first property is in their substance and the second is in their time, either new laid or old. The third is in the manner of their roasting, poaching, or seething. New-laid eggs of hens poached and supped

New-laid eggs [*O1* omits.]	upon an empty stomach do cleanse the lungs and reins of the back. Hard eggs be greatly discommended, unless it be to stop fluxes,
Eggs a mean to stop fluxes [*O1* omits.]	but it were better to seethe eggs hard in vinegar and then undoubtedly it will dry up the flux of the belly. Fried eggs be very hurtful
Fried eggs hurteth [*O1* omits.]	for choleric people and them which have the stone. Ducks' and geese's eggs be gross and noisome but partridge, pheasants, and hens' eggs engender good blood.

JOHN   What is the property of wine?

---

i choler] chollere, and thus I leaue mylke *O1*.   ii of] off *O4*.
iii learned men] doctours *O1*.   iv Tell me somewhat of] What be *O1*.
v the] *O1* omits.

---

1 *and milk ... night*] milk should be poured through the cloth into the basin and left over night.
2 *discommend*] advise against, not recommend.

HUMPHREY Hippocrates sayeth of a customable[1] thing cometh less hurt, whereof I gather that they that drink wine customably with measure, it doth profit them much and maketh good digestion, but those people that use to drink wine seldom times be distemperated. White wine, if it be clear, is wholesome to be drunk before meat for it pierceth quickly to the bladder, but if it be drunk upon a full stomach it will rather make oppilation and stopping of the meserates[2] because it doth swiftly drive food down before nature hath of himself digested it; and the nature of white wine is of least warmness. The second wine is pure claret, of a clear hyacinth or yellow colour;[3] this wine doth greatly nourish and warm the body, and is a wholesome wine with meat, and is good for phlegmatic folk, but very unwholesome for young children, or them which have hot livers or pains in their head occasioned of hot vapours or smokes, for it is like unto fire and flax. The third is black or deep-red wine, which is thick, a stopper of the belly, a corrupter of the blood, a breeder of the stone, hurtful to old men and profitable to few men, except they have the flux. And for the election[4] of wine, sayeth Avicenna that wine is best that is between new and old,[5] clear, declining somewhat to red, of good odour, neither sharp nor sweet but equal between two, for it hath virtue not only to make humours temperate, warm, and moist, but also to expel evil matter, which corrupteth the stomach and blood. In summer it ought to be delayed[6] with pure, clear water (as Aristotle sayeth in his *Problems*). And note this, that in dry years wines be best and most wholesome but in watery years the grapes be corrupted, which wine doth bring to the body many evil diseases, as dropsies, tympanies,[7] fluxes, rheums, winds, and such like (as Galen sayeth). And thus to conclude of wine, almighty God did ordain it for the great comfort of mankind to be taken moderately. But to be drunken with excess it is a poison most venomous: it relaxeth the sinews, bringeth palsey, falling-sickness in cold persons, hot fevers, frenzies, fighting, lechery, and a consuming of the liver to the choleric. And generally there is no credence to be given to drunkards, although they be mighty men.[8] It maketh men like unto monsters, with countenances like unto

Hippocrates in 2 *Aphorisms* This comment appears in section 2, aphorism 50.]

White wine. Averroes in 6 *Colliget*; Rasis in *libra 26, con capitulum 1* [White wine] *O1 omits*.]

Claret wine warmeth the body [*O1 omits*.]

Red wine corrupteth the blood [*O1 omits*.]

Avicenna in 3 *primo* 2. *doc. capitulum* 8 [2 *doc.*] presumably '2nd doctrine']

When wines be best [*O1 omits*.]

Galen in *reg. acu.* [reg. acu.] It is not clear which work by Galen is here referred to.]

Wine moderately drunk comforteth [*O1 omits*.]

A glass for all excess wine-bibbers to look in [The heat of excesse in drinking *O1*.]

---

1 *customable*] customary, habitual.
2 *stopping of the meserates*] possibly the obstruction of the mesentery surrounding the small intestine, where the milky fluid chyle is formed during the digestion of foods and passed to the liver.
3 *claret ... yellow colour*] The term claret was originally used to describe wines that were yellow or pale red.
4 *election*] choosing.
5 *wine is ... old*] In his *Regiment Against the Pleurisy*, Bullein claims that the disease can be caused by "drinkyng moche newe Wine" (Bullein 1562a, B4r).
6 *delayed*] diluted.
7 *tympanies*] morbid swellings or tumours.
8 *although they be mighty men*] even if they are powerful men.

burning coals,¹ it dishonoureth noble men and beggareth poor men, and generally killeth as many as be slain in cruel battles, the more it is to be lamented.

JOHN   What is beer or ale?

Of ale and beer [O1 omits.]
For whom ale is wholesome [O1 omits.]
Sweet ale [O1 omits.]
Sour ale [O1 omits.]
Clean brewed beer wholesome [O1 omits.]
Rotten hops [O1 omits.]

English hops [O1 omits.]
Surfeits of ale and beer [O1 omits.]
Avicenna 2 ter tra. 2, capitulum 8; Averroes in comen; Rasis in 4 Almansorem capitulum 5. [ter tra. 2] presumably '3rd section, 2nd tract']

HUMPHREY   Ale doth engender gross humours in the body, but if it be made of good barley malt, and of wholesome water, and very well sodden, and stand five or six days until it be clear it is very wholesome, especially for hot, choleric folks having hot burning fevers. But if ale be very sweet and not well sodden in the brewing, it bringeth inflamation of wind and choler into the belly. If it be very sour it fretteth and nippeth the guts and is evil for the eyes. To them that be very phlegmatic ale is very gross, but to temperate bodies it increaseth blood; it is partly laxative and provoketh urine. Clean brewed beer, if it be not very strong, brewed with good hops, doth cleanse the body from corruption and is very wholesome for the liver. It is a usual or common drink in most places of England, which indeed is hurt and made worse with many rotten hops, or hops dried like dust, which cometh from beyond the sea.² But although there come many good hops from thence, yet it is known that the goodly stills and fruitful grounds of England do bring forth to man's use as good hops as groweth in any place of the world, as by proof I know in many places of the country³ of Suffolk ⁱwhere they brew their beer with the hops that grow upon their own grounds. And thus to conclude of ale and beer: they have no such virtue nor goodness as wine hath and the surfeits which be taken of them through drunkenness be worse than the surfeits taken of wine. Know this: that to drink ale or beer of an empty stomach moderately hurteth not but doth good, but if one be fasting, hungry, or empty and drink much wine it will hurt the sinews, bringeth cramp, sharp agues, and palsies, as Avicenna, Averroes, and Rasis say.

JOHN   ⁱⁱTell me somewhat of bread.

Of bread [O1 omits.]
The mean baken bread best [O1 omits.]

HUMPHREY   The best bread is made of clean, sweet wheat, which groweth in clay ground and maketh but little bran when it is ground, light-leavened, meanly salted, and the bread to be baken in an oven not extremely hot, ⁱⁱⁱlest it be burned, nor less than

---

i where] whereas O1.   ii Tell me somewhat of] What is O1.
iii lest it be burned] for burning of the bread O1.

---

1 *burning coals*] In Shakespeare's *Henry V* the drunkard Bardolph is said to have a nose "like a coal of fire" (Shakespeare 1988, 3.6.105).
2 *rotten hops ... from beyond the sea*] hops used to make beer were often imported from Holland.
3 *country*] county.

mean hot, ⁱlest the bread be heavy and raw. The lighter the bread is, and the more full of holes it is, the wholesomer (as Averroes and Rasis say). And also, bread must neither be eaten new baken nor very stale or old, for the one causeth dryness, thirst, and smoking into the head, troubling the brains and eyes through the heat thereof; the other dryeth the body and bringeth melancholy humours, hurting memory. The best bread is that which is of a day old and the loaves or manchets¹ may neither be great nor little but mean. For the fire in small loaves dryeth up the moistness or virtue of the bread and in great loaves it leaveth rawness and grossness. Read Galen in the properties of bread. Sodden bread, which be called simnels or cracknels, be very unwholesome and hurteth many one;² rye bread is windy and hurtful to many, therefore it should be well salted and baken with aniseeds. And commonly crusts of bread be very dry and burneth; they do engender melancholy humours, therefore in great men's houses the bread is chipped and largely pared³ and ordinarily is made in brews and soss⁴ for dogs, which ⁱⁱwould help to feed a great number of poor people but that many be more affectionate to dogs than to men. Barley bread doth cleanse, cool, and make the body lean.

Averroes in quint *Colliget;* Rasis in 30 *Almansorem capitulum* 3.

Bread of a day old [*O1 omits.*]

Galen 2 *De alimentorum facultatibus, capitulum* 2. Sodden bread not wholesome [Sodden ... wholesome] *O1 omits.*]

Barley bread [*O1 omits.*]

JOHN   What is the virtue of rice?

HUMPHREY   There be many opinions ⁱⁱⁱconcerning rice but I shall stay myself with the judgement of Avicenna: rice, sayeth he, is hot and dry and hath virtue to stop⁵ the belly. It doth nourish much if it be sodden with milk, but it ought to be steeped in water a whole night before. If blanched almonds be stamped, and with rosewater strained into them, and sodden with cow's milk, it is very ⁱᵛnourishing.

Of rice

Avicenna in 2 *Cantica, capitulum* 500.78 [78] *O1*; lxxviii *O2.*]

JOHN   ᵛShow me the virtue of almonds.

HUMPHREY   The bitter almonds be hotter than the sweet almonds; dry almonds be hurtful. The milk of moist almonds wherein burning steel is quenched stoppeth the flux.⁶ To eat almonds before meat preserveth against drunkenness. Walnuts be

The diversity of almonds [*O1 omits.*]

Almonds before meat

Of walnuts

---

i lest the bread be] for causing the bread to be *O1.*
ii would] wyl *O1.*   iii concerning rice] in the vertue therof *O1.*
iv nourishing] nutramentall *O1.*   v Show me the virtue of] What be *O1.*

---

1 *manchets*] loaves of the finest wheaten bread.
2 *simnels or cracknels*] simnels would be boiled and sometimes then subsequently baked; cracknels were a twice-baked biscuit-like bread and similar in consistency to simnels.
3 *chipped and ... pared*] cut up into small pieces and the crusts cut off.
4 *soss*] a messy mixture.
5 *stop*] bind.
6 *burning steel ... flux*] hot steel or iron filings quenched in water were thought to render the liquid medicinal; it seems almond milk was also treated in this manner (*OED* steel, $n.^1$. 6. a.).

Pliny in *Liber* 22, *capitulum* 8 [Pliny's *Natural History* has no Book 22]	wholesome when they be new (to be eaten after fish) for they hinder engendering of phlegm. Simeon Sethi sayeth they are hot in the first and dry in the second degree; not wholesome before meat. Pliny, speaking of Mithridates (the great king of ⁱPontus),[1] found of his own handwriting that two nuts, and two figs, and twenty rue leaves stamped together with a little salt and eaten fasting doth defend a man both from poison and pestilence that day. Filberts and hazelnuts be hard of digestion, ill before meat, hurtful to the head and lungs; if they be roasted and eaten with a little pepper they will help the running and distillation of rheums. Chesnuts, if they be roasted and eaten with a little honey fasting, they help the cough; if they be eaten raw, although they greatly nourish the body yet they be hurtful for the spleen and filleth the belly full of wind. Nutmegs be very good for cold persons, comforteth the sight and memory (as Avicenna sayeth) but, without doubt, nutmegs doth combust or burn sanguine men and dry their blood. And thus much have I spoken shortly of ⁱⁱnutmegs.
Of filberts	
Of chestnuts	
Of nutmegs	
Avicenna *capitulum de nuce*	

Rasis in *liber* 4 acho. [*acho* perhaps an error for 'apho', that is 'aphorism', a reference to Rasis' work *The Guide*, also known as *The Book of Aphorisms*.]

Isaac in parti dic[.]bus [*parti dic[.]bus* possibly a reference to Isaac Israeli's *Diaetae particulares*. The indistinct character may be a line-ending hyphen and the preceding "c" may be an 'e', giving "diebus" (Latin for 'days').]

A practice

JOHN   What be cloves, galangal, and pepper?

HUMPHREY   They be hot and dry and (as Rasis sayeth) doth comfort cold stomachs, and make sweet breath, and is good in the meats of them that hath ill digestion. Black pepper is hotter than long pepper and doth mightily warm the body; the grosser[2] it is eaten, with fish or fruit, the better it provoketh urine. It is hot and dry in the fourth degree, therefore they do err that say pepper is hot in the mouth and cold in the stomach. Although pepper be good to them that use it well yet unto artificial women – that have more beastliness than beauty and cannot be content with their natural complexions but would fain be fair – they eat pepper, dried corn, and drink vinegar, with such like baggage, to dry up their blood and this is the very cause that a great number, though not all, fall into a weakness, green sickness, stinking breaths, and oftentimes sudden death.

JOHN   What is sweet *calamus odoratus*?[3]

---

i Pontus] Pompius *O1*.   ii nutmegs] Nuttes *O1*.

1 *Mithridates ... Pontus*] Mithridates VI, King of Pontus after whom *mithridatum* is named; he is also referred to by Bullein in his section on almonds (pp. 293–4).

2 *grosser*] coarser.

3 calamus odoratus] sweet calamus; referred to as as a "principal spice" in the Bible (Exodus 30.23).

HUMPHREY   An excellent sweet root and profitable for men, if the apothecaries keep it not until it be rotten. It is hot and dry in the beginning to the mids of the second degree; it hath power to cleanse, to dry, to waste all winds within the body without hurt. Galen doth greatly commend the savour of it. They that drink of this root sodden in wine shall have remedy of the white morphew and recover good colours; and this have I proved, it helpeth cramps and sickness in the sinews being drunk in wine. Sodden with sage it helpeth the spleen and liver and reins and will cleanse the secret terms of women and augment natural seed.[1] *Calamus odoratus* [*O1 omits.*]

A remedy for the white morphew [*O1 omits.*]

JOHN   What is ginger?

HUMPHREY   It is hot in the third degree and moist in the end of the first. If it be uncoloured, white, and not rotten it is very good, most chiefly if it be conserved. And green[2] (as Mesue sayeth) it maketh warm a cold stomach and consumeth winds, helpeth evil digestion, and maketh meat go easily down into the stomach. Averroes in 5 *Colliget*

Mesue in 4. distin. [4. *distin.*] It is not clear what is meant here.]

JOHN   What is setwall?

HUMPHREY   Hot and dry in the second degree, and is good; the powder thereof to be drunk is most of effect against the pestilence except *mithridatum*.[3] It is good against poison, wind, choleric and cold passions of the heart, and doth restrain vomits; the weight of eight grams doth suffice to be drunk in ale or wine upon an empty stomach. The operation of setwall [*O1 omits.*]

JOHN   What is cinnamon?

HUMPHREY   Dioscorides doth say there be many kinds of cinnamon but generally their virtue is this: to help dropsies, winds, or stopping of the liver.[4] And is hot and dry in the third degree. Diverse kinds of cinnamon [*O1 omits.*]

JOHN   What is *cassia fistula*, senna, and rhubarb?

HUMPHREY   *Cassia fistula*, if the cane be heavy and the cassia within black and shining, that is good cassia. If this be drawn out of the cane half an ounce or more at one time, and mingled with sugar, and eaten of a fasting stomach in the morning, it hath power to purge choler, to cleanse the reins of the back. It will fret and consume the stone, it purgeth very easily, and is pleasant in taking, and may be taken of children, weak women, and sick men in the To know good *cassia fistula* [*O1 omits.*]

To purge choler [*O1 omits.*]

---

1 *augment natural seed*] increase sperm.
2 *green*] the fresh root of ginger, often in preserve.
3 *is most of effect ... except* mithridatum] is the most effective remedy against the pestilence apart from mithridate.
4 *stopping of the liver*] an obstruction in the liver, which it was believed would prevent blood flowing properly from the liver through the body.

Of rhubarb and his operation	time of their fevers, the access of their fits excepted.[1] Rhubarb doth purge yellow choler by himself; two or three drams may be taken, or a little more, so that there be a dram of spikenard or

cinnamon put into it. In summer to drink it with whey, in winter with white wine; but the clean yellow rhubarb – sliced and put into infusion all the night with whey,

Purging of blood and liver [O1 omits.]	white wine, or endive-water, and strain it in the morning – doth greatly purge the blood and liver. Three or four drams with spikenard, a dram or more senna Alexandria,[2] if it be sodden in the broth of a cock or a hen doth purge the blood and melancholy

very gently and comfort the heart. One ounce of the clean small leaves of senna without cods[3] or stalks, half a quarter of one ounce of ginger, twelve cloves, fennel

To purge the head [O1 omits.]	seed two drams or else two drams of cinnamon, tartar[4] half a dram, beaten all together in powder, these do purge the head nightly to be taken before supper the weight of one dram in a little white wine.

JOHN   I would be glad to learn the virtue of aloes.

Two kinds of aloes [O1 omits.]	HUMPHREY There be two kinds of aloes, one is named *succotrina*, which is like a liver: clear, brittle, bitter, coloured between
To help watery eyes [O1 omits.]	red and yellow. This is best for medicines; a little of this ⁱtempered with rose water, being put ⁱⁱinto the eyes helpeth the dropping of
Against the pestilence [O1 omits.]	watery eyes. Also, it is put in many excellent medicines laxative, as saffron, myrrh, aloes mingled together in the form of pills is the most excellent medicine against the pestilence, as it is written
Marks of stripes [O1 omits.]	in this book following.[5] Honey and aloes mingled together do take away the marks of stripes[6] and also doth mundify sores and ulcers; it doth cleanse the abundance of choler and phlegm from the
Avicenna in li. de. sim. [*li. de. sim.*] This possibly means "book of simples".]	stomach. It is not good to be taken in winter (for Avicenna doth forbid it) but in the springtime or harvest the powder thereof, the weight of a French crown, mingled with the water of honey or mead, and so drunk in the morning, it doth cleanse both choler and phlegm. There is another gross aloes which is good for horse; tempered with ale and ministered, as well to other great beasts as horses, the weight of half an ounce. And thus much have I said of
A cause of the haemorrhoids	aloes. But if aloes be clean washed it is the wholesomer; many unwashed aloes will cause haemorrhoids.

---

i tempered] beinge tempered O1.   ii into] vnto O1.

---

1 *the access of their fits excepted*] unless they are about to have a fit.
2 *senna Alexandria*] Alexandrian senna.
3 *cods*] husks or outer coverings.
4 *tartar*] bitartrate of potash; present in grape juice, it forms a hard crust that sticks to the side of wine-casks.
5 *this book following*] the "Regiment for the Pestilence" at the end of *The Government of Health*.
6 *the marks of stripes*] the marks caused by beatings.

JOHN Is the saffron that grow in England as good as that that come from the other side of the sea?

HUMPHREY Our English honey and saffron is better than any that cometh from any other strange or foreign land.[1] But to thy question of saffron, it hath virtue, either in bread or pottage, to make the heart glad; it warmeth the body, it preserveth from drunkenness, drunk in ale or wine provoketh acts venerous, induceth sleep, purgeth urine. Myrrh, aloes, and saffron make an excellent pill against the pestilence: two pennyweight of saffron powder roasted with the yolk of an egg very hard and the said yolk beaten in powder, twelve grains [i]drunk a-mornings is good against the pestilence. Saffron, plantain, and ivory sodden, the decoction drink helpeth the yellow jaundice. It is dry in the first degree and hath virtue to restrain.

English saffron best

Glad heart

Pillule Ruffe

Against the pestilence

JOHN We plain men in the country dwell far from great cities; our wives and children be often sick and at death's door. We cannot tell what shift to make; we have no acquaintance with the apothecaries. Commonly we send for a quantity of malmsey;[2] whatsoever our diseases be, these be our common medicines or else we send for a box of treacle and when these medicines fail us we cause a great posset[3] to be made and drink up the drink. Thinkest thou these medicines [ii]be not good?

HUMPHREY For lack of medicine God helpeth the people oftentimes by miracle or else a great number of men should perish. But because the almighty God hath covered the whole face of the earth with many precious simples (whereof rich [iii]compositions be made) therefore be neither so rude nor barbarous to think these medicines good that thou hast rehearsed for all diseases, although not hurtful to some. But because many do receive more mischief than medicine in counterfeit treacles I shall rehearse unto thee what Valerius Cordus and [iv]others do write upon the virtue of the precious treacle called *mithridatum*.

God helpeth diverse way

JOHN I would be glad to hear of that precious treacle and his virtues.

HUMPHREY This excellent treacle *mithridatum* is next in quality and virtue of *theriaca* and do differ but little, but only *theriaca* is a little hotter and stronger against venom of snakes,

Mithridatum; theriacha
[O1 omits.]

---

i drunk] drinke *O1*.   ii be not] to be *O4*.   iii compositions] cōpossions *O1*.
iv others] *O3, O4*; other *O1, O2*.

---

1 *Our English honey and saffron*] Saffron was once widely grown in England; the town of Saffron Walden was well known for saffron production and was in fact named after the plant (it was formerly called Chipping Walden). On the growing of saffron in England see Holinshed 1587, 1: 231–4; O'Hara-May 1977, 272–4).

2 *malmsey*] a strong sweet white wine and a variety of Madeira.

3 *posset*] a drink made from hot milk and alcohol (usually wine or ale), with sugar, spices or other ingredients sometimes added; it was often given to the sick and infirm.

	adders, and serpents.¹ It helpeth all pains of the head of men or
Help for the megrim [*O1 omits.*]	women if it come of cold, most chiefly of melancholy and fear. It helpeth megrim, falling-sickness, and all pains of the forehead,
Toothache [*O1 omits.*]	dropping of eyes. It helpeth toothache, pains of the mouth, cheeks if it be put in manner of a plaster or else anoint the pained place.
Pain in the throat [*O1 omits.*]	It helpeth pains of the throat called squinance and also ⁱcoughs, apoplexia, and passion of the lungs and many grievous dolours and pains within the body. Drunk with the decoction of the flowers
Stopping of the flux [*O1 omits.*]	of pomegranates or plantain it helpeth and stoppeth fluxes in the ⁱⁱileum² and long guts, winds or colic. The extension³ or cramps
Help for the cramp [*O1 omits.*]	be helped very much with this *mithridatum* drunken with stilled waters. Palsies, sickness in the midriff, the liver, reins, and bladder
Pestilence and poison [*O1 omits.*]	be cleansed thereby. It provoketh the menstrual terms in women being drunk with posset ale; if hyssop or germander be sodden in the said ale, it is excellent against the pestilence or poison. If it be
Against the stone [*O1 omits.*]	drunk but a little quantity thereof, according to the disease, strength, or age of the person, it is very good against the stone or
Green sickness [*O1 omits.*]	for women, which have a new disease *per accidens* called the green sickness. There is nothing better against the biting of a mad dog than to drink of this and to anoint the wound. If it be given in drink to any sick body a little before the access or coming of the
Of the excellent treacle called *mithridatum*	cold fits of quotidians, tercians, or quartens, so that it be drunk with wine temperately warmed, this *mithridatum* is a medicine of no small price. Democrates hath a goodly composition of it; another excellent composition is of Cleopatra, as Galen writeth. Another, and the most excellent, is the description of Andromachus, physician unto King Nero, but the chief father of this art was King Mithridatus, the noble king of Pontus, after whose name it is called.

JOHN Indeed this is an excellent medicine but, I pray thee, where shall I buy it?

HUMPHREY The blind (fellow John) do eat many a fly and the plain meaning man is oft deceived. There is no trust in some of the apothecaries, for although the ursurpation of *quid pro quo* is tolerable for their succedanes,⁴ yet to abuse their simples or compounds it is not only theft to rob simple men but also murder to kill the hurtless.

JOHN Of late time we have been so afflicted with sundry sicknesses and strange diseases in many places we could get no physicians to help us; and when men be

---

i coughs] coughe *O1*.   ii ileum] *this ed.;* ilias *O2*.

1 theriaca ... *serpents*] an antidote to poison, especially from snake-bites and considered most effective if it contained the flesh of the snake (*OED* theriac, *n* (*a*.)).
2 *ileum*] the third portion of the small intestine.
3 *extension*] distention or swelling.
4 *succedanes*] from the Latin *succedaneum* meaning "substitute".

suddenly sick two hundred miles from London, Cambridge, or Oxford it is too late for the patient to send for help, being infected with the pestilence. I pray thee, tell me some good regiment for me and my family if it please God that it may take place.

HUMPHREY   I shall be glad – for as much as thou hast taken pains to hear me all this while – to teach thee a pretty regiment for the pestilence.

JOHN   Read it fair and softly and I will take my pen and write it.

HUMPHREY   Certainly the occasion of this most fearful sickness cometh many ways, as the change of the air from a good unto an evil quality taking his venomous effect of the vital spirits, which incontinent, with all speed, corrupteth the spiritual blood and suddenly, (as it were) an unmerciful fire, it quickly consumeth the whole body, even to death, unless the wholesome medicine do prevent and come to the heart before the pestilent humour. And because it is a very strong sickness, it is requisite to have a strong, curing medicine for weak things will not prevail against so strong a matter. Therefore, I pray you, note these six sayings: as air, diet, sleep or watch, quietness or trouble, and finally, medicine.[1] First, walk not in stinking mists, nor by corrupt marish[2] ground, nor in extreme hot weather, but in fair, clear air upon high ground in sweet fields or gardens, having fire in your chamber with sweet perfumes of the smoke of olibanum, or benjamin,[3] frankensense being cold weather. And in hot weather roses, willow branches sprinkled with vinegar, and often shifting the chamber is wholesome, fleeing the south wind. Secondly, diet moderate, eating meat of good digestion, as all that have pure, white, flesh, both of beasts and fowls, good bread of wheat, partly leavened. Eat no raw herbs, purslane, lettuce, young lettuce, or sorrel, except with vinegar. Drink of clear, thin wine, not changed, and used oft times vinegar with your meats, and mingle not fish and flesh together in your stomach; and to drink a tisane of barleywater, rose water and sorrel water between meals is good, eight spoonfuls at once. Thirdly, beware you sleep not at noon, it bringeth many sicknesses and giveth place to the pestilence and abateth memory;[4] for as the marigold is spread by the day and closed by the night even so is man of nature disposed, although through custom otherwise altered, unto great

Diffinicio epidinue Gall. [Possibly a reference to Galen's treatise on illness *De morborum differentiis*.]

Six things to be observed in the time of pestilence [Good aire O*1*.]

Beware of raw herbs [yōg lettis O*1*.]

Noon sleep

---

1 *I pray you note ... medicine*] Bullein has apparently miscounted since these are either five or seven sayings but not six.

2 *marish*] marsh.

3 *benjamin*] ben-oil: an edible oil, produced from seeds of the horseradish tree (*Moringa pterygosperma*).

4 *sleep not at noon ... memory*] Elyot also warns against sleeping at noon. In Shakespeare's *King Lear* the Fool's last words (perhaps ominously) are "And I'll go to bed at noon" (Shakespeare 1988, 3.6.43).

Eight hours sleep [O1 omits.]	damage and hurt of body. Eight hours' sleep sufficeth well to nature, but every complexion hath his proper qualities. To sleep upon the right side is best, evil upon the left, and worse upon the
Exercise	back. Fourthly, use moderate exercise and labour for the evacuation of the excrements, as swift going up hills, stretching forth
De sanitate tuenda, Galen	arms and legs, lifting weights not very ponderous; for by labour the first and second digestion is made perfect, and the body strengthened, and this is a mighty defence against the pestilence and many more infirmities whereas through idleness be engendered all diseases both of the soul and body whereof man is compounded and
Mirth	made. Fifthly, above all earthly things mirth is most excellent, and the best companion of life, putter away of all diseases; the contrary

in plague time bringeth on the pestilence through painful melancholy, which maketh the body heavy and earthly. Company, music, honest gaming, or any other virtuous exercise doth help against heaviness of mind. Sixthly, medicine, the party being changed in nature and condition, trembling or burning, vomiting with extreme pain

	in the day, cold in the night, and strange imaginations, *et cetera*,
Signs of the pestilence [*De signis pestilencialis* O1.]	apt to sleep, when these signs do appear, give him medicine before twelve hours or else it will be his death. Take therefore with all
Note this medicine for the pestilence [O1 omits.]	speed sorrel, one handful stamped with rue, *enula campana*,[1] orange rinds, citron seeds, the great thistle roots, juniper berries, walnuts clean-piked,[2] of each one ounce, stamp them all together. Then take pure, sharp vinegar, a quarter of a pint; as much bugloss water; as much white wine, and temper[3] your said receipts[4] with
Mithridatum Andromachi	these liquors. Then put in two ounces of pure *Mithridatum Andromachi*,[5] which is an excellent treacle, and two drams weight of the powder of pure bole armen; mingle them all together in a very close vessel and give the patient a spoonful or more next his
Beware of sleep [O1 omits.]	heart (and eftsoons as much more) and let them that take this sleep not during the next twenty hours. Or else take pure treacle and setwall mingled in posset ale made with white wine wherein sorrel ¡hath boiled a good draught, and let an expert surgeon let the
Mediana Basilica	patient blood upon the middle vein called *mediana* or the heart vein, basilica, a good quanity according to the strength and age

of the patient, except women with child and children, for the retaining the said blood would all turn to venom and incurable poison. And note this, that blood be let upon the same side that the sore doth appear, if any appear, for many causes, and sleep

---

i hath] haue O1.

1 enula campana] horse-heal (*Inula Helenium*); used as a stimulant.
2 *clean-picked*] cleaned and made bare by use of a pick or toothpick (*OED* picked, *ppl. a.* 1.).
3 *temper*] bring to a suitable quality by mixing with something else.
4 *receipts*] recipes.
5 Mithridatum Andromachi] the mithridate or treacle devised bythe Greek physician Andromachus the Elder.

not eight hours after. And use this most excellent pill oftentimes: *Pillule Pestilencialis Ruffi* [pills for the pestilence formulated by Rufus of Ephesus.] take pure aloes hepatic,¹ and myrrh, well washed in clean water or rosewater, of each two drams, and one dram of the power of saffron mingled with ⁱa little of sweet wine and tempered in a very small vessel upon the coals until it be partly thick, or else incorporate all together in a mortar, then roll them up in small, round pills. Use to swallow half a dram of these pills two times a week in the pestilence time a-mornings three hours before meat. Another medicine: tormentil, gentian, setwall, of each one dram; spikenard, drams two; nastic,² drams three; bole armen drams eight; give two drams to the patient (or any that fear the plague) in the water of skabeas³ or *cardus benedictus*,⁴ then drink the broth of a chicken or pure wine. To ripe the sore, roast a great onion, take out the core, put in treacle and ⁱⁱapply it warm to the place three or four times renewed warm. And oil-olive, black soap, sour-leaven,⁵ lily-roots, of each like quantity boiled together, put in the juice of rue and make a plaster, this will break the said sore. Capon's grease, yolks of eggs, swine's grease, barley-flour, linseed powder, incorporated together will make a good healing plaster. *Emplastrum diachylon magnum descriptione filii Zacharia*⁶ doth resolve⁷ and quench the hot ulcer. But in the time of the plague trust not urines. ⁱⁱⁱFINIS

*Again to the gentle reader*⁸

ⁱᵛThou shalt understand (gentle reader) while I was perusing over of this my simple labour, and mending certain faults that were escaped in the print, I heard of some (belike not content with this my poor good will) that found much fault with it and others for that it was handled so grossly and the style so rude, which indeed I confess. But this I am sure of, if these will confer it with those authors which I have alleged⁹

---

   i a] *O1 omits.*   ii apply it warm] warme apply it *O1.*
   iii FINIS] *O1 omits.*   iv Thou shalt understand ... amen] *O1 omits.*

---

1 *hepatic*] liver-coloured.

2 *nastic*] nastic movement is the natural movment of a plant, such as the closing of its flowers or leaves (from the Greek *nastos* meaning "pressed-close"); perhaps Bullein is recommending three drams of spikenard if the plant be closed up.

3 *water of skabeas*] possibly water of scabious, i.e. water derived from herbaceous plants of the genus Scabiosa, which were thought to help cure certain skin diseases.

4 cardus benedictus] blessed thistle or holy thistle.

5 *sour-leaven*] presumably sourdough, which was used as a fermenting agent when baking bread.

6 Emplastrum ... filii Zacharia] diachylum-plaster is an ointment made from various ingredients, put on a piece of cloth and then on to the skin (*OED* diachylon), apparently according to instructions by the son of Zacharia. Bullein provides instructions in his *Bulwark of Defence* for making this particular plaster, which includes, amongst other ingredients, figs, flower-oil, and fat from the belly of a seal (Bullein 1579, Bbb3v).

7 *resolve*] dissolve, disintegrate.

8 *Again to the Gentle Reader*] In O1 the second address to the reader is entirely different from O2 and, since it discusses errors that the author subsequently corrected in O2, it is reprinted as Appendix 3.

9 *confer. . . alleged*] compare with those authorities I have cited.

I doubt not but they shall find it true. And as for the first, I marvel why they should be grieved with this my labour, considering I speak nothing but the health of those whom I see piteously tormented with many kinds of diseases, which good government in time of youth would help all together. This I speak not that I think they are without this care which I allege, but I being as one unable – yet my good will shall not want, whereas occasion and time will serve – to help to the uttermost of my power, and as one espying a poor man overburdened, doth his endeavour to help him up, though his strength be not able yet his good will is to be accepted, though another stronger than he come after and ease him. Even so, I have done mine endeavour and good will in this, trusting that the good learned physicians will help their poor brethren – when their piteous diseases do not only cry unto their consciences but is also present before their eyes – in a much better form than I am able to do. I mean not of such as doth make of their diseases an occupation, using craft and subtlety to beg withal, and had rather to be in that case than to have present remedy whereby they might become profitable members in a commonwealth. But I pray thee (gentle reader) consider to whom I wrote this my Government: to the simple, such as lack wherewithal and be furthest from the physicians, and therefore did temper[1] my style according for their better understanding. I am not ignorant that many in these days in their writing do excellently beautify our English tongue with solely apt words derived from the Latin, and surely they are to be praised, but to hear how the simple place those words in their talk it would make wise men to laugh. And thus, I beseech thee to bear with my rudeness, committing this book once again into thy hands, trusting that I have meant good will unto thee in the setting forth thereof so thou wilt thankfully embrace it and order thyself unto the rules thereof, which is all that I desire. And in the mean season, as I have begun so, through God's help, I intend to make an end of another book of healthful medicines, which like-wise I trust thou wilt take in good worth and in that part that I make it for.[2] And thus I commit thee unto the eternal Father that is able, when all physic faileth, to help thee by his wonderful miracle. To whom, with the Son, and the Holy Ghost, be praise for ever and ever, amen.

Farewell, the 20 of April 1558.
William Bullein[3]
Imprinted at London by John Day dwelling over Aldergate.

---

1 *temper*] modify.
2 *I intend to make an end of another book*] This is his *Bulwark of Defence*, first published in 1562.
3 *Bullein*] At this point in the copy text there is a picture featuring two hands in chains holding a tray on which sits a burning heart.

APPENDIX 1: PROEMS TO THE FIRST AND SECOND EDITIONS OF THOMAS ELYOT'S *CASTLE OF HEALTH*

THE FIRST EDITION (PUBLISHED SOME TIME BETWEEN 1536 AND 1539)

Thomas Elyot, Knight to the right honourable Thomas, Lord Cromwell, Lord Privy Seal.

He, in giving, receiveth a benefit which giveth to him that is worthy to have it. And it may be called a good turn where good and prompt will in neither part lacketh. And benefit in such wise employed may never be barren, but incontinent bringeth forth another good turn, at the least way in will, which continually travaileth until in act it be fully performed. Here perchance your good Lordship is in a great expectation what shall ensue in this proem, the like whereunto I have not before this time used. Pleaseth it you my singular good lord about two months past, according to my custom as duty of old amity bound me, I came to your Lordship's house there to salute you, where it was showed to me by your porters that ye were at that time dyscrased,[1] with the which words, although at the first I felt my heart grieved, as true friendship required, yet reason brought at the last unto my remembrance that whoso is charged with study continual and travail of mind, specially about matters of weighty importance, needs must his body be sometime subject to sickness, either by crudity or lack of digestion or else by unequal temperature in humours, which may be properly called a dyscrasy (which word is taken out of the Greek) for as much as the spirit being occupied in contemplation, the powers natural[2] do cease for that time to do their office and duty, or at the least way doth it not perfectly. With this rememberance, my singular good Lord, I considered what commodity, strength, and consolation it is to a realm to have honourable, wise, and circumspect counsellors attending on the person of the chief governor. Contrariwise, in the lack of them, what incommodity, debility, and desolation happeneth to the realm where the Prince lacketh such counsellors whom Aristotle called his eyes, his ears, his hands, and his feet.[3] For admit[4] that he doth excell all other in wisdom, yet being a man, and but

[*Beneficium dandi accepit, quid digno dedit Publius Minos* [*dandi* should be *dando* and *Publius Minos* should be *Publilius Mimus*. The Latin repeats the point made by Elyot in the first sentence. Publilius Mimus, a contemporary of Cicero, was a performing mime and minor poet whose *Sententiae* were edited by Erasmus.]

---

1 *dyscrased*] affected with a dyscrasy, a bodily disorder resulting from an imbalance among humours or qualities.
2 *the powers natural*] the seven things natural: elements, complexion, humours, members, powers, operations and spirits.
3 *Aristotle ... feet*] See his *Politics* book 3, part 16.
4 *admit*] the word in the first edition is unclear at this point but is apparently "admyt", a Middle English spelling of "admit".

one, like as he cannot hear or see all things, no more can he have at one time in his own remembrance all things necessary which many do think on. In this sort of treasure whereof our most gracious sovereign lord, reigning above all other princes in sapience and most royal courage is nobly adorned, your Lordship may well be esteemed a principal jewel for the incomparable quickness of your Lordship's invention, invincible eloquence, infatigable diligence, gravity in judgement, incredible dexterity, and many other virtues and qualities excellent, which as well because they be more commonly known and of all men found and perceived in you, as also for as much as I would avoid suspicion of flattery, I do now of a purpose pass over. Hereunto I added the particular profit which I might receive by so singular a good lord, by so noble a friend, of whose most happy acquaintance I have oft times rejoiced and given thanks to God when it hath been sundry times told me with what commendable report your Lordship hath advanced most gently my poor estimation, as well to the king's highness as in other honourable and worshipful presence. Also, when I myself have heard you favourably incline to mine humble requests, most gently offering unto me your comfortable assistance in mine honest pursuits, these things justly constrained me to lament your disease. And finally, to the intent that my sincere affection toward your Lordship might in some part appear, in wishing the long preservation of your Lordship in prosperous life, I gathered out of the most ancient and noble authors of physic necessary counsels and doctrines expedient for him to know whose health should be profitable to all them that love virtue, and to dedicate and give it unto your good Lordship, as unto the person which for the causes above mentioned is worthy to have it, taking the receiving thereof by your Lordship for a singular benefice. This little work is named *The Castle of Health*, forasmuch as who so doth diligently read it, and discreetly doth practise the counsels therein contained, he shall perfectly know the state of his body, being in the lattitude of health or declination to sickness, engendered by distemperance of the four natural humours. And knowing so much, if the distemperance be not very great, he shall also find there the means to reduce eftsoons the body to his first temperance. Also, thereby he shall learn how his body, being attached with sickness, he may perfectly instruct his physician so that by conjecture of excrements he be not deceived. Which, by wise physicians considered, they will not disdain that I write in this matter, their estimation (where few men do perish) being thereby increased. And he that thinketh it a great rebuke to a knight to study or write ought in physic, let him now learn that Hadrian and Constantine were Emperors; Apollo, Aesculapius, Euphorbus, Attalus, and Almansor were Kings; Chiron, Hercules, Machaon, Podalirius, Archigenes, and Dioscorides were noble captains and knights; Avicenna and Avenzoar were Princes; Cornelius, Celsus, Nigidius and Quintus Serenus were noble senators.[5] These, with many other equal to them, not only studied physic but also did practise it. And what thing is more honourable than to save thy friend's life when thou seest him in danger? Is it any less the office of a knight to preserve or defend the life of his friend than to slay his enemies in battle? In the heart of a Christian knight is the desire of vengeance

---

5 *Hadrian . . . senators*] Several of the authorities here listed are cited or alluded to in the dietaries by Elyot, Boorde, and Bullein.

and death more to be esteemed (which needs must happen in battle) than good will to save him that is likely to perish, which is the cause final of the study of physic? No, I suppose no man well advised will affirm it. Therefore let not men be offended with my labour, which I have taken for their universal commodity, but let them give thanks unto God and to your good Lordship, whom I confess to be the principal and first occasion that moved me to take in hand this honest enterprise, of the which I firmly trust never to have cause to forethink or repent me, having always your good Lordship, such one as I judge worthy to receive of my gift, such a castle, which being of your Lordship thankfully taken, I shall rejoice not a little at mine own liberality.

THE SECOND EDITION (PUBLISHED 1539)

To the right honourable Thomas Lord Cromwell, Lord Privy Seal, Thomas Elyot, Knight, wisheth long life in honour.

He giveth twice that giveth quickly (sayeth Seneca).[6] The grief which I had for your Lordship's disease, with the desire that ye might live long without sickness, caused such speed in building *The Castle of Health* that therein lacked some part of perfection. But yet the promptness in giving that thing, which I thought necessary to declare mine affection, I doubt not was no less esteemed of your good Lordship than afore is rehearsed. Notwithstanding, when I had eftsoons perused that little fortress and found here and there some things that lacked, I took my pen in the stead of a trowel and amended the faults and added somewhat more where I thought it convenient. And yet perchance some things might happen to escape, which were as needful to be corrected, mine attendance on the parliament (I being a member of the lower house) withdrawing from me leisure convenience to find in this work all the faults which might be amended. May it now like your good Lordship to take in good part not eftsoons the castle, which I already have given you, but my good will and diligence in amending or repairing the same, which is also printed in a much better letter, considering that I no less do behold you continually with mine eye of remembrance than they which at dinner and supper do daily look on you, the cause I will not repeat for suspicion of flattery. Friendship (as men say) should be requited, but yet crave I none other thing but only equal benevolence and faith without any suspicion, whereunto actual demonstration is so much requisite that without it they both seem to be drowned since among us that be mortal, things are most judged by outward tokens. And yet also in them men be sometime deceived, hypocrisy having in this world so great a pre-eminence, but in amity is one rule, which seldom faileth: he that liveth moderately doth love always faithfully, for over him affections and passions have left authority and he that standeth just in the middle standeth most surely. Also, in the world there is no more folly than to choose friends of them which do follow fortune like as swine do follow the maiden which beareth on her head a pail full of milk and if the pail fall, or happen to be empty, they will follow no longer. The moderate person, where both authority and virtue be in his friend equal because that virtue was the only cause of his love, that remaining, his mind is in such wise thereunto

---

6 *sayeth Seneca*] Presumably Seneca the younger, although the saying apparently orginated with Publilius Syrus, the Latin writer of maxims.

joined that although authority happen to slip, yet that love and virtue may never be severed. I have spoken of friendship perchance more than needeth but who will not wish (if it might happen) to have such a treasure, as neither the mountains of Ethiope nor the rivers of Indie do contain in them to be thereto compared. Callimachus, an ancient poet, sayeth "Puissance is dreadful, riches is honourable, but love for surety is most incomparable". Who perceiveth herein more than your good Lordship? which besides the abundant knowledge of histories and natural wit also concerning this matter in your own sundry experiences, I dare say without flattery, are equal to any noble man living. Yet this my long tale is not superfluous, which is told not to teach you but only to renew your Lordship's remembrance, which is not always present, specially where the brain is choked with worldly matters of weighty importance. In such as I am, having little and little to do, remembrance standeth more at liberty and therefore we may more often think on that which we have both heard and seen, and in choosing friends be the more circumspect. But lest I shall make the name of friendship tedious by often rehearsal, I now conclude that I leave this little work a monument of the long continued affection by me born toward your Lordship and a perpetual witness that I have deserved so much of your favour as in mutual friendship is of reason required, which may be as easily paid as it is granted if in place where it ought to be showed ye do not forget it. In the meantime I shall pray to God to add to your good fortune and health continuance, with his grace and favour, wherein only is most perfect surety.

APPENDIX 2: THE PREFACE TO THE FIRST EDITION OF ANDREW BOORDE'S *COMPENDIOUS REGIMENT*

To the precellent[1] and armipotent[2] prince, Lord Thomas, Duke of Norfolk, Andrew Boorde, of physic doctor, doth surrender humile commendation.

Forasmuch as it pleased Your Grace to send for me to Sir Robert Drury, knight, which was the year in which Lord Thomas, Cardinal Bishop of York, was commanded to go to his see of York, to have my counsel in physic in certain urgent causes requiring to the safety of your body. At the time I, being but a young doctor in my science or faculty, durst not to presume to minister any medicine to you without the counsel of Master Doctor Butte, which had a long continuance with you and a great cognition, not only of your infirmity but also of your complexion and diet. But he not coming to Your Grace, thanks be to God Your Grace recuperating your health and convocated[3] through the King's goodness to wait on his prepotent majesty, I then did pass over the seas again and did go to all the universities and schools approbated and being within the precinct of Christendom; and all was done for to have a true cognition of the practise of physic, the which obtained. I then quotidially remembering your bountiful goodness showed to me, and also being at the well-head of physic, did consult with many egregious doctors of physic what matter I should write, the which might be acceptable and profitable for the safety of your body. The said doctors, knowing my true intention, did advertise me to compile and make some book of diet, the which not only should do Your Grace pleasure, but also it should be necessary and profitable for your noble posterity and for many other men the which would follow the efficacy of this book, the which is called *The Regiment or Dietary of Health*. And where that I do speak in this book but of diets and other things concerning the same, if any man therefore would have remedy for any sickness or disease, let him look in a book of my making named *The Breviary of Health*. But if it shall please Your Grace to look on a book the which I did make in Montpellier named *The Introductory of Knowledge*,[4] there shall you see many new matters the

---

1 *precellent*] excelling others, pre-eminent. Notes glossing words, phrases, and people that also appear in the Q2 preface are provided in the main text.

2 *armipotent*] mighty in arms. Shakespeare uses the word armipotent in *Love's Labour's Lost*, *All's Well That Ends Well*, and *The Two Noble Kinsmen* (Shakespeare 1988, LLL 5.2.637, 644; AWW 4.3.239; TNK 5.1.53). As Susan Snyder noted, Shakespeare uses the word "in situations of heightened formality" (Shakespeare, William 1994, 183n239).

3 *convocated*] called or summoned together.

4 The Introductory of Knowledge] The full title of this work indicates its content: *The First Book of the Introduction of Knowledge, the Which doth Teach a Man to Speak Part of all Manner of Languages, and to Know the Usage and Fashion of all Manner of Countries. and for to know the Most Part of all Manner of Coins of Money, the Which is Current in Every Region* (Boorde 1555). The Short Title Catalogue gives 1555 as the date of publication for *The First Book of the Introduction of Knowledge* but Boorde's claim here that the book is currently being printed suggests that 1542 (the year in which Q1 was published) is more likely.

which I have no doubt but that Your Grace will accept, and like the book, the which is a-printing beside Saint Dunstan's Church within Temple Bar, over against the Temple. And where I have dedicated this book to Your Grace and have not ornated and flourished it with eloquent speech and rhetoric terms, the which in all writings is used these modernal[1] days, I do submit me to your bountiful goodness. And also diverse times in my writings I do write words of mirth; truely it is for no other intention but to make Your Grace merry, for mirth is one of the chiefest things of physic, the which doth advertise every man to be merry and to beware of pensivefulness, trusting to your affluent goodness to take no displeasure with any contents of this book but to accept my good will and diligent labour. And, furthermore, I do trust to your superabundant graciousness that you will consider the love and zeal the which I have to your prosperity and that I do it for a common weal, the which I beseech Jesus Christ long to continue to his will and pleasure in this life, and after this transitory life remunerate you with celestial joy and eternal glory. From Montpellier, the fifth day of May, the year of our Lord Jesus Christ, 1542.

---

1 *modernal*] modern, of the present day.

APPENDIX 3: THE SECOND ADDRESS TO THE READER FROM THE FIRST EDITION OF WILLIAM BULLEIN'S *GOVERNMENT OF HEALTH*

The swift runner in his race (gentle reader) in a stubby or rocky ground is in danger eftsoons to stumble or fall, whereas the goer fair and softly in the smooth path is safe. Even so, because I have had no conference with others, nor long time of premeditation in study, but with speed have conciliated this small entitled *Government of Health*, it cannot be but many things have missed in the print: as in folio fifty-two, the eighteenth line, read "sigh" for "fight"; in folio sixty, the second page, eleventh line, read "olibanum" for "olibulom"; and in the end of the epistle to the reader there is imprinted "Wenzoar" for "Avenzoer"; and in folio sixty-six, line fifteen, leave out "because".[1] And thus, to conclude, I will by God's grace join another book called *The Healthful Medicines* unto this *Government*, and at the next impression such amends shall be made that both syllable and sentence shall be diligently kept in true order to thy contentation, God willing, whoever keep thee in health. The first of March, the year of our salvation. 1558. William Bullein.

---

1 *missed ... because*] The second "correction" gives "Olibulom" (in original typography) where the misprinted reading is in fact "Olibbulom" and the fourth seems to be a miscorrection as "because" is not to be found at the place cited.

APPENDIX 4: GLOSSARY OF WORDS COMMONLY USED IN THE DIETARIES

The following words appear frequently in the dietaries and are explained here so as to avoid undue repetition in the explanatory notes.

abstertive cleansing.
adustion, adust the action or process of burning, drying, burnt dry by heat.
affect, affection usually this refers to that which impacts upon the mind or emotions.
ague an acute or violent fever, perhaps specifically malarial and considered a consequence of bad air.
allay dilute.
ambergris a wax-like substance obtained from the intestines of the sperm-whale and used as a perfume.
apoplexia a haemorrhage or embolism in the brain that renders the patient unconscious and then paralysed, commonly termed a 'stroke'; also an efffusion of blood into the lungs or other organs.
appair weaken or damage.
auge increase; the repetition ("auge and augment" or "auge and increase"), which recurs in Boorde, is apparently not an error but rhetorical emphasis.
baken baked.
bind, bound make constipated, costive.
bloody flux an early name for dysentery.
bole armen, bole armeniac, bolus armenus a soft, friable (that is, crumbly) earth, usually pale red in colour (OED bole $n.^2$), used as an astringent and styptic.
boxing making scratches or slight incisions in the skin (see **scarifiy**) and applying boxes or cupping glasses as a surgical treatment.
caudle a warm drink made of thin gruel, mixed with wine or ale, sweetened and spiced; it was usually given to the sick or pregnant women and those visiting them.
cassia fistula the name given to the fruit-pulp from cassia pods, used as a laxative (OED cassia $n.^1$ 4).
choler adust an abnormal form of choler having a black or dark colour (OED choler $n.$ 2. c.).
citron a citrus fruit, similar to the lemon but drier; mostly used in medicine.
clyster like suppositories, this was medicine inserted into the rectum (although a suppository was usually in the form of a capsule and the clyster inserted using a clyster-pipe); Bullein provides instructions for making clysters in his *Regiment Against the Pleurisy* (Bullein 1562a, C2v–C3r).
comfits sweetmeats consisting of a seed, spice, root or piece of fruit encased in sugar.
comfort, comfortable; conformative to strengthen and refresh, reviving; things that have these qualities. In Jonson's *Bartholomew Fair*, Joan Trash's gingerbread is twice referred to as "comfortable bread" (Jonson 1960, 2.5.9; 3.4.92).
commodious, commodity beneficial, benefit.
consumption abnormality or loss of humours, resulting in wasting away, extreme weight loss.

concoction digestion, via boiling or cooking in the stomach. This word and the verb, 'concoct', is most often used by Elyot; it is used by Bullein only once (p. 226) and not at all by Boorde.
condite preserved, pickled.
confection; confectioned, confectionate mixture; mixed, often with sweet things.
cony an adult rabbit; 'cony' was the more usual word since 'rabbit' was used specifically to describe the young animal.
costive constipated.
crudity imperfect concoction of the humours; undigested (or indigestible) matter in the stomach.
cullis a strong broth made of meat, fowl, etc., boiled and strained; used especially as a nourishing food for the sick. Boorde usually refers to the plural "cullises".
cupping see **boxing**.
declare explain.
decoct, decoction the word is used in two senses: (1) digest, digestion and (2) a liquor produced by the action of decocting, whereby a substance, animal or vegetable, is boiled in liquid so as to extract the soluble parts or principles of the substance.
discreet of sound judgement.
distempered, distemperance imbalanced humours or qualities, an instance of this imbalance.
distillations catarrh.
dropsy excess watery fluid in the tissues or cavities of the body.
dryth dryness, dry condition.
dyscrasy used by Elyot to describe a bodily disorder resulting from an imbalance among humours or qualities whereby one is affected with a dyscrasy.
eftsoons a second time, again or soon afterwards.
elecampane horse-heal.
estimation reputation.
excrement superfluous matter produced by the body, for example hair and nails, as well as faeces.
expulse expel.
extenuate emaciate, thin out.
fined refined.
flux an abnormally copious flowing of blood, excrement, etc. from the bowels or other organs.
forseen providing or provided that. Often used by Elyot.
frenzy a mental disorder.
fret; frettings gnaw, chafe; an instance of gnawing, chafing.
fricace; frication a rubbing, massage; the action of rubbing, massaging. Eliot refers to doing this oneself or having a servant do it (in the second book, chapter thirty-three).
fumosities fumes or vapours.
gargarise; gargarism gargarise is used as a noun to describe the gargle itself and the action of gargling; the other terms are used just for the gargle itself.
genitors, genitories testicles. Often used by Elyot.

gravel   urinary crystals.
green sickness   an anaemic disease commonly attributed to a virgin's sexual fantasies, which manifested itself through an unhealthy pallor and could be cured only by a sexual encounter (Williams 1994, 2: "Green sickness").
grief   physical pain.
gross   thick, heavy.
gross meats   heavy and inferior meats; could specifically refer to the flesh of large animals.
heaviness   sorrow.
herb-grace   rue.
hiera picra   a purgative drug made from canella (cinnamon, or cassia bark), aloes, and other ingredients. Information on how to make hiera picra is given in the *Pharmacopoeia Londinensis* (Culpepper 1653, Ll1r).
high countries   mountainous areas.
honeysop   a piece of bread soaked in honey.
humect   moistens.
iliac   ileus, also termed 'iliac passion', was a painful and often fatal condition caused by intestinal obstruction especially in the ileum, the third portion of the small intestine.
impostume   purulent swelling, cyst or abscess.
incontinent   without restraint, immediately.
inwards   innards, entrails.
ireos   the Florentine iris, a species with large, white flowers; the root was commonly used in medicine.
king's evil   scrofula; in England and France it was believed that the condition could be cured by the monarch's touch.
lassitude   weariness.
let   hinder or prevent.
loose, looseth   a verb used mostly by Elyot to describe the laxative effect of certain foods – and also actions such as rubbing the body – by which the bowels or stomach become "loose".
maidenhair   a type of fern.
manna   A dried, sweet exudate or gum from various trees, including the manna ash; dried juice from incision of the bark resulted in whitish pieces of manna that were used as a mild laxative and also in enemas (Matthews 1978, 170).
matrix   womb.
meat   depending on context either food in general or animal flesh specifically.
megrim   a headache, specifically a migrane.
melliot   more commonly known as melilot; the dried flowers of this plant were used medicinally, for example in plasters and poultices.
mercury   a plant often used in enemas (*OED* mercury, n. IV. 10. a.).
metheglin   a spiced or medicated variety of mead.
milt   spleen.
mithridatum   or mithridate, a medicine made from a long list of ingredients and considered an antidote or preservative against disease and poison. Named after Mithridates VI, King of Pontus, who is referred to by Bullein in his section on almonds (pp. 293–4). Bullein provides a recipe for mithridatum in his *Bulwark of Defence* (Bullein 1579, Ccc1r).

morphew a skin disease causing lesions on the skin. A black morphew, causing dark-coloured leisons, was thought to be caused by the humour black bile while a white morphew, causing light-coloured lesions, was thought to be caused by the humour phlegm.

mundify clean, purify.

navew a root, specifically rape, *Brassica napus*.

neezing, "to neeze" the process whereby sneezing is provoked and thus the nasal passage is cleared, usually by the injection of some foreign body such as the leaf of betony recommended by Humphrey in Bullein's dietary (p. 239).

noyful harmful; most often used by Elyot.

official members those serving the needs of the higher organs.

olibanum an aromatic resin from Boswellia trees; also known as frankincense, the term used when the resin is burned rather than consumed orally.

oppilations, oppilated obstructions, obstructed.

organum Latin name for any of the perennial herbs and subshrubs constituting the Eurasian genus Origanum, especially wild marjoram or oregano (*OED* origanum, *n.*).

oxymel, Oxymel Simplex, a medicinal drink made from vinegar and honey; Bullein provides a recipe for this (Bullein 1579, Ccc2r).

palsies paralyses.

passions physical distresses.

pease, peason peas.

pepon pumpkin.

plaster a piece of cloth containing a topical preparation that is placed on the skin.

plummets leaden weights.

polypodium, polypody fern.

poses colds in the head; catarrh.

pottage a thick soup.

powdered spiced.

pretty clever, skilful.

puissance power.

pulses arteries or pulsating veins.

quartan a fever that recurs every fourth day, that is at intervals of approximately seventy-two hours.

quotidian, quotidial every day, daily.

rapes turnip-like vegetables.

raw uncooked or undigested.

rear slightly or imperfectly cooked or underdone; the term usually refers to the cooking of eggs.

refection sustenance, a meal.

reins, reins of the back kidneys or the area in which the kidneys are located, i.e. the loins.

rheum watery or mucous secretion from the eyes, nose, or mouth that was thought to have originated in the brain or head; when abnormal, for example in excess, rheums were believed to provoke disease.

sanders sandalwood.

savour smell.

scarify to make scratches or slight incisions in the body.

setwall   the plant valerian.
seethe, seething   boil, boiling.
siege   excrement, faeces; the action of voiding excrement. Most often used by Elyot.
simples   anything comprised of only one constituent, especially medicine made from one herb or plant; the term might also refer to the herb or plant itself.
sinew   a tendon or nerve.
small ale   weak ale.
sodden   boiled.
soluble   relaxed, free from costiveness.
spike, spikenard   lavender or the aromatic substance obtained from an Indian plant.
squinance   squinsy or quinsy, which is inflamation or swelling of the throat.
stamped   crushed in a mortar with a pestle.
steep   soak.
sternutation   see **neezing**.
stilled   distilled.
stones   testicles.
stone, the   a hard concretition in the body, especially the kidney, bladder, or gallbladder.
styptic   binding.
subtle   fine, delicate.
succade   fruit or vegetables preserved in sugar.
suppositories   see **clyster**.
syrup acetose   sugar boiled in vinegar and water until it has the consistency of a syrup.
temperate   balanced in humours or qualities.
temperature   temperamental balance; a state or condition resulting from that which is tempered or temperate. This word is used only by Elyot.
terms   (also **month-terms, secret terms, women's terms, terms menstrual** and **menstrual terms**) menstrual periods.
tertians   (also **tertian fever** or **tertian ague**) a fever occurring every third day.
theriaca, Theriaca Andromaci   an electuary (medicinal conserve or thick paste) comprising many ingredients and thought to be an antidote to poison and disease; *Theriaca Andromaci*, also known as Venice treacle, was reputedly devised by the Greek physician Andromachus the Elder.
tisane   a medicinal drink made from barley or herbs soaked in water.
travail   labour or work; the spelling 'travel', also used to denote travail by the early moderns, is used specifically when Bullein appears to mean a journey.
treacle   a medicinal compound or salve composed of many ingredients; the word was also used of plants reputed to have medicinal qualities, for example rue and valerian as well as garlic.
venerous   sexual.
venom   poison.
ventosity   wind. A word most often used by Boorde.
virtue   most often used to mean power, e.g. the virtue of specific foods.
watch, watching   wakefulness.
whereas   used by Bullein in the obsolete sense of "where".
while   time.
whole   well, in good condition.

APPENDIX 5: AUTHORITIES AND WORKS CITED OR ALLUDED TO IN THE DIETARIES

These are listed under the name by which they were commonly known in Europe.

Abbas, Haly (first century). Arabic physician Ali ibn Abbas al-Majusi who wrote *The Complete Book of the Medical Art* (also known as *The Royal Book*). Mentioned once by Elyot in the revised proem to the fourth edition of his dietary (upon which this edition is based). Bullein refers to him many times: in his address to the reader (p. 211) and on the value of avoiding sudden passion (p. 254). Regarding particular foods, Abbas is referred to in the sections on animal flesh (pp. 277, 279), birds (p. 283), fish (p. 284), honey (p. 288), and butter and cheese (pp. 289, 290).

Actuarius, Johannes (*c.* 1275 – *c.* 1328). Last great Byzantine Greek writer on medicine and author of *De urinis*, a treatise on urine. Mentioned once by Bullein (p. 249) and twice by Elyot in the fourth book, chapters nine and ten.

Aetius of Amida (sixth to fifth century BCE). Byzantine physician and medical writer; author of *Sixteen Books on Medicine* later divided into four books, *Tetrabiblion*. Mentioned several times by Elyot but only once by Bullein in the section "What is sage?" (p. 257). Elyot refers to him in the second book, chapters fourteen, twenty, thirty-three, and thirty-five; the third book, chapters three, and four to eight; the fourth book, chapters one, and three to five.

Andromachus the Elder (first century). Physican to Emperor Nero who was reputed to have devised the medicine *Theriaca Andromachi*, which was thus named after him and was also known as Venice treacle. He is mentioned in the context of this medicine by Bullein (p. 298).

Apollodorus of Pergamon (first century BCE). Greek rhetorician and teacher of the first Roman Emperor Caesar Augustus, born Gaius Octavius and known as Octavian. Mentioned by Elyot in the third book, chapter twelve, when discussing ire.

Aristotle (fourth century BCE). Greek philosopher who wrote on a wide range of topics including medicine. Author of the following:

De generatione et corruptione (*On Generation and Corruption*);
De somno et vigilia (*On Sleep and Wakefulness*);
Politics;
Problemata (*Problems*).

Politics is alluded to by Elyot in the proem to the first edition of his dietary but is not mentioned in the subsequent editions' proems. Bullein makes numerous references to Aristotle, citing all the works listed above aside from *Politics*, in his verse warning against excess (p. 209); discussion of elements (p. 228), complexions (p. 232), the best time for bloodletting and purging (p. 237), sleep (p. 248), and the value of avoiding sudden passion (p. 254). Regarding particular foods, Aristotle is referred to in Bullein's sections on cabbage (p. 264), fish (p. 284), and wine (p. 291).

Arnaldus de Villanova or Arnold of Villanova (1235–1311). Catalan physician and translator. Author of a number of medical works including a short treatise on bloodletting, *De flebotomia*, and a Latin prose commentary on the influential poem *Regimen sanitatis Salerni*. His work on bloodletting is cited by Elyot in the third book, chapter seven.

Augustine de Angustinis (sixteenth century). Venetian doctor who was personal physician to Cardinal Wolsey and royal physician from 1540 to 1546. He is mentioned favourably by Elyot in the fourth book, chapter one, for the treatment he received from him.

Avenzoar (twelfth century). Arab physican and empiricist Ibn Zuhr who lived in Seville, Spain. He was the first to discover the scabies mite and advocated the use of medical innovations such as tracheotomy. His most important work was his *Teisir* (*Practical Manual of Treatments and Diets*). Mentioned twice by Bullein, in his address to the reader and when discussing the merits of chicken (p. 281), and once by Elyot in the proem to his dietary (the first edition and the revised fourth edition upon which this edition is based).

Averroes (twelfth century). Arab philosopher Ibn Rushd. A student of **Avenzoar**, Averroes wrote *Kulliyat* (*Generalities*, i.e. the general rules of medicine), a seven-volume medical encyclopaedia, which was better known by its Latin name *Colliget*. He is referred to once by Elyot (in the revised proem to the fourth edition of his dietary, upon which this edition is based) and twice by Boorde (in chapter sixteen, the sections "Of mutton and lamb" and "Of kid"). He is referred to by Bullein in his discussion of digestion (p. 244), exercise (p. 247), oil (p. 286), honey (p. 288), beer and ale (p. 292), and bread (p. 293).

Avicenna (eleventh century). Persian physician Ibn Sina who wrote the following:

Cantica (a poem on medicine, translated into Latin);
Canon of Medicine (a key medical text in medieval universities with numerous Latin editions).

Avicenna is mentioned by all the dietary authors but most often by Bullein. Elyot refers to him in his proem to the fourth edition (on which this one is based) and the second book, chapter eight. Boorde refers to him in chapters eleven, twelve, sixteen, and twenty-one. Bullein refers to Avicenna in his address to the reader (p. 211); description of the humours (p. 231); discussion of whether men or women are of colder complexion (p. 232); description of bodily members (p. 233); and discussions of bones (p. 236), purging/vomiting (p. 239), the value of food and a good diet in general (p. 241), digestion (p. 244), good air and the position of one's dwelling (p. 246), and sleep (p. 248). Regarding particular foods, Avicenna is referred to by Bullein in his sections on herbs (pp. 255, 256, 264), animal flesh (pp. 277, 280), birds (pp. 281, 282, 283), fish (p. 285), water (p. 286), honey (p. 288), butter and cheese (p. 290), wine (p. 291), beer and ale (p. 292), rice (p. 293), and spices (pp. 294, 296).

Cato the Elder (234–149 BCE). Elyot mentions the Roman statesman and clearly alludes to his book *De agri cultura* (*On Farming* or *On Agriculture*) in the second book, chapter fifteen, in the section "Coleworts and cabbages".

Cicero, Marcus Tullius also known as **Tully** (106–43 BCE). Roman philosopher, lawyer, political theorist and orator. Author of the following:

Tusculanae disputationes (*Questions Debated at Tuscum*) printed in Latin in London, 1574;
De senectute (*On Old Age*) in two editions before 1558: 1481 and 1535, both in English.

Both works are cited by Bullein (p. 253 and p. 248).

Cunningham, William (sixteenth century). English physician, cartographer, astronomer, and author of *A New Almanac and Prognostication*, written in English and first published in 1558. Mentioned by Bullein (p. 238).

Damascene, John or Yuhanna ibn Masawaih, or John of Damascus, or Mesue the Elder (*c.* 777–837). A Syrian monk and priest, he wrote a number of medical treatises on a range of topics. Often cited as the author of *The Book of Aphorisms*, which it seems was actually written by Mesue the Younger (see below). *The Book of Aphorisms* was one of thirteen supplements to the *Ars medicine* (*The Art of Medicine*), a collection used to teach medicine in early modern universities. Damascene is not mentioned by Boorde. Elyot most often uses the name "Damascene" and refers to him in the second book, chapter twenty-four and the third book, chapters three and seven. He once refers to "Mesue", in his proem to the fourth edition (on which this one is based). Bullein refers to "Mesue" when discussing medicine in the section on bodily members (p. 235) and his discussion of the best time for purgations (p. 238). Regarding particular foods, Mesue is referred to in Bullein's section on herbs (p. 269), oil (p. 286), and spices (p. 295). It is not always clear whether Elyot and Bullein are actually referring to Damascene or to Mesue the Younger.

Digges, Leonard (1520–59). English mathematician and surveyor who wrote *Prognostication of Right Good Effect*, an almanac written in English that was first published in 1555, with a second revised edition in 1556. Mentioned by Bullein in the context of the best time for purgations (p. 238).

Diocles of Carystus (fourth century BCE). Greek physician who was apparently the author of a letter addressed to king Antigonus, *A Letter on Preserving Health*. The letter appears at the end of the first book of Paul of Aegina's medical compendium and the king in question is probably Antigonus II Gonatas, King of Macedon. Elyot presents a diet apparently written by Diocles for King Antigonus in the second book, chapter twenty-five, and Diocles' precepts, also for Antigonus, in the fourth book, chapter eleven.

Dioscorides, Pendanius (first century). Greek physician, pharmacologist, and botanist who wrote *Materia medica* (*Of Medical Materials*). This authoritative work on herbs and other medicines was translated into Arabic but not Latin, although it appears that some chapters in Arabic encyclopaedias and treatises were translated into Latin for European readers. Mentioned by all of the dietary authors, although only once by Boorde, at the end of chapter twenty on herbs. Elyot refers to him in his proem (to first edition and the revised fourth edition, upon which this edition is based); in the second book, chapters eight and thirteen to seventeen; and in the third book, chapter six. He is referred to most often by Bullein: in his verse warning against excess (p. 209), his address to the reader (p. 211), and his discussion of the division amongs physicians (p. 222). Regarding particular foods, Dioscorides is referred to in the sections on herbs (pp. 256–269), birds (p. 284), salt (p. 287), and spices (p. 285).

Elyot, Thomas (c. 1490 – 1546). Bullein mentions Elyot's *Castle of Health* for its advice on radish roots (pp. 269–70).

Ficino, Marsilio (1433–99). Italian humanist philosopher and Neoplatonist. Most famous for his theological treatise on the immortality of the soul, *Theologia Platonica de immortalitate animae*. In the third book, chapter twenty-one, on melancholy, Elyot cites his *De vita libri tres* or *De triplici vita* (*Three Books on Life*), published in 1489, which offers advice for maintaining good health. He is also mentioned in the fourth book, chapter fourteen, which discusses a diet in the time of pestilence.

Fuchs, Leonhart (1501–1566). German physican and author of the herbal *Historia stirpium* (*History of Plants*). Mentioned by Bullein in his address to the reader (p. 211), his discussion of physicians (p. 225), and, when referring specifically to food, in his section on herbs (pp. 256–7, 268).

Galen (second century), also known as Galen of Pergamon, Aelius Galenus or Claudius Galenus. Greek physician who was arguably the best-known and most influential medical authority during the early modern period. He is referred to many times by all the dietary authors although least of all by Boorde. Elyot refers to him in his proem to the fourth edition (on which this one is based); the first book, chapter one; the second book, chapters one, three, eight, ten, fourteen to nineteen, twenty-two, twenty-four, twenty-six to twenty-eight, thirty, thirty-two to thirty-four; the third book, chapters one, three, four, six, eight, twenty-one; the fourth book, chapters to three, seven, and ten. Boorde refers to Galen in chapter three, nine, twelve, and sixteen. Bullein refers to Galen in his epistle to Hilton (p. 208); verse warning against excess (p. 209); address to the reader (p. 211); and discussions of physic (pp. 224, 225), the temperaments and complexions (pp. 226, 229–232), anatomy (pp. 233, 236), bloodletting (p. 237), scarifying or boxing (p. 239), the value of food and a good diet in general (pp. 241–3), good air (p. 245), exercise (pp. 244, 247), and the value of mirth and joy (p. 254). Regarding particular foods, Galen is referred to in the sections on herbs (pp. 255–7, 260, 263, 265–9); fruit (pp. 274–6); animal flesh (pp. 278–9, 281); birds (p. 282); fish (pp. 284–5), honey (p. 288); eggs (p. 290); wine (p. 291); bread (p. 293); spices (p. 295); and on the virtues of *mithridatum* (p. 298).

Galen is author of the following:

Arte parva (*Small Art*);
Commentary on Hippocrates' *Aphorisms*;
De alimentorum facultatibus (*On the Properties of Foodstuffs*);
De diebus decretoriis (*Critical Days*);
De elementis (*The Elements*);
De euchymia et cacochymia: seu de malisbonusque succis generandis (*On Good and Bad Digestion or Generating Good and Bad Chime*);

APPENDIX 5   319

De juvamentis memborum (*On the Uses of the Parts*), a twelfth-century Latin version of an Arabic translation of Galen's *De usu partium*, shorter and more simplified than the original. It is cited by Bullein (p. 241);

De locis affectis (*On Affected Places*);

De methodo medendi (*On the Therapeutic Method*);

De naturalibus facultatibus (*On the Natural Faculties*);

De ossibus (*On Bones*);

De plenitudine (*On Fullness*);

De sectis (*On Sects*);

De simplicium medicamentorum facultatibus (*On the Powers of Simple Remedies*);

De sanitate tuenda (*On Hygiene*);

De temperamentis (*On Mixtures*);

De usu partium corporis humani (*On the Uses of the Different Parts of the Human Body*);

De venesection ... (*On Bloodletting*) – Galen wrote three books on the topic: *On Venesection Against Erasistratus*, *On Venesection Against the Erasistrateans in Rome*, and *On Treatment by Venesection*;

De victu attenuante (*On the Thinning Diet*);

Quod animi mores corporis temperatura sequantur (*That the Qualities of the Mind Depend on the Temperament of the Body*) – Elyot seems to mean this work rather than *De sanitate tuenda* (*On Hygiene*) when discussing the moderate consumption of wine at the end of the first chapter from the first book.

The following are four related treatises; Bullein apparently cites the first three:

De morborum differentiis (*On Various Diseases*);

De causis morborum (*On the Causes of Diseases*);

De symptomatum causis (*On the Causes of Symptoms*);

De symptomatum differentiis (*On Various Symptoms*).

Gazio, Antonio (fifteenth century). Paduan physician and author of a dietary in Latin entitled *Florida corona* that is cited by Bullein (p. 278).

Gesner, Conrad (1516–65). Swiss naturalist, also known by the pseudonym Euonymus Philiatri and author of the following:

Thesaurus Euonymus Philiatri (*The Treasure of Euonymus Philiatri*), a work on distillation, printed in Zurich, 1552: an English translation by Peter Morwyng (STC 11800) appeared in 1559, the year after Bullein's *Goverment of Health* was first published);

Historiae animalium (*History of Animals*), printed in Zurich, 4 vols, 1551–58. A comprehensive encyclopaedia of all known animals; Edward Topsell's *History of Four-Footed Beasts* (STC 24123) is a translation and abridgement of Gesner's work, published in 1607.

Bullein refers to him in his address to the reader (p. 211) and, referring to food specifically, in his sections on distillation (p. 270), animal flesh (pp. 277, 279), and birds (p. 282).

Hippocrates (*c.* 460–377 BCE). Influential Greek physician, called "the Prince" and "the Prince of Physicians" by Bullein and others. All the works listed below are from the Hippocratic Corpus, which indicates that they are associated with Hippocrates' name but were likely written by a number of authors:

Airs, Waters, and Places;
Aphorisms;
De humoribus (On the Humours);
De natura humana (On the Nature of Man);
De ratione victus in morbis acutis (On Regimen in Acute Diseases);
The Book of Prognostics.

Hippocrates is referred to many times in all of the dietaries but less by Boorde than by Elyot and Bullein. Elyot refers to him in his proem to the fourth edition (on which this one is based); the second book, chapters three, eight, eighteen, twenty-four, twenty-seven, twenty-eight, and thirty-three; the third book, chapters one, three, four, six, and nineteen; the fourth book, chapters seven and ten. Boorde refers to him only once, in chapter nine. Bullein refers to him in his verse warning against excess (p. 209); address to the reader (p. 211); discussion of physic (pp. 224, 225); description of the four elements (p. 227) and of purging (pp. 237–9), the value of a good diet in general (p. 241), good air (pp. 245, 246), and exercise (p. 247). Regarding particular foods, Hippocrates is referred to in the sections on fruit (pp. 273, 275), animal flesh (pp. 279, 280), birds (p. 282), and wine (p. 291).

Israeli, Isaac Ben Solomon (ninth to tenth century). Jewish physician writing in Arabic and called simply "Isaac" by Elyot, Bullein, and Boorde; author of the *Diaetae particulares (Particular Diets)*. He is mentioned by Elyot in the revised proem to the fourth edition of his dietary (upon which this edition is based), by Boorde at the end of the fifteenth chapter ("Of birds"), and by Bullein in the section "What be pigeons, turtles or doves?" (p. 282).

Johannitius (ninth century). Latin name for the Assyrian Christian physician and scholar Hunain ibn Ishaq (also Hunayn or Hunein) who translated Greek works into Arabic and was author of the *Isagoge* (intended as an introduction to Galen's *Tegni*), which became a standard text for medical students. Mentioned by Elyot in the penultimate paragraph of the revised proem to the fourth edition of his dietary (upon which this edition is based) and in the first book, chapter two.

Macer, Floridus or Aemelius (died in 16 BCE). Roman poet and reputed author of the herbal *De viribus herbarum carmen (A Song on the Properties of Plants)*, a work first published in 1477. Cited by Boorde at the end of chapter twenty on herbs.

Machaon (12 BCE). Greek surgeon; son of Aesculapius and brother of Podalirius, he was a member of the Greek force led by Agamemnon at the siege of Troy. Mentioned by Elyot in the proem to the first edition of his dietary and in the revised proem to the fourth edition (upon which this edition is based) and by Bullein in his discussion of physicians (p. 224).

Mesue the Younger (ninth to tenth century). Arabic physician Masawaih al-Mardini or Yahya ibn Masawaih al-Mardini, also called "John Mesue" by Bullein; author of *Antidotarium sive grabadin medicamentorum* (also known as the *Pharmacopoeia*). Cited by Elyot and Bullein (see the entry for **Damascene**), although it is not always clear whether they mean this Mesue or John Damascene, also known as Mesue (the Elder).

Oribasius (c. 320–400). Greek medical writer and physican to Roman Emperor Julian the Apostate. He is best known for a medical compendium called the *Collectiones medicae*, which gathered together excerpts from Galen and other ancient medical authorities. He is referred to several times by Elyot: in his proem to the fourth edition (on which this one is based); the second book, chapters twenty, twenty-six, and thirty-three; the third book, chapters six to nine; and the fourth book, chapter thirteen. Oribasius is mentioned only once by Bullein, in his section on salt (p. 287).

Ovid, Publius Ovidius Naso (43 BCE – c. 17 CE). Roman poet whose *Metamorphoses* is cited twice by Bullein (p. 223 and p. 253). Arthur Golding's full English translation of Ovid's work was published in 1567, with the first four books published in 1565, seven years after the publication of the first edition of Bullein's dietary.

Paul of Aegina or Paulus Aegineta (seventh century). Byzantine Greek physician and author of the influential encyclopaedia *Epitomae medicae libri septem* or *De re medicina* (*Medical Compendium in Seven Books*). Referred to several times by Elyot: in the second book, chapters sixteen, seventeen, twenty, twenty-three, twenty-six, thirty-three, and thirty-five; the third book, chapter six; and the fourth book, chapters one and ten.

Pliny the Elder (23–79). Natural philosopher and author of the *Naturalis historia* (*Natural History*). Mentioned by Elyot in the revised prologue to the fourth edition of his dietary (upon which this edition is based); in the second book, chapter twenty-two "Of honey"; and possibly also in the second book, chapter eight, in the section "Hare, Cony". Boorde refers to Pliny when discussing honey in chapter twelve and in chapter twenty on herbs. Bullein refers to Pliny in his verse warning against excess (p. 209); address to the reader (p. 211); and discussion of physic (p. 223). Regarding particular foods, Pliny is referred to in the sections on herbs (pp. 261, 263–6); animal flesh (p. 279); birds (p. 284); and almonds (p. 294).

Podalirius (12 BCE). Greek surgeon; son of Aesculapius and brother of Machaon, he was a member of the Greek force led by Agamemnon at the siege of Troy. Mentioned by Elyot in his proem (to the first edition and revised fourth edition, upon which this edition is based) and by Bullein (p. 224).

Rasis or Rhazes, Muhammad ibn Zakariya al-Razi (c. 850–923). The most prolific Arabic physician and author of the following:

> *Book of Medicine for Mansur* known as *Liber ad almansorem*, translated into Latin by Gerard of Cremona (many editions were printed in Renaissance with commentaries by prominent physicians including Andreas Vesalius);
> *The Guide* sometimes known as *The Book of Aphorisms* (apparently never translated into Latin).

Rasis is referred to by all three dietary authors. Elyot refers to him in his proem to the fourth edition (on which this one is based) and in the fourth book, chapter fourteen. Boorde refers to Rasis in chapters fifteen and sixteen. Bullein refers to him most often: in his address to the reader (p. 211), his discussion of what pill to take before purging (p. 234) and for toothache (p. 236), his discussion of purgations (pp. 237, 238), digestion (p. 244), and the position of one's dwelling (p. 246). Regarding particular foods, Rasis is referred to in the sections on: herbs (p. 264); fruit (pp. 275, 276); animal flesh (pp. 277, 280); birds (pp. 281, 283); salt (p. 287); milk (p. 289); beer and ale (p. 292); bread (p. 293); and spices (p. 294).

Salerno Italian medieval medical school that was said to have produced the anonymous *Regimen sanitatis Salernitanum* (*The Salernitan Rule of Health*), a regimen or dietary in verse attributed to Joannes De Mediolano. It was first translated into English by Thomas Paynell in 1528 with a verse translation by Sir John Harington in 1607. The book and the school are mentioned by Elyot in the revised proem to the fourth edition of his dietary (upon which this edition is based) and the book by Bullein in the section "What is sage?" (p. 257).

Seneca the Younger (*c.* 4 BCE – 65 CE). Roman stoic philosopher and dramatist; author of *De beneficiis* (*On Benefits*). He is referred to by Elyot in the proem to the second edition of his dietary and in the third book, chapter thirteen, in the discussion of sorrow that is a consequence of ingratitude.

Serenus, Quintus (third century). Roman medical writer and author of a didactic poem on medicine *Liber medicinalis*, also known as *De medicina praecepta saluberrima*. Mentioned by Elyot in the proem to the first edition and revised fourth edition of his dietary (upon which this edition is based).

Sethi, Simeon (eleventh century). Byzantine scholar whose *Syntagma peri trophon dynameon*, or *Syntagma de alimentorum facultatibus* (*Lexicon on the Properties of Food*), was a compilation of works by Galen and others, printed in Basel, 1538 and 1561. Referred to by Bullein in his section on herbs (pp. 265, 266, 268), animal flesh (pp. 276, 279, 280), birds (pp. 282, 283), milk (p. 289), eggs (p. 290), and almonds (p. 294).

Sirach, Jesus (second century BCE). Jewish scribe also known as Ben Sira, and author of Ecclesiasticus, the apocryphal Biblical book also known as The Wisdom of Jesus, Son of Sirach or The Wisdom of Ben Sira. Cited once by Elyot, in the second book, chapter nineteen ("Of wine"), and twice by Bullein, once in the epistle (p. 207) and again when discussing physic (p. 223).

Solomon (*c.* 970 – *c.* 931 BCE). Old Testament King of Israel and son of David who was reputed to have written the Biblical books Ecclesiastes and Proverbs. Referred to twice by Elyot, in the third book, chapter thirteen, and in the fourth book, chapter two. Boorde cites his Cantica Canticorum, also known as the Biblical Song of Solomon, in chapter two. Solomon is referred to several times by Bullein: in his discussion of physic (p. 223), greed (p. 242), the value of good health (p. 248) and joy (p. 254).

Soranus of Ephesus (first century). Greek physician who practised medicine in Alexandria and then in Rome; known for *In artem medendi isagoge* (*The Art of Healing*), *De morbis acutis & chronicis* (*On Acute and Chronic Diseases*), and a treatise on gynaecology. Elyot cites his *Art of Healing* when discussing the distemperance of humours in the third book, chapter seventeen, in the discussion of "Peculiar remedies against the distemperance of every humour".

Tully see **Cicero**

Ulstad, Philipp (sixteenth century). German medical author and teacher who wrote *Coelum Philosophorum, seu, De secretis naturae liber* (*The Heaven of the Philosophers, or, Concerning the Secrets of the Book of Nature*), a work on distillation, printed in Freiburg, 1525. This work is mentioned by Bullein in the section "What be the virtues of leeks and roots of radish, turnips, parsnips, rapes or navews?" (p. 270).

Vesalius, Andreas (1514–64). Physician and expert on anatomy, specifically via dissecting the human body. His *De humani corporis fabrica libri septem* (*On the Fabric of the Human Body in Seven Books*), printed in Latin in 1543, was a hugely influential work, not least due to the anatomical detail of its woodcut illustrations of the human body; the illustrations are apparently the work of a number of artists, including Vesalius himself. Bullein's dietary appears to feature an illustration copied from this work (p. 236).

Virgil or Publius Vergilius Maro (70–19 BCE). Roman poet. The first book of his *Eclogues* is quoted by Bullein on the order and peace of bees compared to the discord of men in the section "What is honey of the virtue thereof?" (p. 288).

The following authorities are cited or alluded to but their works' titles are not given or it is unclear which works are intended.

Alexander of Tralles (*c.* 525 – *c.* 605). Byzantine Greek medical writer whose chief work was his *Twelve Books on Medicine*. Mentioned by Elyot in the revised proem to the fourth edition of his dietary (upon which this edition is based) and in the second book, chapter twenty-two, on honey.

Ambrose, St (*c.* 340–97). Archbishop of Milan and influential theologian. Referred to by Boorde in the seventh chapter when he observes that a man ought to prepare his soul for death, and by Elyot as an authority on what priests ought to wear in the fourth book, chapter two.

Apollonius Antiochenus or Apollonius of Antioch (second or first century BCE). The name given to two physicians (father and son) who were members of the Empiric school of medicine; they were also known as Apollonius Senior and Apollonius Empiricus. Mentioned by Bullein in his discussion of the Empiric school (p. 225).

Apollonius of Tyana (*c.* 15–100). Greek Neopythagorean philosopher from the town of Tyana. This is presumably the Apollonius meant by Elyot when he refers to the followers of Pythagoras in the section on water in the second book, chapter eighteen.

Appianus or Appian of Alexandria (*c* .95 – *c.* 165). Roman historian of Greek origin and author of *De natura animalium* (*On the Nature of Animals*) and *Varia historia* (*Various History*). The latter work is mentioned by Elyot in a marginal note to the third book, chapter thirteen, but since the note is regarding elephants it is possible he meant to cite Appianus' *On the Nature of Animals*.

Aristoxenus (fourth century BCE). Greek philosopher and pupil of Aristotle. His only extant work is on the subject of music. Mentioned by Elyot in relation to the virtues of honey in the second book, chapter twenty-two.

Asclepiades of Bithynia (first century CE). Greek physician who practised medicine in Rome and whose views would later influence the Methodic school of medicine. Mentioned by Bullein in his discussion of physic (p. 225).

Barthelmew of Montagnaue probably Bartholomeus Anglicus (also known as Bartholomew of England) (*c.* 1202–72). Franciscan friar and encyclopaedist who wrote *De proprietatibus rerum* (*On the Properties of Things*), which was translated into English in 1398 by John Trevisa. Referred to by Boorde in chapter twenty-seven.

Buttes, Master Doctor probably the physician, Sir William Butts (c. 1485–1545). Mentioned by Boorde in the preface to his dietary.

Callimachus (c. 310–240 BCE). Greek poet, critic and scholar whose poetry is mentioned by Elyot in the proem to the second edition of his dietary but not in subsequent proems.

Celius, Paulus probably Caeius Aurelianus, a fifth-century Roman writer known mainly for his translation of *On Acute and Chronic Diseases* by Soranus of Ephesus. Cited by Elyot in the revised proem to the fourth edition of his dietary (upon which this edition is based).

Celsus, Cornelius (first century). Roman scholar who wrote on medicine and husbandry. His book *De medicina* (*On Medicine*), published in 1478, was reprinted many times and is probably the work alluded to by Elyot in his proem to the first and second edition of his dietary; the second book, chapters thirty, thirty-two, thirty-four, and thirty-five; the third book, chapters four, five, and seven; the fourth book, chapter ten.

Chrysostom, John (347–407). Archbishop of Constantinople and important early church father who wrote on the priesthood and other matters pertaining to religion. Presumably the Chrisostomus referred to by Elyot as an authority on what priests ought to wear (in chapter two of the fourth book).

Cordus, Valerius (sixteenth century). German physician and botanist whose two great Latin works were his pharmacopoeia, the *Dispensatorium*, and his herbal *Historia plantarum* (*History of Plants*). Bullein mentions him twice (p. 238 and p. 297) and both times is probably referring to the *Dispensatorium*.

Cyprian, St (third century). Bishop of Carthage and early Christian writer. Referred to by Elyot as an authority on what priests ought to wear (in the fourth book, chapter two).

Cyrus, St (fourth century). Egyptian martyr who was reputed to have treated the sick for free. This might be whom Bullein means when he refers to "Sirus" in his discussion of physic (p. 225) but he is probably refering to Themison of Laodicea.

De Apono, Petrus (thirteenth to fourteenth century). Italian physician; Bullein recommends pills devised by him (p. 235) and mentions him when discussing fear (p. 254).

Democritus (*c.* 460 – c. 370 BCE). Greek philosopher with an interest in numerous subjects, amongst them mathematics, ethics, and nature. Mentioned by Elyot when discussing the virtues of eating honey (second book, chapter twenty-two).

Diodorus Siculus (first century BCE). Greek historian and author of *Bibliotecha historica* (*Historical Library*). He is apparently mentioned by Bullein in his discussion of physic (p. 223).

Fulgentius, Fabius Planciades (late fifth to early sixth century). Latin grammarian and mythographer referred to by Bullein as praising exercise (p. 247).

Glaucias (third century BCE). Greek physician of the Empiric school who was known for his commentaries on works by Hippocrates. He is mentioned by Bullein when discussing the empiricist physicians (p. 225).

Guainerius, Antonius (fifteenth century). Italian physician who wrote a treatise on fevers as well as being an authority on women's health. Mentioned by Elyot in the second book, chapter fifteen, in the section on sorrel, which is probably a reference to *Poisons*, Guainerius' book on plants.

Herodotus (fifth century). Greek historian mentioned by Bullein when discussing physic (p. 224).

Jerome, St (*c.* 347 – 420). Priest, theologian, and historian who wrote extensively on religious matters. Referred to by Elyot as an authority on what priests ought to wear in the fourth book, chapter two.

Linacre, Thomas (*c.* 1460–1524). Humanist scholar, physician, and probably tutor to Elyot. He was appointed royal physician in 1509 and taught Greek to Sir Thomas More. His translation of Galen into Latin is mentioned by Elyot in the second book, chapter thirty-three.

Livius, Titus (59 BCE – 17 CE). Roman historian, known as Livy in English and author of *Ab urbe condita* (*The Founding of the City* [*of Rome*]). Mentioned by Elyot in the third book, chapter fourteen, in the discussion of joy.

Lucian of Samosata (second century). Classical rhetorician and satirist; called simply "Lucian" by Bullein when explaining that women have hot tongues (p. 232).

Marsilius (1275 1342). Italian scholar trained in medicine and known as Marsilius of Padua. He is referred to by Elyot as a physician in the final chapter of his dietary but is best known for his political and anti-clerical treatise *Defensor pacis* (*The Defender of Peace*).

Martial (first century). Latin poet Martial Valerius Martialis who was best known for his book *Epigrams*. Mentioned by Bullein in his discussion of lettuce (p. 261).

Menodotus of Nicomedia (second century). Physician who belonged to the Empiric school and who is presumably the Menodotus mentioned by Bullein in his discussion of the school (p. 225).

Myrepsos, Nicholas (thirteenth century), also known as **Nicholas Alexandrinus**. A Byzantine physician whose pills are presumably those recommended by Bullein when he cites "Nicholai" or a variant of the name, which he does several times in his section on bodily members (pp. 234, 236). This physician is presumably also the "Nicholas" Bullein refers to in his discussion of purging (p. 238). Myrepsos' *Dynameron* contains numerous remedies, many of which are indebted to other authorities.

Perusinus, Matheolus (fifteenth-century). Physician, his second name indicating that he was from Perugia in Italy. Presumably this is whom Bullein refers to in his discussion of physic (p. 225).

Philinus of Cos (third century BCE). Greek physician who reputedly founded the Empiric school of medicine. Mentioned by Bullein when discussing the Empiricist physicians (p. 224).

Pindar (c. 522 – c. 443 BCE). Greek lyric poet. Mentioned by Elyot when praising water in the second book, chapter eighteen.

Rufus of Ephesus (first century). Greek physician who wrote numerous medical treatises; pills formulated by him to protect against pestilence are recommended by Elyot in the fourth book, chapter fourteen, and by Bullein (p. 235).

Serapion of Alexandria (third century BCE). Greek physician who was a member of the Empiric school of medicine and was thought by some to have founded it. The name Serapion is mentioned twice by Bullein, once when discussing Empiricist physicians (p. 225) and once when discussing the merits of dates preserved in sugar (p. 273). It is possible that the second reference is to Serapion the Elder (ninth century) or Serapion the Younger (twelfth or thirteenth century), both of whom were medical authors.

Sextus Empiricus (c. 160–210). Physician who was traditionally aligned with the Empiric school of medicine. He is referred to by Bullein in this context (p. 225).

Themison of Laodicea (123–43 BCE). A pupil of Asclepiades Bithynia and founder of the Methodic school of medicine. Probably whom Bullein means when he refers to "Sirus" in his discussion of the Methodics (p. 225).

Theognes (late sixth century BCE). Greek poet and author of a collection of proverbial sayings. Mentioned by Elyot twice in relation to wine-drinking in the second book, chapter one, and the second book, chapter nineteen.

WORKS CITED

Albala, Ken 2002. *Eating Right in the Renaissance*. California Studies in Food and Culture. Berkeley: University of California Press.

Anon. 1910. "Euphorbium" in *The Encyclopaedia Britannica: A Dictionary of Arts, Sciences, Literature and General Information*, edited by Hugh Chisholm, 11th ed., 894. Cambridge: Cambridge University Press.

Arber, Edward 1875. *A Transcript of the Registers of the Company of Stationers of London, 1554–1640 A.D*. 5 vols. London: Privately Printed.

Barnes 1541. [*The Treatise Answering the Book of Beards*] *The Treatyse Answerynge the Boke of Berdes. Compyled by Collyn Clowte* ... London: Robert Wyer.

Barwick, Humfrey 1592. [*A Brief Discourse Concerning the Force and Effect of All Manual Weapons*] *A Breefe Discourse, Concerning the Force and Effect of All Manuall Weapons of Fire, and the Disability of the Long Bowe or Archery, in Respect of Others of Greater Force Now in vse*. London: [E. Allde] for Richard Oliffe.

Beaumont, Francis 2002. *The Knight of the Burning Pestle*. Edited by Michael Hattaway. 2nd ed. New Mermaids. London: A. & C. Black.

Bennett, Judith M. 1996. *Ale, Beer, and Brewsters in England: Women's Work in a Changing World, 1300–1600*. New York: Oxford University Press.

Boorde, Andrew 1547. [*The Breviary of Health*] *The Breuiary of Helthe, for All Maner of Sycknesses and Diseases the Whiche May Be in Man or Woman Doth Folowe* ... London: William Middleton.

——— 1550. [*Book for to Learn a Man to Be Wise in Building of His House*] *The Boke for to Learne a Man to Be Wyse in Buyldyng of His Howse for the Helth of Body [and] to Holde Quyetnes for the Helth of His Soule, and Body*. London: Robert Wyer.

——— 1555. [*The First Book of the Introduction of Knowledge*] *The Fyrst Boke of the Introduction of Knowledge, the Whych Dothe Teache a Man to Speake Parte of All Maner of Languages and to Know the Usage and Fashion of All Maner of Countreys* ... London: William Copland.

——— 1565. [*Merry Tales of the Mad Men of Gotham*] *Merie Tales of the Mad Men of Gotam, Gathered Together by A. B., of Physicke Doctour*. London: Thomas Colwell.

——— 1625. [*Scoggin's Jests*] *The First and Best Part of Scoggins Jests: Full of Witty Mirth and Pleasant Shifts, Done by Him in France, and Other Places: Being a Preseruatiue against Melancholy*. London: [Miles Flesher] for Francis Williams.

——— 1870. *The Fyrst Boke of the Introduction of Knowledge Made by Andrew Borde, of Physycke Doctor. A Compendyous Regyment Or, A Dyetary of Helth Made in Mountpyllier Compyled by Andrewe Boorde, of Physycke Doctou. Barnes in the Defence of the Berde: A Treatyse Made, Answerynge the Treatyse of Doctor Borde upon Berdes. With a Life of Andrew Boorde, and Large Extracts from His Breuyary*. Edited by F. J. Furnivall. Early English Texts Society 10. London: N. Trübner and Co.

——— 1936. *The Wisdom of Andrew Boorde*. Edited by Edmund H. Poole. Leicester: Falconer Scott for Edgar Backus.

Bullein, William 1558. [*The Government of Health*] *A Newe Booke Entituled the Gouernement of Healthe, Wherein Is Vttered Manye Notable Rules for Mannes Preseruacion, with Sondry Symples and Other Matters, No Lesse Fruiteful Then Profitable* ... London: John Day.

——— 1562a. [*A Comfortable Regiment ... against the Most Perilous Pleurisy*] *A Comfortable Regiment and a Very Wholsome Order against the Moste Perilous Pleurisi Whereof Many Doe Daily Die within This Citee of London and Other Places, and What the Cause Is of the Same* ... London: John Kingston.

——— 1562b. [*Bulwark of Defence*] *Bulleins Bulwarke of Defe[n]ce Againste All Sicknes, Sornes, and Woundes, That Dooe Daily Assaulte Mankinde, Whiche Bulwarke Is Kepte with Hillarius the Gardiner, Health the Phisician, with Their Chyrurgian, to Helpe the Wounded Soldiers.* London: John Kingston.

———.1564. [*A Dialogue against the Fever Pestilence*] *A Dialogue Bothe Pleasaunte and Pietifull, Wherein Is a Goodly Regimente against the Feuer Pestilence with a Consolacion and Comfort against Death.* London: John Kingston.

——— 1579. [*Bulwark of Defence*] *Bulleins Bulwarke of Defence against All Sicknesse, Soarenesse, and Woundes That Doe Dayly Assaulte Mankinde, Which Bulwarke Is Kept with Hilarius the Gardener and Health the Phisicion, with the Chirurgian, to Helpe the Wounded Souldiours.* London: Thomas Marshe.

Carlino, Andrea 1999. *Books of the Body: Anatomical Ritual and Renaissance Learning.* Translated by John Tedeschi and Anne C Tedeschi. Chicago: University of Chicago Press.

Chaucer, Geoffrey. 1989. *The Canterbury Tales: Nine Tales and the General Prologue.* Edited by V.A. Kolve and Glending Olson. New York: W.W. Norton.

Culpepper, Nicholas. 1653. [*Pharmacopoeia Londinensis*] *Pharmacopoeia Londinensis, or The London Dispensatory Further Adorned by the Studies and Collections of the Fellows, Now Living of the Said Colledg.* London: Printed for Peter Cole.

De Mediolano, Joannes 1528. [*Regimen sanitatis Salerni (The Salernitan Rule of Health)*] *Regimen Sanitatis Salerni, This Boke Techyng Al People to Gouerne Them in Helthe* ... Translated by Thomas Paynell. London: Thomas Berthelet.

———.1607. [*Regimen sanitatis Salerni*] *The Englishman's Docter, Or the Schoole of Salerne.* Translated by John Harington. London: [William Jaggard] for John Helme and John Busby Junior.

Diodorus 1933. *Library of History.* Translated by C.H. Oldfather. 12 vols. Loeb Classical Library. London: Heinemann.

Dorrell, Hadrian. 1594. [*Willoughby His Avisa*] *Willobie His Auisa, Or the True Picture of a Modest Maid, and of a Chast and Constant Wife.* London: Windet.

Ekirch, A. Roger 2001. "Sleep We Have Lost: Pre-Industrial Slumber in the British Isles." *The American Historical Review* 106: 343–86.

———. 2005. *At Day's Close: Night in Times Past.* New York: W.W. Norton.

Elyot, Thomas Undated. Letter to Thomas Cromwell in British Library MS Cotton Cleopatra E. Iv, fol. 260.

——— 1970. *The First Edition of Thomas Elyot's "Castell of Helthe" with Introduction and Critical Notes.* Edited by John Villads Skov. Los Angeles: University of California.

Erasmus, Desiderius 1537. [*Praise of Physic*] *Declamacion in the Prayse and Commendation of the Most Hygh and Excellent Science of Phisyke.* London: Robert Redman.

Flavius, Vegetius Renatus 1572. [*De re militari*] *The Foure Bookes of Flauius Vegetius Renatus, Briefelye Contayninge a Plaine Forme, and Perfect Knowledge of Martiall Policye, Feates of Chiualrie, and Whatsoeuer Pertayneth to Warre*. Translated by John Sadler. London: Thomas Marsh.

Fossa, Ove 1995. "A Whale of a Dish: Whalemeat as Food" in *Disappearing Foods: Studies in Foods and Dishes at Risk*, edited by Harlan Walker, 78–102. Proceedings of the Oxford Symposium on Food and Cookery 1994. Totnes: Prospect Books.

Furdell, Elizabeth Lane 2004. "Boorde, Andrew (c. 1490–1549)" in *Oxford Dictionary of National Biography*. Oxford: Oxford University Press.

Gerard, John 1633. [*The Herbal*] *The Herball or Generall Historie of Plantes. Gathered by Iohn Gerarde of London Master in Chirurgerie Very Much Enlarged and Amended by Thomas Iohnson Citizen and Apothecarye of London*. London: Adam Islip, Joyce Norton, Richard Whitakers.

Guthrie, Douglas 1943. "The 'Breviary' and 'Dietary' of Andrew Boorde (1490–1549), Physician, Priest and Traveller." *Proceedings of the Royal Society of Medicine* 37: 507–9.

Hogrefe, Pearl 1967. *The Life and Times of Sir Thomas Elyot, Englishman*. Ames: Iowa State University Press.

Holinshed, Raphael 1587. [*Holinshed's Chronicles*] *The First and Second Volume of Chronicles ... Newlie Augmented and Continued by J. Hooker Alias Vowell Gent. and Others*. 3 vols. London: [H. Bynneman for] J. Harrison,

Homer 1919. *The Odyssey*. Translated by A.T. Murray. 2 vols. The Loeb Classical Library. London: Heinemann.

Hyde, Patricia 2004. "Drury, Sir Robert" in *Oxford Dictionary of National Biography*. Oxford: Oxford University Press.

Jonson, Ben 1960. *Bartholomew Fair*. Edited by E.A. Horsman. The Revels Plays. London: Methuen.

—— 1967. *The Alchemist*. Edited by F.H. Mares. The Revels Plays. London: Methuen.

—— 1983. *Volpone, or The Fox*. Edited by Brian Parker. The Revels Plays. Manchester: Manchester University Press.

Lehmberg, Stanford 2004a. "Elyot, Sir Richard" in *Oxford Dictionary of National Biography*. Oxford: Oxford University Press.

—— 2004b. "Elyot, Sir Thomas (c. 1490–1546)" in *Oxford Dictionary of National Biography*. Oxford: Oxford University Press.

Lewis, Robert E. 1988. *Middle English Dictionary: S8*. Ann Arbor: University of Michigan Press.

Llewelyn Davies, John 1877. "Ambrosius" in *A Dictionary of Christian Biography: Literature, Sects, and Doctrines*, edited by William Smith and Henry Wace. London: John Murray.

Mambretti, Catherine Cole 1974. "William Bullein and the 'Lively Fashions' in Tudor Medical Literature." *Clio Medica* 9 (4): 285–97.

Marmion, Shackerley 1632. [*Holland's Leaguer*] *Hollands Leaguer, an Excellent Comedy as It Hath Bin Lately and Often Acted with Great Applause ...* London: J[ohn] B[eale] for John Grove.

Martin, C.T., and Rachel E. Davies. 2004. "Butts, Sir William" in *Oxford Dictionary of National Biography*. Oxford: Oxford University Press.

Maslen, R.W. 2008. "The Healing Dialogues of Doctor Bullein." *Yearbook of English Studies* 38: 119–35.

Matthews, Leslie G. 1978. "Day Book of the Court Apothecary in the Time of William and Mary, 1691." *Medical History* 22: 161–73.

McCutcheon, Elizabeth 1996. "William Bullein" in *Sixteenth-Century British Nondramatic Writers Third Series*. Edited by David A. Richardson, 8–12. Dictionary of Literary Biography. Detroit: Gale Research.

Middleton, Thomas 2007. *The Collected Works*. Edited by Gary Taylor and John Lavagnino. Oxford: Clarendon Press.

Mitchell, William S. 1959. "William Bullein, Elizabethan Physician and Author." *Medical History* 3: 188–200.

More, Thomas 1551. [*Utopia*] *A Fruteful, and Pleasaunt Worke of the Beste State of a Publyque Weale, and of the Newe Yle Called Vtopia*. London: [S. Mierdman for] Abraham Vele.

—— 1553. [*Dialogue of Comfort*] *A Dialoge of Comfort against Tribulacion, Made by Syr Thomas More Knyght*. London: Richard Tottel.

Moulton, Thomas 1531. [*Mirror or Glass of Health*] *This Is the Myrour or Glasse of Helth, Necessary and Nedefull for Euery Person to Loke In, That Wyll Kepe Theyr Body from the Syckenes of the Pestylence*. London: Robert Wyer.

Muffett, Thomas 1655. [*Health's Improvement*] *Healths Improvement, or Rules Comprizing and Discovering the Nature, Method, and Manner of Preparing All Sorts of Food Used in This Nation*. London: Tho[mas] Newcomb for Samuel Thomson.

O'Hara-May, Jane 1977. *Elizabethan Dietary of Health*. Lawrence, KS: Coronado Press.

Patai, Raphael 1994. *The Jewish Alchemists: A History and Source Book*. Princeton, NJ: Princeton University Press.

Pliny 1952. *Natural History*. Translated by H. Rackham. 10 vols. Loeb Classical Library. London: Heinemann.

—— 1956. *Natural History*. Translated by W.H.S. Jones. 10 vols. Loeb Classical Library. London: William Heinemann.

Plutarch 1919. *Parallel Lives*. Translated by Bernadotte Perrin. 11 vols. Loeb Classical Library. London: Heinemann.

Porter, Roy 1987. *Disease, Medicine and Society in England, 1550–1860*. Basingstoke: Macmillan Education.

Roper, William 1935. *The Life of Sir Thomas More, Knight*. Edited by Elsie Vaughan Hitchcock. Early English Text Society 197. Oxford: Oxford University Press.

Scurlock, Jo Ann, and Burton R. Andersen 2005. *Diagnoses in Assyrian and Babylonian Medicine: Ancient Sources, Translations, and Modern Medical analyses*. Translated and with Commentary by Jo Ann Scurlock, Burton R. Andersen. Urbana: University of Illinois Press.

Setton, Kenneth M. 1992. *Western Hostility to Islam and the Prophecies of Turkish Doom*. Memoirs of the American Philosophical Society. Philadelphia: American Philosophical Society.

Shakespeare, William 1988. *The Complete Works: Compact Edition*. Edited by Stanley Wells, Gary Taylor, John Jowett, and William Montgomery. Oxford: Clarendon Press.

Shakespeare, William 1994. *All's Well That Ends Well*. Edited by Susan Snyder. The Oxford Shakespeare. Oxford: Oxford University Press.
Skeat, Walter W. 1993. *The Concise Dictionary of English Etymology*. Wordsworth Reference. Ware: Wordsworth Editions.
Swain, David W. 2008. "'Not Lernyd in Physicke': Thomas Elyot, the Medical Humanists, and Vernacular Medical Literature" in *Renaissance Historicisms: Essays in Honor of Arthur F. Kinney* Edited by James M. Dutcher and Anne Lake Prescott, 54–68. Newark: University of Delaware Press.
Taylor, C.C.W. 1999. *The Atomists: Leucippus and Democritus: Fragments, a Text, and Translation, with a Commentary*. Toronto: University of Toronto Press.
Thornton, John L. 1948. "Andrew Boorde, Thomas Linacre and the 'Dyetary of Helth.'" *Bulletin of the Medical Library Association* 36: 204–9.
Tracy, P.B. 1980. "Robert Wyer: A Brief Analysis of His Types and a Suggested Chronology for the Output of His Press." *The Library (=Transactions of the Bibliographical Society)*, Sixth series (=Fourth of the *Transactions of the Bibliographical Society*) 2: 293–303.
Udall, Nicholas, and Joannes Ravisius Textor. 1562. [*Thersytes*] *A New Enterlude Called Thersytes, Thys Enterlude Folowynge Dothe Declare Howe That the Greatest Boesters Are Not the Greatest Doers*. An Adaptation, Possibly by Nicholas Udall, of a Dialogue of Joannes Ravisius. London: John Tysdale.
Vesalius, Andreas 1543. *De Humani Corporis Fabrica Libri Septem (On the Fabric of the Human Body in Seven Books)*. Basel: Joannis Oporini.
Wallis, Patrick 2004. "Bullein, William (c. 1515–1576)" in *Oxford Dictionary of National Biography*. Oxford: Oxford University Press.
Wayne, Don E. 1984. *Penshurst: The Semiotics of Place and the Poetics of History*. London: Metheun.
Williams, Gordon 1994. *A Dictionary of Sexual Language and Imagery in Shakespearean and Stuart Literature*. 3 vols. London: Athlone.

EU authorised representative for GPSR:
Easy Access System Europe, Mustamäe tee 50,
10621 Tallinn, Estonia
gpsr.requests@easproject.com